GCE A2 Level

D1350262

A2 Level for **OCR**

Applied **ICT**

Series editor: **K. Mary Reid**

www.heinemann.co.uk

✓ Free online support
✓ Useful weblinks
✓ 24 hour online ordering

01865 888058

Heinemann

Inspiring generations

Heinemann Educational Publishers
Halley Court, Jordan Hill, Oxford OX2 8EJ
Part of Harcourt Education

Heinemann is the registered trademark of
Harcourt Education Limited

© Graham Manson, Maggie Banks, Karen Scott, Sonia Stuart 2006

First published 2006

10 09 08 07 06
10 9 8 7 6 5 4 3 2 1

British Library Cataloguing in Publication Data is available
from the British Library on request.

10-digit ISBN: 0 435 462 14 8
13-digit ISBN: 978 0 435 462 14 7

Edited by Susan Ross
Typeset by Planman

Original illustrations © Harcourt Education Limited, 2006
Illustrated by Planman
Cover design by Wooden Ark
Printed in the UK by CPI Bath
Cover photo © Getty Images/Stone

Websites

Please note that the examples of websites suggested in this book were up to date at the time of writing.
It is essential for tutors to preview each site before using it to ensure that the URL is still accurate and
the content is appropriate. We suggest that tutors bookmark useful sites and consider enabling students
to access them through the school of college intranet.

Contents

Unit 18 is available from the Heinemann website (www.heinemann.co.uk/vocational). Click on **IT & Office Technology** and select **Free Resources**. The password is **A2ICTU18**

Database design

Acknowledgements

Every effort has been made to contact copyright holders of material reproduced in this book. Any omissions will be rectified in subsequent printings if notice is given to the publishers.

Microsoft product screenshots courtesy of Microsoft Corporation.

The publisher would like to thank the individuals and organisations who granted permission to reproduce materials in this book.

Page 1 – Getty Images / Stone
Page 19 (Figure 9.8) – Getty Images / PhotoDisc
Page 43 – pintailpictures / Alamy
Page 101 – James Leynse / Corbis
Page 136 (Figure 11.25) – Google
Pages 153, 154 – AAF / Richard Smith
Page 160 (Figure 12.6) – Philipp Mohr / Alamy
Page 201 – Jeremy Hoare / Alamy
Page 245 – Getty Images / Stone
Pages 257, 277 – Yahoo!
Page 299 – Getty Images / PhotoDisc
Page 335 – ImageState / Alamy
Page 357 (Figure 16.20) – Corbis
Page 358 (Figure 16.21) – 3com
Page 360 (Figure 16.22) – Andrew Smith
Page 360 (Figure 16.23) – Andrew Smith
Page 425 – Getty Images / PhotoDisc

Websites

There are links to relevant websites in this book. In order to ensure that the links are up to date, that the links work, and that the sites are not inadvertently linked to sites that could be considered offensive, we have made the links available on the Heinemann website at www.heinemann.co.uk/hotlinks. When you access the site the express code is 2148P.

Tel: 01865 888058
www.heinemann.co.uk

Introduction

This is one in a series of three volumes that support the OCR qualifications in Applied Information and Communication Technology for GCE.
The books are organised like this:

* AS (Single Award), which covers units 1 to 3

* AS (Double Award), which covers units 1 to 8

* A2 (Single and Double Award), which covers units 9 to 16, and Unit 18.

A Level (Single Award)

This book covers the six units that are offered at A2 Level for the A Level (Single Award):

* Unit 9: Working to a brief

* Unit 10: Numerical modelling using spreadsheets

* Unit 11: Interactive multimedia products

* Unit 12: Publishing

* Unit 13: Artwork and imaging

* Unit 14: Developing and creating websites

If you have already taken the AS (Single Award) then you can complete the A Level (Single Award) by studying three further units. These should be selected as follows:

* Unit 9

* two units chosen from Units 10 to 14.

A Level (Double Award)

This book covers the six units that are offered at A2 Level for the A Level (Single Award) – see above. In addition, it covers three further units that are offered at A2 Level in the A Level (Double Award):

* Unit 15: Software development

* Unit 16: Networking solutions

* Unit 18: Database design.

If you have already taken the AS (Double Award) then you can complete the A Level (Double Award) by studying six further units. These should be selected as follows:

* Unit 9
* two units chosen from Units 10 to 14
* one unit chosen from Units 15 and 16
* two units chosen from Units 17 to 20. (Note that only one of these is covered in this book.)

Assessment

Your achievements at A2 Level on this qualification will generally be assessed through portfolios of evidence. The only exception to this is if you are taking the Double Award, when one of your units will be assessed through an examination.

Unit 9, which is mandatory for both the Single and Double Awards, is externally assessed. You will be required to assemble a portfolio of evidence in response to tasks set by the examination board. This will initially be marked internally, but will be moderated by the examination board.

Units 15 and 16, one of which must be selected if you are entering for the Double Award, are both externally assessed. For either unit you will be given a case study to read and some tasks to complete. You will then take these into a 90-minute examination, which will ask you questions on the work you have done and on other aspects of the unit.

All other units will be assessed internally. You will be expected to construct a portfolio for each unit. Further guidance on this is given in each unit.

Quality of written communication

The quality of your written communication will be assessed in all the units for which you submit a portfolio. In general, the extended pieces of written work that are included in the portfolio will be assessed in terms of the level of errors in spelling, punctuation and grammar. For you to achieve the highest marks, your written work should be consistently well-structured with few, if any, errors.

Further information

You can find further information about these qualifications at the OCR website (via www.heinemann.co.uk/hotlinks, express code 2148P, where you will find other links to useful sites). Remember to search for GCE Applied ICT. You can download the complete specification, which gives full details of all the units, both AS and A2, and how they are assessed. This document is nearly 300 pages long.

We hope you enjoy your studies and wish you every success.

K Mary Reid
April 2006

Working to a brief

Unit 9

By studying this unit, you will

* learn to improve your own performance and working relationships with others

* be able to apply different techniques for planning a project

* practise and further develop skills used to produce a solution to a brief

* practise and further develop the skills needed to work with others

* practise and further develop the skills needed to reflect on work you have completed.

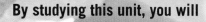

Introduction

This unit is about the process of working on a set task and assesses your ability to plan and deliver a project as well as your ability to reflect and learn from the experience. To a very large degree, this unit assesses the techniques you use to produce the solution, rather than the solution itself.

You will be asked to plan and produce a solution to a brief set by the exam board. As part of your preparation, you will be expected to carry out some research into current working practice and use this research to inform the plan you then develop to produce the solution. Once you begin working, you will need to keep a record of the work you carry out as well as how your skills develop to meet the demands of the brief. The work you carry out will be the production of the solution as well as any support materials you may need to make the solution easier to use. Finally, having produced your solution, you will produce a final report that comments on various aspects of the project, including how well you think you have met the brief. You will need some user feedback to help you with this, but the ongoing record you have completed will also provide you with evidence to help you at this stage.

Overall, this mandatory unit allows you to practise some extremely useful skills. You may also be able to combine your work for this unit with work for other units included in the qualification.

How you will be assessed

This unit will be assessed through a report that highlights the planning, development and evaluation of the process of producing a response to a brief set by the examination board. The report will include seven separate elements as follows:

* a report into current working practice
* a project plan
* a record of work completed
* any support materials
* an evaluation of how well you planned the project
* an evaluation of how well you implemented the project
* an evaluation of the finished solution.

9.1 Understanding a set brief and planning to meet the requirements of the brief

In this context, the term 'brief' originally meant the instructions for a flight given to an air crew, and so a brief can be understood as the instructions for a task.

The brief

You will be well aware from the work you have already completed for this qualification that, when you are set a task, you will be given certain targets that you will need to hit as you work through the task. With other projects in other subjects, these targets may include a requirement about the areas you could consider. A geography project might ask you to consider examples of landforms from one continent, or a history project might ask you to consider the implications of the work of one prime minister or president. Because these targets limit how you work, they actually go a long way to defining what the final product will look like. In the same way, you may be asked to produce a report using a certain font size or line spacing. These requirements would again define the form that your final report will take.

These targets combine to make up a brief. In this unit, you will be asked to choose a brief from a set list. The brief you choose will include a clear indication of what targets your final brief should achieve. These targets will include the function of the completed solution as well as an indication of any other targets that you will need to take into consideration.

Choosing a brief

The choice of which brief to work to is a big one. Whilst this unit is more focused on assessing the process of working to the brief, rather than the quality of the finished solution, you will still need to make a wise choice. Whichever brief you choose, you will need to ensure that your work:

* meets the technical and resource constraints
* is fit for purpose
* allows you to work with others.

Theory into practice

Below are two possible briefs that you could be set for this module.

Brief 1: City Zoo needs to increase its income. It would like to change the entry price for the zoo, but is not sure whether to raise the price and hope people still visit, or to lower the price and hope more people visit. Create a system which would allow the zoo to model the effects of any changes in entry price on the income of the zoo.

Brief 2: Sara's Staff is an employment agency specialising in supplying catering staff. Sara currently advertises her staff using a monthly newsletter. She would like to have a website that can advertise the staff she has available and that can deal with enquiries.

You have been asked to choose one of these briefs. Write a short report explaining what each of the briefs requires and which of the two briefs you would prefer. Your report should fully explain the reasons behind your decision.

The following section looks at these considerations and, hopefully, will give you some hints that will make the choice of a final brief easier to make.

Technical and resource constraints

Have you ever had to explain to a friend or relative that the document they are trying to open was produced on a piece of software that does not exist on their computer, or that they have the correct software, but the wrong version? Perhaps you have had to explain that a new computer game will not work because the computer on which it is being installed does not have a sufficiently powerful video card. This can be a frustrating experience, both for the person trying to open the document or install the computer game and for the person doing the explaining. Now try to imagine completing many hours of work to produce a solution to a brief, only to find that the solution will not work because it was produced on software that the client does not have or requires hardware or peripherals that the client does not possess.

When choosing a brief, you must ensure that the work you produce meets the technical and resource constraints of the client. These restraints may be some or all of the following:

✳ the speed and capacity of the client's computer system

✳ the type of software the client is using

✳ the version of the software the client is using

✳ the quality of any peripherals, such as printers or scanners, which the client owns.

There will be others, but when planning to avoid the problems caused by technical and resource constraints, you must be very clear about the questions you are asking. A good example is a printer. There are many types of printer available, all with different capabilities and functions. Do not assume that the client has the same printer as you, or that the printer they have can do what yours can. If you merely ask the client if they have a printer and are told that they do, all you know for sure is that they have a printer. You do not know what type it is, whether it can print in colour or what paper it can print to. All these factors may affect the success of your finished solution, so make sure you ask these questions before you begin. Remember, once you have accepted a brief, it is your responsibility to complete it to the client's requirements. If you do not ask the correct questions at the start, and produce a finished solution that will not work with the client's hardware or software, then it will be your responsibility to remedy the situation. Of course, at the same time as asking the client specific questions about their software and hardware, you could make some recommendations that they may want to consider upgrading their ten-year-old printer or buying an A3 scanner, if that would suit their needs.

Fitness for purpose

As well as ensuring that your finished solution actually works with the hardware and software that your client owns, your solution must fit the task that it was designed to do. *Fitness for purpose* refers to how well a product or system actually carries out what it was designed to do.

The design process tries to ensure that the finished product meets all the criteria set by the project. There are many different factors which determine the criteria that a design has to meet. However, the main considerations are:

✳ the task the product or system is meant to do

✳ the way in which the product does the task

✳ the needs of the end user.

The extent to which a product is fit for purpose is the extent to which the product meets the criteria which come from these considerations.

For example, a software programmer has been asked to write a piece of software for use at a golf club. The golf club charges members for each game of golf they play and charges different rates for games played at different times or on different days of the week.

This software should do the following tasks:

✳ store members' details

✳ record when members play golf at the club

✳ charge each member the correct amount for each game of golf they play.

CONSIDERATION	CRITERIA TO BE MET
What the software must do	The software must meet the demands of the client. Contact details must be stored and must be easy to access, bills must go out every month, etc.
How the product does the task	The software must use different rates per game for each member; these rates need to be updated when necessary, etc.
Who will use the final product	The end user will have specific requirements such as a specific font or font size or a very straightforward data entry process. The age or gender of the end user may have to be taken into consideration. You may also have to consider more than one end user.

TABLE 9.1 *Criteria to be met to ensure that the golf club software is fit for purpose*

This information will then be combined to create a monthly bill that is sent to each member's home address. The software should then record whether this monthly bill has been paid.

As well as the details above, the programmer has been told what format the output from the software will need to have, as well as who will use the information once it has been processed.

This project therefore has a range of criteria which need to be met if it is to be considered fit for purpose. These are shown in Table 9.1.

This is a fairly simple list of requirements, but if the programmer fails to meet these criteria then the finished product will not be fit for purpose and will have failed to meet the needs of the client.

When you are choosing a brief, be sure to consider the criteria you need to meet and, once you have started working, regularly refer to these criteria. As we shall see, if you are able to reflect on how well you are meeting the criteria, your chances of scoring well in this unit will be improved.

Working with others

An important part of working on any project is how well you interact with others. Whether you consider yourself a team player or someone who works best on your own, you will need some form of interaction with others as you work through your project.

As we will see later in the unit, there are many ways of deciding who the others are, but it is clear from the exam board specification that you will need to be able to assess how well you have worked with others, whoever they may be, if you are to do well in this unit. As you are choosing and planning your brief, you should bear this requirement in mind.

In conclusion

We have now discussed the three main considerations that need to be taken into account when you are choosing your brief: technical and resource constraints, fitness for purpose and working with others. Each brief will have some very clear constraints and you will need to be aware of these, but you have certain constraints also. Try to choose a brief that will interest you, that will allow you to develop your skills and on which you will enjoy working. At the same time, be realistic and try to choose a brief which you have some chance of completing. A brief asking you to work with a piece of software you do not own or to which you cannot get access is clearly one you may wish to avoid. Equally, one that does not interest you is also probably worth avoiding. However, do not dismiss a brief simply because you do not have the necessary skills, as skills development is a very important aspect of this unit.

> **Knowledge check**
>
> 1 (a) Give three factors that will influence your choice of brief.
>
> (b) Explain the importance of each of these factors.

Working to a brief

Hilary and her friend Patrick have been working on a set brief to produce a website to advertise a travel agency. They have just submitted their completed response to the client for approval and had the following letter back. It seems that the plan which Hilary and Patrick followed may not have been the best.

Dear Hilary and Patrick

Thank you for the website you sent me to check. I am afraid that there are a few problems which I need to pass on.

Firstly, we asked for a website of at least four pages. Your website had three. We also asked that each page of the website should include our logo. When we checked, only two of the three pages included a logo.

You also sent us instructions for loading the website. Despite having the same word processing software as you, we are unable to open this document.

Lastly, we have checked with some of our customers and the website does not appeal to them at all. I did explain that due to the tours we offer, our customers tend to be older than for other travel agents in the area. Unfortunately, some of the materials you chose to include in your website do not reflect the average age of our customers nor their interests.

I do remember you saying that you would each take responsibility for separate pages in the website. It seems that one person has produced the successful pages whilst another has produced the one, unsuccessful, page.

I look forward to hearing from you soon.

**Robert Lockheed
Manager, Fastway Travel**

1 Explain why Robert Lockheed is unhappy with the website that Hilary and Patrick have produced.

2 Explain how this problem might have occurred.

3 Write a short 'how to improve' report to Hilary and Patrick explaining how they may avoid making these mistakes again.

9.2 Identifying your own skills

As you work through your solution to the brief, you will need to show that you are aware of the strengths and weaknesses in your work. You will also need to identify areas where you have been successful and other areas where there is room for improvement. This may seem like quite a difficult task, as you are probably used to celebrating what you do well and trying to hide what you do less well, but if you are able to focus on your work, warts and all, then you can score well in this area. The areas you should consider are:

* skills and techniques

* use of new software

* skills for working with others

* the degree to which your work meets professional standards.

This is an important section of your work, so it is worth looking at each of these areas in turn.

Skills and techniques

You will have used a range of software and other techniques already. As part of *Unit 1: Using ICT to Communicate*, you will have used word processing and possibly desktop publishing software. As part of *Unit 3: ICT Solutions for Individuals and Society*, you will have used spreadsheets and databases.

You will also have planned projects for other units and for other subjects, and may even be working on other coursework projects already. You will have gained knowledge of different techniques when working on these projects and we will look at some of these later. Where you already have techniques for planning a project, you need to be given recognition for this knowledge as well as recognition for any knowledge you develop as you work through the project.

As you work on your solution to the brief, your knowledge of skills and techniques will improve. These may include:

* planning
* use of software
* timekeeping
* gathering data.

These are just a few suggestions. What is important is that you are aware of the skills you have at the start of the project and are able to record how your knowledge of a range of skills and techniques improves as you are working.

Use of new software

You will not be surprised to know that you will be using software to produce your solution to the brief. The software you use will, obviously, depend on the brief you choose, but, as you work through the brief, your skills in using different software packages will increase. Just like with the previous section, you need to be clear how your skills have developed as you progress through your project.

There are many ways you can show progress in the use of software. Fundamentally, you need to compare your skills at the start of the project with those you have at the end. The difference is the development. Where you have not used a piece of software, any progress will be obvious, but for other types of applications software, such as word processing or desktop publishing, you will already have some experience. There are various ways in which you could show your proficiency in using a piece of software at the start of the project. A simple list of skills or a statement that you are a beginner or intermediate user signed by the project supervisor should give you the opportunity to gauge your progress in the summative report at the end of your project. As we shall see, another method would be to highlight at the planning stage that a particular task will require some increased understanding of how to use a particular software package. This may range from something reasonably straightforward through to some quite complicated tasks, but by highlighting that you need to increase your understanding at this stage, you will be able to reflect on how well your understanding and knowledge have increased as you have worked through the project.

Skills for working with others

In the next section, we will look at specific issues to do with working with others. For now, it is enough to know that there are as many skills involved in working with others as there are in any other areas of this unit. Think about the teams with which you are involved. Do you play a leading role – always making suggestions and prepared to take a lead – or do you play a supporting role – happy to follow other people? Whichever role you play, in order to be good at it, you will need skills.

Each group of people you work with will have different expectations of you. These different expectations will mean that you must have a range of skills for working with different people and be able to use them at the correct time.

We will also look at how teams work. Successful teams need a range of people with different skills. It may be that you will need to take on a different role within your team from the one you usually adopt and so will need to develop your skills accordingly.

Meeting professional standards

Every profession has rules and expectations which govern the quality of work that members of the profession produce. These rules and expectations define the standard or quality of work that is required. Sometimes, these are based on legal requirements, such as health and safety. In other cases, these may be standards that a group of professionals have imposed on themselves.

In your daily life, you will be aware of the effects of these standards. For example, there is a huge difference between the quality of a home video and a professionally produced documentary. This difference is not due solely to the equipment being used, but also to the care and attention to detail shown at all stages of the production of the documentary.

Similarly, an image you created with graphic manipulation software may not be as professional as that produced by a full-time graphics artist. Whilst both you and the graphics artist may have a similar level of talent, the experience and, again, attention to detail shown by the graphic artist will be likely to result in an image of superior quality.

At the start of working on the solution to the brief, your standard of work may not come up to the quality of a piece of work produced by someone who would be creating the piece as part of their full-time job. However, as you make progress, gain experience and benefit from input from others, you will become more aware of the standard of work which exists in the area on which you are focusing. As you apply these standards to your work, so the quality of the work you produce will become increasingly professional. You should monitor this progress and be prepared to comment on it at the end of your project.

9.3 Working with others

Now is the time to think some more about working with others. The first thing to do is to decide who the others are. We will then go on to consider the skills that are needed.

Who are the others?

Introduction

Whether you choose to create a solution as part of a team or as an individual, you will work with others. These others may be any of the following:

* the other members of your team
* the client who has commissioned the work
* those to whom you go for support during the lifetime of the project, such as project supervisors or others who have specialist knowledge
* those around you, such as your parents or friends, with whom you share some ideas as you are working.

As you work through your project, you will have both **formal interaction** with others, such as between yourself and the client during meetings, and **informal interaction**, such as between yourself and friends. In fact, you could argue that everyone you meet during the time you are working on your project, and even some you do not meet, will be affected by the work you are doing and will, themselves, possibly affect how you work.

> **Key terms**
>
> *Formal and informal interaction:* Two different forms of communication, bound by different rules. Formal interaction will be more businesslike and less relaxed than informal interaction, which will be more like a conversation between friends.

Identifying others

Who will you be working with on this project? If you work in a group, who will be in the group with you? Maybe you can choose who is in your group, or you may have to work with all those who have chosen to complete the same project. You may decide to work on your own. This does not mean that you will not interact with others. For example, where will you get advice when you need it? Who will explain how a piece of software

is programmed? Remember that anyone you meet during the lifetime of the project will be affected by the work you are doing. If they also support you with practical help or advice, then you have worked with them.

At various stages of the project you will also need feedback from a client. Because of the nature of the briefs set by the exam board, you may need to find a contact who knows something about the area on which your brief focuses and who can take on the role of client, or it may be that your teacher or college lecturer will take on this role. Your work with these people will require just as much skill as you will need to work with any team-mates you may have.

The stakeholder model

One method of identifying who the 'others' are is to look at groups of people as **stakeholders**. Stakeholders can be defined as those who have an interest in the project itself. This means that they will be affected by the project in some way, maybe because they are working on it or are dependent on its outcome. Stakeholders are divided into internal or external stakeholders. **Internal stakeholders** are those who are members of the team working on the project, whilst **external stakeholders** are all the rest of the people affected. Basically, external stakeholders are all those groups who will be affected by the project but who are not part of the team.

Let's look at an example to make things clear. Suppose you have been asked to write a website for your friend's band. The website is intended to increase bookings for the band in the local area, and maybe beyond. You will need to work with one member of the band, who will supply design ideas and write some text. You will also work with a photographer, who will take any photographs you need for the website.

In this case, the stakeholders are the people in the team producing the website and the band, because they will all be affected. Even though working on the website and being in the band are obviously different things, it should be clear that these groups of people are all involved. However, what may not be immediately obvious is that there are other

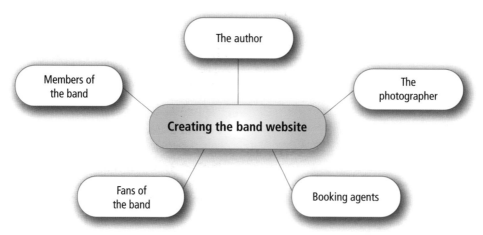

FIGURE 9.1 *The stakeholder model for the band website*

people who will be affected by the website. The following may all be considered as stakeholders:

* people who book bands will depend on the website for information

* fans of the band may access the website to check when the band is playing.

In short, anyone who is affected by the website is a stakeholder.

This idea of being affected by the website is important. The band is clearly affected, but if they decide to ask someone else, other than you, to produce the website, they will still get a website; anyone initially working on the website might find themselves unemployed if such a decision was made. We can therefore talk about two groups of people. These are the internal and the external stakeholders. The internal stakeholders are the people working on the website, which is the one member of the band, the photographer and you, whilst the external stakeholders are the band, the fans and the people making bookings. (You may notice that, as the team producing the website includes one member of the band, this person is both an internal and external stakeholder.)

The stakeholder model is best shown as a diagram. Figure 9.1 shows the stakeholders for the website.

How to...

Construct a stakeholder diagram

A stakeholder diagram may take many forms. Figure 9.1 is only one version.

To construct a stakeholder diagram for a project, start by creating a list of all people or organisations which would be affected by the project. Some of these will be people working on the project, others will be those who act as users or customers for the project. Others may be affected in other ways. For example, the stakeholders for an annual outdoor concert would be included, as they would be affected by the noise and the crowds.

You can then use this list to create your stakeholder diagram.

Extension
It is possible to create a diagram which shows internal and external stakeholders separately. A ring or doughnut diagram, with the project at the centre, internal stakeholders in the first ring and external stakeholders in the outer ring, would be suitable.

The stakeholder model is a very useful way of identifying who you will be working with on a project. Your project will have many stakeholders, so one of the first tasks you should do is to complete a stakeholder model diagram for your project, showing all the groups with which you will have to work.

CASE STUDY

You work as a reporter for the *Ridgeway Times*. The following article appeared in yesterday's issue.

New sports facilities for Ridgeway Village
After many years of campaigning by the local pressure group, 'No sleep 'til we get a playground', Ridgeway Council has announced that funding has been approved to provide a skateboard and cycling area to the south of the village. There will also be funding for a youth club on the site. It is hoped that the facility, which will be built on land left derelict since the failure of the village's park and ride scheme, will provide an area for young people to meet and take part in sports and social activities. At the moment, no facilities exist for any organised activity of any sort.

Also present at the meeting were members of the Acton Road Action Committee. Acton Road backs onto the derelict site, and the action committee has been campaigning for the site to be cleaned up for some years. At present, the site is used mainly for fly-tipping. The group were said to be 'generally pleased' with the decision to transform the site.

As yet, no dates for the completion of the project have been announced, but local builders JMB Construction are understood to be interested in the contract.

1   Who are the stakeholders in the Ridgeway Village sports ground project?

2   Create a diagram to show who the internal and external stakeholders in this project are.

3   Explain how each of the stakeholders will be affected by the project.

Theory into practice

The following is a list of projects. For each project, complete a stakeholder diagram showing both the internal and external stakeholders.

Project 1: A bypass for Ridgeway Village.

Project 2: A new supermarket for Ridgeway Village.

Project 3: A new secondary school for Ridgeway Village, so that students do not have to travel 24 miles each day to the school in Meltone.

It should be clear that you will be working with a lot of other people. Some of these people will be directly involved in the project, as fellow team members or as clients or end users, whilst others will be indirectly involved, as teachers or advisers. You will have a relationship with each of these groups, and the quality of these relationships can have a direct effect on the quality of the solution you produce. The skills you have at the start of the project and the skills you develop during the lifetime of the project will go a long way to ensuring that your relationship with each of these groups is effective.

The roles people play

The four main roles

One of the major factors for determining how you work with others is the role that these others play. These roles may be thought of as job titles, as they define what people do. The four main roles are:

* experts
* users
* team members
* project supervisors.

These are assigned roles that carry with them set expectations and patterns of behaviour. It should be clear from the outset who is playing these roles.

Experts

Experts are there to give advice. They will differ from project supervisors due to the quality of the advice they give. Experts are really people who know a great deal about the area in which you are working. This knowledge has probably been gained by working in the relevant area.

FIGURE 9.2 *Experts are for advice. Do not treat them as team members*

As well as practitioner experts, you should think of your teachers or lecturers as another form of expert. Whilst they may not know a great deal about the actual topic on which you are working, they will know about working in a team and may be able to suggest techniques you could use in the day-to-day running of your project. You may find that your teacher or lecturer knows a good deal about conflict resolution, for example.

Users

All of the four different roles are important, but possibly the user is the most important of all. The user is the person who will use your completed product. That sounds simple, but, if you stop to think, you may realise that your project has two different end users. The first is the client who wants a new system, maybe to organise an aspect of his or her business. However, the client may never actually use the system, as he or she does not work in the section which will use the system. In this case, there is a second user: the person or group of people who will actually use the system in their day-to-day work. Both of these groups can be important sources of information, but can also have different needs and expectations. Tread carefully and be prepared to use different skills with each group.

Team members

A team member is someone you work with every day. They are there to be relied on, but not exploited. Working with people and passing all your work over to them are two very different things!

Project supervisors

These are the people who will take control and really drive the project forward. These people will be the ones who take responsibility for making sure that the project is on time because everyone is working well. They will ensure that all the little tasks, which go to making up the big project, get done. There is no reason why the project supervisor may not be you, for example!

Each of these roles is strictly defined and those playing the roles will have a different interaction with you. If you choose to work as part of a team,

FIGURE 9.3 *Team members share the workload*

your team members will be there to share tasks. This sharing of tasks between team members fits the team member role. However, you would not expect the expert to share work in the same way that a team member would. The role of the expert is to provide advice. They may be happy to help out occasionally by giving some practical help as well; by doing so, they are effectively changing their role and, at some stage, will want to change back. Do not expect your friendly expert to remain friendly for too long if you keep asking them to carry out tasks that are really yours to do.

Similarly, the project supervisors (these will usually be your teachers or lecturers) will be there to supervise, which means to look over and ensure that everything is going reasonably well. This is another very well defined role, which does not really include playing a practical part in the production of the finished solution. Obviously, these project supervisors can also be experts, so use them wisely!

The role that the client will play is a difficult one to predict. As we have discussed elsewhere in this unit, you may not even have a client and your project supervisor may be playing this role as well. Whoever the client is, they will want the solution to the brief to be effective and so it is likely that they will be happy to spend time with you at the start of the project to ensure that you have a clear understanding of what is required. If you are lucky (or maybe have the necessary skills), you may be able to get your client to give you some very useful help with the project, which may include some practical help. However, you need to be aware that this is again a change of role and so your request may be politely, but firmly, turned down.

✱ Remember

As you work through your project, you will meet people playing different roles. Some of these people may be willing to take on different roles, but this is likely to be short-term and you should expect these people to want to revert to their original role at some stage. You can ask people to change roles, but be prepared for when they want to change back.

The successful team

The other members of your team are likely to be the people you work with most closely. They are also the source of most conflict. You should spend some time thinking about how teams work, as this may avoid a good deal of problems.

Firstly, what is a team? The business expert Charles B. Handy gives the following definition of a team: 'any collection of people who perceive themselves to be a group'.

This may seem a bit vague, but put yourself into a position where you are with a random group of people, maybe at a cinema or on a bus or even at the start of this course. At that stage, you all have the same aim, which may be to get into the city centre or to see a film or even to pass a qualification, but you are not a team. However, if you are all faced with a common problem, such as the bus breaking down or the cinema catching fire or your course tutor being ill, then you begin to see yourselves as a team, working together.

Once in a group or a team, different people will behave differently. Much research has gone into how these different patterns of behaviour may make up specific roles within a team. An expert on team-working, R. M. Belbin, argued that there were seven roles necessary within a successful team. Some of the titles for the roles may seem strange, but, if you spend a few moments thinking about the definitions, you should be able to apply the labels to friends and colleagues with whom you have worked in the past. The roles are as follows:

✱ The **chairman**: the person who organises.

✱ The **shaper**: the person who spurs others into action by being the task leader.

✱ The **plant**: the person who can be relied upon to come up with new ideas.

✱ The **evaluator**: the person who thinks about ideas and may see flaws in solutions.

✱ The **resource-investigator**: the person who knows where to get hold of materials, or knows people who can help.

✱ The **company worker**: the person who turns even the craziest ideas into manageable tasks.

✱ The **finisher**: the person who checks details and makes sure that targets are met.

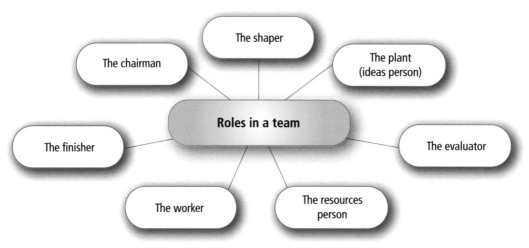

FIGURE 9.4 *Roles in a team*

If the group with which you are to work is to be successful, you must be aware that the roles people play within groups are all of equal importance.

Each of the roles listed above is important within a group. It is as important to have someone who is full of ideas as it is to have someone who points out the flaws in an idea. As you are working in your group, be aware of the different roles people are playing and learn to value them. As your team-working skills increase, you may develop different skills

for dealing with each of these types of group members. As you do, record your experiences in your diary or log.

Skills for working with others

The skills required when working with others may be broken down into four groups:

✳ interpersonal skills

✳ technical skills

✳ effort skills

✳ economic skills.

Each of these groups has set skills within them.

Interpersonal skills

Interpersonal skills are all those skills which you use to make everyday relationships with people easier. They may range from knowing when to smile at someone to knowing when to be assertive or submissive. However, in a working situation, whilst all these everyday skills are important, we concentrate on a small group of what may be considered essential tools. If you use these well, they can improve not only your work but also the work of others.

The first topic with which we shall deal is the issue of stress. The ability to deal with stress is not strictly an interpersonal skill, but more of a personal skill that, when learned, improves the way you work with others. It has been included in this section because of the benefits it can bring to working in teams.

The remaining skills are as follows:

* cooperation
* exchange of information
* clarification of responsibility
* leadership
* enthusiasm
* adaptability.

Dealing with stress

As you work through the solution to the brief, you will be faced with different forms of stress. With some forethought, you should be able to deal with these issues and so avoid conflict within the team.

You will, at times, be under stress to meet a certain deadline or to program a piece of software to do a specific task. How you cope with that stress and whether you allow that stress to influence your relationship with others are important issues. You may have a potentially difficult working relationship with someone who is maybe having their own stress issues, or with whom you have argued in the past. Some of the strategies you adopt will prove to be the wrong ones, but this is all part of the learning experience and you can earn as many marks reflecting on a poor strategy as you can reflecting on one that worked.

* Remember

You can earn as many marks reflecting on a strategy that did not work as you can by reflecting on one that did.

As you work through the project, you will need to cope with these issues and it is likely that you will develop your own coping strategies, which you may then go on to use in the future.

Theory into practice

This activity will explore some of the ways in which you cope with different situations. The intention is that you spend some time thinking about how you would respond to each situation and then compare your responses to those of others in your group. For each situation, your aim is to clarify the situation and reduce the conflict you are facing.

Situation 1: You have been blamed for some damage at your school or college. You know who did the damage, but the teacher who is making the accusation is one with whom you have never got on.

Situation 2: You work at a restaurant during the evening. One customer has been extremely difficult throughout his meal and has called you over to complain about the quality of the dessert. He has already complained that the soup was too cold and that his steak was overcooked.

Situation 3: You dealt with the customer well and thought that he was now satisfied. You are called over by your manager, who explains that the customer has now complained about the quality of service he received during the meal. You are convinced that you were as polite and attentive as you could have been during the meal, and by now are extremely irritated by what you see to be an extremely difficult customer. Your manager is concerned that the restaurant may have lost an influential and high-spending customer.

Cooperation

Cooperation is working together with someone else to achieve the same target or goal. By working with someone else, you are able to share tasks and, by doing so, become more efficient. It was cooperation within the very earliest groups (see Figure 9.5) which allowed people to concentrate on the tasks to which they were suited rather than all those to which they were not; this led to a general increase in production, which benefited all. It is this spirit of cooperation for the

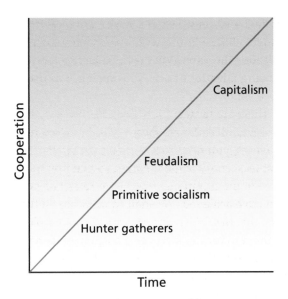

FIGURE 9.5 *Cooperation as part of human development*

benefit of all that is so important when working with others, whoever those others may be.

Whichever brief you choose to work towards, the overall project will involve many different tasks. If you are able to work with others, you will find it beneficial for these tasks to be shared. However you choose to share these tasks, if the members of your team do not share common targets and do not work together, then the separate tasks will remain separate. By cooperating with each other, you will be able to combine your separate tasks into one overall package.

There are many ways in which you can achieve the cooperation and mutual support that successful team-working demands. We will discuss some during this section, but, whichever method you choose, remember that this is an extremely important aspect of any successful team.

> **Think it over...**
>
> Think of a time when you were able to achieve a target by cooperating with others.
>
> Give five strategies you employed to reach your target.
>
> Evaluate the importance of each of these strategies to achieving successful cooperation.

Exchange of information

The exchange of information is vital to the success of any project. At the start of the project, the only person with knowledge of the project is the client. If they fail to share this information with you, the project is doomed to failure. The result will be the same if you fail to share information with others in your group.

Similarly, if you know how to program a piece of applications software to perform a specific task, by sharing that knowledge with others in your group, you can improve the efficiency of the group as a whole. You may also find that this process works in reverse and someone else helps you.

Exchange of information and cooperation are both central to the success of any collaborative project. As you plan and develop your response to the brief, you need to factor in opportunities to share ideas and knowledge. This may take the form of group meetings or discussions or, if you are working on your own, may be a planned meeting with the client to discuss progress. You may be able to set up a group discussion area on your school's network. All members of the group may then contribute to the discussion in a safe and unthreatening

FIGURE 9.6 *The mutual exchange of information is vital to the success of any project*

manner. Alternatively, you could have a policy within the group that each member of the group oversees and supports the work of someone else in the group.

Experiment with other ideas that allow for the sharing of ideas and tasks, but ensure that you keep a record of doing so, as this can be part of your final report.

Whichever method you choose, the better you can share tasks, ideas and problems, the better will be your chance of success.

Clarification of responsibility

Clarification of responsibility refers to how well defined are the tasks within a group. If tasks are well defined then everyone is clear about who is responsible for the completion of a task. This breaks group responsibility into the responsibility of a member of the group and so is likely to ensure that the task is both done well and on time.

Failure to make it clear who is responsible for separate tasks will not only result in problems with achieving your end result but may also cause stress within the group, as members of the group assume that other members are responsible for tasks. This **role ambiguity** may lead to friction within the group.

Key terms

Role ambiguity: A lack of clear understanding about the specific roles that members of a group may play.

As with all aspects of this unit, time spent planning can save many problems. The section on planning will look at techniques for successful planning of a project.

Leadership

Leadership is the ability to organise or motivate others. A leader can be someone who has organised a night out for a group of friends or may be someone who has ensured that the most work-shy individual completes their share of work on time.

Any successful leader will use skills to ensure success for the team. The skills used can be

learned and, as we shall see, the skills which leaders choose to use will depend on which sort of leader they are. Whether you have experience of being a leader or not, you can learn to use these skills.

There are far too many theories of what makes a successful leader for these to be discussed here. However, you need to have some understanding of at least some of the theories, so that you may try some of the techniques and better reflect on what you have achieved. We shall concentrate on the style theories. These theories argue that employees respond to certain styles of management better than others. There are a range of different styles, but the three which are usually considered are **authoritarian**, **democratic** and **paternalistic**.

Key terms

Authoritarian: A style of management where the manager is fully in control of all decisions and resources.

Democratic: A style of leadership which involves all team members equally.

Paternalistic: A style of management where the leader treats the team as a family and plays out the role of a father, who may allow some discussion but, ultimately, makes most decisions.

Which style are you? Which style do you prefer? The fundamental difference between the three styles of leadership is in their assumption of where the power lies. In the democratic style, the power is shared amongst the group and the group as a whole is responsible for all decisions about the running of the project. In the authoritarian model, there is one leader, who makes all decisions and tells the workers what to do. In the paternalistic model, power lies somewhere between the two extremes, and the leader acts like a parent, caring about the welfare of workers. The staff may be consulted, but the ultimate decision lies with the leader.

It is unlikely that any leader would employ either a fully democratic or a fully authoritarian style of leadership, as these are very much the extremes of management style. Whilst working on your solution to the brief, you will be called upon to make decisions and to work with others. When you do so, you may stop and consider which style of leadership you want to use. You may decide that you want to have a style which allows debate and discussion, where everyone has the chance to comment and to criticise, and so you may opt for a democratic style of leadership. This will require certain skills. As well as a thick skin, you will need to be able to allow all members of the team to have their say; this may include asking the quieter members of the group to make a contribution. You may also need to control any issues which may be caused by a frank exchange of opinions. Some people find criticism extremely threatening and this can lead to conflict. However, the positives may be that, by allowing members of the group to express their frustration at this stage, you can stop small issues becoming big ones by giving everyone the opportunity to express their frustrations.

Alternatively, you may decide that you do not want to have any discussion at all in your group, as you know best what is required. This approach also requires specific skills. The lack of debate and open discussion will mean that team members do not have any process whereby they can express their frustration. This can lead to informal moaning and griping within the team. You may decide that this is not a problem, but, if left unchecked, this can soon lead to bigger problems. As you continue working on the project, this frustration may lead to a direct challenge to your authority. This may be by one or more team members putting forward their own point of view and demanding to be heard, or a refusal by some or all of the group members to work with you. Whatever form this rebellion may take, the end results are potentially disastrous.

Groups need leaders, and, at some time during the lifetime of the project, it is extremely likely that you will need to employ leadership skills. These may be used with one person or the team as a whole. They may be in response to a crisis or used on a daily basis. However the situation arises, use it as the opportunity to learn and develop skills and remember to reflect on both the process and what you have learned.

Enthusiasm

It is a simple fact of human nature that we prefer those tasks we enjoy over those we dislike. You will undoubtedly love doing the work for this unit and so will approach each task with commitment and joy and your enthusiasm for the task will be huge! However, you will probably be working on other tasks, maybe for other subjects, to which you do not look forward and so your enthusiasm will suffer.

The ability to generate enthusiasm for a task is a skill like anything else. You can learn to like tasks that you previously hated, or at least you can learn to do a task you previously avoided. This may be because you see a value in the task which was not obvious before, or because you have simply accepted that the task

FIGURE 9.7 *Enthusiasm is a key skill for success*

FIGURE 9.8 *Chameleon: survival through adapting*

needs doing. As you have progressed through your school career, you will have changed your opinion of some aspects of school and college life. This change of opinion and ability to develop enthusiasm for a project, sometimes despite a lack of initial interest, is a skill well worth having, especially as enthusiastic employees and team members are generally regarded with more favour by employers and team leaders.

Adaptability

We have already discussed roles within teams. At that stage, we said that there were many roles within a team, but that one person may play more than one role. An important skill for working with other people is the skill to change, to adapt to changing circumstances. This may be a change of role or a change of plan. As you work through your solution to the brief, there will be changing circumstances. If you are unable to adapt to meet these changing circumstances, your project will, in extreme cases, fail.

For example, your plan may have involved the use of a certain program or peripheral device. If this program or device is unavailable or will not work, can you change your plans to suit the changing situation or will you prefer to complain? One of the few certainties in life is that it is full of uncertainties. You need to have the skills to deal with these uncertainties. These skills may be ones which you have already or you may surprise yourself with an ability to change plans at the last minute. A good approach is to be aware that there are often many ways in which to achieve the same result and to be prepared to use these other methods should the need arise.

Negotiation

Negotiation is the process of discussing with others so that an agreement may be reached. As part of this process, those involved in the discussion will each put forward their point of view so that it may be considered. For negotiation to be considered successful, the final output of the process should be a policy or plan which everyone involved in the discussion can support. This will be achieved because everyone involved in the discussion will feel that they have contributed to the final plan or policy, and so will either feel some loyalty to the plan or responsibility for the overall success of what has been agreed.

Where some or all of the parties fail to complete the process of negotiation, and therefore have not contributed to the overall policy or plan, the process of negotiation may be considered to have failed. Similarly, if some or all parties involved in the final agreement then fail to carry through what has been agreed, the process has failed also. The root cause of this failure is often that some of the participants did not feel sufficiently involved. This would usually be because their views and suggestions have been ignored. The following section will look at some negotiating skills you could use to ensure that negotiations are a success.

As you know, you will be working with many others as part of this project. Each of these groups of others may have a different opinion on the work you are about to do, each of which may be different from the view you hold. Obviously, where their view is irrelevant to you, you will be able to ignore the views of some of these groups. However, you will have to deal with some of the groups and, where there is a difference of opinion, you will need to employ negotiating skills.

A good starting point for negotiation is to fully understand the other person's point of view. When working on your solution to the brief, you may find that you develop what you are convinced is an excellent response. When you discuss this strategy with others, such as the client or other members of the group, you may find that they also have a response which they also feel is excellent. How you deal with these conflicting responses may be critical to the success of the project. If you allow the discussion to descend into a shouting match, there is no guarantee that you will end up with the best plan. What is more likely to happen is that the team will either break up or will accept the plan proposed by the person who shouts longest or loudest. There is no guarantee that this will be the better of the two options.

By approaching the discussion with a view to avoiding conflict, you may actually end up with a plan which combines the best parts of each proposal into a superb project. Not only will this be a better plan, but the relationships between yourself and the others with whom you work will be improved.

Here are some ways you may avoid conflict when you are working with others:

* Create an atmosphere where all members involved in the discussion can do so openly and without fear.

* Listen to others, rather than just waiting for them to stop talking and then having your say.

* Try to fully understand the other person's point of view by asking questions that make the other person's point of view more clear.

* Prove to the other person that you have both listened to and understood their point of view by summarising their argument once they have finished.

One further technique you may choose is to use the **win–win approach**. This technique attempts to reduce conflict by removing the competition from the discussion. If this technique is used successfully, then all involved in the discussion will feel that they have made some contribution to the plan or policy.

The central skill in this technique is the ability to see competitors in an argument as potential partners. As we have discussed in the section on roles in groups, in a successful team there is room both for an ideas person and a person who points out possible issues with plans. If these two people are to be used most constructively, their potentially conflicting roles must be seen as part of the process of deciding on an ultimately successful plan. The first stage of the win–win technique is 'I want to win and I want you to win also.'

This is an incredibly powerful statement, as it says that I will gain if I win, but I will gain more if you win *as well*.

The second stage of the technique is to acknowledge each person's motivation. This will help you to analyse the conflict more fully and to decide whether the two arguments really are in competition or may both be achieved to some extent. You may, for example, find that one person is arguing for a particular approach because they wish to use their favourite software package rather than learn new skills. One way of describing this is to say they are working within their *comfort zone*. When you stop to think about it, you may decide that this is a perfectly understandable reaction, as your solution requires in-depth knowledge of an obscure software package with which only you are familiar. If that is the case, there may be room for training. You may also find that the alternative plan would allow the person who is arguing with you so strongly to achieve another target, maybe a particular key skill or some other completely valid target. If that is the case, try to build their needs into the plan that is finally adopted.

The win–win approach works because it focuses on solving the problem, not on competition between competing solutions. Not only will argument and competition in the group have been lessened, but trust and cooperation will also have increased. One side-effect of this increase in trust and cooperation is that the team as a whole will benefit from energy being spent on solving the problem rather than arguing about solutions.

Key terms

Win–win approach: A strategy for avoiding conflict by concentrating on solving the problem rather than arguing about possible solutions.

✱ Remember

When working in a group, negotiation is not about winning an argument but deciding on what is best for the group as a whole.

Technical skills

Technical skills are the skills which you have developed for using software and hardware. You will already have skills in this area, but these skills will develop further as you progress through the project. You will also find that the people you are working with will have different technical skills. This is not a problem in itself, in that different people can carry out different tasks. You will need to be aware of the range of skills that you and your group have and take account of these at the planning stage.

Knowledge of specific software and hardware

The brief you choose will go a long way towards deciding which type of applications software you will use when working on the project. A number-based brief may require you to work with spreadsheets, or a brief using a lot of data and information may require you to use a database. You may be required to use presentation software or multimedia software to create a presentation, or image manipulation software to produce a range of images for a project. Once you have decided which type of applications software you will use, you then have to decide which software package is most suitable. You will probably have used at least one example of each of the software types already mentioned, but you will need to assess whether the package you know meets the needs of the project. You will also need to assess whether you are able to use the software to produce the results which the client and the brief require.

It will hopefully become clear during the planning stage what software skills you need to meet the requirements of the brief. A quick check will then identify whether your favourite software package is sufficient and whether you need to practise or learn new skills.

You will also have used some items of computer hardware and will probably be planning to use them again. Table 9.2 shows some of the hardware items you may use when working to the brief and some of the features you may want to use. Use the table as the beginnings of a check-list to help your planning.

ICT skills in general

ICT as a subject is more than just a study of how different software packages and hardware items work. The 'C' part refers to *communications*, and it is as important that you understand issues such as how you put a message across as it is that you know how to program a particular software package.

Apart from the skills involved in using software packages and items of hardware, possibly the most important skill you need to develop is **awareness of audience**. This is the ability to meet the needs of the **target audience**.

DEVICE	FEATURES
Scanner	Set scan area Set scanning resolution Set scan colour
Digital camera/ digital video camera	Set format of saved image files Manipulate image files whilst on the camera Download images from the camera
Video capture device	Connect device Capture images from a video or DVD
Microphone or other sound capture device	Connect device Capture sound files of the quality required
Printer	Choose printer formats Change printer resolution Change paper type Change paper orientation

TABLE 9.2 *Some devices and the features you may use*

The target audience is the group of people at whom the completed work is aimed. Each target audience will have different needs, tastes and interests. The better able you are to identify these different needs, tastes and interests and to interpret those needs in your work, the more successful you are likely to be.

Key terms

Awareness of audience: The ability to produce work that meets the needs of the target audience.

Target audience: The audience for which a piece of work has been produced. Each target audience will have different needs, tastes and interests.

The end user and the target audience are not necessarily the same group of people. The end user for a piece of animation may be a cinema, but the target audience will be those people who the animation is attempting to interest or attract. As you will be aware from the section on fitness for purpose, the needs of the end user will influence the design and structure of your final solution to the set brief, but the needs of the target audience, the people at whom the product is aimed, will affect many aspects of the style and content of the project itself.

There are various different considerations that will need to be taken into account if you are to meet the needs of the target audience. The following checklist will help you decide how to meet those needs.

* What do you know about the target audience? Are factors such as age, gender, interests, job or where they live important?

* What is the importance of the message that you are attempting to put across?

* What is the mood of the message? Is it a fun or a serious message?

* On whose behalf are you creating the document?

The answers to each of these questions will allow you to come to some conclusions about the style and content of any materials you produce. You are then ready to decide on other aspects of your work.

Do you remember when you first learnt how to format the font colour in a word processing package? You probably used as many different colours as you could and were immensely proud of the fact that you used a different one for each letter. (If you still do this, it is probably best to stop now.) You may even have formatted each letter in the title to be in a different font. At some stage in your school career, you will have been told that a title page for a piece of coursework need only have basic details such as your name, school and the title of the piece. Despite this, you may have spent hours producing a front page that used every single formatting technique you knew, only to be told that it was not worth any marks in the mark scheme. At this stage, you may have dismissed the examiners as boring, because your front

FIGURE 9.9 *Less is definitely more – front of a magazine*

page looked exciting and that was surely worth something. Have you now noticed that actually most magazines only have a few colours on the front page and, at most, two or three fonts? The same is true of most published material, whether it is the front of this book or a huge advertising poster. It seems that the examiner might just have been right, as what you are now aware of is that when you are producing a document, the message you are trying to put across is the message contained in the text or images used and not how skilled you are at using different fonts and font colours.

Images can play an important role in any document you produce. The images used in this unit have been chosen to emphasise points, provide clarification or to act as prompts.

As you choose images, you need to be aware of the different effects that they will have. In some cases, what might be a relevant image for one purpose will be irrelevant for another.

Before you choose an image, ask yourself the following questions:

* Why are you using the image?
* Who is the target audience?
* What is the message you are trying to convey with the image?

The answers to these questions will help you in your choice of image. If you were choosing an image to emphasise a serious story about pollution, you would be unlikely to choose a cartoon image. Conversely, a cartoon image would be wholly appropriate for including in a children's book about the pleasures to be gained from looking after rabbits.

Theory into practice

The images shown in Figure 9.10 have been chosen to illustrate a government report into the dangers of alcohol abuse. They have been chosen because they combine a generally serious tone with a clear message and an appeal to young people.

You have been asked to find suitable images to use with the following projects. Using whichever source is appropriate, find images that suit the content and the style of the message as well as appeal to the target audience.

Project 1: A campaign to reduce smoking amongst under-16s.

Project 2: An advertising campaign for a new fruity milk drink aimed at young children.

Project 3: An advert trying to tempt young couples to visit Paris and sample the romantic delights of 'the city of love'.

One further thing you need to think about in the communications area is **house style**. Basically, the house style is the subtle and not-so-subtle visual clues that enable you to realise that two products are made by the same group of people. These

FIGURE 9.10 *Images used as part of a government advertising campaign*

may be pieces of furniture made by the same manufacturer or magazines produced by the same publisher.

Your client may have a very clear house style, and you may be required to take account of this in your work. Any house style should be clear from the brief. However, if it is not, the initial research you do may give you some clues about professional standards and the needs of the target audience. When working with documents, the features which may be affected by house style include the following:

* fonts
* colours
* the quantity, quality and type of images used
* the writing style (how articles are written and the type of words that are used)
* the quality and type of paper on which the document is printed
* the quality of the final printout.

You may come across other factors of which you need to take account. Some house styles will dictate that there must be a logo on each page, or that each page must have the name of the publication or the page number. There may also be set standards about where these items are to appear on the page.

Giving and taking advice or support

Before reading on, consider the difference between giving support and patronising someone. A cynic may say that the only difference is how much the person being given the advice wanted to hear it. Both may involve giving advice, but, when you patronise someone, you give advice in a way that makes the other person seem inferior to you.

It can be difficult to give advice. Some people will see it as an attempt to gain some authority over them and will resent the advice being given. It can also be difficult to accept advice, particularly when the advice means that you have to go back over a piece of work or review a long-held opinion. These responses to what can be constructive input are almost guaranteed to restrict the flow of advice.

Advice, in its purest sense, is not meant to be threatening. It is simply someone trying to help someone else. If someone knows how to use a software package and you do not, would you rather spend hours and days learning how to use the package or would you rather ask someone else to show you the main tasks and a few shortcuts? The whole idea behind this book is to give you advice on how you may complete tasks that will, hopefully, lead eventually towards a good exam grade. We trust that you are not finding the content of this unit too threatening!

There are some techniques you can employ when giving and seeking advice. A simple technique is the use of a **critical friend**. This method relies on you having a person whom you trust – a friend – who gives you advice in a non-threatening manner. Another technique which the critical friend may employ, but which may be employed by others as well, is to give advice using *non-judgemental language*. This means that you use language that does not criticise the person for the problems with their work, but rather tells them how they can improve their work even further. In other words, do not tell somebody their work is rubbish, but rather that it can be even better if they follow your advice.

FIGURE 9.11 *Criticism need not be threatening*

> ## Key terms
>
> *Critical friend:* A person you trust to give you constructive advice in a non-threatening manner.

The giving and taking of advice is an important skill to be developed when working with others. When you are giving advice, try to be sympathetic to the amount of effort that the other person has already given to the task. When you are given advice, try to remember that the person advising you is trying to help and that they at least deserve to be listened to. As you progress through this project, try to develop an open attitude to the giving and taking of advice, as it can be an important contributing factor in the ultimate success of any team.

Effort skills

Whether you work as part of a team, or on your own working directly with the client, the solution you produce in response to the brief will require a good deal of effort on your part. The ability to work well and to a high quality are both skills which you need to develop further during the lifetime of this project.

The amount of work you do

When you think of work, what do you imagine? Perhaps you think of work as hard physical labour, or hours spent in a shop on a Saturday. Perhaps you imagine the effort you will need to spend on completing this project or the time you spent revising for a recent exam. Work may be all of these things and more, and your project will involve many different activities, ranging from the initial planning stage, through to the production of the finished solution and the writing up of your summative report. If you decide to work on this project as part of a team, you may share some of these activities with others. As you do so, remember that work can take many forms. It is probably better to think of work in terms of the

FIGURE 9.12 *Life is all about effort!*

FIGURE 9.13 *Quality or quantity?*

hours that each task will take to complete rather than whether the task may be seen as simple or complicated.

However you organise your work, you will need to ensure that you complete sufficient work to carry out the task and to produce a report that shows how you ensured your project was a success. This will be a major task and you will need to balance these demands against the demands of your other studies. You will also have to accept that others may have the same level of demands placed upon them as you do and so the group as a whole may need to prioritise these competing demands. You must accept that other people may not have the same priorities as you and so you must be prepared to compromise on deadlines. This can apply to other members of your group as well as the client, and you will need all the interpersonal skills identified in the previous section if you are to be able to balance your priorities and timetable against the priorities and timetables of others with whom you work.

The quality of work you do

As well as the amount of work you do, the quality is important. The people with whom you work, whether they are fellow team members or the client, will have an expectation that the work you complete will be of an acceptable standard. This standard may vary according to the values of the team and the expectations of the client. However this standard is established, it should be clear to all what the requirement is.

Depending on your skills level at the start of the project, you may take time to achieve this standard. As you work, either share your concerns with others in the group or ask for interim meetings with the client to check that the work you are completing meets the required standard. By including regular review meetings in the overall plan for the project, you will be giving yourself the opportunity to identify any problems that may occur and any further training that may be required. These meetings should be minuted and included in your final report as evidence of your development of ideas and skills.

How well you meet deadlines

Deadlines are an important aspect of any project. Whether you are working with others as part of a team, or the project just involves you and the client, others will be waiting for you to complete the work you have been allocated. If you miss deadlines, this will affect others, either in the team or those waiting for the finished product.

The skill of **time management** is essential to learn. It involves **setting priorities**. It is very easy to be distracted from tasks, either by other people or by your own competing priorities. Some people have the ability to look busy and yet achieve nothing, simply because the task they are working on is a low priority. When challenged about this apparent inability to prioritise, these people may explain that they have chosen tasks based on the ones they enjoy, rather than the importance of each task to the success of the team. In this case, the criteria applied to prioritise need to be addressed and you may need to support the person to help them re-evaluate their priorities.

Key terms

Time management: The ability to use the time you have available to complete the most relevant and necessary tasks in an efficient manner.

Setting priorities: The ability to analyse a list of competing tasks and decide which are more important than others.

There are various techniques you can employ to achieve effective time management:

* an action diary
* a daily action sheet
* project planning.

The **action diary** is simply an ongoing diary in which you note down things that have to be done. The things you may list would include practising specific tasks using a software package or researching a concept that needs some clarification. Keep this diary with you at all times, as you never know when inspiration may strike! At the end of each week, allocate time in the coming week to the tasks that have been listed.

The **daily action sheet** is a list of all tasks that you need to complete in a day, with some indication of priorities. As you work through the tasks, cross off those you have completed. At the end of the day, start a new action sheet. Include the tasks that you did not complete today and also any new tasks you have allocated yourself in the action diary.

Project planning is covered on page 28.

Economic skills

Economic skills are to do with resources and how well you use them. As we shall see, it is as important to choose the correct resources as it is to use those resources wisely.

Identification of resources

We discussed the importance of the resource-investigator in the section on roles in teams.

There, we described this person as the person who knows where to get hold of materials. Knowing which resource to use for a specific task and who to go to for help are skills that are central to the success of your project. Without these skills, you may waste time using software that is inappropriate or asking advice from someone who is unable to help.

Decisions about which resources you will use need to be made at the initial planning stage. Having identified resources, you may then identify any skills which need improving and plan training accordingly.

Efficient use of resources

Efficiency is all about how well you use your resources. These resources may include how much disk storage space your project has been allocated, restricted printer credits or access to textbooks. Time is also a resource, whether it is your time or the time you are given with experts. It may be tempting to have a five-minute settling-in period at the start of a meeting, where everyone ensures they are sufficiently topped up with coffee, but, if this then leaves you with insufficient time in your meeting, you may regret the slow start. You will need to employ techniques to ensure that you do not waste any resources.

Knowledge check

1 Explain the role of a critical friend in reducing tension in a group and improving performance.

2 (a) List the seven main roles in a successful team.

(b) Explain how each of these roles helps to contribute to the success of the team as a whole.

3 Explain what is meant by each of the following forms of leadership: autocratic, paternalistic and democratic.

4 (a) How may a leader measure success?

(b) Under what circumstances might it be better to have an autocratic leader rather than a democratic leader?

9.4 Planning, developing and delivering a project

The importance of planning

Throughout this unit, we have referred to the importance of planning. Whichever brief you choose, you will be involved in many different tasks. These tasks will need to be prioritised and these priorities used to develop a project plan.

A good plan will make you more organised and more likely to achieve success. A successful plan will control the resources available to you, such as people, equipment, materials and maybe even money. It will help you hit deadlines and will also help to achieve agreement within the group about what are the common targets and goals. Such a plan does not occur by itself but will be the result of time spent thinking, analysing and maybe even arguing. However, whatever process you have to go through to create a plan, it will be worth it, as the project will be immeasurably easier and more successful with a plan than without one.

Planning a project
Top-down design

There are many different techniques that you may employ when planning your project, and you should use as many as you need to ensure success. However, one of the fundamental tasks is to break down the plan into manageable parts. This process is sometimes called **chunking down** and may be achieved by following a process called **top-down design**. These techniques are part of the planning process but are better thought of as being part of the initial analysis of the brief.

Your first thought when considering any brief may be that it is a huge task that you will never complete. The process of breaking a project down into smaller tasks means that rather than be faced with a project that seems huge, you are faced with a series of small tasks, which you will eventually combine to form the completed solution.

How to...

Use the top-down approach to planning

Let's start with a simple brief. You work for a newsagent who operates a delivery service. Customers are expected to settle their bills at the end of the calendar month. Your employer wants to be able to send reminder letters to customers who have not settled their bills after two further weeks.

Stage 1: Decide what are the main tasks that need to be completed. These may be called the **headline tasks**. In this case, the main tasks are to create a database, if one does not already exist, to plan a standard letter and to mail merge these two elements so that the process of sending letters is automated. The database will be queried to identify late payers.

Stage 2: Reduce each of the main tasks into smaller components. For the database, this will mean designing the structure of the database and the query that will be used to identify late payers. For the standard letter, this will be to design the layout and wording of the letter. For the mail merge, it will involve deciding which elements of the database may be used in the mail merged letter and then combining these elements with the standard wording to create the late payment letter.

FIGURE 9.14 *The importance of planning*

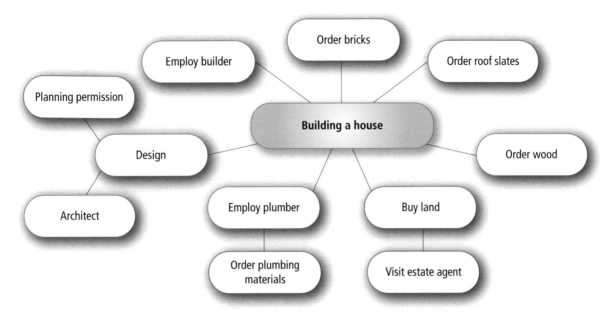

FIGURE 9.15 *Even the biggest project is made up of little ones!*

Once you have completed the process of chunking down, you will need to give some thought to how you are going to produce the solution. There are many ways in which you can do this. One of the most useful is a process called **mind mapping**.

Mind mapping

The technique of mind mapping has been given many names over the years. You may know the mind maps as spider diagrams for example.

Mind mapping involves starting with the idea from which all other ideas or points will come. This may be an essay title, or a specific target, such as 'I want to achieve an A grade in Applied GCE ICT'. Once you have this central idea, you will then add key words or concepts around it. These concepts or key words will be linked to the main concept in some way. To continue with the target of getting an A grade for this qualification, you may have thought of the following points:

* Study hard.

* Work with the specifications for each unit.

* Target the higher skills.

* Research properly.

* Work to a plan for each unit.

* Prepare fully for all exams.

Each of these points is linked to the main target because they will all, in some way, contribute to your success if you follow them.

If you were producing a mind map of how to achieve this target, you would now put these new points on the diagram and link them to the main point to show that there is a relationship.

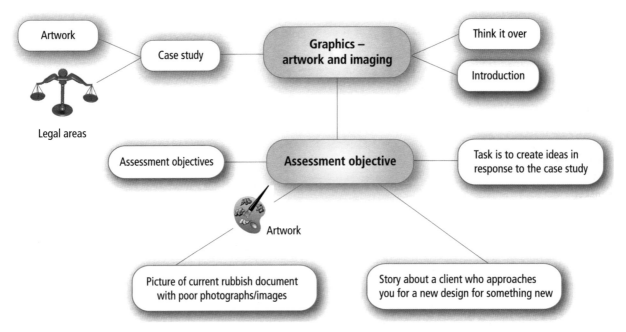

FIGURE 9.16 *A mind map*

This link may be a line or an arrow. You may want to use different colours for each of these ideas, to show that they are different branches or groups of ideas. As you work, you may think of other ideas or points that need to be linked to these new ideas. These may be thought of as sub-ideas or sub-themes. If you have used different colours for each main idea, continue using the same colour for each sub-theme. You may, for example, decide to add the following points to the 'Work with the specifications for each unit' idea:

✳ What are the specifications?

✳ How is each unit graded?

✳ How many tasks are needed for each unit?

As you work, you will develop a diagram of ideas or themes that will help you achieve your target. You could also add your own images to jog your memory or to make the diagram clearer.

Here are a few hints for creating really successful mind maps:

✳ use blank paper

✳ draw quickly and write ideas as they come into your head

✳ use capitals

✳ leave space.

Blank paper is important because lined paper may force you to work in a linear way. Your brain probably does not work like that! The aim is to get as many ideas down as you can and really give your brain the chance to come up with great ideas. If you restrict your brain, you will probably restrict the ideas. This is also why you should draw quickly and use capital letters. You can come back later and reject ideas that would not work, but by quickly writing down all ideas, you are more likely to come up with something unique. Capital letters also encourage you to make short, sharp points, which will make you work more quickly and will help you keep up with the flow of excellent ideas. Finally, leave space to add ideas later. You never know when yet another great idea may come to you and it would be a shame to have to leave it out because you had no space to make a note of it.

The strength of this technique is that you are producing a plan using your own words. By then adding colour, you are making your plan easier to remember. You are also making it easier to refine your plan, as you will have begun the process of breaking down the task into smaller groups of tasks.

Clearly, producing a mind map may be useful to you when you are producing your solution to the brief. As you will see, you could use this technique to come up with initial ideas about how to meet the demands of the brief or, once you have decided on the bare bones of an idea, you could use the technique to put flesh on the plan.

Management tools

There are several more formal tools that you can also use to help your planning. Each of these techniques assumes that you are able both to break down tasks into smaller manageable sections and to accurately predict how long a particular task will take to complete. With some tasks, your estimates will be based on past experience. However, simply because of the nature of the briefs that will be set, you are bound to be faced with some activities that are new to you. In these cases, you will need to look to your experts, project supervisors, or even the client, for advice; any of them may be able to help you make an informed estimate rather than a guess.

Critical path analysis

If chunking down is the first part of the analysis of a task, **critical path analysis** is the first stage of the planning process. This analysis helps you to plan in which order the separate tasks in a project should take place. By doing so, you can then plan how resources may be allocated and also have a firmer idea of when individual tasks and the project as a whole may be completed. The analysis is based on the assumption that certain tasks have to be completed before others begin. It plots the path through these tasks so that each task is completed in the correct order. In this sense, the analysis is plotting the path that must be followed if the project is to be successful. Any task that is dependent on another being completed is called a *dependent* or *sequential* activity. Any task that can happen at any time is called a *non-dependent* or *parallel* activity.

How to...

Develop a critical path analysis

✳ List all the tasks that need to be completed. For each task, show the earliest start date, the estimated time it will take to complete the task and whether the task is dependent or non-dependent.

✳ The next stage is best done on graph paper. Set up a chart with the days or weeks you have available for the process across the top.

✳ Plot the tasks, one per line, on the chart. Start each task at the earliest start date and draw a solid horizontal line to show how long you expect the task to take. End each task with a dot, and label each duration line with the name of the task.

✳ Link any dependent tasks.

You will now have a chart looking something like the critical path analysis shown in Figure 9.17.

Once you have completed your draft analysis, you can use it to create a plan of when different tasks need to take place. Take care not to schedule tasks before their earliest start date or, if they are dependent tasks, before the completion of the task on which they are dependent. As you are working on the plan, be aware of the allocation of resources, including time. Be realistic at this stage and build in any restrictions you know about. These restrictions may be the time you can allocate to a project per week or that there is a piece of hardware unavailable for some time. Similarly, it is probably best to include some slack time in your plan to take account of unforeseen problems such as computer downtime or illness.

Theory into practice

Use critical path analysis to create an initial plan for the production of a roast meal including meat (or a vegetarian substitute) and a range of vegetables of your choice.

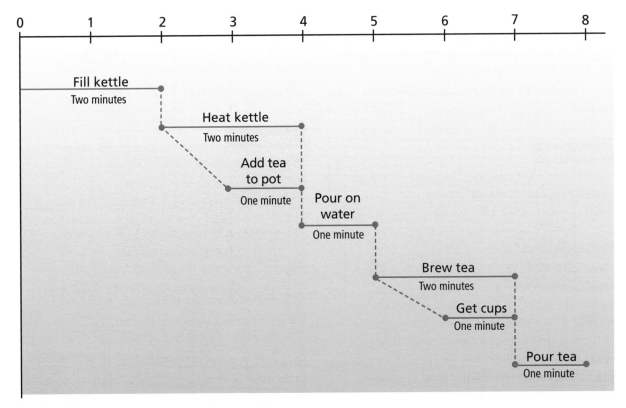

FIGURE 9.17 *The first draft of a critical path analysis diagram*

Having completed your critical flow analysis and transferred your timings onto your plan, you may now represent your final plan to show when individual tasks may start and finish. There are two techniques that you could use to represent this plan: a Gantt chart or a PERT chart. The choice of which technique to use is up to you.

Gantt charts

A Gantt chart is a diagram that shows each distinct activity as a block of time. Each block of time is labelled with a title to show what the task is and also the amount of time that the block represents. This is shown in the Gantt chart in Figure 9.18. The critical path through the tasks is shown as the longest sequence of dependent activities.

Gantt charts aid planning, as they show how long each activity is expected to take and the order in which activities should occur. Your Gantt chart will also allow you to model how long the overall project will take and where the pressure points in the project will occur. These may be

times when a number of tasks need completing or all members of any team with which you are working are involved in tasks.

PERT charts

PERT stands for **P**rogramme **E**valuation and **R**eview Technique. A completed PERT diagram looks something like a railway network and you may see PERT diagrams referred to as network models. A PERT chart will use circles to represent the milestones and linking lines to represent the time taken to complete the task. The linking lines are labelled to show the time allocated to each task.

Each milestone is labelled with a number so that the end milestone of an activity has a higher number than the beginning milestone. It is a good idea to use milestones numbered in units of ten

	Minutes							
Task	**1**	**2**	**3**	**4**	**5**	**6**	**7**	**8**
Fill kettle	▓	▓						
Heat kettle			▓	▓				
Put tea in pot			▓	▓				
Pour on water					▓			
Let tea brew						▓	▓	
Get cups							▓	
Pour tea								▓

FIGURE 9.18 *A Gantt chart*

so that new milestones may be added later with little disruption (for example, a new milestone between the first and what you thought was going to be the second could be given the number 15 and drawn off to the side).

When you are constructing a PERT chart, the critical path will be the longest chain of consecutive tasks and will usually be the main horizontal path on the chart.

As with Gantt charts, PERT charts allow you to show visually how different tasks interact.

Each task within the production of your response to the brief is shown, and it will be clear from the diagram how resources need to be organised for efficiency.

Theory into practice

Produce a PERT chart to represent the tasks involved in the production of a roast meal including meat (or a vegetarian substitute) and a range of vegetables of your choice.

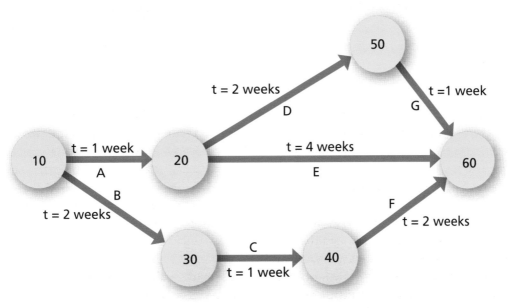

FIGURE 9.19 *A PERT chart*

Timelines

Timelines are another method of showing the progress of a project over time. You will probably have seen timelines representing events in history, with events in one country shown on one timeline and events in another country shown on a second. Where the timelines meet, the events are linked. The lead up to some sort of conflict is usually shown as a pair or more of timelines that eventually meet.

A timeline is constructed by showing how events occur at times throughout a project. Typically, you may write 'Task A started' and then later 'Task A completed'. It should be clear that timelines are a bit like diaries completed in advance of events. The simplest timeline will be one line with various events shown at different times. This is not a very clear method of showing your plans, as it may not be immediately clear when events begin and end or how many events are happening at the same time. However, timelines are probably the easiest of the three techniques described here for showing how the different tasks in a project may combine to create the finished solution.

CASE tools

CASE stands for **C**omputer **A**ided **S**oftware **E**ngineering and refers to automated tools that are specifically designed to support the software engineer or designer. When first introduced, these tools were mainly intended to help with software programming. Tools such as translators and assemblers were specifically created to aid the process of software development. However, as technology has advanced, so the range of available tools has increased. It is now possible to use tools that help with most aspects of software, including analysing software to identify bugs.

If, in producing your solution to a brief, you choose to use programming language to produce anything more than the simplest of tasks, you will need the help of at least some CASE tools. The area of programming is a specialist area within

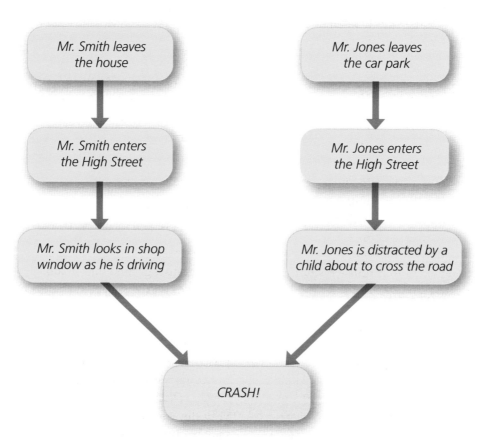

FIGURE 9.20 *A simple timeline showing the events leading up to a car crash*

ICT and requires more space and consideration than can be given here. Similarly, a more in-depth analysis and discussion of CASE tools would be considered part of a specialist programming textbook.

Other activities

We have just looked at some very powerful tools that will help you plan your project once you have decided what your project will actually do. This next section will look at some methods you could use to help you decide what you will include in the solution to the brief.

Reviewing current practice

When you first choose a brief, it is unlikely that you will know enough about the focus area to be able to produce anything more than an extremely simple response. A review of current practice, which will involve you analysing how things are done at the moment and identifying areas that you need to take into account, will allow you to talk about the focus area in more depth and with more clarity. Not only is this an important starting point for deciding what your finished solution will need to achieve, but it is also a task required by the exam board.

Your review of current practice should be at least a description of how tasks are currently done in the focus area. Ideally, you should include a discussion of the issues that need to be taken into account when producing the project. You may decide to discuss what the current working practice is trying to achieve or in what form it publishes the final product.

As you carry out your research, you may discover that there are some restrictions, such as restricted access to resources, that need to be taken into account. Any points you discover at this stage should be included in your report and taken into account when you plan and develop your solution to the brief.

Your review of current practice will focus on those tasks that are in some way linked with your project. For example, your brief may ask you to produce a spreadsheet that will be used in modelling the effects of a price change on sales and total revenue of a small bookseller. Your review of current practice could then be a description of how the effects of a price change are currently modelled in such a business. Another possibility is a brief that asks you to produce images for use in a school or college publication. In this case, you could focus on current publications and the methods used to produce these images. In both cases, you may find that the task is not currently done, and so your review would include commentary on the possible effects that this failure to carry out this task would have on the organisation.

So that you can review how things are done at the moment in the focus area, you will need to conduct some research. This can be a huge task, so where do you start? The best place is with information that already exists. This is called **secondary research**. The three main sources for secondary research are:

* the trade press

* trade associations

* market intelligence reports.

Each of these sources of data can give you some excellent background information. If the brief you have chosen is based on a new business or is a general task then secondary sources of information could prove extremely useful.

Most industries in the UK have a trade press. They are quite easy to find, as they tend to have names that describe what they do, such as *Drapers*, which is a magazine dealing with the fashion industry. Further examples may be found at the Trade Media Planner (via www.heinemann.co.uk/hotlinks, express code 2148P). They can provide excellent information and, if you are really lucky, may even include a specific article on the area on which you are focusing. Most public libraries will be able to give you advice on which industries have a trade magazine.

Trade associations and market intelligence reports may give you some useful information, but tend to be more statistical, with articles about trends in industries and the value of the industry as a whole. It is unlikely that you will need such in-depth information, but it is worth knowing that these sources exist.

Once you have found out all you can from secondary sources, it is time to carry out some research of your own. Research that you carry out will produce information and data that has not existed before, which is called **primary data**.

<table>
<tr><td>**Key terms**</td></tr>
</table>

Secondary research: Research based on information that already exists.

Primary data: Information obtained through your own research.

There are three main methods of finding your own data:

* questionnaires
* observation
* interviews.

A questionnaire asks questions! Ask the correct questions and the answers you need will come tumbling off the page. Ask the wrong questions, or the correct questions but in a wrong way, and you will have problems. For example, you may word a question in a way that prompts the respondent (the person answering the questions) to give you a certain answer. This means that your question, and maybe even the whole questionnaire, has been a total waste of time, because you have influenced the answers given by those answering the questions.

The main things to remember when writing a questionnaire are as follows:

* be sure about what you want to know
* avoid any bias or hints in questions which point the respondent towards a specific answer
* be sure to ask questions in a clear and concise way.

Once the questionnaire has been completed, you will need to look at the answers and try to see patterns. Patterns will only be clear if you are able to group the answers that your respondents give. If, for example, you asked a group of people for their eye colour and asked them to write the answer in a text box, you would probably get a huge list. When you came to analyse the data to see if any patterns existed, how would you cope with the following answers?

RESPONDENT	EYE COLOUR
A	Light blue
B	Blue
C	Greeny blue
D	Bluey green

Would you be prepared to put all these people down as having the same eye colour? Maybe you could put respondents A and B down as both having 'blue' eyes, but what about respondents C and D? Is respondent C in the 'blue group' and respondent D in the 'green group'?

To avoid problems caused by being given a range of answers, do not ask open questions; instead, try to ask closed questions, which restrict the answer the respondents may give. For example, you could ask the respondents to tick a box for the eye colour that most closely matches their own. This would give you a set of answers that were far easier to analyse.

You should also ask some questions about the respondents themselves. This will let you see if there are any links between the type of person who is answering the questions and the answers they are giving. These questions will be in a section on their own, either at the start of the questionnaire or at the end.

It is a good idea to test a questionnaire on a small group of people before you actually use it. This will give you the chance to see if there is any direction being given in questions or if the meaning of a question is clear.

Theory into practice

This activity will give you the opportunity to practise writing closed questions. Below is a list of open questions. For each question, suggest a closed question which could replace it.

1   What colour hair do you have?

2   What is your favourite food?

3   Describe your favourite restaurant.

Now consider this list of vague questions. For each question, suggest a question with more clarity.

4   How many pints of water do you drink?

5   Do you watch too much television?

6   Are you a regular cinema-goer?

A second research method is one where you watch people going about their daily routines. This method is called observation and, if done well, can be extremely useful. You may be able to see patterns in behaviour that would not be obvious if you had not carried out the observation. For example, watch a friend or classmate doing a task they do every day and take notes. You may notice that, when they concentrate, they scratch their left ear or poke their tongue out. Some time later, ask them to describe what they do when they are concentrating, such as how they hold their pen or any other aspect of their behaviour. It will be highly unlikely that they will be able to answer the question correctly. In this case, because you are watching out for certain actions or for what happens during a set period, the observation you have carried out will yield more worthwhile results than you would have gained from a questionnaire.

Observations are also a useful way of identifying patterns in group behaviour. You may, for example, be interested in whether a business should purchase a second photocopier. The answers to questionnaires have suggested that there are always queues and yet secondary research has told you that the photocopier is of sufficient capacity to cope with the amount of photocopies that are done. By sitting and watching the photocopier and seeing whether queues build up, you can assess whether a second photocopier may be an efficient purchase. If you do see significant queues then a second photocopier may be the answer; if these queues only happen at certain times in the day, you may decide that the solution to the problem may be a change in working practice.

Interviews allow you to talk to people and ask questions that need longer answers. They can be extremely useful, as you can gain an impression from the person to whom you are talking and can tease out any answers that you suspect may be lying beneath the surface. You will also be able to further explain any questions that the person being interviewed does not understand. However, as with questionnaires, be careful not to lead the person being interviewed to give you the answers you want to hear.

Drafting initial ideas

Whether you are working with others or on your own, you will need to consider different methods of meeting the needs of the brief. This is important because, whilst considering different possible responses in depth, you will be forced to reject what might have seemed completely reasonable ideas at one time but which, when properly thought through, prove to be ideas that are either too simple, too complicated or just would never work. By rejecting some of these initial ideas, you will be far more likely to settle on a solution that is achievable and does what the client needs.

There are stages to settling on a final solution to the brief. These are explained below.

Step 1: Once you have completed your observation and a report on current practice, you will have a better idea of how the target organisation currently does the task on which you will be working. Now is the time to reconsider what the brief is asking you to do. This may have seemed obvious when you first chose your brief, but, after carrying out some research, you may have further ideas. Before you make much more progress on the solution to the brief, you will need to discuss them with your client. Having a very clear understanding of the needs of the brief, improved by the insight gained from your research, will allow you to develop ideas which are far more focused than if you had not spent this time thinking through the project.

Step 2: Now is the time to consider how you are going to meet the demands of the brief. This will be a discussion of the big ideas, such as which software you will use, how the software will be configured or programmed and what your finished product will look like. If you are working as a team, call a group meeting, get hold of a huge piece of paper (a flip chart is ideal) and get scribbling. Encourage all of the team to put in ideas and do not criticise anything that is suggested. Once everyone is out of ideas, have a group discussion about what has been suggested and try to whittle the ideas down to a few that could be successful. These ideas will then be taken away and given some further thought. At the end of the process, you will have the basis of a working plan.

Step 3: You are now ready to set up your meeting with the client to agree on a solution to the brief. At this meeting, you may want to present your client either with one final design for the solution or a few competing ones. The choice of how many ideas to present at this meeting is a difficult one. If you produce one only and the client is not impressed, it may be some time before you can meet to discuss any further designs. If you produce too many, it can look like you are really unclear about the whole of the project and are desperate for guidance. To avoid these dangers,

you should probably present three different ideas equally well and be prepared to discuss each of them.

Assessing your ICT skills and identifying areas for development

Now that you have agreed a plan with the client, you will be able to complete your review of your software skills to identify the skills that you will need to develop if you are to be successful. Where your plan needs specific technical tasks or the use of advanced skills, include time on your plan for this training to take place. You may also choose to include the source of this training. By doing so, you make it clear to any reader of your plan that you have identified any skills gap that either you or a member of your group may have and how you intend to bridge that gap.

Reviewing the plan on completion of the project

One of the final tasks you will need to complete is a reflection of how well your plan worked for you. It is tempting to allow little to no time for this to take place, but this task is as vital as any other you will have carried out. If this is to be a meaningful exercise, this process will need time.

There are two possible approaches to this task. First, you could meet as a group to discuss the plan. Alternatively, each member of the group may wish to reflect on the success of the plan on their own. Either of these methods could be successful, as both have the potential to bring out some honest and critical comments.

How to...

Review a plan

1 Start by considering each stage of the plan on its own.

2 Compare each stage of the plan against the initial mind map or any other planning tools you may have used.

3 As you compare each stage, make a list of good and bad points.

4 Finally, decide whether each stage of the plan was a success or a failure.

Keeping a log of work or diary

As you are working through your solution, you should keep a record of your experiences. Whichever format you decide to use to record these experiences, you need to build up evidence that will allow you to reflect on how effective your project was in meeting the needs of the brief and how your skills have developed as you have worked on this solution.

This section will now consider in more detail the format you may use to record the experiences you have whilst working on your solution.

This unit is about how you respond to a brief, and your thoughts as your skills develop are a vital piece of evidence, as they allow you to show what you have learned as you have produced your solution. It is important that you keep a log of how these skills develop, as this will allow you to complete your summative report. This log can take many forms, but a diary completed at the end of each session would seem to be the best method. If the diary is set out using headings, it will develop into an important piece of evidence that will help you when it comes to writing your final report. As you are writing, you will be able to reflect on the work you have completed during the day, the challenges with which you were faced and the techniques you employed to cope with them. Some of these techniques and strategies will be ones you have used before,

in which case you will be able to comment on how effective your knowledge and understanding was in helping you meet the challenge. Other techniques and strategies will be completely new to you, in which case you can comment both on the learning process and how successful the new approach was.

The log itself should include the following elements:

* a list of all tasks completed when working on the solution

* a frank discussion of your contribution to the task

* a list of any skills you have used in meeting the needs of the brief

* an ongoing discussion of how your skills are developing in order to meet the demands of the brief.

9.5 Continually evaluating your work

Continual self-evaluation is stressed throughout this unit. Your summative report for this unit will focus on seven key areas:

* How has the work others have done influenced how your work has developed?

* How have you supported others?

* The process of making important decisions and then informing others of these decisions

* How did you deal with conflict whilst producing your solution to the brief?

* The effectiveness of the processes and techniques you developed in allowing you to meet the demands of the brief.

* How well did your project meet the demands of the brief?

* How would you alter your finished solution if you were to do it again?

By self-evaluating at all stages of your project, you will build up a body of evidence that will not only give you a reference point for when you write your summative report but will also make

DATE	ACTIVITY	THOUGHTS
12/1	Research	Good questionnaire, but I needed to ask some questions to back it up.
13/1	Analysing data	Data covers the topics I need, but I need to find out some more details about working practice.
16/1	Contacting the client	Had to apologise for needing to go back, but managed to deal with an angry client and am going back tomorrow.

FIGURE 9.21 *Excerpt from a diary*

SOURCE OF CONFLICT	HOW I DEALT WITH IT	HOW EFFECTIVELY I DEALT WITH IT	WHAT I LEARNED
Martin handed his report in late	I lost my temper with Martin. Martin then left the team.	Not very well. Martin had been ill and needed support, not me shouting at him.	Patience!
The client decided to change his mind about the colour scheme on the front page.	Set up a meeting between the client and myself. Explained that we were almost finished and that a change would cause delay.	Well. Client agreed to reduce changes to only one new colour and to accept completion a week later than planned.	Negotiation skills.

FIGURE 9.22 *Example of self-evaluation within a diary*

the process of writing the report itself easier. The previous section discussed the importance of keeping a diary of your experiences. This diary should not just be a record of events, but should include reflection on the areas listed above. As you are writing, consider issues such as how you dealt with events, how your skills had to develop to do this and the implications for the next time an issue like the one with which you have just dealt comes up again. In short, as you are writing this diary and adding your reflections, you are effectively writing your summative report and, if well written, your task at the end will be much reduced.

Think it over...

Reflecting on the progress you have made

You will remember that you assessed your skills at the start of this unit by completing a box to show how you had developed skills whilst working on different units.

When you complete your project, you will need to reflect on how your skills have developed. Figure 9.22 may be used to help you with this. It shows how you may assess how well you dealt with conflict. The excerpt from a diary has been competed to show how a team member has dealt with conflict in a group.

In the first example, the team has suffered because of a lack of skill. In the second, the team has benefited from some well-used negotiating skills.

9.6 Producing a summative project

When you have completed your solution to the brief and passed it over to the client, you will need to produce a summative report of your experiences. This will be a large body of work and, as discussed elsewhere in this unit, you should build up as much evidence as you can as you are working through the response.

This summative report must include the following elements:

* a discussion of the needs of the chosen brief
* an analysis of your ICT and project management skills at the start of the project
* research you have conducted into current working practices
* a report on current working practices
* any planning you conducted
* your diary or log
* all support materials produced in response to the brief
* a summative report evaluating your response to the brief
* a summative report evaluating your overall performance in creating the finished solution
* a report on the effectiveness of your ICT solution to the brief.

We have already discussed some of these tasks in some detail. However, this section will now expand on some of these elements to give you further insight into what should be included.

The needs of the brief

The first stage in producing a list showing the needs of the brief is to break the brief down into manageable chunks. The process of chunking down has been discussed earlier and you should be fully aware of the importance of this task. Start by trying to identify the main headines for each task. For example, you may have been asked to produce a school magazine. Chunking down the section dealing with images and photographs may result in a list that includes some or all of the following headlines:

* Take photographs.
* Edit photographs to suit style of the magazine.
* Print completed photographs and pass copy to editor.

From these headline tasks, you may discuss the needs further. There are various ways in which you could do this. A spider diagram or mind map expanding these issues may be sufficient, or you may decide to discuss each requirement in a written section. However you choose to present this analysis, the discussion will focus on the two main areas of hardware and software.

The discussion of hardware is basically a discussion of what you need in order to do the project. In the hardware section, you may wish to consider the following:

* the quality of computer required, including memory and storage devices or capacity
* which peripheral items, such as printers and scanners, are required and of what type.

To continue with the example of images for a school magazine, you would include a discussion of hardware issues under two headline tasks, 'Take photographs' and 'Print completed photographs'.

The software discussion is a discussion of how you will 'do' the project. When discussing software, you may wish to consider the following issues:

* Which type of applications software package is required?

* Which tools or facilities are included in this type of applications package?
* How will these tools be used to meet the demands of the brief?
* Which particular package is sufficient to meet the needs?

Again, to continue with the school magazine example, the headline task to 'edit photographs' would be expanded by discussing how this editing process may be achieved.

Support materials

Your solution to the brief will require a range of support materials. These materials will need to be fit for purpose and to meet the needs of the client. The choice of support materials and the format they will take will be based on the brief you choose. For example, if you decide to produce a program, you will need to produce both **user documentation** and **technical documentation**. Such a brief may also require data to be gathered, in which case you should also produce the data-gathering sheets. A brief asking you to produce a series of images may require a list of images with where they were taken and the tools used to create the effects. You may be asked to produce teaching units, in which case the list of support materials will depend on the age and ability level of the class at which any package is aimed.

User documentation

There are specific requirements for what should be included in user documentation. User documentation is any documentation included with a program to help the user run the package. Another term for user documentation is a **user guide**. Your user guide should fully explain to the user how to install and run all aspects of the package. It should include a trouble-shooting section, which would deal with common problems, and a list of error messages that may appear and how they may be dealt with or avoided. Increasingly, a user guide would include a frequently asked questions (FAQ) section.

Think it over...

User documents

For this activity, you will need at least three forms of user documents.

For each user document, analyse the content of the document and produce an idiot's guide to writing a user document. Your guide should include the purpose of a user guide and a list of what should be included.

The summative reports

The summative reports require a discussion of three separate areas. The discussion of your performance should focus on the skills discussed in the section on working with others. This section highlighted four skills areas:

* interpersonal skills
* technical skills
* effort skills
* economic skills.

Your report should focus on each of these areas and may be supported by the diary you have written as well as any other evidence you may have gathered, such as notes or minutes from meetings or witness statements from your project supervisors.

The evaluation of the project as a whole should be a discussion of how well your project met each of the objectives for the project you set out at the start. You should discuss the success of each of the tasks identified as part of the chunking down process and be prepared to explain why some aspects of your work did not perform as well as intended. There are many reasons why a particular task may not have been successful, ranging from lack of skills through to problems with team members, but remember that you may gain as many marks for fully explaining an unsuccessful project or part of a project as for explaining a successful one.

Technical documentation

Any technical documentation should show how the program works. This document is not intended for the user and it is expected that it would be written in technical language using terms that the average user would not fully understand.

This document would include a description of all the technical aspects of the program: the type of software used to produce the program, a description of the purpose of the software in technical terms, a flowchart or other representation of how data is processed, and some indications of how any modifications to the program itself may be achieved.

Knowledge check

1 Why is it important to assess the success of a project once it has been completed?

2 Explain the difference between user documentation and technical documentation.

3 Explain the difference between primary and secondary research.

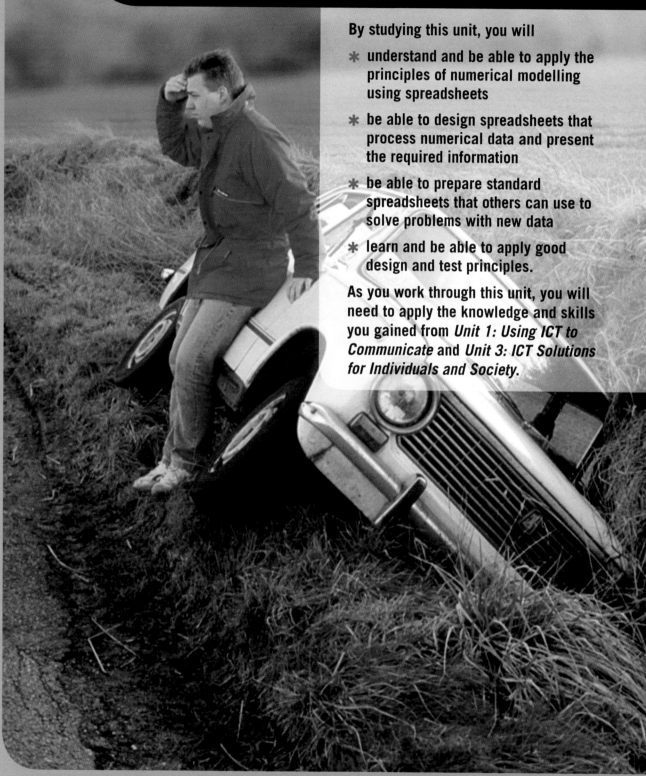

Numerical modelling using spreadsheets

By studying this unit, you will

* understand and be able to apply the principles of numerical modelling using spreadsheets

* be able to design spreadsheets that process numerical data and present the required information

* be able to prepare standard spreadsheets that others can use to solve problems with new data

* learn and be able to apply good design and test principles.

As you work through this unit, you will need to apply the knowledge and skills you gained from *Unit 1: Using ICT to Communicate* and *Unit 3: ICT Solutions for Individuals and Society.*

Introduction

As part of a Young Enterprise scheme, you have decided to make and sell greetings cards. You know how much the raw materials to make each card will cost and the amount of other costs such as hiring equipment. What should you charge for each card? How many will you need to sell to start making a profit? A spreadsheet will help to answer these questions and many others. Modern spreadsheet software includes specialist facilities that can be used to create complex models to predict what will happen in the future. One example is calculating the likely value of a pension based on different interest rate predictions; another is calculating car insurance premiums for different groups of drivers based on how likely they are to make a claim.

How you will be assessed

This unit will be assessed on a portfolio of evidence that you will produce. The assignment at the end of this unit will provide you with the evidence to complete the portfolio.

What you need to learn

In this unit you will create a spreadsheet to meet specified requirements that will involve the use of some of the specialist and complex spreadsheet facilities. To do this, you need to learn about

* developing a working specification
* using spreadsheet facilities
* designing and developing spreadsheets
* implementing a spreadsheet solution
* presenting spreadsheet information
* testing spreadsheets
* documenting the development
* evaluating the effectiveness of your solution and your performance.

10.1 Developing a working specification

Before you can begin to design a spreadsheet, you will need to find out exactly what the user of your spreadsheet requires it to do. You will need to find out what data will be input and what output is required. This will help you to decide what **numerical processing** needs to take place. You will also need to find out how the results should be presented; for example, does the user want output as numerical values or charts? You will also need to consider how you can make it easier for the user to input the correct data into the spreadsheet and to obtain the required results.

> **Key terms**
>
> *Numerical processing:* The calculations that will be needed to obtain the required information.

Analysing user requirements

To analyse the user's requirements there are a number of questions to which you will need to obtain the answers. You might find it helpful to create a list of questions to ask the user before you interview them. However, you should be prepared to ask other questions to ensure you get all the information you need. Your interview(s) with the user will need to find the answers to the following questions.

What output information does the user want?

You may have been asked to produce a spreadsheet to replace an existing system, or the spreadsheet might be required to solve a new problem. In either case, you will need to question the user carefully to find out exactly what results the spreadsheet must produce. This might be how long it will take for a company to **break even** based on different levels of income and expenditure, what the likely **return on an investment** will be after different **investment periods** and based on different **interest rate**

predictions, or predictions for the final positions of teams in the Premiership based on the match results to date.

> **Key terms**
>
> *Break-even:* When a company's income becomes equal to the amount it spends (expenditure) so that it can start to make a profit.
>
> *Investment:* Money that is put into a bank, business or stocks and shares to make a profit.
>
> *Return on an investment:* Profit made.
>
> *Investment period:* The length of time the money is invested.
>
> *Interest:* The money earned by the investment.
>
> *Interest rate:* The percentage of the investment paid as interest. This will vary over time.

How is the information currently obtained?

If you are replacing an existing system, you will need to find out exactly how the information is currently obtained. You will need to find out what is good about the current system – what works well – so you can take this forward into the new system. You will also need to find out what does not work so well, so that you can improve it in your spreadsheet. It might help to watch the system being used and to collect and study documents, such as **data capture forms** and printed output, that are currently used.

Where will the input data come from?

All spreadsheets will require input data. In the break-even model above, the input will be the values of income and expenditure; in the Premiership model, it will be the results of matches played to date. You will need to find out from where and how the input data is obtained. Is a data capture form needed to collect the data? If you are replacing an existing system, does a data capture form already exist? If it does, you may need to consider designing the input to your spreadsheet to match the existing form. In some cases, the data may be collected automatically, for example using a **data-logging** system. You will need to design the inputs to your spreadsheet to match the sources of input data.

What numerical processing is needed?

Having found out what output is required and the data that will be input, you must now find out what numerical processing is needed. In the break-even model, in simple terms, this will involve subtracting expenditure from income to determine when this becomes a positive quantity. The Premiership model will require more complex processing based on the probability of teams winning or losing particular matches. The return on investment model will require the use of financial functions, for example to calculate interest rates and future value. You will need to find out about the mathematics needed to obtain the required output from the inputs. This will help you decide which formulae and functions are needed in your spreadsheet and how these will be linked.

What user aids can be provided?

Most spreadsheet users will not be ICT experts. The system you create will need to make it as easy as possible for the user to input the correct data and obtain the output required. You will need to consider how you can achieve this. This may include:

* providing forms for data input
* validating inputs to reject values that are too large, too small or of the wrong type
* providing drop-down lists to restrict the values that can be input

* providing buttons backed by macros to carry out common tasks
* providing input messages to tell the user what they must input.

Your aim should be to hide as much as possible of the actual spreadsheet from the user.

You will need to discuss the user aids that you can provide with the end user to ensure that what you include meets their needs.

How does the output need to be presented?

Another important aspect that you will need to discuss with the user is how the output should be presented. This may be in a particular format: as an invoice, in a table, mail merged into a letter or as graphs or charts. You will need to find out exactly what is required and design the output of your spreadsheet to meet these requirements. You may need to draw up some initial designs for outputs and refine them as a result of discussions with the user to ensure their requirements are met.

Creating a design specification

When you have interviewed the user of your spreadsheet thoroughly and gathered together the answers to the questions described, the next stage is to create a design specification. Your design specification needs to state the user's requirements in detail so that the scope of the project is clear. It also needs to make clear the work that must be done to meet the user's requirements. Your design specification should include the following:

* a clear and detailed statement of the user's requirements in terms of the information they want from the spreadsheet model
* a description of how the information is currently obtained (if at all), any aspects of the current system that work well and will be retained, and any aspects that need to be improved or replaced
* details of data sources and how the data will be collected
* details of the numerical processing required

* details of the user aids that will be incorporated and the layout of data input screens, including sketches

* details of how the output will be presented, again including sketches.

Your design specification should also include details of how your spreadsheet will be tested – a test specification. You will learn more about what this should include when we discuss testing later in this unit.

When you have completed your design specification, you will need to discuss it with the user to check that they agree with what you have produced. You will need to make any changes they require so that you and the user agree the design specification before you begin work on the detailed design and implementation of your spreadsheet.

CASE STUDY

The Sovereign Hill amateur dramatics group stages a number of plays each year. The plays are performed in a small theatre owned by the group. Each play is performed for six nights from Monday to Saturday and there is usually a matinee performance on Saturday afternoon. The bookings manager is responsible for selling tickets for each performance. Ticket booking is currently done manually. The group has recently been given a computer with spreadsheet software installed. The booking manager would like you to produce a spreadsheet to keep a record of the seats booked for each performance and the revenue generated, and to print the tickets. She would also like to be able to carry out some analysis of the ticket sales to compare revenue from different performances of a play, to compare revenue from different plays and the breakdown of the types of tickets sold. She would also like to model the effect of changing ticket prices.

The booking manager currently uses a paper seating plan for each performance. This is a simple grid with two side-by-side blocks of seats, each with 25 rows of 15 seats with a central aisle. The booking manager asks the customer how many seats they want to book and where they would prefer to sit. If the seats are available, the customer is asked which type of tickets he or she requires. For most plays, adult, child and concession (student, unemployed, pensioner) tickets are available. The booking manager writes A, Ch or Con in the relevant squares on the seating plan to indicate that the seats have been booked. She must then write the row and seat numbers on the appropriate number of tickets and use a calculator to calculate the total due from the customer. The amount paid is recorded in a column beside the seating plan. After each performance, the booking manager counts up the number of each type of ticket sold and multiplies each by the relevant ticket price. These are added and compared with the total amount paid. Customers often buy tickets immediately before a performance and frequently errors are made in recording these sales because of the rush to get everyone seated in the auditorium before the curtain goes up.

1 Analyse the user requirements of the booking manager of the Sovereign Hill amateur dramatics group.

2 Create a design specification for a spreadsheet solution to this problem.

10.2 Using spreadsheet facilities

Spreadsheet software offers a wide range of standard and specialised facilities. You may be familiar with some of the standard facilities from your work for *Unit 3: ICT Solutions for Individuals and Society*. You need to be able to use the standard facilities described below to independently carry out activities including:

✳ selecting and setting cell formats to match the data format

✳ selecting and using suitable cell presentation formats

✳ using and processing numerical spreadsheet data

✳ using cell referencing facilities appropriately

✳ correctly applying and using operators and formulae

✳ using common built-in spreadsheet functions appropriately.

You also need to be able to selectively apply at least one type of specialised built-in spreadsheet function.

Setting cell formats to match the data format

The cell format is the way that the data in a cell is displayed. Selecting Cell in the Format menu and then the Number tab will provide a list of the formats available. It is important that the format chosen matches the data in the cell.

Decimal number

Decimal numbers are numbers that have digits after the decimal point (decimal places). For example, if a cell contains someone's height in metres, the value will be a decimal number because most people's height is between 1 and 2 metres.

If you select Number from the list of formats, you can select how many decimal places are displayed. If a value has more decimal places than the format will display, the number is

rounded to that number of decimal places, but the complete number is used in any further calculations.

Theory into practice

1 Make sure the format of cell A1 of a spreadsheet is set to General.

2 Enter the formula =100/6 in cell A1. The answer to this sum is 16.666666666 . . ., i.e. 16.6 recurring. The number of decimal places shown depends on the width of the cell to a maximum of eight, i.e. 16.66666667.

3 Now format cell A1 as a number with two decimal places. What value does the cell show?

4 Key this value into cell A2 – do not copy and paste.

5 Format cells B1 and B2 to number with two decimal places.

6 Enter formulae in these cells to divide each number by 2, i.e. =A1/2 and =A2/2.

Are both results the same? If they are not, why is this?

When deciding how many decimal places to display, you need to consider the accuracy of the data. If the input data only has values to two decimal places, the results should not show more than two.

Integer number

An integer is a whole number that does not have a decimal part. For example, if a cell contains a number of people, the value will be an integer. Microsoft Excel does not provide a separate integer format, although it does have an INT function that discards the fractional part. You can, however, set the number of decimal places to zero in the number format.

Percentage

This format multiplies the value of a cell by 100 and displays it with a percentage symbol (%). For example, at the time of writing, value added tax (VAT) is calculated at 17.5% on most goods and services. To find how much VAT must be paid, the net price must be multiplied by 0.175. If the cell containing the VAT rate is formatted as percentage, the value stored and used in calculations will be 0.175, but the cell will display 17.5%.

Date

All dates are stored as a number, normally counting from 1st January 1900 – today's date happens to be 38602. The Date format determines how the date will be displayed. There are several different options available for you to select from. Make sure that your PC's regional settings are set up correctly for the UK. Otherwise, you may find that dates are formatted in the US style (mm/dd/yy) and the currencies default to dollars.

Fractions

The Fraction format displays decimal numbers as fractions. You can choose to display fractions with up to one, two or three digits in the numerator and the denominator. You can also choose to display a number as specific fractions – halves, quarters, eighths, sixteenths, tenths and hundredths. If the number is not an exact multiple of the fractions selected, the nearest will be displayed.

Text

All UK telephone numbers start with the digit 0. If you enter a telephone number into a cell of a spreadsheet, the software treats it as a number and deletes the leading zero. Formatting the cell as Text retains the leading zero, as data is displayed exactly as it is entered.

Currency

As you would expect, the currency format displays values as money. The default is most likely to show the £ sign and two decimal places. However, this can be changed to any currency symbol such as € (euros) or GBP (the international currency code for British pounds). You can also select how negative values are displayed. It is often a good idea to show negative values in red – either with or without a minus sign – so that the user's attention is drawn to a situation that might need action, such as payments exceeding income.

Scientific

Scientific notation is usually used for very large or very small numbers. For example, a 40 GB hard disk can hold 42,949,672,960 bytes of data. In scientific notation, this would be written as 4.29×10^{10}. The Scientific format in Excel would display this as 4.29E+10. At the other extreme, the connections between components in a processor chip are only 0.00000009 metres thick. In scientific notation this would be 9.00×10^{-8} metres and would be displayed as 9.00E-08. You can select how many decimal places are displayed, but there will always be a single digit (other than 0) before the decimal point. If you enter a number of 100,000,000,000 or larger, Excel will automatically display it in Scientific format. Similarly, a number like 0.0000000001, with nine or more 0s after the decimal point, will be automatically displayed in scientific format.

Custom or Special

Custom format type allows you to create your own display format for the content of a cell, but it does provide you with some starting points. In these starting formats, a 0 denotes that a digit will always be displayed, even if it is zero; a # indicates that the digit will only be displayed if it has a value. Table 10.1 shows examples of how data would be displayed if the format #,##0.00 were selected.

Special provides mostly American formats for values such as zip codes, telephone and social security numbers.

DATA INPUT	DISPLAYED AS
66000	66,000.00
6600	6,600.00
660	660.00
0660	660.00
66	66.00
6.6	6.60
0.66	0.66
0.066	0.07

TABLE 10.1 *The effect of the format #,##0.00*

Setting cell presentation formats

Cell presentation formats allow you to improve the appearance of a spreadsheet to make it easier to read and understand. You need to be able to use all of the following presentation formats effectively.

Horizontal alignment

By default, most spreadsheet packages align text to the left edge of the cell and numbers to the right. The logical values TRUE and FALSE are centred. Whilst this allows for quick differentiation between the two types of data, it does not always make the data as easy to read as it could, for example when a column heading is left aligned and the numbers below it are aligned to the right. The alignment of any cell can be made left, centred or right. However, it is not a good idea to centre numeric values, unless they are all single digits, because any sense of place value will be lost. These options can usually be selected using buttons on the toolbar as well as selecting Cells from the Format menu and then the Alignment tab.

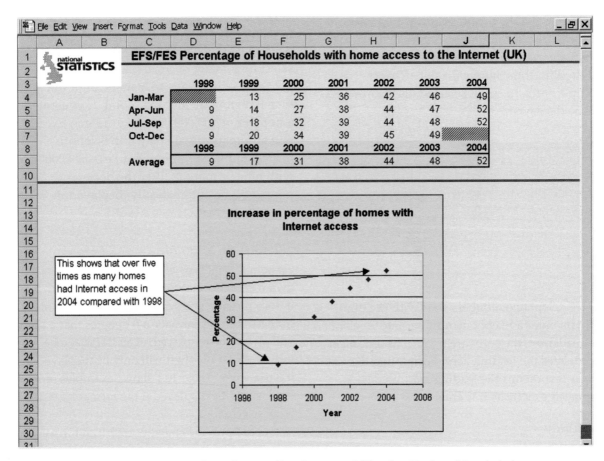

FIGURE 10.1 *Good use of colour aids understanding (Source: Office for National Statistics)*

The Alignment dialogue box provides additional options. If a cell contains a block of text, it is possible to justify it. This breaks the cell contents into multiple lines within the cell and adjusts the spacing between words so that all lines are as wide as the cell. It is also possible to centre across a selection. This is useful for centring a heading across a number of columns of a spreadsheet. You need to enter the title in the left-most cell. You then select the range of cells and select Centre across selection.

Colour

Colour can be used to enhance the appearance and readability of a spreadsheet (see Figure 10.1). Cells can be filled with colour and the colour of the cell content can also be changed. Filling different areas of a spreadsheet with different colours can help to differentiate them. For example, all cells where the user must enter data can be filled with one colour, whilst the cells that contain the results of calculations can be filled with another. One convention for showing negative numbers, as already indicated, is to display them in red. However, care is needed when choosing colours. Red text or numbers on a green background will appear as a brown blur to someone who is red/green colour-blind. Too many different colours or colours that clash are more likely to annoy the user than to help them understand the spreadsheet (Figure 10.2).

One other way that colour can be used is with conditional formatting. This is where the formatting of a cell can be made to change depending on its content. This is useful to highlight when action is needed, for example when stock levels have fallen below a set value and an order needs to be made.

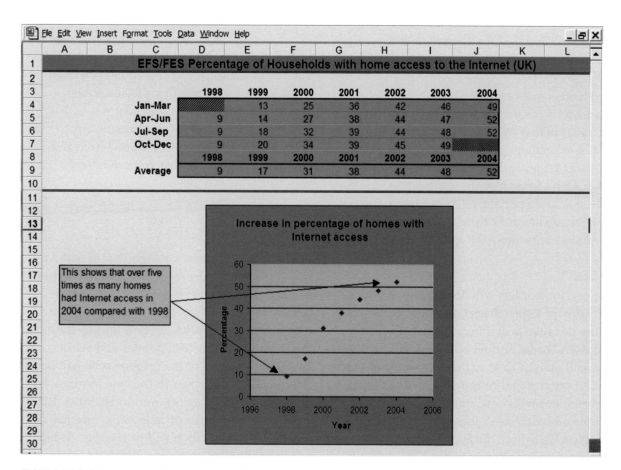

FIGURE 10.2 *Too many colours annoy the user*

Vertical alignment

Vertical alignment determines whether the cell content appears at the top of the cell, in the centre, or at the bottom. It only applies when a cell is deeper than the height of the characters within it. Normally, the height of a row automatically adjusts to fit the height of the characters (autofit), but row height can be set to be a specific value. The vertical alignment options can also be found on the Alignment tab of the dialogue box that is accessed by selecting Cells from the Format menu.

Shading

As well as solid colour fill, there is a range of patterns that can be applied to the cells on a spreadsheet. These can be found by selecting Cells from the Format menu and then the Patterns tab. The colour selected for the cell shading and the pattern must be different or you will simply end up with a solid colour fill. Care is needed when using patterns and shading that any text or numbers in the cells can still be read easily.

Fonts

As with other software packages, when using spreadsheet software you will have access to a wide range of font styles and sizes. Other than for titles or headings, it is best to stick to standard, easy-to-read fonts such as Arial or Times New Roman. Don't forget that, in a spreadsheet, it is the results that are important: cell presentation formats should be used to make these easier to understand; fancy fonts may achieve the opposite effect.

Borders

How you use borders will do much to aid the readability of a spreadsheet. A border below the column headings will differentiate them from the data. A border around cells that require data input will make it clear to the user where to enter data. A border round cells that show the results of calculations will draw attention to them. To apply a border, select the group of cells and then select Cells from the Format menu. The Borders tab will allow you to select the type of line you want to use and where you want the border to appear.

Using and manipulating your spreadsheet

Spreadsheet software provides tools that help you to manipulate data. Some of these are similar to those you will be familiar with from using other types of software, such as word-processing software. All of these tools can be found in the Edit menu.

Find, search and replace data

Find allows you to locate each occurrence of a particular data item, whilst Replace allows you to find a particular data item and replace it with something else.

You can choose to search by row or by column, whether you want to match the case, and whether the result must match the entire content of a cell. Find Next will move to the next occurrence of the data item, which you can then choose to replace or not. Replace All will change every occurrence of the data item.

Go to a specified cell

The Go To facility is useful if you have a large spreadsheet that is not all visible on screen. Typing in a cell reference will take you to that cell. What's more, the Go To dialogue box keeps a record of where you started from and any cells you go to, so that you can retrace your steps.

Cut, copy, paste, move and paste special

These facilities work in a slightly different way from those in word-processing software. When you select a block of cells and select Cut, the content of the cells does not disappear, but a flashing border appears around the selection. When you move the cell pointer and select Paste, the contents of the original cells will be cleared and will appear in the new location. For the Paste facility to work, you must either select exactly the same area of cells as the original, or just a single cell, which will be the top left-hand corner of the new block of cells. Copy works in the same way, but the content of the original cells is not cleared.

If you want to paste the cut or copied cells within the area of the spreadsheet that contains data, you can use Insert Copied Cells. This works best when a whole row or column is being pasted, otherwise you will need to decide in which direction the existing cells are to be shifted. This may result in formulae referring to the wrong cells and giving the wrong value or an error message. It is also possible to move the content of cells by selecting the cells and dragging them to a new position on the spreadsheet. If the destination cells already contain data, you will be asked if you want to replace it.

Paste Special allows you to choose what you want to paste. For example, if you are pasting values that are the results of calculations to somewhere else on the spreadsheet, or to another spreadsheet, you may need to use Paste Special and paste the values. If you paste the formulae, the cell references may not be correct and you will get error messages or different values from what you expect. Using Paste Link will ensure that any changes in the value in the original cell will be reflected in the pasted cell.

Clear

If you select a cell and press the Delete key on the keyboard, it will clear the contents of the cell but leave any formatting intact. By selecting Clear in the Edit menu, you can choose whether you want to clear everything from the cell, just the formatting, just the content or just a comment that is attached to it.

Using cell referencing facilities

Cell referencing allows you to include the contents of particular cells in a formula or function. This is what allows results to be recalculated if the values in the cells are changed.

Relative referencing

Most cell referencing used in formulae is **relative cell referencing**. This means that if the formula is copied down a column of cells, the cell references change to match as shown in Table 10.2.

	A	B	C
1			=A1+B1
2			=A2+B2
3			=A3+B3

TABLE 10.2 *Relative references*

Absolute cell referencing

Absolute cell referencing is used when you want to always use the value in a particular cell in a formula. An example of this would be the hourly rate in the spreadsheet shown in Table 10.3. The wages for each member of staff are calculated by multiplying their total hours by the hourly rate. The formula in cell H4 is =G4*$B$1. The $ symbols show that this is an absolute cell reference. To make a cell reference absolute, you move the cell pointer onto that cell so that it appears in the formula

	A	B	C	D	E	F	G	H
1	Hourly rate	£8.50						
2				Hours worked				
3			Week 1	Week 2	Week 3	Week 4	Total Hours	Wages
4		Maggie	36	29	40	27	132	£1,122.00
5		Deepak	25	30	29	44	128	£1,088.00
6		Surinder	28	31	29	40	128	£1,088.00
7		Judith	15	20	17	12	64	£544.00
8		John	25	36	29	26	116	£986.00

TABLE 10.3 *Example spreadsheet using absolute cell referencing*

and then press F4 on the keyboard. When the formula is copied into cells H5 to H8, the first cell reference will change, but $B$1 will stay the same. So the formula in H8 will be =G8*$B$1. The advantage of this is that, if the hourly rate changes or you want to see the effect of changing it, only one value needs to be changed in the spreadsheet.

Mixed cell referencing

Mixed referencing is when either the row or the column is absolute and the other is relative, for example $B2, or B$2. In the first example, the value will always be found in column B, but the row will change from cell to cell. In the second example, the values will always be found in row 2, but the column will change from cell to cell.

Cell ranges

Another way of achieving the same thing as absolute referencing is to name the cell. You do this by selecting the cell and then selecting Name in the Insert menu. You then select Define. If, as in the example in Table 10.3, there is a label next to the cell to say what it contains, this label will be used to name the cell, i.e. Hourly_rate. Otherwise, you can type in a name. The name can then be used in formulae, rather than an absolute reference. It is also possible to name a **range of cells**. Using the wage calculation example, the range of cells G4 to G8 can be named as Total_hours. The formulae in cells H4 to H8 can then be entered as =Hourly_rate*Total_hours. This makes the spreadsheet calculations a lot easier to follow. Named cell ranges can also be used with functions.

Multi-sheet referencing

A spreadsheet workbook can consist of a number of linked worksheets. You can reference cells on different sheets in a formula. This is known as 3D referencing. This will appear as, for example, =Sheet1!B2.

Applying common operators in formulae

Formulae in a spreadsheet use operators and cell references to perform calculations on the contents of the cells so that useful results may be obtained.

OPERATOR	EXAMPLE	WHAT IT DOES
+	A1+A2	Adds the contents of the two cells together
-	A1-A2	Subtracts the contents of A2 from that of A1
*	A1*A2	Multiplies the content of the two cells together
/	A1/A2	Divides the content of A1 by the content of A2
%	A1/A2%	Divides the content of A1 by the content of A2, then multiplies the answer by 100 to give it as a percentage
^	A1^3	Raises the content of A1 to the power 3, i.e. A1*A1*A1

TABLE 10.4 *Arithmetic operators*

Arithmetic operators

Operators are used with cell references to create formulae. When describing cell referencing, we have used the arithmetic operators + (add) and * (multiply). A list of other arithmetic operators that you need to be able to use are listed in Table 10.4.

Relational operators and logical values

It is also possible to use relational operators in formulae. This tests whether the relationship is true or false. The result of this will be the logical value TRUE if the relationship is true or the logical value FALSE if it is not. Relational operators are most often used with the IF function. As you will find out shortly, this function returns one outcome if the relationship is true and another if it is false. The relational operators you should be able to use are shown in Table 10.5. The cells used in the relationship will usually contain the results of other calculations – most people can tell whether one number is bigger, smaller or equal to another!

Parentheses ( )

As with any mathematics, there is an order or precedence for operators. The order in which operations will be evaluated is %, ^, * and /, + and –, and then the relational operators =, <, >, <=, >= and <>. You can change the order by using brackets, more correctly called parentheses. Whatever is in the brackets will be evaluated first. This is best shown by an example using simple numbers. The sum 2+3*4 will give the answer 14. The multiplication is done first 3*4=12 and then the

OPERATOR	EXAMPLE	RELATIONSHIP
=	A1=B1	Is equal to
>	A1>B1	Is greater than
<	A1<B1	Is less than
>=	A1>=B1	Is greater than or equal to
<=	A1<=B1	Is less than or equal to
<>	A1<>B1	Is not equal to

TABLE 10.5 *Relational operators*

2 is added to give 14. However, using parentheses, (2+3)*4 will give an answer of 20. The bracket is evaluated first to give 5, which is then multiplied by 4 to give 20. When you are creating formulae in a spreadsheet, you need to take great care over the order of precedence and use parentheses when necessary. If you do not, you may find the results of calculations are not what you expected.

Applying common built-in spreadsheet functions

Spreadsheet software offers a range of built-in functions that you can use. You will need to be able to use the common built-in functions effectively.

SUM

The SUM function is one of the most commonly used, and the one that is most often used incorrectly! Excel even provides an AutoSum button (Σ) on the toolbar. The purpose of the SUM function, as its name suggests, is to add up the values in a range of cells; for example, =SUM(A1:A6) will add up the contents of cells 1 to 6 in column A. The range of cells does not have to be a single row or column; for example, =SUM(A1:B6) would add the values in cells 1 to 6 in both columns A and B. The content of the bracket could also be a named cell range. Going back to the wage calculation spreadsheet in Table 10.3, the total hours worked by all the employees could be calculated using =SUM(Total_hours). The same result could be obtained by naming the cell range C4 to F8 Weekly_hours and using =SUM(Weekly_hours).

Unfortunately, by clicking on the AutoSum button, it is possible to include a formula rather than a cell range in the bracket; for example, =SUM(A1*B1). This is *not* good practice and should be avoided. If you want to enter a formula, press the = key or click on the = sign on the Formula toolbar – do *not* use the AutoSum button.

RAND

This function generates a random number between zero and one. If you paste =RAND()

into a number of cells, each value generated is independent of every other value and each is equally likely to assume any value between 0 and 1, although never actually 1. Each time the spreadsheet is opened or new information is added to the spreadsheet, the random values are recalculated and new values are displayed. Pressing F9 on the keyboard will also cause the values to be recalculated. You can generate other ranges of random numbers by multiplying by a number. For example, =RAND()*100 will give random values between 0 and 100, but not 100 itself. The RAND function is useful in spreadsheet models involving probability, as it allows many trials to be carried out with different random values.

DATE

We have already mentioned when describing cell formats that dates are stored as numbers, usually counting from 1 January 1900. The DATE function returns the numerical value of a particular date. For example, =DATE(2005,09,09) will return the value for 9 September 2005, which is 38604 (although this will still be displayed as a date unless the General cell format is selected). A more useful way of using this function is if the day, month and year are in different cells and you want to combine them so that you can, for example, calculate the number of days between two dates. For example, if the day is held in cell D12, the month in cell E12 and the year in cell F12, =DATE (F12,E12,D12) will give the complete date. You will need to enter the year as four digits, i.e. 2006 rather than just 06, or the returned date will be for 1906, rather than 2006.

AVERAGE

The AVERAGE function calculates the **mathematical mean** or average of the values in a range of cells. For example, =AVERAGE(A1: A6) will give the mean of the values in cells A1 to A6. As with the SUM function, a named cell range can be used. Returning to the example in Table 10.3, =AVERAGE(Total_hours) will give the average number of hours worked each month by all employees.

IF

We mentioned the IF function when we were describing relational operators. The output of this function is dependent on whether a relationship is true or false. An expression using the IF function takes the form =IF(relationship, value if true, value if false). For example, =IF(A1>A2,"profit","loss") will display the word 'profit' if the value in A1 is bigger than that in A2. If the value in A1 is equal to or less than that in A2, the function will display the word 'loss'. The *value if true* and *value if false* could be formulae or functions. For example, you might want to subtract the value in A2 if it is less than the value in A1 but otherwise add the two values. This could be achieved as follows: =IF(A2<A1,A1-A2,A1+A2).

MAX and MIN

The MAX function returns the largest value in a range of cells, whilst the MIN function returns the smallest value. They are used in the same way as SUM or AVERAGE.

INT

The INT function returns the whole number (integer) part of a decimal number. The value is truncated (rounded down) rather than rounded to the nearest whole number; so =INT(2.9), for example, would return 2 rather than 3. If you want the value rounded to the nearest whole number, or any other number of digits, you can use the ROUND function. One use for the INT function is to obtain whole number random values. =RAND()*6, for example, will give random decimal numbers between 0 and 6, but not 6 itself. If you want to simulate the throws of a dice, you need whole number values. =INT(RAND()*6) will give the whole numbers 0 to 5 (because of the rounding down). Adding 1 to the result will give the required numbers 1 to 6, i.e. =INT(RAND()*6)+1.

Why can you not simply multiply the random number by 7 and then take the integer value?

COUNT

The COUNT function counts up the number of cells in a range that contain a numeric value. This includes cells containing dates and those containing formulae that return numeric values.

In the example in Table 10.6, =COUNT (B2:B6) will give the value 3. The date in B2 and the formula in B3 will be counted as numbers, but the word 'Red' in cell B4 will not. Since cell A2 is empty, the formula in B6 will produce a #DIV/0! error message, which will also not be counted.

Applying specialist built-in functions

As well as the commonly used functions that have just been described – most of which you may have met before – spreadsheets offer many specialist functions and facilities to provide solutions to specific types of problem. You will not be expected to use all of these, but you will need to know what they do and when they might be used, so that you can select the ones you might need for a particular problem.

	A	B
1	21	24
2		09/09/2005
3		=A1+B1
4		Red
5		54
6		=A1/A2
7		=COUNT(B2:B5)

TABLE 10.6 *Using the COUNT function*

Iterative problem-solving or rounding features and functions

Problems requiring **iterative problem-solving** techniques could be quite time consuming, even using a spreadsheet, as many different sets of values might need to be entered to narrow down the solution. Facilities such as Goal Seek and Solver can try many different values automatically to find a solution. The FLOOR and CEILING functions determine how values, such as the solution found, are rounded.

Iterative problem solving: A method that is sometimes called trial and improvement. This involves entering values and then refining them to obtain the required solution.

Goal Seek

The Goal Seek feature allows you to work out what the input value needs to be so that a formula in the spreadsheet will match a certain value. To do this, you need to provide three pieces of information in the Goal Seek dialogue box:

1   Set Cell – this is the cell that contains the formula to calculate the answer you want.

2   To Value – this is the numerical value you want the formula to match.

3   By Changing Cell – this is the input cell whose value will be changed until the value of the Set Cell matches the To Value.

CASE STUDY
Ticket price

Sonia is organising a charity dance and wants your help to work out how much she should charge for tickets. The cost of the venue, band and DJ is £9,525.00. A buffet will be provided at a cost of £3.25 per person. The venue can hold a maximum of 1,500 people and Sonia wants to make a profit of at least £2,500 if she sells all the tickets. What is the minimum price she can charge for a ticket?

Solving Sonia's problem is an ideal candidate for using Goal Seek. The How to… box below explains how to solve this problem, but first you need to understand the mathematics behind the problem and a few business terms.

The amount of £9,525.00 is Sonia's **fixed cost**. Sonia will have to pay this even if she only sells half of the tickets. The buffet cost is the **variable cost**. The cost will depend on the number of tickets sold. Sonia will only buy enough food for the number of people who have bought tickets. The variable cost will be the number of tickets sold multiplied by the unit cost of £3.25. The income (or revenue) will be the ticket price multiplied by the number sold. To calculate the profit you need to subtract both the fixed and the variable costs from the income.

Key terms

Fixed cost: Costs, such as rent or mortgage payments, wages or the cost of machinery, which stay the same regardless how many items are made or sold.

Variable cost: Costs, such as raw materials, which will change depending on the number of items made or sold.

Knowledge check

How much would the ticket price have to go up to if Sonia could only sell 900 tickets, if she wanted to make the same profit? What other questions can you answer using this model?

FLOOR and CEILING

As mentioned at the start of this section, these two functions determine how a value is rounded.

How to...

Work out the minimum ticket price

Now you need to set up the spreadsheet. Starting in cell C1 on a blank spreadsheet, enter the following labels in cells C1 to C7:

price
tickets sold
unit cost
fixed cost
income
variable cost
profit.

Next, select the block of cells C1 to D7, i.e. the labelled cells and the ones to the right of them. Select Insert, Name and then Create and in the Create Names dialogue box click on the box that says Left column. This will use the labels in column C to name the cells in column D. Select one of the cells in column D and you will see the name, rather than the cell reference, in the Name box on the Formula bar. This means you can use names in the formulae. Format all the cells in column D, except D2, as currency.

Now enter the data and formulae. Leave D1 blank and enter 1500 in D2, as this is the maximum number of tickets. Enter the unit cost of £3.25 in D3 and the fixed cost of £9525 in D4. Enter the formula **=tickets_sold*price** in D5, by either typing it or clicking on the relevant cells. In D5 enter **=unit_cost*tickets_sold** and finally in D7 enter **=income–fixed_cost–variable_cost** (see Figure 10.3).

Currently, the income should be zero and the profit a negative value, as no ticket price has been entered. Now you will use Goal Seek to find the minimum price for the tickets.

Select Goal Seek from the Tools menu. The Goal Seek dialogue box shown in Figure 10.4 will appear.

With the Set Cell box highlighted, click on cell D7, press the Tab key or use the mouse to move to the To Value box and type in 2500 (Sonia needed a profit of £2,500). Move down to the final box and click on cell D1 as the cell that needs to be changed. Finally click on OK. Another box will appear to say that a solution has been found. Click OK to get rid of it.

Cell D1 will show the price Sonia needs to charge for a ticket to make £2,500 profit if she sells all 1,500 tickets.

	C	D
	price	
	tickets sold	1500
	unit cost	3.25
	fixed cost	9525
	income	=tickets_sold*price
	variable cost	=unit_cost*tickets_sold
	profit	=income-fixed_cost-variable_cost

FIGURE 10.3 *Entering the data and formulae*

FLOOR rounds a value down, whilst CEILING rounds a value up. The special feature of these functions is that you can determine what multiple of the number it is rounded to. Suppose, in the future, 2p and 1p coins become obsolete and all prices are rounded down to the nearest 5p. The function =FLOOR(2.99,0.05) would return £2.95, i.e. the price of £2.99 is rounded down to £2.95. If, on the other hand, it was decided prices should be rounded up to the nearest 5p, =CEILING(2.99,0.05) would give the value £3.00. Obviously, the first **argument** is more likely to be a cell reference, a cell range or a formula. For example =CEILING(A1*A2,100) would multiply the values in cells A1 and A2 and then give the answer rounded up to the nearest 100.

Key terms

Argument: The values or cell references that appear in brackets after a function. For example, the arguments for CEILING are the number to be rounded and the multiple (or significance) it is to be rounded to.

Solver

Solver is another facility, like Goal Seek, that takes the hard work out of trial and error calculations. However, Solver is more powerful than Goal Seek because it can change values in more than one cell. It will also find a solution that gives a maximum or minimum value in the Set Cell, as well as finding a solution to

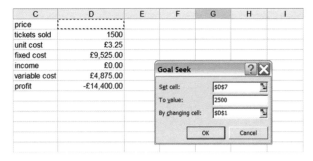

FIGURE 10.4 *Using Goal Seek*

give a specific value. To access Solver, you need to click on Tools. If Solver does not appear in the Tools menu, you will need to install it from the Microsoft Office CD-ROM, or get the System Administrator to do this for you. The Solver Parameters dialogue box is shown in Figure 10.5.

CASE STUDY
Planning for a pension

Gurmeet has just graduated from university and started his first job. He has read a lot in the newspapers about the need to start saving early for retirement and, although this seems a very long way off, he has decided to do something about it.

Gurmeet has decided that at the beginning of each of the next 40 years he will make a contribution to a pension fund. As he is hopeful that his salary will increase each year, he plans to increase the contribution by £250 each year. When he retires in 40 years' time, he wants to be able to withdraw £75,000 from his pension fund at the beginning of each of the following 20 years.

Gurmeet has done some research that suggests that for the first 20 years his investment will grow by 10 per cent each year and after that it will grow by 5 per cent each year.

Gurmeet has asked you to find out what the minimum contribution will be in the first year to give sufficient funds for all 20 pension withdrawals.

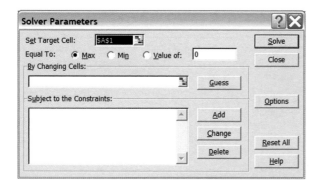

FIGURE 10.5 *The Solver Parameters dialogue box*

Creating a balance sheet for Gurmeet's pension fund for the next 60 years and using Solver to calculate the minimum initial contribution can solve this problem.

The end-of-year balance (the amount of money in the fund at the end of the year) will be calculated from the initial balance (how much there was at the start of the year), plus any contribution, minus any withdrawal. This will then be increased by the rate of growth. The end-of-year balance then becomes the initial balance for the following year. Table 10.7 shows the start of the spreadsheet you need to set up. The initial balance in year 1 is zero. You need to enter a trial value in C2 (1000) – this is the cell that Solver will change. Also, in year 1 the growth is 10 per cent (0.1) and the withdrawal is zero. Cells F2, B3 and C3 show the formulae you need to enter. The formula in C3 shows the contribution increase of £250 a year.

Format columns B, C, E and F as currency and format column D as percentage, so that 0.1 is displayed as 10%. Fill down column A to cell A61 so that the years go from 1 to 60. Next, copy the formula from B3 into cells B4 to B61 and the formula from F2 into cells F3 to F61.

How to...

Use Solver

Select cell C2 and then select Solver from the Tools menu. The Solver Parameters dialogue box will appear with cell C2 showing as the target cell.

You need Solver to find the minimum value, so click on the radio button to select Min. The cell you want to change is also C2. Click on the By Changing Cells box and then select cell C2 on the spreadsheet to enter this cell in the box. Although in this case you are changing a single cell, in other models a range of cells might be changed.

A constraint is a restriction you place on the model. In this case, you need to ensure that there is always money available to cover the withdrawals. That is, the values in cells F42 to F61 must be greater than or, in the case of F61, equal to zero. Click on the Subject to the Constraints box and then click the Add button. Select the block of cells F42 to F61 on the spreadsheet so that it appears in the Cell Reference box in the Add Constraint dialogue box (see Figure 10.6). Now select >= from the dropdown list and type 0 (zero) in the Constraint box before clicking on OK. For problems with more than one constraint, clicking Add instead of OK will enable you to enter the next one.

The Solver Parameters dialogue box should look like Figure 10.7. Click the Solve button to find the answer to Gurmeet's question.

	A	B	C	D	E	F
1	Year	Initial balance	Contribution	Growth	Withdrawal	End of year balance
2	1	0	1000	0.1	0	= (B2+C2-E2)*(1+D2)
3	2	=F2	=C2+250			
4	3					
5	4					

TABLE 10.7 *Starting the balance sheet for Gurmeet's pension fund*

Gurmeet will only make contributions for 40 years, so the formula in C3 only needs to be copied into cells C4 to C41. Copy the value 0.1 into cells D3 to D21, as growth is only 10 per cent for the first 20 years. Then enter 0.05 (5 per cent) in cell D22 and copy this down to D61. Finally, fill cells E3 to E41 with zero – there are no withdrawals for the first 40 years – and fill cells E42 to E61 with 75000.

You will find that, with an initial contribution of £1,000, Gurmeet would run out of money in the fifty-third year. You could simply change the value in cell C2 yourself until all the values in column F are positive, but this would be time-consuming and there is no guarantee that the value you find would be the minimum. This is where Solver takes over. The How to… box below explains how to use it.

Knowledge check

The initial contribution is a little higher than Gurmeet feels he can afford. He thinks that in 10 years' time, when he has finished paying off his student loan, he will be able to increase his contributions by £500 a year rather than £250. By how much would this reduce his initial contribution? How much would the initial contribution need to be to enable Gurmeet to withdraw £70,000 a year for 25 years?

Hint: Don't forget to change the cell range in the constraint. Select the constraint and then click the Change button.

Financial functions

Spreadsheets provide a set of functions that allow you to calculate important financial values that would otherwise need quite complex formulae to perform the calculation. These functions are particularly useful when you need to create a spreadsheet to solve a problem about savings or loans, or the finances for a business.

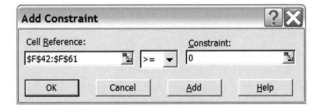

FIGURE 10.6 *Adding the constraint*

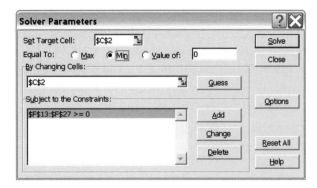

FIGURE 10.7 *The completed Solver Parameters dialogue box*

Interest rates

Earlier in the unit we described the term **interest rate** as the rate of increase of an investment. Interest rate can also be the percentage of the amount you owe that you must pay when you take out a loan. Suppose an advertisement for a car says that it costs £8,000 and that it can be bought for 36 monthly payments of £275.

It is relatively easy to work out how much extra you would have to pay if you paid by monthly instalments – £275 × 36 = £9,900 – so it would cost £1,900 more. However, if you wanted to see if you could borrow the money more cheaply, you would need to know what rate of interest is being charged. This would be a much more complex sum, but you can find out using the RATE function.

Select Function from the Insert menu or click on the Paste Function (*f*ₓ) button on the tool bar. Select Financial as the function category

FIGURE 10.8 *What's the interest rate?*

and then scroll down to select RATE. The RATE function has five arguments, but the last two are optional (Excel assumes they are zero if no value is given). The first argument is the **period** of the loan, i.e. how many payments you must make, so enter 36. The next is the amount of each payment. As this is reducing the amount owed, you need to enter –275. The final argument you need to enter is the present value of the loan, i.e. how much you want to borrow, which will be 8000 – the cost of the car. When you click OK, the cell should show that the monthly interest rate will be 1.2%. If it just shows 1%, you will need to change the number of decimal places displayed with the percentage format.

Future value

Future value is best explained with an example. Suppose, when you were born, a rich relative deposited £1,000 in a savings account with a fixed rate of interest of 4 per cent per year. The relative deposited the same amount every year the day after your birthday. How much would be in the savings account when it is handed over to you on your eighteenth birthday? As the amount deposited stays the same and the interest rate is fixed, this problem can be solved using the FV (future value) function.

Select the FV function from the financial category of Paste Function. As with RATE, there are five arguments and, again, the last two will be given the value zero if you do not enter a value. The first argument is the interest rate (0.04). The second argument is the number of payment periods. As payments started when you were born and end immediately after your seventeenth birthday, this figure is 18. The third argument is the payment amount (–1000). The minus sign is because the account is receiving money.

This time we are going to give a value for the fifth argument. This indicates whether the payment is made at the beginning of the period or the end. In this case, payments are made at the beginning of each year. This means when the account is handed over to you, a year's interest will have been added based on the amount after the final payment. To indicate this, the final argument needs to be 1 (the default value of 0 indicates end of period payments). When you click OK, the cell will show how much money would be in the savings account.

Loan payments

So far, we have looked at how to find the interest rate of a loan based on the amount borrowed and the amount and number of payments. We have also found the future value of savings. There is also a function to calculate what the monthly or annual payments would be. This is the PMT (payment) function. In this case, the arguments are as follows:

1   interest rate (either monthly or annual)

2   number of payments (monthly or yearly to match interest rate)

3   present value of the loan (i.e. how much was borrowed)

4   an optional argument that allows you to indicate if you want to leave some of the loan unpaid – if you leave it blank, Excel assumes a value of zero

5   0 or 1 to indicate whether payments are made at the end or beginning of each period.

To find out what the payments would be on a £7,000 loan to be paid back by 36 monthly payments (at the end of each month) at a monthly interest rate of 0.8 per cent, the function would be: =PMT(0.008,36,7000).

Rate of return

This is similar to the interest rate but is used when money is being paid out as well as received. For example, Bronwyn is starting a business. It costs her £80,000 to buy premises and set up the business. Bronwyn's business

	A	C
1	Initial cost	−80000
2	Year 1	15000
3	Year 2	18000
4	Year 3	21000
5	Year 4	27000
6	Year 5	30000
7	Rate of return over 5 years	
8	Rate of return over 4 years	

TABLE 10.8 *Calculating the rate of return*

plan suggests she will make £15,000 in the first year, £18,000 in the second, £21,000 in the third, £27,000 in the fourth and £30,000 in the fifth year of trading. She wants to know what the **rate of return** will be.

Set up the spreadsheet shown in Table 10.8. Select cell B7 and insert the IRR (internal rate of return) function from the Financial category. Select the range of cells B1:B6 as the Value argument and click OK. The second argument, Guess, is set to 10% (0.1) by default.

If the result is a #NUM error message, it is because the actual value is too far away from 10 per cent for Excel to find it in the set number of attempts. Entering a different value for Guess may solve the problem.

Net present value

The **net present value** of a series of incomes and payments is how much they would be worth today. It is linked to the IRR function that we have just discussed, as the rate of return is calculated by making the net present value equal to zero.

Table 10.9 shows three different ways of investing £12,000 over 5 years. If an interest rate of 5 per cent is assumed, which method gives the best value in today's money?

	A	B	C	D
1	Now	2000	500	3500
2	In 1 year	2000	1000	3000
3	In 2 years	2000	1500	2500
4	In 3 years	2000	2500	1500
5	In 4 years	2000	3000	1000
6	In 5 years	2000	3500	500

TABLE 10.9 *Three ways of investing £12,000*

The first investment is already in today's money, so this can be added on when the present value of the other investments have been calculated. In cell B7, insert the NPV (net present value) function. The first argument is the rate (0.05). For the Value 1 argument, select the range of cells B2:B6 and then click OK. With cell B7 selected, click after the last bracket in the formula bar and add +B1 to the formula and click on the ✓ or press Enter. Now copy the formula to C7 and D7. Which method has the highest value in today's money?

Asset depreciation

If you buy a car or a computer, the longer you keep it, the less it will be worth if you try to sell it. The car or computer is known as an **asset** and the reduction in its value is called **depreciation**. Businesses need to know what the depreciation will be on the assets they own, such as machinery or computers, partly to know what the company is worth and partly for tax purposes. This will be based on the original cost, the useful life of the asset and the salvage value – how much it is worth at the end of its useful life. There are a number of different methods of calculating depreciation. One of the simplest is straight line depreciation (SLN). This assumes that the depreciation will be the same every year. Suppose a company buys computer equipment for £5,000 and considers its useful life to be three years. At the end of three years, the salvage value will be £1,000. How much will this asset depreciate each year? This can be found by =SLN(5000,1000,3), which gives £1,333 to the nearest whole number.

In fact, most assets depreciate more when they are new. A slightly more complex way of calculating depreciation is called declining balance (DB). This calculates and subtracts the depreciation for the first year. The depreciation for the second year is then calculated on the reduced value, and so on. The function to do this is DB. Using the example above, the depreciation for the first year would be: =DB(5000,1000,3,1) which gives £2,075. For the second year, the depreciation would be: =DB(5000,1000,3,2), which gives £1,214, and the depreciation for the third year would be: =DB(5000,1000,3,3), which gives £710 to the nearest whole number. There is a fifth argument, Month. This is used when an asset is bought part way through a financial year to indicate how many months need to be included in the first year calculation. If the argument is left blank, Excel assumes a full year, i.e. 12 months.

Key terms

Interest rate: The monthly or annual rate of increase of an investment, or the monthly or annual cost for a loan.

Period: The length of time between payments, usually a month or a year. The interest rate and the period must match, i.e. months and monthly interest rate or years and annual interest rate.

Future value: How much an investment will be worth at a certain time in the future.

Rate of return: The percentage increase or decrease in value of a series of payments and/or incomes over a period of time.

Net present value: The value of a series of investments and/or payments in today's money.

Asset: Anything of value that is owned by a company.

Depreciation: The decrease in value of assets over time.

Mathematic and trigonometric functions

As their name suggests, these are functions for solving mathematical problems.

Trigonometry

Cosine (COS), sine (SIN) and tangent (TAN) are three commonly used trigonometric ratios associated with right-angled triangles. If you know the size of one of the angles and the length of one of the sides, one of these ratios can be used to find the length of another side. For the triangle in Figure 10.9, COS θ = a/h, SIN θ = o/h and TAN θ = o/a. Excel provides functions to give the value of COS, SIN or TAN for a given angle. The only complication is that the angle must be in **radians**, rather than degrees.

Key terms

Radian: A unit for measuring angles. If you draw two radii of a circle so that the arc between the two points where they touch the circumference is the same length as the radius, the angle between the radii will be one radian. A right angle is equal to $\Pi/2$ radians.

To convert an angle from degrees to radians, either multiply by PI()/180 or use the RADIANS function. So, for example, to find the cosine of 60°, you could use either =COS(60*PI()/180) or =COS(RADIANS(60)). If the hypotenuse (h) is 32 cm and you wanted to find the length of the side a, you would simply multiply the result by 32.

One use for the TAN function is to measure the height of a tall tree, building or even a mountain. If you stand a known distance away

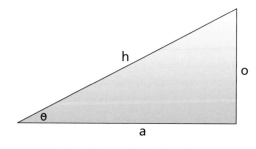

FIGURE 10.9 *A right-angled triangle*

and measure the angle between the horizontal and a line from your eye to the top of the object, you have the value of an angle and the adjacent side in a right-angled triangle. The height of the object (o) will be the TAN of the angle multiplied by the distance you are from it (a). You will, of course, need to add on the distance from the ground to your eyes, but this is unlikely to be significant, particularly if the object is a mountain.

FLOOR and CEILING

These are the rounding functions that have been described in the section on iterative problem-solving or rounding features and functions.

Power

The power of a number is the number of times it is multiplied by itself. 2 squared is 2 to the power 2, or 2×2; 2 cubed is 2 to the power 3 or $2 \times 2 \times 2$. 1 kilobyte is 2 to the power 10 (2^{10}) bytes or $2 \times 2 \times 2 \times 2 \times 2 \times 2 \times 2 \times 2 \times 2 \times 2 = 1024$. A negative power gives the reciprocal value, so 2^{-10} equals $1/1024$. One way of finding the value of a number to a particular power is to use the $^\wedge$ operator, for example $=5^\wedge 4$. Another way is to use the POWER function, for example $=POWER(5,4)$.

Combinations

Suppose you had a squad of 15 basketball players. How many different teams of five players are possible? This is an example of combination; the order of the items in the subset is not significant. There is a useful function to solve this problem and bypass some tricky arithmetic. $=COMBIN(15,5)$ provides the answer – 3,003! Obviously, in practice, different players specialise in particular positions on court, which would reduce the number of possibilities, but if any player could play in any position, over 3,000 different teams would be possible.

A similar function is PERMUT. This finds the number of possible permutations of a set of numbers. This is used where the order of items within the subset is significant. For example, a door entry keypad has keys with the digits 0 to 9. An entry code consists of four different digits, e.g. 1234. How many different entry codes are possible? Using $=PERMUT(10,4)$ shows that there are 5,040 possible codes.

Product

The product is simply the result of multiplying numbers together. In a spreadsheet, this can be achieved by simply using the * operator. However, the function PRODUCT can also be used. For example, to multiply the values in cells A1, B1 and C1, you could use $=A1*B1*C1$ or $=PRODUCT(A1,B1,C1)$.

Statistical functions

This group of functions allows you to carry out statistical analysis of the data in a spreadsheet. Although some attempt will be made here to explain the statistics behind these functions, you may need to refer to mathematics or statistics textbooks to understand them fully.

Count if

This is one of the more straightforward functions in this category. It is used to count the number of cells in a range of cells that fulfils the condition you specify. Table 10.10 gives an example.

The result of using this function would be 4; four of the cells in the range contain the word Apple. The condition could be a number – it could include a relational operator or it could be a cell reference. If the condition includes a relational operator, it needs to be enclosed by speech marks, e.g. $=COUNTIF(A1:A6,"< 20")$ would find how many cells in the range contain a number less than 20.

	A	B	C
1	Apple	Pear	Banana
2	Banana	Apple	Apple
3	Pear	Pear	Pear
4	Banana	Apple	Banana
5			
6		=COUNTIF(A1:C4,"Apple")	

TABLE 10.10 *Using the COUNTIF function*

A company employs a number of salespeople. A spreadsheet is used to keep a record of all sales. For each sale, the date, value of the sale and the name of the salesperson is recorded. How would you find out how many sales each salesperson has made? How would you find out how many high-value (say more than £1,000) sales had been made?

Create this spreadsheet and make up and enter some sales data. Find the answer to the above questions for your data.

Forecast

The FORECAST function allows you to predict or calculate a future value by using existing values. Table 10.11 shows the annual sales figures for a business between 2000 and 2005. You can use the FORECAST function to predict what the annual sales will be for 2006.

Firstly, try plotting a graph of this data. Select the cells A1:G2 and then click on the Chart Wizard button (or select Chart from the Insert menu). Select XY (Scatter) as the chart type and click Next. Check that the radio button by Rows is selected and click Next again. Enter Year as the X-axis label and Sales (£) as the Y-axis label and click Next. Finally, select the As new sheet option and click Finish. Notice that the years are along the horizontal (x) axis and sales are on the vertical (y) axis. Notice also that the points are approximately in a straight line (**linear**). In Figure 10.10, a **trend line** has been added to show this. As the FORECAST function uses a mathematical concept called linear regression, this means that it will give a reasonably accurate prediction, all things being equal.

Add a trend line to a graph

To add a trend line to your graph, click on one of the points to select all of them. Now choose Add Trendline from the Chart menu. Choose Linear as the type (it should already be selected) and click OK.

The syntax for the FORECAST function is:

```
=FORECAST(x, known y values,
known x values)
```

To use this to predict sales for 2006, insert the FORECAST function from the statistical category in cell H2. Type 2006 as the first argument – the x value for which you want to predict a y value. For the second argument, select the range of cells B2:G2 – the known y values. For the third argument, select the range of cells B1:G1 – the known x values. When you click OK, you should get a value of 46,266.67. Since all the other sales are given as multiples of 1,000, you could use the FLOOR function to round this down to 46,000 to match.

Correlation coefficient

The **correlation coefficient** between two variables is a measure of how dependent one is on the other. A positive coefficient means that if one variable increases, the other also increases. The nearer the value is to one, the stronger the dependence is. The nearer the value is to zero, the weaker the dependence is. A coefficient of zero means there is no dependence between the two variables at all, while a negative coefficient means that as one variable increases, the other decreases. Again, this dependence becomes stronger as the value moves towards (minus) one.

	A	B	C	D	E	F	G	H
1	Year	2000	2001	2002	2003	2004	2005	2006
2	Sales	21,000	26,000	32,000	34,000	39,000	41,000	

TABLE 10.11 *Sales figures*

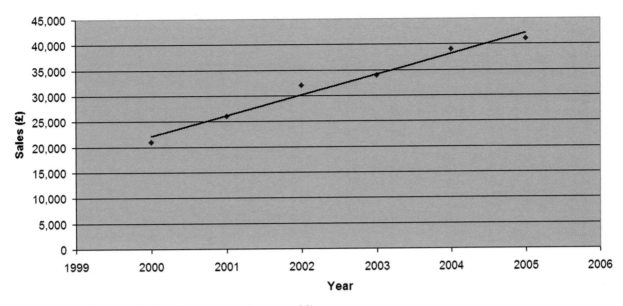

Annual Sales

FIGURE 10.10 *Graph of sales figures showing trend line*

For example, the data in Table 10.12 shows the relationship between the number of televisions sold in a particular store and their price. How dependent is the number sold on the price of the television? We can use the CORREL function to find out.

Use the CORREL function

In a blank cell, insert the CORREL function from the statistical category. Select the range B1:K1 as the first argument and the range B2:K2 as the second argument and click OK. What is the value of the correlation coefficient? What does this mean? Try plotting these values as an XY (Scatter) chart. Add a linear trend line. How are most of the points arranged in relation to the trend line?

Measure the height of a number of people and ask them for their shoe size – try to measure people with a range of different heights. Is there any correlation between height and shoe size? Use a spreadsheet and the CORREL function to find out.

What about height and weight? What other pairs of variables could you find the correlation coefficient for?

Frequency

The COUNTIF function allows you to count how many times a certain value appears in a range of cells; the FREQUENCY function allows you to count how many numeric values are within particular ranges – their **frequency**. The FREQUENCY function is a type of function

	A	B	C	D	E	F	G	H	I	J	K
1	Price	310	325	350	390	440	480	510	620	750	800
2	No. sold	180	218	243	196	148	136	107	96	12	3

TABLE 10.12 *Sales of television sets*

	A	B	C	D	E
1	45	57	52	89	59
2	57	27	81	66	25
3	57	34	48	76	66
4	84	66	43	51	55
5	63	42	62	54	87
6	70	51	66	35	79
7	44	42	78	65	42
8	48	50	78	66	41
9	35	79	8	27	54
10					
11	39	U			
12	49	E			
13	59	D			
14	69	C			
15	79	B			
16		A			

TABLE 10.13 *Student grade distribution*

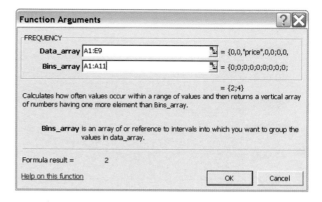

FIGURE 10.11 *The FREQUENCY function arguments*

known as an **array function**. It works on an array (a range) of cells and the results, in this case, will require a range of cells, rather than a single cell.

For example, in Table 10.13, the range of cells A1:E9 holds the marks scored by a number of students in one examination. Grades are awarded as follows:

* U   0–39
* E   40–49
* D   50–59
* C   60–69
* B   70–79
* A   80–100

The FREQUENCY function will allow you to find out how many students achieved each grade.

In cells A11:A15 are the top boundary marks for each mark band. This is called the **bins array**. It is not necessary to enter the maximum mark for grade A, as FREQUENCY automatically includes the number of values that are above the top boundary you specify – you have to remember to add an extra cell in the results range to allow for this. The range of cells A1:E9 is called the **data array**. The number achieving each grade will go in the range C11:C16. The grade letters have been entered in B11:B16 so that they can be used as labels on a chart.

Select the cell range C11:C16, then select the FREQUENCY function from the statistical category. The dialogue box is shown in Figure 10.11. Select the cell range A1:E9 as the data array and the cell range A11:A15 as the bins array. Do *not* click the OK button. Instead, press CTRL, SHIFT and ENTER simultaneously on the keyboard. The numbers 7, 9, 11, 8, 6 and 4 should appear in cells C11 to C16, i.e. the number of students with each grade. The formula in the Formula bar will have braces { } round it to signify that it is an array function. By selecting the cells B11:C16 and using the Chart Wizard, you can graph the results as shown in Figure 10.12.

The FREQUENCY function would also be useful for analysing the results of surveys, for example.

Standard deviation and variance

To understand **standard deviation** and **variance**, you need to know about some terms used in statistics. Suppose you wanted to find the average (**mean**) height of 18-year-old girls in the UK. You would not go out and measure the height of every 18-year-old girl – in statistics called the **population**. You would measure the height of a **sample** of them. Providing the sample is

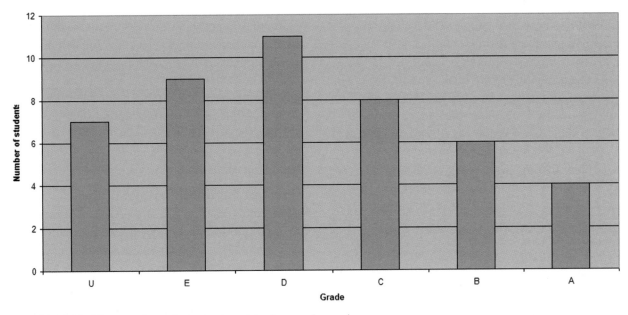

FIGURE 10.12 *The number of students achieving each grade*

large enough, you assume that the distribution of heights in your sample matches that of the population. The other thing you can assume is that, for the population, the heights will have a **normal distribution**, i.e. if they are plotted on a graph, the graph will be a symmetrical bell shape (a normal curve), as shown in Figure 10.13. Many measurements, given a large enough population, appear to have a normal distribution and so this is used as the basis for many statistical calculations.

Standard deviation and variance are two linked measures of how widely the values of a variable are dispersed. The standard deviation is given by the square root of the variance. The standard deviation is particularly important as it and the mean define the distribution of values, based on a normal distribution. The units on the horizontal axis of the normal curve are, in fact, multiples of the standard deviation. You can see from the curve that the majority of values are within two standard deviations of the mean.

The functions STDEV and VAR estimate the standard deviation and variance by assuming that the values used are a sample of the population. Suppose the marks given in Table 10.13 are a random sample of all the marks awarded by an examination board for an ICT exam. You can use them to estimate the standard deviation and variance for this population as a whole. Insert the STDEV function in a blank cell on the spreadsheet and then select the range of cells containing the marks as the first argument. STDEV allows up to 30 arguments, each of which can be a value in the sample or a range of cells, as in this case. Click on OK to display the value. VAR works in exactly the same way. What is the estimate for the variance?

If the marks were for the whole population, such as for an internal school or college exam that no one else had taken, you would use STDEVP and VARP to find the standard deviation and variance. What difference does this make to the standard deviation and variance?

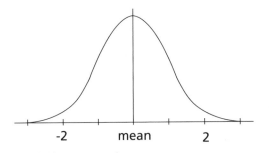

FIGURE 10.13 *A normal curve*

Confidence intervals

The **confidence interval** is a range on either side of the mean of a sample. The mean of the population will be within this range with a particular level of confidence.

Let's apply this to the sample of marks in Table 10.13. First you need to use the AVERAGE function to find the mean mark for the sample, which should be 55.64 to two decimal places (dp).

What is the range that we are 95 per cent confident that the mean mark for the population of students will be in?

The syntax for the CONFIDENCE function is:

```
=CONFIDENCE (alpha, standard_dev, size)
```

where:

* alpha = 1 − confidence level/100 (e.g. if the confidence level is 95%, alpha = 1 − 0.95 = 0.05)

* standard_dev is the standard deviation for the population (18.19 to 2dp as found using the STDEV function)

* size is the size of the sample (45).

Insert the CONFIDENCE function in a blank cell, enter 0.05, 18.19 and 45 as the three arguments and click OK. The value for the confidence interval should be 5.31 to 2dp. This means we are 95 per cent confident that the mean mark for all students who took the exam will be between 50.33 and 60.95, i.e. 55.64 ± 5.31.

Rank

The **rank** of a value is simply its position if all the values were put in numerical order. Use the marks in Table 10.13 again. Firstly, insert the RANK function in a single blank cell. There are three arguments. The first is simply the number whose rank you want to find; select any of the cells with marks in, such as A1. The second argument is the range containing all the values, so select A1:E9. The final argument can be 0 (or left blank) or 1. Zero means you want to rank the values in descending order and one means you want to rank them in ascending order. Exam marks are usually ranked in descending order, so leave this argument blank. Clicking OK will give you the rank of the mark in A1.

It is also possible to use RANK as an array function. Select a range of cells that matches the original range, say G1:K9. This time, select the range A1:E9 for both the first and second arguments. Instead of clicking OK, press the CTRL, SHIFT and ENTER keys on the keyboard to signify an array function. The rank of each mark should appear in the corresponding cell. Notice that where two or more marks are the same, they have the same rank, but the next number down has a rank that assumes they were different. For example, there are two marks of 79 which both have the rank 5, so there is no mark with rank 6; the next mark down (78) has a rank of 7.

Binomial distribution probability

A **binomial** situation is one where there are only two possible and **mutually exclusive** outcomes to an event. These are often labelled success and failure. For example, a tossed coin can land heads or tails, a seed can either germinate and grow or fail to do so, widgets on a production line either meet quality assurance standards or they are rejected. **Binomial distribution probability** allows us to determine the probability of an exact number of successes in a series of trials or the probability of there being a number of successes at most in a series of trials (cumulative probability).

The easiest example to consider is tossing a coin. For each toss of a coin, the probability of it being heads is 0.5. Suppose you toss a coin ten times (ten trials); what is the probability of exactly six tosses landing heads?

To find out, insert the BINOMDIST function in a spreadsheet cell. The arguments are:

* the number of successes you want to find the probability of – 6 in this case

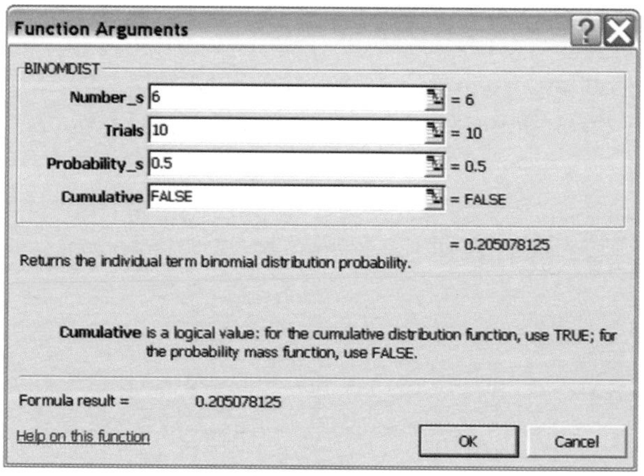

FIGURE 10.14 *The BINOMDIST dialogue box*

* the number of trials – 10

* the probability for each trial – 0.5

* the logical values TRUE or FALSE to indicate whether a cumulative probability (TRUE) or the probability of an exact number of successes (FALSE) is required – FALSE in this case.

As you can see, the probability of exactly six heads out of ten trials is 0.205078125, or just over 20 per cent.

Lookup and referencing functions

These functions allow you to locate and use values stored in other areas of a spreadsheet or on another sheet in a workbook.

Vlookup

The VLOOKUP function will look up a value in the leftmost column of a table and return the value in the same row of a specified column.

Suppose you wanted to calculate the highest rate of income tax a person would have to pay based on their taxable income (after personal allowances and other deductions have been subtracted). The current (2005–2006) tax rates are shown in Table 10.14.

This is an example of a **range lookup**. If the taxable income does not exactly match one of

Key terms

Linear: When values plotted on a graph form, or are close to, a straight line.

Trend line: A line drawn on a graph to fit the measured values.

Correlation: The level of dependence between two variables.

Correlation coefficient: A measure of the correlation between two variables. It has values between –1 and +1. 0 means the variables are independent of one another.

Frequency: The number of values that fall in particular ranges.

Array function: A function that acts on a range of cells and whose results can appear in a range of cells. Pressing CTRL, SHIFT + ENTER signifies an array function and will insert braces { } round the formula in the Formula bar.

Population: All possible individuals for a particular statistical measure.

Sample: A subset of the population that is measured and assumed to behave like the population as a whole.

Normal distribution: A distribution of values that produces a symmetrical bell-shaped curve when

plotted. Many measurements are approximately normally distributed.

Mean: The mathematical average of a set of values, i.e. the total value divided by the number of values.

Standard deviation (sd): A measure of the distribution of values or the width of a normal curve; 68 per cent of all values fall within 1sd of the mean.

Variance: The square of the standard deviation.

Confidence interval: A range on either side of the mean of a sample. The mean of the population will be within this range with a particular level of confidence.

Rank: The position of a value within a list of values if they were placed in numerical order.

Mutually exclusive: If one value is true, the other cannot be.

Binomial distribution probability: The probability of a number of successes in a number of trials when there are two possible and mutually exclusive outcomes – success and failure.

TAXABLE INCOME	TAX RATE
Up to £2,090	10%
£2,091 - £32,400	22%
From £32,401	40%

TABLE 10.14 *Income tax thresholds*

	A	B
1	Taxable income	Tax rate
2	0	0.1
3	2091	0.22
4	32401	0.4

TABLE 10.15 *Income tax lookup table*

the values in the lookup table, the nearest value below will be used. Also, if the taxable income is less than the lowest value in the lookup table, a #N/A error will be displayed. This means that the bottom value in each range must be used in the lookup table – see Table 10.15.

Enter this table in cells A1:B4 of a spreadsheet. Name the range of cells A2:B4 tax_rate. It is always best to name the range of cells that contains the lookup data, as it makes the formula easier to understand and it means that you can copy the formula anywhere on the spreadsheet without having to worry about cell references.

Now enter the headings and data as shown in Table 10.16. Enter a formula in column D to subtract deductions from salary. Name these cells taxable_income. To input the maximum tax rate, you need to insert the VLOOKUP

function in cell E7. Figure 10.15 shows the dialogue box.

Enter the values shown for the arguments. The lookup values are in the cells you have just named taxable_income; the table array that contains the lookup table is the range you named tax_rate; the column of the lookup table that contains the tax rate values is column 2. As we are using a range lookup, the final argument is the logical value TRUE. It does not matter if you do not enter this, as TRUE is the default value. Notice, however, that the values in the left column of the lookup table must be in ascending order. Click OK and copy the formula into the other cells in column E.

Theory into practice

The price of air tickets to Australia varies according to the time of year. A particular airline offers the following prices for departure dates:

01 Apr 06 to 31 Jul 06	£650
01 Aug 06 to 09 Dec 06	£799
10 Dec 06 to 24 Dec 06	£999
25 Dec 06 to 31 Mar 07	£899

Remembering that dates are treated as numbers by Excel, use a lookup table and the VLOOKUP function to write a formula to find the price of a ticket for any date between 01 Apr 06 and 31 Mar 07.

If you enter the range_lookup argument as FALSE, the VLOOKUP function will only find values that exactly match the lookup value. If this value does not exist in the lookup table, a #N/A error will be displayed. When you are using this

	A	B	C	D	E
6	Name	Salary	Deductions	Taxable income	Max. tax rate
7	Banks T	21000	4320		
8	Murphy A	14500	12500		
9	Khan A	56000	11800		

TABLE 10.16 *Calculating maximum tax rates*

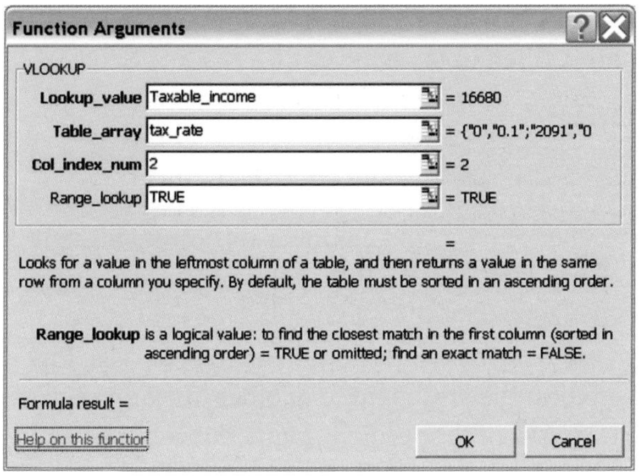

FIGURE 10.15 *The VLOOKUP dialogue box*

type of lookup, the lookup table does not have to be in ascending order.

Typical uses for this would be to insert the description and price of a product on an invoice by looking up its product ID, or to insert the customer's name and address by looking up the customer ID. In both cases, the lookup table will have more than two columns. For example, the product lookup table may have product ID in the left column (1), description in the next column (2) and price in the next column (3). The description and price will need to be inserted in different cells on the invoice, so each will need a lookup formula. These will be the same except for the column index number. This will be 2 for the description and 3 for the price.

Theory into practice

Use a spreadsheet to create an invoice. Use lookup tables to input the customer details and the product descriptions and prices by inputting the customer and product IDs.

Hlookup

This works in exactly the same way as Vlookup except that the lookup values are in the top row and the value returned is in the same column. In the HLOOKUP dialogue box, the third argument is, therefore, Row_index_num, rather than Col_index_num.

Theory into practice

Rearrange the air tickets data and use HLOOKUP to write the formula.

Row

The ROW function simply returns the row number of the cell reference in its argument. For example, =ROW(A6) = 6. If the argument is left blank, the function will return the row number of the cell it is inserted in. For example, if =ROW( ) is inserted in cell D7, it will return the value 7.

Theory into practice

What will the COLUMN function do?

Transpose

The TRANSPOSE function is an array function that copies rows in a selected range into columns and vice versa. If a value in the original range is changed, the corresponding value in the transposed range will also change.

You were asked earlier to rearrange the air tickets data so that you could use HLOOKUP rather than VLOOKUP. You can do this using the TRANSPOSE function. The original lookup table had two columns and four rows (five if you added column headings), so the transposed table will require four (or five) columns and two rows. Select a range of cells of the correct size and insert the TRANSPOSE function. This only requires one argument; the original cell range you are copying. Select this and then remember to press CTRL, SHIFT and Enter, rather than clicking OK. The dates should appear as the top row with the prices in the row below. Change one of the dates or prices in the original table. Does the corresponding value in the transposed table change? The transposed table does not need to be on the same worksheet as the original table.

Match

The MATCH function is similar to the lookup functions but it returns the relative position of the item, rather than the item itself. Add an extra heading 'Tax band' in cell F6 of the spreadsheet shown in Table 10.16. You will need to make one or two minor changes to the spreadsheet. First, name the cell range A2:A4 taxable_income – keep the name tax_rate for A2:B4. Change the heading in D6 to 'For tax' and name the cells in that column for_tax. Finally, change the lookup_value argument in the VLOOKUP formula to match.

Insert the MATCH function in cell F7. The dialogue box is shown in Figure 10.16.

Enter the arguments as shown. Notice the lookup_array argument only includes the taxable income column. The third argument, match_type, is similar to the range_lookup argument in the lookup functions. It is 1 by default, which acts in the same way as TRUE in the lookup argument, which is what we require here. A match_type of 0 matches exact values only, whilst –1 finds the nearest number that is greater than the lookup value. For this to work, the values in the lookup table must be in descending order.

Click on OK and copy the formula into the other cells in column F. You should find that

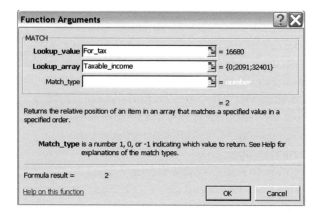

FIGURE 10.16 *The MATCH dialogue box*

T Banks is in tax band 2, A Murphy in tax band 1 and A Khan in tax band 3.

Offset

The OFFSET function is used to create a reference to a rectangular range of cells that is a specified number of rows and columns away from a single cell or range of cells. If the reference is to a single cell, the result will be to display the contents of that cell. If the reference is to a range of cells, this can form the argument to another function such as SUM. Also, the specified number of columns and rows can be calculated using another function such as MATCH. The syntax of the OFFSET function is:

```
=OFFSET(reference, rows moved,
columns moved, height, width)
```

where:

* reference is the cell or range of cells from which the offset begins

* rows moved is the number of rows from the reference that you want the new range to start (top left corner), e.g. –1 moves up a row, (+)1 moves down a row

* columns moved is the number of columns, e.g. –1 moves one column left, (+)1 moves one column right

* height and width are optional arguments; height is the number of rows in the new range, width is the number of columns; if left blank, the new range is the same height and width as reference.

Set up the spreadsheet shown in Table 10.17. In cell B10, enter the formula

```
=SUM(OFFSET(A1,5,1,3,4))
```

The result should be 78 – the sum of all the numbers in the range B6:E8.

	A	B	C	D	E
1					
2					
3					
4					
5					
6		1	2	3	4
7		5	6	7	8
8		9	10	11	12
9					
10					

TABLE 10.17 *Preparing to sum offset cells*

Table 10.18 shows an example of using the OFFSET function with the MATCH function. Suppose the sales figures for each product are downloaded monthly and do not always appear in the same order on the spreadsheet.

Enter the following formula into cell B12 and copy it to C12:

```
=OFFSET($A$1,MATCH($A12,$A$2:$A$8,
0),B11)
```

The formula in B12:C12 will always pick out the values for Colour laser, irrespective of where

it appears in the list. The reference cell is A1. The MATCH function gives the rows moved by finding the position of the value that matches that in A12 (colour laser) in the list of products. As the third argument in MATCH is 0, an exact match will be found and the list can be in any order. This will return the value 4. The columns moved is given by the value in B11, which is 1. As height and width are omitted, they will match the reference, which is a single cell. The result in B12 is the value from the cell that is 4 rows down and 1 column to the right of A1 (454, the number of colour lasers sold). When the formula is copied to C12, the columns moved becomes C11, which is 2, giving the value 2 columns to the right – the income from colour lasers. Try changing the order of the rows in the table. Do cells B12 and C12 still give the correct values?

Think it over...

How could you extend the spreadsheet in Table 10.18 so that you could put the product details in the same order each month?

Add columns for cost price and profit and extract this data as well.

Date and time functions

The date and time functions, as you would expect, allow you to manipulate dates and times. As they are so interlinked, we will not describe them separately.

The best way to explain how these functions can be used is with an example. Set up the spreadsheet shown in Table 10.19. The =NOW() function simply puts the current date and time in cell B1. As will become obvious, the HOUR, MINUTE, SECOND, DAY, MONTH and YEAR functions extract the appropriate part of the date and time. DATE and TIME allow you to combine the constituent parts of a date or time that are held in separate cells into a single cell. Incidentally, the NOW function is a volatile function (like RAND). Every time you make a change to the spreadsheet, the value changes. If you have not made any changes to the spreadsheet, and you want to update the NOW value, press F9 on the keyboard.

	A	B	C
1	Product	Units sold	Income
2	TFT monitor	541	4328.00
3	CPU	1000	5000.00
4	Laser printer	577	2308.00
5	Colour laser	454	3632.00
6	Motherboard	141	705.00
7	Graphics card	221	1105.00
8	Scanner	223	1115.00
9			
10		Units sold	Income
11	Product	1	2
12	Colour laser		

TABLE 10.18 *Using OFFSET and MATCH*

	A	B	C	D
1	Now	=NOW()		
2				
3	Hour	=HOUR(B1)	Time	=TIME(B3,B4,B5)
4	Minute	=MINUTE(B1)		
5	Second	=SECOND(B1)		
6	Day	=DAY(B1)	Date	=DATE(B8,B7,B6)
7	Month	=MONTH(B1)		
8	Year	=YEAR(B1)		

TABLE 10.19 *Date and time functions*

10.3 Designing and developing spreadsheets

In previous sections, we have considered what you need to do to determine the needs of the user of your spreadsheet and we have described some of the spreadsheet facilities and functions that are available for you to use. Now it is time to consider how to design and develop the spreadsheet to match the design specification and to make use of the appropriate facilities and functions.

Data entry

We said earlier that most spreadsheet users will not be experts. The spreadsheet you produce, therefore, will need to provide simple but effective ways of entering data and of helping users to input meaningful data. There are several ways that you can achieve this:

✳ creating sheets that have the appearance of a form

✳ using data entry forms

✳ providing data entry messages

✳ using data validation and associated messages.

Creating sheets that have the appearance of a form

If asked to enter data directly into a standard spreadsheet table, a novice user might become intimidated and confused. One way of simplifying data entry is to make the spreadsheet look like a form and make it

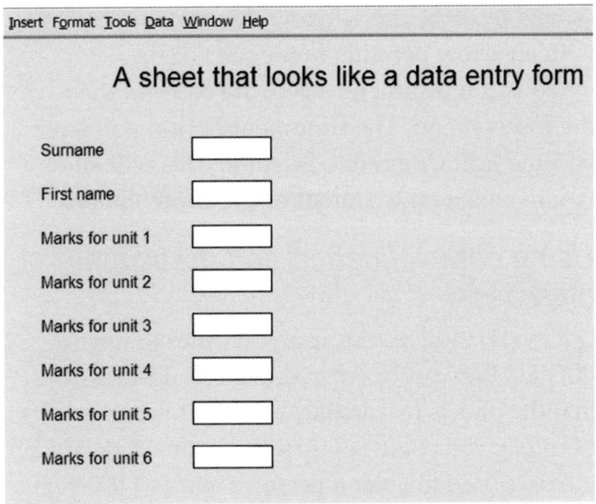

FIGURE 10.17 *A sheet with the appearance of a form*

obvious which data should be entered where. You will need to change the View options so that the gridlines are not displayed on screen. To do this, select Options from the Tools menu and then select the View tab. To hide the gridlines, click on the box next to it to remove the tick.

You will need to use labels, borders, colour and shading to make it clear which data should be entered where. If data has been collected using a paper data collection form, you should try to make the layout of your on-screen 'form' as similar as possible to that of the paper form. Figure 10.17 shows a very simple screen that looks like a form – you will be able to do much better. The background has been coloured yellow, but the cells that require data entry have been left clear with a border round them. There is a label to tell the user what needs to be entered in each cell.

The results of any calculations can appear elsewhere on the same sheet or the data can be copied to another sheet to calculate and display any output. If the output is to appear on the same sheet, you should consider using cell presentation formats to differentiate between the input data and the output.

Incidentally, there are a number of other options that you can switch on or off in the View tab of the Options dialogue box. These include row and column headers, scroll bars and sheet tabs. Row and column headers are not required by the user and can be switched off. If each sheet fits on

the screen and you provide buttons to move from sheet to sheet (see later), scroll bars and sheet tabs can be switched off too. All of this will help to make your spreadsheet appear more user friendly.

Using data entry forms

Microsoft Excel provides the facility to use data entry forms to input data into a spreadsheet. To create a form, you must first enter the labels for the data that needs to be input. These should be in a row in the spreadsheet. With the cell pointer on one of the label cells, select Form from the Data menu. A warning dialogue box will appear. The first bullet says: 'If you want the first row of the selection or list used as labels and not as data, click OK.' As this is exactly what you want to happen, do exactly as the instruction tells you to – click OK. A form will appear like the one shown in Figure 10.18. You can then enter the data. When you click on New, the data will be entered in the first blank row of the spreadsheet under the labels and the form will be cleared for the next entry.

If there is already at least one row of data in the list, the warning dialogue box will not appear; the form will appear straight away with the first row of data displayed in it.

The Find Prev and Find Next buttons can be used to locate a particular row of data (record),

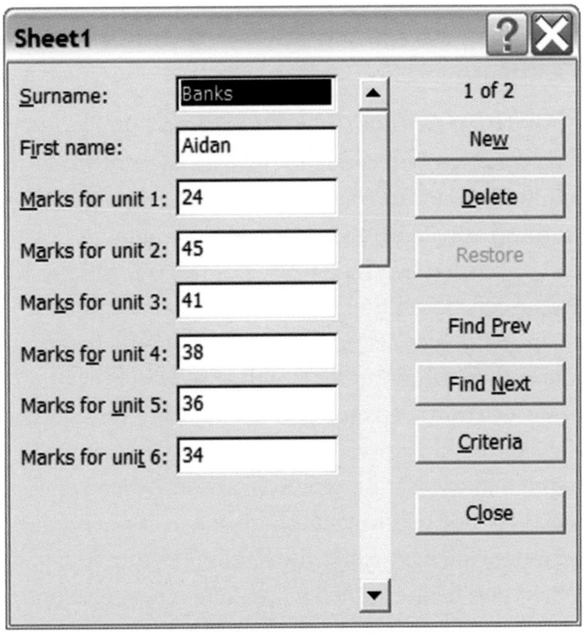

FIGURE 10.18 *A data entry form*

which can then be edited or deleted. You would not expect the user to use the Data menu to access the form, so you would need to record a macro and provide a button to open it.

This type of data entry form clearly has limitations. The data can only be entered into rows in a table and there is no option for providing facilities, such as drop-down lists, to limit the values that can be entered. Also, if **validation** is applied to a cell, the data entry form will override it. You can use the Visual Basic for Applications (VBA) Editor to create more flexible forms. You can access this by selecting Macro from the Tools menu and then Visual Basic Editor. We are not going to explain how to create forms and link them to your spreadsheet using VBA, as it goes beyond the scope of the unit. If you want to find out about how to use VBA, you can access Help from the Visual Basic Editor, or there are many tutorials available, both in books and on the internet.

Key terms

Validation: A method of ensuring the data that is input is reasonable, i.e. that it meets the validation rule applied. For example, a rule that requires values between 1 and 20 would reject values outside that range, such as 0 or 21. Validation does *not* ensure data is correct.

Prompts

Providing data entry messages

One way that you can help the user to enter the required data is to provide data entry messages. The simplest way to do this is to insert a comment box that appears when the mouse pointer is positioned on the cell. Select the cell where you want to insert a comment. Now select Comment from the Insert menu. A small red triangle will appear in the corner of the cell and a box for you to enter the comment. The comment box will probably show the user name that was set up when Microsoft Office was installed, but you can simply delete it. Type in your comment such as 'Enter the date as dd/mm/yyyy'. When you have finished, click somewhere else on the spreadsheet. The comment box will disappear but the red triangle will remain. Moving the mouse

pointer over the cell will reveal the comment box with an arrow pointing to the cell.

To edit a comment, select the cell and then the Insert menu. The Comment option will have become Edit Comment. Selecting this will allow you to change the content of the comment box.

Using data validation and associated messages

Data validation means applying rules to restrict the data that can be entered in a cell. This ensures that the data is reasonable; *not* that it is correct. For example, you could set up a rule to reject the data if the user tried to enter a person's age as 1,000 years, but an incorrect age of 45 would not be rejected if it was within the range set by the rule.

Figure 10.19 shows the Data Validation dialogue box. You select Validation from the Data menu to access this. There are three tabs. The Settings tab is where you set up the rule to restrict the data that can be entered. The Allow drop-down list offers several different options. These include *any value* (the default), *whole number*, *decimal*, *list*, *date*, *time* and *text length*. There is also a custom option to allow you to enter a formula to place a specific restriction on the data entered. The other options will depend to some extent on which of the Allow options you select. Most offer similar options to those shown in Figure 10.19 for *whole number*. The second drop-down box offers a range of relational operators. *Between* and *not between*

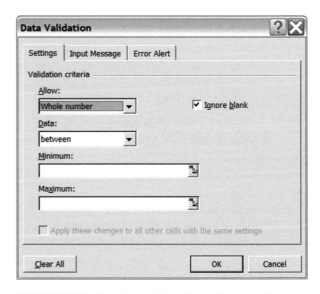

FIGURE 10.19 *The Data Validation dialogue box*

require both a maximum and minimum value; all the other operators require just one value. Notice the symbol at the end of these boxes. This means that you can minimise the dialogue box and select a cell containing a formula to give the value. We will consider the list option a little later.

In this qualification, you will receive a mark between 0 and 50 for the units assessed by a portfolio and a mark between 0 and 100 for the externally assessed units. All marks are whole numbers. If you were setting up a spreadsheet to record your group's marks for each unit, it would be sensible to add a validation rule to ensure only values between those limits could be entered. In both cases, you would need to select *Allow whole number* and *Data between*. For portfolio units, you would need to enter 0 and 50 as the maximum and minimum boxes respectively; for externally assessed units, this would be 0 and 100.

The Input Message tab allows you to enter a message, much as you did using a comment box, that will appear when the cell is selected and that will tell the user what should be entered. A possible input message for entering a mark for a portfolio unit would be 'Enter a value between 0 and 50'. You can also enter a title for the comment, such as 'Mark for Unit 1'.

The third tab, Error Alert, allows you to determine what will be displayed if invalid data is entered. If you do not set up your own message, a default message will be displayed. These do little to help the user correct the error.

Figure 10.20 shows the setting up of a more helpful error message for an externally assessed unit.

FIGURE 10.20 *Setting up a helpful error message*

Presenting results

Results need to be presented so that they are easy to understand. Some of the means of improving the way that results are presented have already been described and you may be familiar with others from your work on *Unit 3: ICT Solutions for Individuals and Society*. They include:

* cell formatting, such as colours and borders
* drawing tools and graphic images
* charts and line graphs.

Cell formatting

Careful use of colours and borders, as already suggested, will differentiate between cells for data entry and those that show the results of processing. Techniques such as the use of a border round the cells containing the results, coloured background or text and a larger font size will all draw the user's attention to the results.

Theory into practice

Set up validation, including input messages and error alerts, for the following data inputs:

1 A person's height in metres. This must be greater than zero, and the height of the tallest man is recorded as 2.72 metres.

2 The date of travel when the booking must be made at least two days in advance.

3 The time you woke up today – assuming you are awake!

---

* Remember

When using colour, make sure that the results are still easy to read – after all, it is the results that are important. Make sure also that the colours chosen can be distinguished by all users, including those who are colour-blind.

Drawing tools and graphic images

As part of the Microsoft Office suite, Excel provides you with the same range of drawing tools as Word. This means that you can add lines or arrows to point to a specific area on the spreadsheet, you can add text boxes or callouts to add notes or explanations and you can use WordArt for titles or headings. You can also insert graphic images, such as a company logo. However, do not get too carried away. Always remember that it is the results of processing that are the reason for creating the spreadsheet in the first place, so any drawings, WordArt or graphic images should not detract from these results.

Charts and line graphs

You will have already come across charts and graphs earlier in this unit. We plotted an XY (Scatter) graph when we were describing the FORECAST function and a bar chart when we were describing the FREQUENCY function. You will also, almost certainly, have produced different types of graphs and charts when analysing data and presenting the results of your investigation for *Unit 3: ICT Solutions for Individuals and Society*. We will not, therefore, provide a detailed description of how to create a chart or graph. You should, however, remember the following:

* Take care when positioning and selecting the data to chart, e.g. blank rows or columns between data will appear on the chart – you may need to copy data to somewhere else on your spreadsheet to ensure its layout is suitable.

* Ensure the chart type you choose is suitable for the results you are trying to convey – chart types such as Radar, Surface or Stock may look impressive, but have very specialist applications and will not be understood by most.

* Ensure that the chart or graph is suitably labelled – a graph or chart with no labels is meaningless.

Macros

If you are going to make your spreadsheet as simple as possible for the user, you will need to use macros, linked to control buttons, to help the user carry out a number of different tasks. At its simplest level, this may be moving from one sheet to another within a workbook, but you will also need to create macros to carry out more complex tasks. You do not need to be able to write a macro from scratch in the Visual Basic Editor; you can record it using the Record New Macro option. However, you will find it helpful to be able to edit a macro you have recorded, rather than having to record the whole thing again.

To record a macro, make sure you are on the sheet where you want the macro to start. Select Macro from the Tools menu and then Record New Macro. Enter a name for the macro in the dialogue box. You can also enter a shortcut key to run the macro. You might also want to edit the Description box to include your own name, rather than the system user name.

When you click OK, the Macro toolbar will appear. Carry out the procedures you want to include in your macro and, when you have finished, click on the Stop button. As everything you do will be recorded in the macro, it is important that you work out beforehand exactly what needs to be done and the best way to do it. It may be helpful to carry out the task first without recording it, as a rehearsal. This will help to avoid recording unnecessary actions that make the macro coding more complicated than it needs to be.

Having recorded the macro, you can run it by selecting Macro from the Tools menu and then Macros. Select the name of your macro and then click Run in the dialogue box that appears. If you set up a shortcut key, you can run the macro by pressing that instead. The best way to run the macro is to provide a button on the spreadsheet to do so. We will describe how to do this a little later.

The Macros dialogue box also provides a button to edit the macro. Clicking on this takes you to the Visual Basic Editor where you can view and make changes to the macro code.

Macros to replace multiple key depressions for a required action

There may be many opportunities for you to provide macros to replace multiple key depressions (or mouse clicks). For example, you could record a macro to copy the contents of some cells on one sheet of a workbook to another and then clear the cells on the original sheet ready for new data. The following sections of code are part of a macro that copies data from individual named cells on a sheet called Invoice to the next blank row of a sheet called Summary and then deletes the data from the Invoice sheet. We will use these to explain the main features of this code.

```
Sub ToSummary()
```

This indicates the start of the macro and assigns it a name.

```
'
' ToSummary Macro
' Macro recorded 26/09/2005 by
Maggie
'
```

Any lines that have ' at the beginning are comments and are ignored.

```
Application.ScreenUpdating = False
```

This ensures that the screen does not flash as the macro is run.

```
Sheets("Summary").Select
Range("A3").Select
Selection.CurrentRegion.Select
If Range("A4") <> " " Then
   Selection.End(xlDown).Select
End If
```

The first line selects the Summary sheet. The rest defines the range that currently holds data – the headings are in row 3 and the first line of data is in row 4. Selection.End(xlDown).Select moves the selection down to the last row with data in it. The If statement is to overcome a problem caused by the first row being empty. The Selection.End command is only carried out if A4 is not empty.

```
ActiveCell.Offset(1, 0).
Range("A1").Select
Sheets("Invoice").Select
Range("Date").Select
Selection.Copy
Sheets("Summary").Select
ActiveSheet.Paste ActiveCell.
Offset(0, 1).Range("A1").Select
```

Offset (1,0) moves the active cell down one row to the first empty row. The Invoice sheet is selected and then the cell named Date. The data in this cell is copied, the Summary sheet is selected and the data pasted into the active cell. Offset (0,1) then moves the active cell one column to the right, ready for the next data item. This would need to be repeated for each cell to be copied.

```
Range("VAT").Select
Application.CutCopyMode = False
Selection.Copy
Sheets("Summary").Select
Selection.PasteSpecial
   Paste:=xlValues,
   Operation:=xlNone,
   SkipBlanks:= False,
   Transpose:=False
```

The cell named VAT contains a formula, so Paste Special was used to paste just the values to the appropriate cell on the Summary sheet.

```
Sheets("Invoice").Select
Application.CutCopyMode = False
Range("Date").Select
Selection.ClearContents
```

Having copied the required data, this section of code moves back to the Invoice sheet, switches off copy mode and then clears the contents of the Date cell. The last two lines would need to be repeated for each cell that needs to be cleared.

```
End Sub
```

This denotes the end of the macro.

The use of named cells overcomes problems with relative cell references if the cell pointer is not in the same place each time the macro is run. However, if you record a macro, you will need to edit the code to replace relative cell references such as:

```
ActiveCell.Offset
(1,3).Range ("A1").Select
```

with:

```
Range("CellName").Select
```

Macros to enable or simplify data input

Earlier, when discussing forms, we said that you would need to create macros so that users did not need to access commands from the Data menu. In fact, you might have more than one button that will have essentially the same macro attached to it, as the form can be used for editing and deleting, as well as entering data. This macro will be far less complex than the one described above, as it will simply need to select the correct sheet and then open the form. If you have created user forms in VBA, you will need to write code to put the data in the correct cells of your spreadsheet.

Macros to produce printed or screen reports

A macro to produce a printed report will involve selecting the area you want in the report and then setting it as the print area. You might then want to set margins, headers, footers, etc., before sending the report to the printer. Producing a screen report might simply involve moving to another sheet where the results are displayed or it could involve recording a macro to create a chart or graph.

More complex spreadsheet facilities

When you are designing and developing your spreadsheet, you need to try to incorporate some of the more complex spreadsheet facilities described in the following sections. Some of these have already been described elsewhere. Where this is the case, we will indicate that they form part of this list of facilities, but you will need to refer back to the relevant section to find out more.

Lists and tables

Sorting

Data that is arranged in columns in a table can be sorted in either ascending or descending order. Clicking the buttons on the toolbar will do just that, based on the column selected. However, if you select Sort from the Data menu, the dialogue box shown in Figure 10.21 will offer additional options. In the example shown, the data will first be sorted in reverse date order. Next, where there is more than one invoice for a particular date, these will be sorted by invoice number. Finally, where there is more than one cost for an invoice, these will also be sorted. If you select the column labels with the data – or

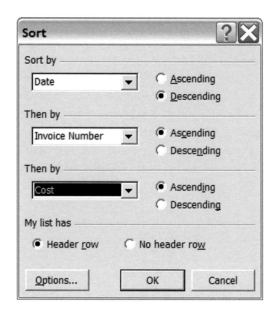

FIGURE 10.21 *The Sort dialogue box*

Excel thinks you have – the header row will not be included in the sort. If there is no header row, you can click on the appropriate radio button to indicate this.

If your data is arranged in rows, rather than columns, click on Options and you can select Sort left to right, rather than Sort top to bottom.

Lookup tables

One use for the Sort facility might be to ensure lookup tables are in ascending order – see the sections on VLOOKUP and HLOOKUP.

Subtotals and totals

Subtotal works on lists like the one shown in Table 10.20. We will use this example to explain what Subtotal does. Enter this data into a spreadsheet – the VAT and Total columns are actually calculated using formulae, but that is not important here.

	A	B	C	D
1	Date	Cost	VAT	Total
2	29/09/2005	£250.00	£43.75	£293.75
3	29/09/2005	£175.00	£30.63	£205.63
4	30/09/2005	£250.00	£43.75	£293.75
5	30/09/2005	£300.00	£52.50	£352.50
6	30/09/2005	£275.00	£48.13	£323.13

TABLE 10.20 *Data for subtotalling*

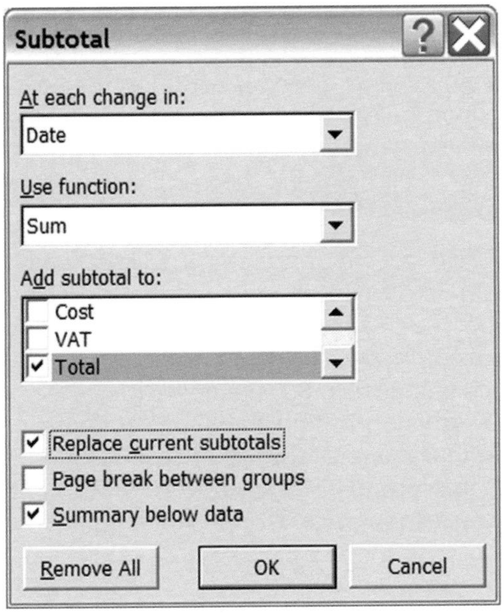

FIGURE 10.22 *The Subtotal dialogue box*

The easiest way to set up subtotals is to select one of the cells containing data and then to select the Subtotal dialogue box from the Data menu. The dialogue box shown in Figure 10.22 will appear.

The dialogue box picks up the headings from the list. Currently, a subtotal will be inserted each time the date changes – the only logical option in this example. However, the drop-down list includes all four headings. The list must be sorted on the column you are going to use. We will stick with SUM, but click on the arrow to show the functions that could be used. Make sure SUM is still selected when you have finished. You can get subtotals for just one column of values or more than one. In this case, just select Total. Make sure the Replace current subtotals and the Summary below data boxes are checked before clicking OK. The spreadsheet should show a subtotal for each date and the grand total.

Think it over...

What has happened to the spreadsheet screen?

What is being indicated?

What formulae are in cells D4, D8 and D9?

Use the Help menu to find out what the argument 9 refers to.

List boxes and drop-down boxes

List boxes and drop-down boxes are ways of restricting the values that a user can enter in a cell. They also speed up the process of data entry, as the user can simply select from the list with the mouse, rather than having to enter the data using the keyboard.

The simplest way to set up a drop-down list is to select the List option from the Allow box in the Validation dialogue box. The Source will be the range of cells that contain the allowed values. These need to be on the same sheet as the cell being validated. For example, in a theatre booking system, there are three ticket prices: adult, child and concession. When a user is entering the type of ticket required, only these three options are valid. If the values 'adult', 'child' and 'concession' are stored elsewhere on the spreadsheet in a range of cells named 'ticket_type', Figure 10.23 shows the Validation dialogue box.

When the mouse pointer is on the validated cell, an arrow head will appear to show there is a drop-down list. You could also add an input comment to tell the user to select from the list.

The other way of creating list boxes and drop-down boxes is to use the Forms menu. Suppose that, instead of just entering the type of ticket in the theatre booking system, we want to enter the price for that type of ticket. A combo box is an ideal way of doing this.

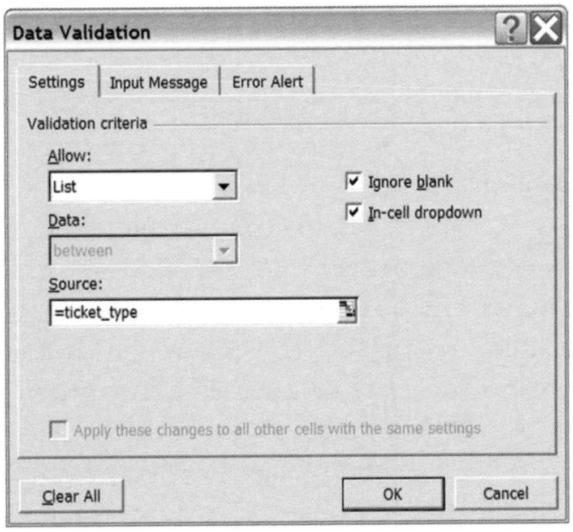

FIGURE 10.23 *Creating a drop-down list using data validation*

Set up a combo box

Firstly, set up a table that includes the ticket types and prices – D1:E4 in Figure 10.24, but this could be on a different sheet in the workbook. Select this range of cells and select Name and then Create from the Insert menu. Choose Top Row to take the names from so that D2:D4 is named ticket_type and E2:E4 is named price.

Next, select the Combo Box button on the Forms toolbar and drag from the top left corner of cell A3 to the bottom right. An empty box with an arrowhead will appear in that cell. Right-click on it and then select Format Control from the menu. The dialogue box shown in Figure 10.24 will appear. Select the Control tab. Type ticket_type as

the Input range and then select C3 as the Cell link. This is *not* the cell that the price will eventually appear in, for reasons that will become obvious in a moment. Click OK and then click anywhere on the spreadsheet to deselect the combo box.

Now, click on the arrow and the list should appear. Select concession from the list. The number 3 will appear in cell C3 because concession is the third item in the list. To make the price appear in B3, we need to use the INDEX function to find the item in the price range that matches the ticket type selected. Enter the formula =INDEX(price,C3) in cell B3. The concession price of £25 should appear in B3.

A list box is similar to a combo box, but, rather than an empty box being displayed, one or more of the items in the list is shown with both up and down arrows to scroll through the items.

Styles

You will have come across named styles for headings and body text in word-processing software. It is also possible to set up a named

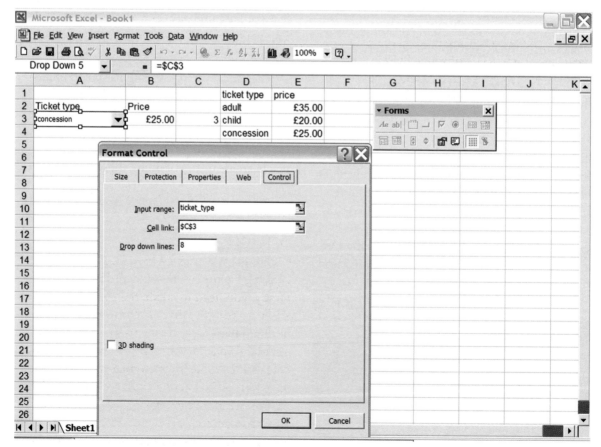

FIGURE 10.24 *Using the Forms toolbar to create a combo (drop-down) box*

style and apply it to particular cells in a spreadsheet.

Selecting Style from the Format menu will bring up the Style dialogue box. Enter a name for the style and then click Modify to open the Format Cells dialogue box, where you can select the formatting options you want to apply. When you have finished, click OK to return to the Style dialogue box. The Add button will no longer be greyed out. Click on it to add your new style to the list. When you want to apply the style, open the Style dialogue box and select its name from the drop-down list.

Named cells and ranges

The use of named cells and ranges has been mentioned many times throughout this unit. The advantages of using names, rather than absolute cell references, are that formulae are easier to understand and the data can be moved to somewhere else on the spreadsheet without having to change the formula. The How to… box earlier describes how to name cell ranges using Create when data is in columns or rows with headings – the headings are used as the names. You can also name a cell or range by selecting it and then selecting Name and Define. This allows you to type in a name for the cell or range.

Auto-fill lists

Auto-fill lists can be useful when you need to enter a series of dates, days of the week or months of the year into a spreadsheet. The Custom Lists tab in Options shows two different options for lists of days and months – three-letter abbreviations or the full names. The easiest way to fill a row or column of cells with days of the week, for example, is to enter Monday in the first cell. Position the mouse on the square at the bottom right corner of the cell, so the cell pointer becomes a black +, and drag to the right or down six more cells to fill them with the remaining days of the week. You can use the same method to fill a range of cells with consecutive dates. However, if you want only weekday dates, or you want the month or year rather than the day to change, you will need to use the Fill option from the Edit menu.

Enter the first date in the topmost cell of a column or the left most cell of a row and select the cells that you want the dates in (including the first one). Select Fill from the Edit menu and then Series to open the dialogue box shown in Figure 10.25.

If you have only selected a single column or row, the correct radio button will be selected. Excel will also recognise that you have entered a date. Entering the value 7 as the Step value will give the dates of the same day each week. Changing the Step value to 1 and selecting Weekday will omit any dates that fall on Saturday or Sunday from the list; Month will give the same day in each month and Year will give the same date each year.

Validation

We have discussed data validation in the section on data entry earlier in this unit. We also described the use of drop-down lists as a validation method in the section on list boxes and drop-down boxes.

Templates

Creating a spreadsheet template is very similar to creating a template in word-processing software. Firstly, you need to create the spreadsheet with all the headings, labels and formulae in place, but no data. The next stage is to save it as a template. Select Save As from the File menu and enter a file name. Select Template(*.xlt) in the Save as type box and click Save. The template will be saved in the default Templates folder. To use the template, select New from the File menu and then select the template and click OK. When you have entered the data into the spreadsheet,

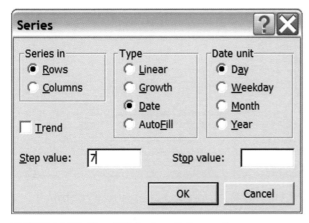

FIGURE 10.25 *The Fill Series dialogue box*

you can save it as a normal workbook file (.xls). You will find it useful to create a template when the same spreadsheet needs to be used again and again.

Protecting cells

If you spend time and energy creating a spreadsheet for a user, the last thing you want is for important formulae to be deleted. There may also be cells that you do not want the user to see, such as the table containing the values for a drop-down list. The first of these problems can be addressed by locking all cells except those that you want the user to be able to change. The second problem can be addressed by hiding the cells – they can still be referenced, but cannot be seen.

There are two stages to locking cells. By default, Excel locks all cells when you protect a worksheet, so first you need to unlock the cells where data will be entered. To do this, select the cell and then select Cells from the Format menu. Finally, select the Protection tab.

Click on the check box next to Locked to unlock the cell and then click OK. Next select Protection and then Protect Sheet from the Tools menu to open the Protect Sheet dialogue box.

You can enter a password so that the worksheet can only be unlocked if the password is entered. If you click on OK without entering a password, the sheet will still be protected, but you will be able to turn the sheet protection off at any time by selecting Protection and the Unprotect Sheet. It is probably best to apply a password only when you have completely finished developing your spreadsheet. It would be disastrous if you needed to make changes and you forgot the password.

To hide a column, either right-click on the column header and select Hide from the menu that appears or select Column and then Hide from the Format menu. To unhide the column, select the columns on either side and select Unhide.

Control buttons

Users will not want to remember key combinations or use the Run macro command to run the macros that you record or write to help them use your spreadsheet. You will need to create control buttons on the sheets of your workbook and assign macros to them. It is possible to use the rectangle or oval on the Drawing toolbar to create buttons, but the best method is to use the Button option on the Forms toolbar. You can either assign a pre-written macro to the button, or you can record the macro from the Assign Macro dialogue box (Figure 10.26).

FIGURE 10.26 *Assigning a macro to a control button*

Assign a macro to a control button

Switch on the Forms toolbar via the View, Toolbars menu. Select the Button option and then drag out a rectangle where you want the button to be. The Assign Macro dialogue box will appear automatically. Either select the name of the macro you want the button to run, or click on Record to record a new macro and follow the normal steps. Click OK to exit the dialogue box. Right-clicking on the new button opens a menu that will allow you to edit the text and format it using Format Control. Clicking elsewhere on the spreadsheet will deselect the button. When you move the mouse pointer onto the button, it will change to a pointing finger, and clicking will activate the macro.

Theory into practice

Record a macro to print out the quotation you created for Rod. Create a control button to run the macro. Make sure that the Print Object check box in the Properties tab of the Format Control dialogue box is not checked: you don't want the button to be printed out on the quotation.

Multiple sheets

A spreadsheet solution to anything but the most straightforward problem is unlikely to consist of a single sheet. Earlier in this unit we described multiple sheet referencing, which enables you to reference cells from a different sheet in a formula. Numerous other references have been made to using multiple sheets, such as for storing a lookup table.

You need to be able to work with multiple sheets. At least some of these sheets should be linked by formulae; others may be used to separate different sections of the system you are designing. These should be linked using macros with control buttons to move from one to the other. You may also want to provide a front sheet that the user will see first, which simply provides buttons to take the user to different parts of the workbook.

When working with multiple sheets, you should change the sheet names so that the sheet tabs give an idea of what each contains, and multiple sheet formulae are easier to follow. The macro code listed earlier would have been more difficult to follow if the sheet names had not been changed to Summary and Invoice. To change the name of a sheet, select Sheet from the Format menu and then Rename. The name on the sheet tab will be highlighted and you can simply replace it. Although it is sensible to leave the sheet tabs visible whilst you are developing your spreadsheet, if you have provided buttons for the user to move from sheet to sheet, these can be removed from the final system. Use the View tab in the Options dialogue box to do this.

Multiple views or windows

It is possible to set up a number of different custom views for a workbook. Custom views change the way the workbook, worksheets, and other objects are displayed. You can give names to sets of particular display and print settings and save them as views. Then you can switch to any of the views whenever you want to display or print the workbook in a different way. To set up a custom view, you first need to set up the workbook exactly as you want to view and print it. You then select Custom Views from the View menu and click Add. You can then enter a name for the view and select the options you want. To apply the view, you also select Custom View and then the name of the view from the list offered.

Multiple windows allow you to view more than one part of a sheet or workbook at the same time. For example, you might want to have two different sheets from a workbook on screen together. To do this, with one sheet on screen, select New Window, switch to the new window and select the other sheet you want to view. Next, select Arrange from the Window menu and select the option you want. (See Figure 10.27 on next page.)

Multiple panes are also useful. If you have a large sheet that does not fit on the screen, scrolling down or right is likely to mean that column or row labels are no longer visible.

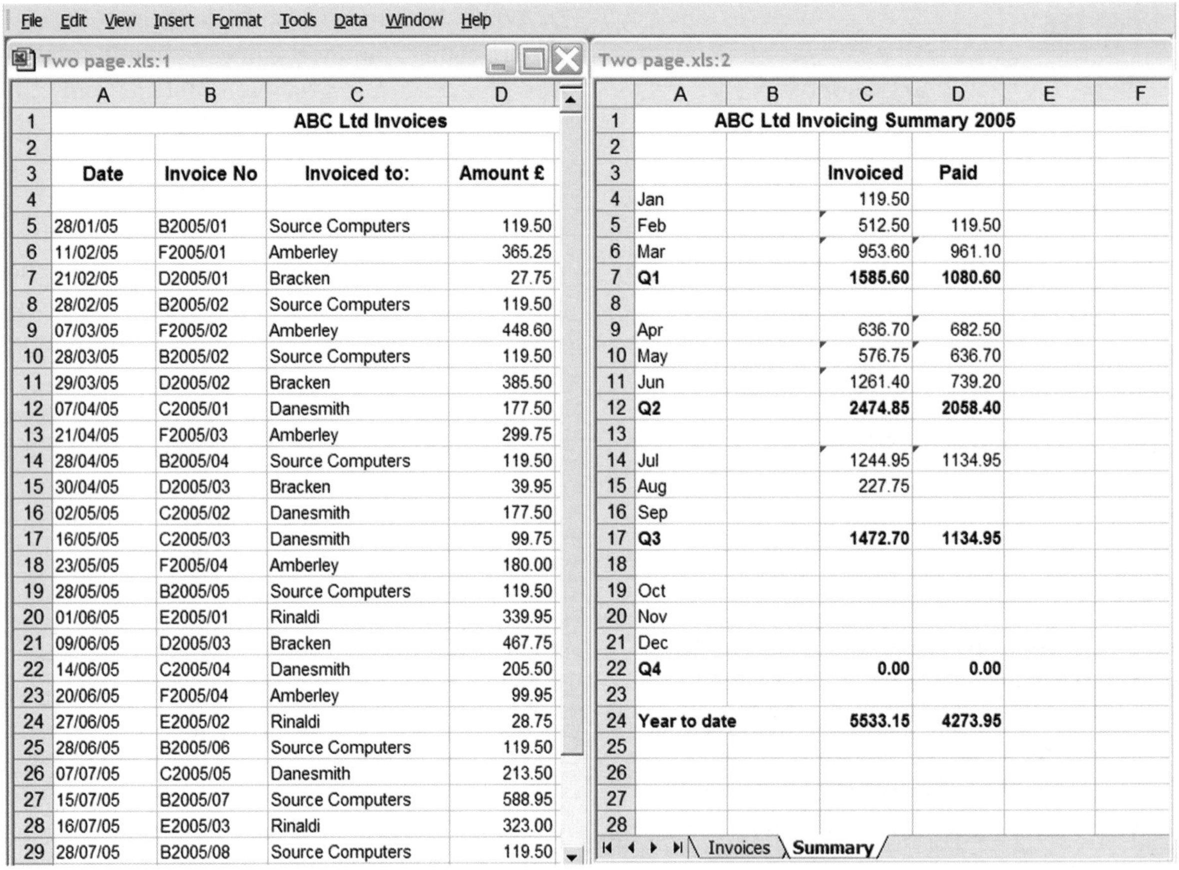

Two page.xls:1

	A	B	C	D
1			ABC Ltd Invoices	
2				
3	Date	Invoice No	Invoiced to:	Amount £
4				
5	28/01/05	B2005/01	Source Computers	119.50
6	11/02/05	F2005/01	Amberley	365.25
7	21/02/05	D2005/01	Bracken	27.75
8	28/02/05	B2005/02	Source Computers	119.50
9	07/03/05	F2005/02	Amberley	448.60
10	28/03/05	B2005/02	Source Computers	119.50
11	29/03/05	D2005/02	Bracken	385.50
12	07/04/05	C2005/01	Danesmith	177.50
13	21/04/05	F2005/03	Amberley	299.75
14	28/04/05	B2005/04	Source Computers	119.50
15	30/04/05	D2005/03	Bracken	39.95
16	02/05/05	C2005/02	Danesmith	177.50
17	16/05/05	C2005/03	Danesmith	99.75
18	23/05/05	F2005/04	Amberley	180.00
19	28/05/05	B2005/05	Source Computers	119.50
20	01/06/05	E2005/01	Rinaldi	339.95
21	09/06/05	D2005/03	Bracken	467.75
22	14/06/05	C2005/04	Danesmith	205.50
23	20/06/05	F2005/04	Amberley	99.95
24	27/06/05	E2005/02	Rinaldi	28.75
25	28/06/05	B2005/06	Source Computers	119.50
26	07/07/05	C2005/05	Danesmith	213.50
27	15/07/05	B2005/07	Source Computers	588.95
28	16/07/05	E2005/03	Rinaldi	323.00
29	28/07/05	B2005/08	Source Computers	119.50

Two page.xls:2

	A	B	C	D	E	F
1			ABC Ltd Invoicing Summary 2005			
2						
3			Invoiced	Paid		
4	Jan		119.50			
5	Feb		512.50	119.50		
6	Mar		953.60	961.10		
7	Q1		1585.60	1080.60		
8						
9	Apr		636.70	682.50		
10	May		576.75	636.70		
11	Jun		1261.40	739.20		
12	Q2		2474.85	2058.40		
13						
14	Jul		1244.95	1134.95		
15	Aug		227.75			
16	Sep					
17	Q3		1472.70	1134.95		
18						
19	Oct					
20	Nov					
21	Dec					
22	Q4		0.00	0.00		
23						
24	Year to date		5533.15	4273.95		
25						
26						
27						
28						

Invoices \ Summary

FIGURE 10.27 *Multiple windows allow you to view more than one sheet at a time*

You can overcome this problem by creating separate panes for the labels and then freezing the panes so that they do not move when you scroll through the sheet.

There are two ways of doing this. Selecting Split from the Window menu will split the spreadsheet into panes. You can then move the pane boundaries to where you want them to be. Alternatively, move the mouse pointer to just above the vertical scroll bar so that it changes to parallel lines with arrows pointing up and down. You can then click and drag a pane boundary down to where you want it. You can add a vertical frame boundary by moving the mouse pointer to the right-hand end of the horizontal scroll bar. Notice that rows or columns will appear in more than one pane. Now select Freeze Panes from the Windows menu. The thick pane boundaries and any duplicated rows or columns will disappear. Now when you scroll through the spreadsheet, the labels or data in the frozen panes will remain visible.

> **✳ Remember**
>
> When designing and developing spreadsheets you need to
>
> ✳ provide simple but effective ways of entering data
>
> ✳ provide users with helpful prompts
>
> ✳ present results in appropriate ways
>
> ✳ make good use of macros to simplify the use of the spreadsheet
>
> ✳ use some of the more complex spreadsheet facilities.

10.4 Implementing a spreadsheet solution

When you are developing any system, you should follow a process called the system life cycle, although the process you will follow is

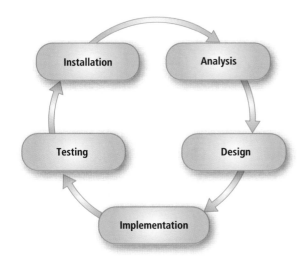

FIGURE 10.28 *The system development cycle*

more correctly called the **system development cycle**. The stages of the system development cycle are shown in Figure 10.28.

So far in this unit, we have covered the analysis and design phases. You now need to implement the system. You need to plan how you will approach this implementation.

One approach would be to break the task down into sections or modules. You will then need to develop each module and test it. When each module is working as it should, you will need to combine the modules and test the system to check that the modules work together.

Another approach that you could use is prototyping. This might involve designing basic worksheets, a sample user interface and outline reports that will give the user an idea of how the system will operate. The user can then suggest any changes they would like made before you continue development.

Whichever strategy you use, you must document it and keep a record of your progress, including any ad hoc testing you carry out and any problems that arise. You will then need to keep a record of how you solve these problems, including any consultation with your user. You might find, for example, that you are not able to implement part of your solution as you planned, requiring you to check with your user that an alternative approach is acceptable.

10.5 Presenting spreadsheet information

There are two ways that the output from your spreadsheet solution will be presented: on screen and on paper. In both cases, the information may be presented numerically or graphically. You will need to consider how the information will be presented from the outset, and you will need to apply what you learnt about presenting information in *Unit 1: Using ICT to Communicate*. We described the tools and techniques for presenting results – such as cell formatting, colour and borders, and the use of charts and line graphs – in the section on the design and development of spreadsheets. Here we will consider issues to do with page layout of printed reports and the appropriate labelling and presentation of charts and line graphs.

Page layout

As with any printed document, when printing out information from a spreadsheet, you will need to consider the layout of the page. You will need to set the page size to match the paper you are printing on. You will also need to consider the page orientation – would it be better to print landscape or portrait? As the screen layout is wider than it is high, landscape orientation is often more appropriate for printing spreadsheet information. You can access the Page Setup dialogue box by selecting Page Setup from the File menu.

As well as the paper size and orientation, you may need to adjust the margins. The Margins tab allows you to change the top, bottom, left, and right margins as well as the header and footer margins. You can also centre

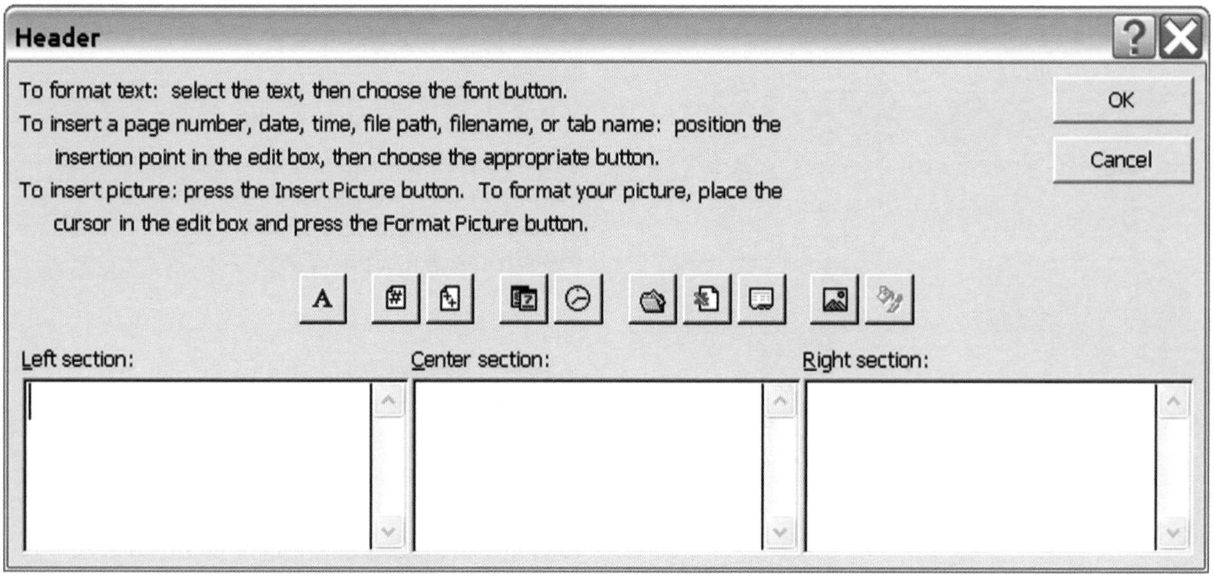

FIGURE 10.29 *The Header dialogue box*

the information on the page both horizontally and vertically.

Another important aspect of page layout is the use of headers and footers. The Header/Footer tab provides a list of standard headers and footers that you can select from. However, it is more likely that you will need to create your own. Clicking the Custom Header button will open the dialogue box shown in Figure 10.29. A similar dialogue box will be displayed if you click the Custom Footer button.

As you can see, you can enter header text on the left, in the centre or on the right of the page. The buttons allow you to enter data that will change, such as the page number, the date or the filename. Including such information may be important if a number of different spreadsheets are to be printed at different times.

The Print Preview button will show you what the printout will look like and you can make final adjustments to margins, for example, by physically moving them with the mouse.

Presenting charts and line graphs

Whether charts and graphs are to be displayed on screen or printed on paper, there are important items that must be included and other aspects that need to be considered to improve the display and ease of understanding of the information being presented. If you use the Chart Wizard to create a

chart or graph, you will be given the opportunity to add a title and labels, depending on the type of chart you select. However, you can also change these and other features by selecting Chart Options from the Chart menu.

Chart or graph title

This should make it clear what the chart or graph is designed to show, such as 'Yearly sales by region, 2000 to 2006', or 'Distribution of grades for GCE Applied ICT'.

Axis labels

Both the x and y axes should be given suitable labels to indicate the value or category of the data that has been used to plot the chart. In the first example above, the x axis would be labelled Year and the y axis Sales (£) (Figure 10.30). If the cells containing the sales figures had already been formatted as currency, the £ sign would not be needed.

Note: In this example, the cells containing the years were formatted as text, otherwise they would have been treated as data rather than category labels.

Knowledge check

What would the axis labels be for the distribution of grades example?

Background

It is possible to insert a picture as the background to a chart by selecting Sheet from the Format menu and then Background. However, the likelihood is that this would distract the viewer rather than improve their understanding of the information being conveyed.

A more useful way of changing the background is by right-clicking on the area surrounding the chart (the chart area) or the background of the chart itself (the plot area). In either case, there will be a Format option in the menu that appears. This will allow you to change the colour of the background, or to apply effects and patterns. You still need to be careful that these too do not detract from, rather than enhance, the presentation.

Incidentally, right-clicking on a bar will allow you to format that **data series**. This means that you can change the colour of the bars, or, if the chart is to be printed in black and white, use patterns, rather than colours, to distinguish between the different data series.

> ### Key terms
>
> *Data series:* One row or column of data in the spreadsheet that is used to create a chart or graph.

Legend data series labels

Where more than one series of data is being plotted, or a pie chart is being used, a key is needed. This will tell the viewer which bar or line shows which data series, or which section of pie relates to which data category. If you select the labels as well as the data when you select the area of the spreadsheet to plot, this key (more properly called the legend) will be set up automatically. Table 10.21 shows the data used to create the chart in Figure 10.30. This shows the sales by region from 2000 to 2006. The whole range of cells from A1 to H5 was selected. The data series are in rows 2 to 5 and the labels in column A have been used in the legend for the chart. The Legend tab in the Chart Options dialogue box allows you to choose where the legend will appear, and whether it will be shown or not. Where you are plotting a single data series, you should switch off the legend.

Data and category labels

Data labels allow you to show the value and category label for each bar in a bar chart (or each point in a line graph), but this rarely does much to aid the viewer's understanding. However, adding such labels or percentages to a pie chart adds additional information and makes the information easier to understand.

Figure 10.31 shows a pie chart for just one year's data from Table 10.21. The category labels and percentages make it immediately obvious which segment relates to which region, so a legend is not needed. Also, it is possible to see that the North region had a slightly higher percentage of sales than the East region. Without the percentages, it would be difficult to see this.

	A	B	C	D	E	F	G	H
1		2000	2001	2002	2003	2004	2005	2006
2	South	860000	101000	169000	784000	206000	82000	238000
3	East	148000	89000	763000	211000	161000	120000	631000
4	West	78000	768000	150000	15000	892000	665000	857000
5	North	804000	277000	862000	257000	902000	46000	683000

TABLE 10.21 *Sales by region*

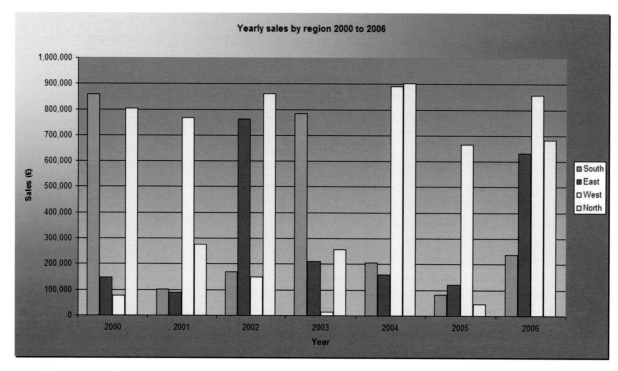

FIGURE 10.30 *Using shading effects in the chart and plot areas*

Axis formats and values

Right-clicking within the *x* or *y* axis area will allow you to format that axis. In both cases, you will be able to change the font and number format and the alignment of the axis label. For the *y* axis, also called the value axis, you will also be able to change items such as the maximum and minimum values displayed and the interval between the major and minor gridlines (see the next section). For the *x* axis, also called the category axis, you can change where the *y* axis crosses, the number of categories between the tick marks on the axis and the number of category labels between tick marks.

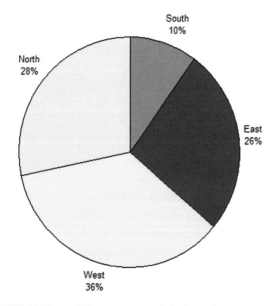

FIGURE 10.31 *Adding category labels and percentages to a pie chart makes the information clearer*

Gridlines

By default, Excel displays the major gridlines for the *y* axis. These are the values that are displayed on this axis. Using the Gridlines tab in the Chart Options dialogue box, it is possible turn these gridlines off or add minor gridlines as well. Adding the minor gridlines allows values to be read more accurately, but can be distracting if a general impression of the distribution of values is required. There is also an option to add *x* axis gridlines. These are only relevant if an XY (Scatter) chart is plotted so that there are values on both the *x* and *y* axes.

When presenting spreadsheet information on paper, you will need to create an appropriate page layout including selection of suitable

* page size
* page orientation
* margins
* headers
* footers.

Charts or graphs must have, as appropriate

* a title
* axis labels
* a legend.

The presentation of charts and graphs can be enhanced by adding or formatting

* the background
* data labels
* category labels
* axis formats
* axis values
* gridlines.

However, care is needed to ensure that such changes enhance rather than detract from the information being presented.

10.6 Testing spreadsheets

The spreadsheet you create will be of little use if the results are not accurate or it does not meet your user's needs. It is, therefore, vital that you test your spreadsheet solution thoroughly. In the section on implementation, we mentioned that you might carry out ad hoc testing as you develop the spreadsheet. You will also need to test the final solution.

Questions to ask

There are several important questions that you will need to answer through your testing.

Does the solution meet the agreed specification?

The ease with which you can answer this question will depend on how clearly the user's requirements have been set out (and agreed) within your design specification. If within the specification you have listed a clear set of objectives, you will be able to test whether each of these objectives has been met in your solution.

Do your results agree with manual methods?

Comparing your results with manual methods of doing the same problem will help to identify whether the formulae and functions you have used are correct.

Can the spreadsheet cope with normal, abnormal and extreme data?

Normal data is data that is of the correct type and within the range that you would normally expect – the acceptable range. *Abnormal data* is data that is of the wrong type; for example, text when a number is expected, or data that is outside the acceptable range. *Extreme data* is data that is acceptable but that is on the boundary of the acceptable range. For example, if the acceptable data range is between 16 and 65 inclusive, the values 16 and 65 would be extreme data. You need to ensure that your spreadsheet copes with each type of data appropriately. Normal and extreme data should be accepted without any problem. Abnormal data should be rejected with a user-friendly error message that allows the user to enter an acceptable value.

Can other people use your solution?

It may seem obvious to you how to use your solution, but is it as obvious to other people? The only way to find out is to give it to someone else to use. The best person to try to use it is the user you are creating it for. If this is not possible, you will need to find someone else with similar ICT skills to try to use it.

Is the spreadsheet robust?

A robust system is one that can deal with anything the user does without an irretrievable error occurring. It is virtually impossible to test every single thing that a user might do when using your spreadsheet. Software companies often have to issue upgrades or patches to overcome problems that have only been found as a result of use. You should, however, test to see if you can make your solution fail. For example, you should test that all buttons and macros do what they should without run-time errors being displayed.

Test specification

To ensure that you test your spreadsheet thoroughly, you need to create a test specification. Ideally, this should be developed at the same time as your design specification. A test specification should consist of a table with the following column headings:

* test number
* what is being tested
* test data
* expected result
* actual result
* action required.

Obviously, the last two columns will be filled in when you actually carry out the test. Hopefully, the actual result will match the expected result so no action will be needed. Your test specification will need to define tests for the following.

Acceptable data input values

You should include tests for all data inputs using acceptable data. The test value column should include the actual value of the data to be input. Where a range validation rule has been applied, you should test with a value in the middle of the range and with the values at the maximum and minimum boundaries.

TEST NUMBER	WHAT IS BEING TESTED	TEST DATA	EXPECTED RESULT	ACTUAL RESULT	ACTION REQUIRED
1	Input Age – Normal data	44	Accepted		
2	Input Age – Boundary data (min)	16	Accepted		
3	Input Age – Boundary data (max)	65	Accepted		
4	Input Age – Unacceptable data rejected – below range	15	Rejected – error message		
5	Input Age – Unacceptable data rejected – above range	66	Rejected – error message		
6	Input Age – Unacceptable data rejected – decimal number	44.5	Rejected – error message		
7	Input Age – Unacceptable data rejected – wrong type	sixteen	Rejected – error message		

TABLE 10.22 *Part of a test specification*

Unacceptable data values

You should include tests for all possible types of unacceptable data. Table 10.22 shows part of a test specification. The input being tested is Age, which must be a whole number from 16 to 65. The table shows the minimum testing that should be applied to this input. This includes a value below the range, one within the range that is not a whole number, a value above the range and data of the wrong data type. Similar testing should be planned and carried out for all inputs where a range validation rule has been applied. The unacceptable data for other inputs will depend on the type of validation rules applied.

Checking functions and formulae

Your test specification will also need to include tests to check that all the functions and formulae in your spreadsheet work correctly. You can do this either by entering simple values so that you can easily work out what the result should be, or you can use a calculator to work out what the result should be for particular input values. The likelihood is that one formula or function will use the results of another. You need to work through each step to ensure that it gives the result you expect. This is sometimes called dry running. Excel provides a set of auditing tools in the Tools menu that helps you to see how formulae are linked and to trace any errors.

Checking the system meets user requirements

One of the most important aspects of your test specification will be to check that your spreadsheet does what your user wants it to. As mentioned earlier, this will be easier to determine if there is a clear agreed set of measurable objectives within your design specification. You can then define tests in your test specification to check these objectives have been met.

10.7 Documenting the development

There are two types of documentation that you need to develop alongside your spreadsheet solution. These two types of documentation are for very different audiences, so the content and the language used for each should be appropriate for its particular audience. You should apply your knowledge of presentation techniques from *Unit 1: Using ICT to Communicate* to help you create documents that are suitable for each audience. You should certainly include page numbers and a contents page to help the reader find information and make good use of screen prints and other graphic images to illustrate the text. However, when you use screen prints, you need to ensure that they are large enough for their content to be read. It may be better to include just the relevant dialogue box (by pressing ALT at the same time as the PRT SCR key) or to crop and enlarge the relevant section of the screen.

Technical documentation

Technical documentation is for specialists, so it can use suitable technical language. It should allow someone else to extend or maintain your spreadsheet solution. As such, it should not be a diary of how you created the spreadsheet – a specialist will know how to set up a validation rule, for example – but should include all the details specific to your solution. This will include the following.

A copy of the agreed design specification

This is self-explanatory. If someone is to extend or maintain your spreadsheet solution, they need to know what it was designed to do. You simply need to include the specification you produced and agreed after your initial discussions with the user.

✱ Remember

You must test your spreadsheet solution thoroughly by creating a test specification. This should include tests to check that

✱ normal data, including boundary data, is accepted

✱ abnormal data is rejected

✱ formulae and functions work correctly

✱ the system meets user requirements.

You should also check that other people can use your system and that it is robust.

Resource requirements

You need to list the hardware and software needed to run your spreadsheet solution; for example, the software version used to create it and whether it will run on other versions of the software. You should also include details of any other resources that are needed.

Instructions for opening and configuring the spreadsheet

This will include details of the location of the file and its name. If the spreadsheet requires a password to open it, you will need to say what this is. Also, where sheets have been protected with a password, you will need to include this as well, so that the protection can be removed when any changes need to be made to the spreadsheet.

Details of numerical processing

You must include clear details of all the formulae and functions you have used in your spreadsheet solution. This should include the location of each formula or function and its purpose. This is best shown by including formula printouts of each sheet in your spreadsheet with annotations to indicate how formulae are linked. You should also include annotated listings of any macros you use.

Validation and verification

You need to indicate which validation rules you have applied to which inputs. You also need to describe any **verification** procedures you have used. This may include requiring the user to enter important information twice, or providing a button to enter the data only when the user has checked it.

Input and output screens and printed designs

You will need to include in your technical documentation details of all the input and output screens you use. These will need to be annotated to show how data is transferred from any input forms or screens and from where the information on output screens is obtained. You should also show any formatting that has been applied. As well as screen output, you will need to show the design and layout of any printed output.

Throughout your development of the technical documentation, you should keep in mind that it should include enough detail for someone else to know exactly how your spreadsheet works.

User documentation

User documentation, on the other hand, should enable someone else – possibly with few ICT skills – to use the spreadsheet you have created. The user documentation should explain how to use your spreadsheet, not the software you used to create it.

As user documentation could be used by people with limited ICT knowledge, instructions need to be simple and straightforward with little or no technical language. If you need to use technical terms, you need to explain them. You should also consider the saying 'a picture is worth a thousand words' and make good use of well-annotated screen prints to show the user what they need to do.

Although you will need to produce hard-copy evidence of the user documentation for the spreadsheet you create, user documentation can also be provided on a CD or as an online help file.

Your user guide should include the following.

How to start the spreadsheet program

The amount of detail in this section will depend on how you have set up the spreadsheet. You may, for example, have created a button on the desktop that will open the spreadsheet software and the file, in which case the instructions will be very simple. However, if the user needs to open the spreadsheet software and then find the file in a particular folder, more detailed instructions will be needed. You will also need to tell the user how to enable macros, and possibly how to change the security setting if macros are blocked.

Routes through spreadsheet menus

You will need to include examples of all the menus offered within your spreadsheet and describe the route each menu item provides. You need to do this systematically, possibly describing each route in a separate section with its own heading so that the user can find it easily. Don't forget to include options for saving, printing and exiting the spreadsheet.

Examples of screens and data entry forms

Your user guide should include screen prints of all the data entry screens that the user will encounter and examples of important screens that they will need to use. These should be carefully annotated to identify the features the user needs to recognise.

Instructions about data entry

Alongside the screen prints, you need to provide instructions about how to enter data. This will include details of the type of data required, how to enter it – for example, by typing it in or selecting it from a drop-down list – and how to move from one entry point to another.

Common error messages

Errors inevitably occur when software is being used. The most likely cause is the user entering unacceptable data. Hopefully, you will have created user-friendly error messages that explain what the user has done wrong and how to put it right. You should include examples of these error messages in your user guide. You might also want to include examples of common system error messages and what to do if they appear.

Data output screens and printed copy

Finally, in your user guide you should include annotated screen prints of any data output screens.

You should also print out and include examples of any printed reports available to the user, explaining what they show and how to produce them.

> ### ✷ Remember
>
> Technical documentation is for specialists. It can use technical language and should enable someone else to extend or maintain your spreadsheet system.
>
> User documentation is for possibly novice users. It must explain how to use your spreadsheet solution using simple instructions in non-technical language.
>
> Both types of documentation should use headings, subheadings and page numbers and include a contents page.
>
> You should use annotated screen prints effectively in both types of documentation.

10.8 Evaluating the effectiveness of your solution and your performance

An important part of the assessment evidence for this unit and, indeed, of any project is evaluating its effectiveness. You also need to evaluate your own performance in arriving at the solution and consider how you could be more effective when carrying out a similar project in future.

You need to provide a critical analysis of the effectiveness of your solution. How well does the solution meet the brief? What are the strengths of your solution? What are its weaknesses? How could you improve your solution in future? You also need to get feedback from your user and take this into account so that you can refine your solution to meet the user's needs more closely.

When evaluating your own performance, you need to think about what you did and how you went about solving the problem. What went well – what were your strengths? What didn't go so well – what were your weaknesses? What could you do to overcome these weaknesses? Are there aspects of your performance that you could improve upon? How could you be more effective in future?

UNIT ASSESSMENT

The assessment evidence for this unit requires you to design and implement a spreadsheet solution to a user's problem. Ideally you should find a user so that you can discuss their requirements with them before developing a design specification. Alternatively, your teacher may act as the user and provide you with the information you need. You will need to ask your teacher questions, as if they were the user, to make sure you have all the information you need. Another possibility is to use the Sovereign Hill amateur dramatics group case study at the start of this unit. You may have already produced a design specification for this, but you will need to revisit and amend it in the light of what you have learnt by studying the rest of the unit. You may also be able to think of other information the spreadsheet could provide.

Whichever problem you solve, you will need to carry out the following tasks.

Task A

Produce a design specification that analyses the problem and describes how you will solve it by numerical modelling.

Mark Band 1
Your design specification will take account of the user's requirements.

Mark Band 2
You will produce a complete design specification that includes details of sources of data, numerical processing required, user aids and how output is to be presented.

Mark Band 3
Your design specification will provide a clear, precise and complete description of a numerical modelling solution to a problem.

Task B

Produce evidence that you have implemented your solution using suitable entry aids and processing facilities.

Mark Band 1
You will produce a numerical modelling spreadsheet solution which can be implemented and includes data entry, numerical processing and output.

Mark Band 2
You will produce a solution that effectively includes specialist numerical processing functions and complex spreadsheet facilities.

Mark Band 3
You will implement a complete solution to a complex problem that consistently shows effective use of complex spreadsheet facilities for data entry, numerical processing and presentation of output.

Task C

Keep a record of how you overcame problems.

Mark Band 1
You will produce a record of the strategy that you used to implement the spreadsheet solution, including methods you used to overcome problems.

Mark Band 2

You will show that the methods you used to overcome problems show an understanding of the user's needs and the effective use of spreadsheet facilities.

Mark Band 3

You will use methodical, analytical and critical approaches to overcome problems during implementation. Your methods should fully address the user's needs and make effective use of spreadsheet facilities.

Task D

Produce a specification for testing your spreadsheet and provide evidence of the results of these tests.

Mark Band 1

You will test the spreadsheet to check that it meets the requirements of the design specification.

Mark Band 2

You will provide evidence that you have followed a test specification that adequately tests the functionality of your spreadsheet solution.

Mark Band 3

You will provide a detailed test specification, which tests all aspects of your solution, with a full range of acceptable and unacceptable input, expected output and any associated error messages.

Task E

Produce technical documentation that explains how your spreadsheet works and user documentation that explains how it is used.

Mark Band 1

You will produce clear technical and user documentation that identifies numerical processing methods used, includes copies of menus and screens used and provides expected outputs.

Mark Band 2

Your technical and user documentation will make good use of graphic images, together with explanations of technical aspects of the solution, examples of menus and data input screens, types of output available and possible error messages.

Mark Band 3

In addition to your technical and user documentation, you will make effective use of graphic images and explain all technical aspects of the solution.

Task F

Evaluate the effectiveness of your solution and your personal performance.

Mark Band 1

You will comment on the effectiveness of your final solution, with some overall indication of how your work might be improved in the future. You will evaluate aspects of your personal performance that affected the solution. Your report may contain errors in spelling, punctuation and grammar.

Mark Band 2
You will provide an analysis of your final solution, identifying the strengths and weaknesses in order to identify how your work may be improved in the future. You will also evaluate aspects of your personal performance by identifying your strengths and weaknesses that affected your solution, with some suggestions for improvement to the overall process. Your report will contain few spelling, punctuation and grammar errors.

Mark Band 3
You will provide a full critical analysis of your final solution identifying how well it meets the initial brief, taking into account user feedback in order to identify how your work might be improved in the future. When evaluating your own performance, you will identify how you may address any weaknesses to be more effective in the future. Your report will be consistently well structured with few, if any, spelling, punctuation and grammar errors.

Interactive multimedia products

By studying this unit, you will

* learn to be critical of commercially produced interactive products

* increase your understanding of the process of designing and creating an interactive multimedia product

* research into commercially produced interactive multimedia products

* produce a range of different elements for inclusion in an interactive multimedia product

* design and create an interactive multimedia product in response to a brief from a client

* produce a final report into the effectiveness of your interactive multimedia product in meeting the client's requirements and the role you played in its creation.

This unit is about reviewing and creating interactive multimedia products. You will review existing multimedia products so that you may have a better understanding of the features included within multimedia products and be able to make informed decisions about including similar features in any interactive multimedia product you produce. You will then be given a brief to produce a multimedia product. This multimedia product should be fully interactive and include a range of different features which suit the requirements of the brief.

Reviewing commercially produced interactive products is extremely important to the success of your project. You will learn to identify the intended audience for a product and to evaluate the impact of the product on the target audience. You will also learn to assess the degree to which the product meets the need of the target audience. Once you have completed your review of commercially produced multimedia products, you should be in a position to produce a multimedia product of your own which is well written, runs efficiently and fully meets the needs of both the target audience and of the brief you accept.

Your brief from the client will explain what sort of product you need to produce. The first stage of meeting the demands of this brief will be to produce initial designs. You will learn about technical terms, such as colour depth and frame rate, and then use these terms in your initial planning. This planning will include a range of skills, including the use of storyboards, designing screen layouts and choosing navigational tools which suit the purpose of the interactive multimedia product you are producing.

Once you have completed your planning, you will go on to learn about using a range of applications software to create elements to include in a multimedia product. You will learn about creating multimedia presentations and will then combine the separate elements into one completed solution to the brief.

This is an extremely interesting and creative unit. You will be taught new skills and encouraged to use these, along with the skills you already have, to produce an interactive multimedia product which should show real imagination, ability and professionalism.

How you will be assessed

This unit will be assessed on a portfolio of evidence that you will produce. The assignment at the end of this unit will provide you with the evidence to complete the portfolio.

What you need to learn

You need to learn about

* reviewing and evaluating interactive multimedia products
* considering design
* designing an interactive multimedia product
* creating elements of an interactive multimedia product
* authoring an interactive multimedia product
* testing and documenting your product
* reviewing your final product.

11.1 Reviewing and evaluating interactive multimedia products

Your target for this unit is to produce an interactive multimedia product. Before you begin the process of creating this product, you need to be aware of what makes a good and what makes a bad interactive product. You will then use this knowledge and understanding to evaluate a number of commercially produced interactive multimedia products. At the end of this exercise, you will have gained some further understanding of which elements you may wish to include in your multimedia product in order to make it effective.

What is an interactive multimedia product?

Multimedia

A multimedia product is used to present information to a viewer or user. There are four main **elements** that may combine to make up a multimedia product:

* graphics
* animation
* sound
* text.

> **Key terms**
>
> *Elements:* The individual parts which are combined together to create a multimedia product.

There are many examples of multimedia presentations in all areas of our life and it is unlikely that you will not come into contact with at least one during the next 24 hours. Many organisations will use them to present information as you walk into their premises. Banks and post offices, for example, use multimedia products set up to run on a loop to give out product information. DIY stores may have multimedia products, again running on a loop, to provide you with decorating tips or advice on how to use a specific tool. When you visit a castle or historic home, you will probably start your tour with a presentation on how the building was created and what it looked like when it was lived in. This technique of letting you see things as they once were may also be used in museums, either as part of a special presentation or as part of the general information that is being presented.

You will also come across multimedia productions in less formal settings. For example, many bands now have a multimedia product playing behind them to add to the atmosphere of the concert.

Multimedia products are not only used to give information. The ability to interact with a multimedia product gives the viewer the opportunity to decide what happens on the screen, thereby making their experience of the multimedia product effectively unique and, potentially, much more exciting. As we shall see, a computer game is an interactive multimedia product. Whilst some of the interactive multimedia products you have may be intended to give a message or include elements of learning, others are pure escapism. This is true whether you are battling your way through a range of incredible monsters, racing around a track or playing chess against your own computer.

Whatever form your multimedia products take, it is the 'multi' bit that is important. As we will discuss below, a true multimedia product will combine most, if not all, of the four types of elements listed above. Other software types allow you to combine some of these elements but do not give sufficient control over what goes on within the multimedia product to be considered true multimedia software. For example, some word-processing packages allow for small amounts of animation to be added to a document, sometimes as a border to further emphasise an area of the document. You may also be able to add a few sound files to a spreadsheet, but this is hardly what we think of when we talk about multimedia software and so we need to define terms accurately so as to avoid confusion.

Presentation software allows the user to combine the four elements listed above and is often confused with multimedia software.

Fundamentally, presentation software does just what the name implies: it allows information to be presented, and although there are some animations included, these are there to allow extra emphasis to be given to a message and the choice of animations is quite limited and lacking in options.

Presentations tend to be created around slides and are sometimes refered to as slide shows, which reflects the suggestion that this type of software has replaced the slide shows based on hundreds of individual photographic slides that used to be shown by relatives around about Christmas time.

Multimedia software, on the other hand, allows far more control over the elements than the author is given when working with presentation software. It also tends to create a product which it is difficult for the user to edit or to stop and restart at will.

The features available in more recent versions of presentation software packages, especially the slide transition options, have undoubtedly blurred the difference between presentation and multimedia software, but there is still a difference between the amount of control over elements included within a true multimedia package and a presentation software package. If in doubt, it is best to consider anything that uses slides as being presentation software.

This therefore gives us the problem about what to call our multimedia equivalent of a slide. The simplest term is **frame**, as this is the term used to describe the smallest section of a film. Some multimedia packages use the term 'stage' and combine elements, which are sometimes known as 'sprites', on the stage. You should use whichever term you feel comfortable with, as long as it is not 'slide'. Throughout this unit, we will use the term 'frame'.

Key terms

Frame: The smallest part of a completed multimedia product. A competed product will be made up of lots of frames.

Interactivity

This unit is concerned with interactive multimedia products. This means that you should be reviewing and creating multimedia products which give the user some control over what happens. At the most simple, this would be letting the user decide when to move onto the next section or to play a message. You may have come across more complex interactive multimedia products, where the user not only decides which sections of the presentation get accessed, but also in what order, or when to play a video or sound file.

There are many different types of multimedia authoring packages, but all will include tools that allow the author to apply different effects to elements within the multimedia product. Interactivity is one of these tools. Most authoring packages include a range of different events that can happen once the viewer clicks on a button or some other interactive element on a frame. Options include moving to another frame or fixed point within a product, or opening another file, such as a sound file or video. The interactivity options from Macromedia Director MX are shown in Figure 11.1.

Whilst Figure 11.1 shows those options in one specific software package, the options shown are fairly standard and you should expect to find at least some of these options in the multimedia authoring software you choose to use.

Multimedia games

Multimedia games are possibly the most widely used form of multimedia product at present. Successful computer games combine the elements of multimedia with interactivity to achieve a product that can command a level of attention and concentration about which producers of other forms of multimedia products may only dream. The most successful multimedia products are not necessarily the most complicated products either, as many of the original computer games which launched the genre over 20 years ago are still highly popular and demand just as much dedication if they are to be completed successfully as do their more complicated modern counterparts.

And the Internet?

You may also be wondering about the Internet. The Internet combines sound, text images and

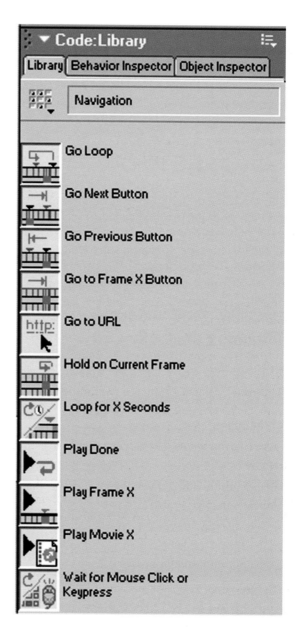

FIGURE 11.1 *Interactivity options within Director MX*

animation, especially when working in some of the more complex languages that may be used on the Internet to produce elements for inclusion on web pages. Surely this means that the Internet should be thought of as a huge multimedia product?

Whilst it is true that the four main features of multimedia products are combined on web pages, the fundamental difference between the Internet and multimedia packages is a practical one. Internet pages are designed to open and run quickly. Multimedia packages are either installed or accessed locally, so that elements that are required for the presentation load quickly. If multimedia products were accessed over the Internet, even with a fast broadband connection, the amount of information that would be needed to be downloaded to run the product would make it run extremely slowly.

> *** Remember**
>
> This unit is about using multimedia authoring software to create multimedia products. It is not about using presentation software to create slide shows or web page authoring software to create websites.

Assessing good and bad interactive multimedia products

There are a number of skills you will need to develop in order to assess the quality of any interactive multimedia product. You will need the ability to:

* identify the intended audience of any multimedia product

* decide on the impact which any product has on the intended audience

* recognise the 'tricks of the trade' which an author may use to create an atmosphere within a multimedia product

* decide whether a multimedia product is appropriate

* decide whether a multimedia product is effective in communicating its message.

We will now look at each of these skills in turn.

Identifying the intended audience

Imagine that you have thought of an idea for a new book. You are so convinced that this book will sell that, when you close your eyes, all you can see are the flashing lights of the paparazzi as you attend the launch party. Having come up with the idea for the book, you may even be lucky enough to be given the chance to explain your book to a publisher. After listening politely, the publisher will ask you one question, 'Who will buy this book?'. If the answer to the question is that you do not know,

but you would find the subject matter fascinating and would definitely buy at least one copy, your chances of seeing the book published are going to be pretty slim. If, however, you are planning to produce a definitive textbook for a rapidly growing exam, and are therefore able to talk about hundreds of thousands of eager readers who will find the book invaluable to their studies, then you may have a deal. The difference between these two scenarios, and the factor which determines whether each will be published, is the size of the target audience and therefore the projections for possible sales.

Target audience

Target audience is a very important concept for any product, as it defines at whom the product is aimed. The target audience may be a very narrow group of people, such as a specialist interest group or people who live in a small geographical area, or it may be a huge group, possibly even worldwide. In the first case above, the target audience was extremely narrow, because the only person who wanted the book was the author. However, in the second scenario, the target audience was much bigger and was based on the many candidates who will be taking the qualification.

It is therefore possible to define the group that a product is aimed at by describing the characteristics or profile of that group. For example, an author may decide to write a book about the adventures of a particularly fluffy rabbit called Gerald. They may decide to aim the book at all children from the age of 3 to 8. The target audience is therefore all children between 3 and 8 years old. Alternatively, a software publishing house may decide that it wants to produce a first-person adventure computer game that appeals to girls between the ages of 15 and 19. In this case, the target audience would be girls between these ages.

> **Key terms**
>
> *Target audience:* The audience for which a piece of work has been produced. Each target audience will have different needs, tastes and interests.

Once the target audience has been decided, the product will be designed to appeal to that agreed target audience. This design process will consider many different factors that may achieve this goal, such as the content and packaging.

The apparent audience

It is important to note that a product may have an apparent audience, as well as a target audience. The apparent audience is the audience at whom the product seems to be aimed, which may differ from the real audience at which the product is aimed. A good example is magazines for teenage girls. A review of the content of some of these magazines would suggest that their target audience was girls aged between 12 and 14. However, the name of the magazine or the front cover may suggest that the product is aimed at a more mature and less naïve audience.

Identifying the target audience

In order to assess the target audience for a product, you need to be able to pick up the clues that may be included. Elements within a product, such as the text or images used, may suggest a certain target audience. If you look closely, you may find that you are given a clear indication of the age range for the product, or even a statement in supporting documentation which explains who the product is aimed at. Similarly, you may gauge products by any free gifts they include or the images and colours used in their packaging.

However, you should be wary of making snap decisions. As suggested in the previous section, you may need to think beyond the title of a product and

FIGURE 11.3 *Is this product well targeted?*

look at the content or design. If a product claims to be aimed at girls aged between 15 and 18, consider whether the content or design actually suits that age range. Manufacturers are aware that many young teenagers are desperate to be treated as young adults rather than older children and will exploit this in their product design. You should be aware of such tactics and be able to see beyond them so that you can identify the true target audience for a product.

When assessing the target audience for a product, it will be helpful if you have a good understanding of other products. If you happen to know that men aged between 18 and 25 like the colours blue and yellow, especially when combined as a tartan, then you can start guessing that products which combine these colours in a tartan pattern are aimed at this particular target audience.

However, it may be that the target audience for a product is so wide that it is virtually impossible to define. For example, the target audience for everyday household items, such as bleach or salt, will be just about everyone.

It is also worth remembering that, with some products, those who use the product may be beyond the target audience. Whilst the target audience will be those the manufacturer intended to buy the product, others may buy the product because it appeals to them, or it helps them make a fashion statement, or, in the case of

PARENTAL ADVISORY EXPLICIT CONTENT

OVER 18s ONLY

FIGURE 11.2 *Age warning on a computer game*

certain age-restricted products, people under that age are aware of the product and want to be customers alongside those at whom the product was initially targeted. This may be especially true for products such as computer games, which may carry an age warning, but which have been bought and are being used by people below the intended age. Bear this factor in mind when assessing target audiences for interactive multimedia products and do not base your decision about the target audience on who you know may buy or use the multimedia product, but rather on who the manufacturer or author intended to use the product. The two groups are often not the same. Similarly, any assessment of the effects of an interactive multimedia package must be based on how the intended audience will view the product. Unless you, as a viewer, fit the profile of the target audience, any opinion you express based on how the multimedia package affects you is largely irrelevant.

Intended impact of the publication on the target audience

An important skill used in evaluating interactive multimedia products is the ability to assess the intended effect of the product. Multimedia products may be created to give information, in which case the intention is to inform. Other multimedia products may have features that are intended to shock or amuse. These features are intended to have the desired effect on the target audience, so in order to assess the impact of a multimedia product, it is necessary to be aware of what audience is being targeted, and what that audience may find amusing or shocking.

Theory into practice

Below is a list of proposals for new multimedia products that have been submitted to a software publishing house. For each proposal, state what you think would be the target audience.

* Conflex – a package that will help predict GCSE grades based on end of Key Stage 3 SATs.

* Shadows and Light – a third-person 'shoot em up' game based on the battle between good and evil, represented by two wizards.

* Horse world – a round-by-round simulation of a horse jumping competition.

* Home tax planner – allows a household to model the total they pay in tax over a year based on variables such as income and expenditure pattern.

* The Ridgeway Elementary School ex-pupils and 'where are they now?' database.

* Plan and cut – a step-by-step interactive guide to making your own clothes at home, from planning the quantity of materials to buy through to manufacturing each garment.

Extension
Put the list of six proposed software titles in the order of the size of their target audience. Explain the reasons for your decision.

Theory into practice

Part A
Think of three separate multimedia products with which you are familiar. Try to choose one which is intended to inform, one to shock and one to amuse.

For each product, write a short report explaining the intended purpose. Your report should include

* a brief discussion of the product

* the intended purpose

* an indication of how you were able to decide on the intended purpose.

Share your report with the rest of your group.

Part B
You should now have feedback from a number of people about multimedia products with which they are familiar. As a group, use this feedback to produce a list of characteristics of each of the three main purposes of a multimedia product.

Tricks of the trade

Tricks of the trade is a term that refers to elements such as the choice of music, the lighting and fonts, which are all chosen to have a desired effect.

Whilst they are not actually tricks, the effects that can be achieved by a well-practised user may seem like magic, especially when the product changes your mood or opinion without you being aware that any pressure has been applied.

Most people do not enjoy being controlled by somebody else, so any pressure that is applied is intended to be very subtle. However, with some thought, you will be able to pick out the pressures as they are being applied.

Think about two scary films you have seen recently. If the films were effective, you will have been scared by what you saw. However, what you saw was happening to somebody else. You knew this, and yet the film made you feel scared. If you now list what was similar about these two films, you will find many common elements. Included in that list will be some elements that were not immediately apparent. It is likely that these elements were intended to set the atmosphere of the film. These techniques may also be used in multimedia packages to the same effect.

Music and sound effects

The effects that we highlighted above may be used in other genres of film or multimedia to different effect. The use of stirring martial music may induce a feeling of patriotism in the viewer, whilst other pieces may induce a feeling of lightness and therefore make the viewer more susceptible to any comedy or openness that the presentation as a whole is trying to portray. As well as music, simple sound effects may have profound effects. The sound of rain, laughter, a baby crying and alarm bells will all have a psychological effect on the viewer.

Pace of animations

The speed at which animations run can have a great effect on the target audience. A feeling of stress and tension may be brought about by running animations at a faster pace. This would increase the rate at which data and information were presented. As the audience then had to increase their concentration, this would cause a certain amount of anxiety in the audience. Alternatively, a slower animation, with a more relaxed feel, may have the opposite effect and relax the audience, as the work rate required to process the information being given was decreased. If this was then combined with music that suited the pace of the message, the effect would be increased. A manic piece of music played alongside the fast-paced presentation may serve to increase the feeling of anxiety, whilst a medium-paced piece of music would further calm the viewer when played alongside the calmer presentation.

Use of colour

Much has been written over the years about the psychological effects of colour. Your local supermarket will have made decisions about the lighting within sections of the store based on analysis of the psychological effects of colours on consumer behaviour. For example, it is likely that the toiletries and health care section will be bathed in a bluey white light. The use of this lighting in this particular area is intended to suggest a clean and efficient atmosphere, both of which are concepts we associate with medicine and health care. It may be that this effect is based on a subconscious awareness of the lighting effect used in hospitals and dental practices, and by using this colour effect, supermarkets are linking their products with these health care experiences.

The use of colours may be based on cultural values. In western cultures, white is usually associated with weddings. However, this association is not true for other cultures. Hindus associate white with widowhood and sadness, whilst, for Buddhists, white is associated with death and mourning. Clearly, any use of the colour white will need to be a decision based on a very clear awareness of the cultural values of the target audience.

As well as being linked to specific cultural events, colours may have more subtle effects. Table 11.1 lists the main colours and the symbolism and effects with which they are associated. As you read through the table, bear in mind that the symbolism may vary for different colours.

As we have seen, colours can be used to create feelings and impressions in the mind of the viewer. Like red, for example, they can also be used to add emphasis. A red word amongst a large group of black text will stand out and so draw the viewer's attention. However, a large block of red with one word in black will not have

COLOUR	EFFECT
Red	Red is the colour of blood, passion, love and excitement. This colour will attract the viewer's attention but is very dominating and should be used sparingly. This colour is great for emphasising one word or phrase.
Blue	This colour represents solitude, loyalty and wisdom. It is a relaxing colour, but avoid using it with food, as it is associated with rotting or spoiled food. The colour could be used to show success or power.
Green	This colour symbolises nature. It can also represent youth and energy as it symbolises natural growth. It is a very calming colour and may be used in areas of high stress, such as hospitals. The use of a calming colour may suit your product, especially in tense or high-pressure situations.
Yellow	This colour can be the hardest on the eye, as it reflects so much light back into the retina. For this reason, it can be an excellent attention grabber. As the colour of the sun, it can bring feelings of joy and warmth. Consider using it where you want people to feel happy.
Black	Be careful with black! Obviously, it is the default colour for text in most programs, but it can give mixed messages when used elsewhere. Black is a strong, powerful, reliable colour, but it is also associated with some of the more unsavoury aspects of life.
White	Generally seen in western cultures as symbolising innocence. This colour symbolises cleanliness and is generally a refreshing, soothing colour.
Purple	Like red, purple may be associated with passion. However, it is more often associated with royalty and is generally seen as an upmarket colour.

TABLE 11.1 *The effects of different colours*

the same effect, as too much red makes a block of text difficult to read.

As well as avoiding large blocks of some colours, anyone creating a multimedia product should avoid using lots of different colours, as this will distract from what is being said. Unless the author is trying to make a point about the use of colour, you should criticise excessive use of different colours within a multimedia product. As a rule of thumb, expect to see a colour scheme limited to maybe three or four colours.

You should also be aware that some colours can be grouped together well and others just do not look good when combined on a page. Many software packages now include a choice of colours from a complementary list. Figure 11.4 shows the font colours available within Microsoft Word.

The colours are shown in complementary groups, so that if you wanted to use colours which combined well on a page, you would choose colours that were immediately above or below

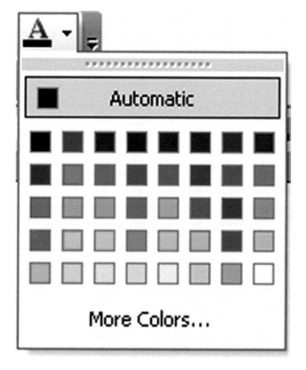

FIGURE 11.4 *Microsoft Word font colour choices*

or to the left or the right of the colour you were currently using. However, as you are assessing different multimedia products, remember that, if the author has chosen colours that clash, this might have been done deliberately. This does not mean you cannot criticise the choice of colours if you think it is wrong, but it does mean that there may be an excuse!

Think it over...

Spend some time experimenting with text and different colours. It does not matter which software package you are using, but try creating titles for documents using both complementary and non-complementary colours.

Using fonts

As with so many other decisions to do with creating a multimedia product, the choice of which font to use will depend on the target audience and intended message of the finished product. If the author wanted to convey a serious message, then he or she should have used a serious-looking font, such as Times New Roman or Arial, both of which are seen as part of the strong, silent group of fonts. For a less serious message, an author should consider using a font such as Desdemona or Comic Sans. Other fonts may be used to convey a historic feel or a more 'arty' feel.

As you read through the products you are evaluating, ask yourself whether the fonts used suit both the intended message and the target audience. If you spend some time experimenting with the fonts available to you within the software package you are using, you should get a better feel for how different fonts may be used for different occasions and you will be able to use this understanding both to criticise any commercially produced product and to choose appropriate fonts for your product.

Times New Roman

A serious message

Comic Sans

A more relaxed message

FIGURE 11.5 *Different fonts suit different purposes*

Theory into practice

Produce a wall display and teacher's notes to explain how different fonts may be used for different effects. Suggest fonts for the following uses on your poster:

1. presenting a serious message
2. presenting a fun message
3. creating a poster with a historic feel
4. creating a poster that includes text which looks like handwriting
5. creating a poster with an arty feel.

The teacher's notes will be used to explain why each font has been chosen as the most suitable. Make sure that you include good reasons for your choice of each font.

You may also come across serif and sans serif fonts. Serif fonts, such as Times New Roman, add a small line, called a serif, to individual characters. Serif fonts are very useful for large quantities of text, as the serif makes it easier to tell the difference between individual letters and so makes the text easier to read. Other fonts do not use a serif. These fonts, such as Verdana, are very useful for titles and headings. These fonts are called sans serif, which is French for 'without serif'.

As you are assessing multimedia products, take note of whether serif or sans serif fonts have been used, where they have been used and whether you think the font used was effective. You may notice that certain fonts are used fairly consistently throughout all the multimedia products you review. This is because certain fonts are more suited to some uses than others. For example, fonts such as Verdana, Tahoma and Bookman were developed for use on web pages and are particularly well suited to this purpose.

You will also need to consider the number of different fonts that have been used. It is

S erif

S ans serif

FIGURE 11.6 *Serif and sans serif fonts*

important that the font used does not become more important than the words and message that it conveys. We have already discussed that a serif font is best used for the main body of a document, whilst a sans serif font is best used for a title. It would therefore make sense to use at least two different fonts in a multimedia product, but, if you start to use a different font on each section of your product, the audience will soon start to notice the font more than the message. Also, as we have seen, each font has a different feel and you may give the audience the wrong message by changing the font for each section, as the audience may interpret the message in a different way because of this use of a different font.

Putting the message across

When authors set out to create an interactive multimedia product, they may be attempting to put across a message. Whether this message is positive or negative, or is intended to amuse or to shock, the intention will be for the audience to both understand and remember that message. It is therefore possible to evaluate the effectiveness of a multimedia product by assessing whether the audience will be able to understand and retain the message.

Similarly, the appropriateness of the multimedia presentation will be an important consideration. If the material is inappropriate, any message expressed may be overwhelmed by the reaction to the inappropriate material. Inappropriate material need not necessarily be offensive. Material that the target audience perceives as being patronising may be considered to be inappropriate and will undermine the product's intended effect.

You will have developed an idea of both the target audience and the intended effect for any multimedia product as you worked through the sections above. These factors will be used to assess the appropriateness and overall effectiveness of presentation, as both should provide the focus for deciding how best to express the message through the design. Put another way, once you know what the author is trying to say and how they intend to say it, you can then assess whether the different elements that they chose to include suited the target audience and clearly put across the message.

Using elements effectively
Content and presentation

An interactive multimedia product of any type will include many separate elements. These may be photographs, images, videos or animations, as well as text, music and the elements that make the product interactive, such as buttons or hot spots. The choice of which type of element to use, as well as the specific examples of each element included, should be based on an analysis of what would appeal to the target audience and a sense of what is appropriate to the message. For example, the cartoon image in Figure 11.7 would be inappropriate for an official report about the threat of bird flu, as it is too flippant for an official report and would not appeal to the target audience.

When analysing products, you need to be able to justify the points you make. For example, you may be analysing a multimedia product aimed at younger teenagers. From your own experience, you will be aware of what images, sounds and other elements will appeal to that target audience. Work through the multimedia product commenting on the elements that have been included. Your comments should include a discussion of the

FIGURE 11.7 *You should use images which are both appropriate and appeal to the target audience*

appropriateness of the elements. However, it will not be enough just to say that a product includes a range of elements that are inappropriate (or words to that effect!) – you will need to explain your viewpoint. This is your opportunity to explain what you do know about your target audience and therefore what you would have expected to find, as well as what you did find.

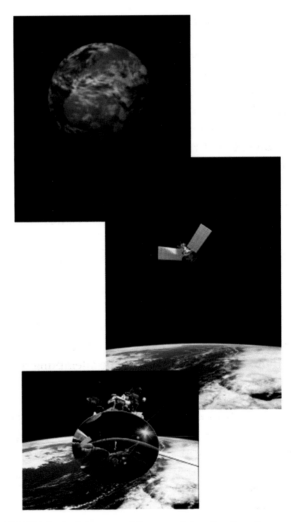

Theory into practice

The images in Figure 11.8 were suggested for a textbook about the history of space flight. The target audience is boys aged 14–17 years.

1 Before you begin, think about what sort of images about space flight would appeal to the target audience.

2 Individually, consider each image. Decide whether the image is suitable for the target audience. You should justify each of your decisions with clear and balanced reasons.

3 Working with others in your group, decide why you think these images have been chosen for the target audience.

Extension

Using your understanding of the target audience for this book, suggest four more images which may be included. These images may be ones you create, or may be found from other sources.

FIGURE 11.8 *Suggested images for a textbook about the history of space flight*

Each element of the interactive multimedia presentation may have an effect associated with it, such as a motion path or a certain reveal, both of which we will discuss later. Each effect may also be considered to be an element of the presentation in its own right. As with the decision about what elements to include, so the decision about how those elements are presented should be based on an understanding of the target audience. A presentation that is intended to inform the audience of facts and uses separate elements to do so, needs to show an awareness of how quickly the target audience may process data. In order to appeal to the majority of the target group, such issues will need to be based on generalisations. For example, a very young or very old audience may need slightly more time to read or to think about any message included in an element. If the author of a multimedia package aimed at either of these groups chose to include elements that change automatically, then sufficient time should be allowed for the target group to read and understand. Whilst the author may get away with the odd element that disappears too quickly, if the target audience fails to read the majority of any information displayed, the multimedia product will have failed in its task.

You should comment on the choice and range of effects that are used in any multimedia product. An interactive multimedia product with too many effects may end up distracting the viewer, who may be more interested in the wide range of effects being used rather than the intended message. A good rule of thumb when assessing the presentation of elements included in the multimedia product is that any presentation effects should enhance the message rather than distract from it. Consider an interactive multimedia product about a school that is attempting to show that it is at the forefront of technology. If the presentation includes no effects, the audience may be left with the impression that the school has all the necessary hardware and software, but little understanding of how it may be used. If, however, the multimedia product includes effects that allow the audience to better access the information, such as emphasising sections of text as they

FIGURE 11.9 *A poorly designed and confusing front page can mean that a product does not get used*

are being read or motion paths which bring an important piece of information to the fore, then the audience may view the school in a more positive light.

Ease of interaction

If an interactive multimedia product uses interactive features that are unclear, the majority of users will not use the product. This means that any subsequent screens or elements will remain unseen. If this is the case, the message will have not been delivered.

Interactivity is an important and potentially very powerful feature of multimedia products, but care must be taken when including such features within a presentation. Where used well and in a manner that suits the target audience, buttons will allow the user to pick their own way through an interactive multimedia product. The user will therefore avoid areas that they feel are irrelevant to them and will be able to choose to go to those areas that include relevant information. By allowing the user to avoid certain areas, the author is likely to achieve a better response to those areas that the user wants to see, as they will have wasted less time and effort accessing them.

When assessing the navigability of an interactive multimedia product, you should remember that different users have differing levels of skills and experience and what is obvious to one person may be totally confusing to another. Inexperienced computer users tend

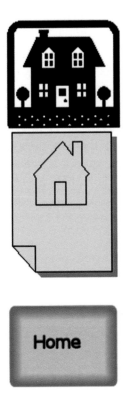

FIGURE 11.10 *Which icon represents home?*

but when faced with lots of different icons all linking to the home page, they may be less confident.

Other conventions include using underlining or emboldening to show that text has been used as a link. If the meaning of such a link is not clear to the target audience then it is unlikely that the user will follow the link. Similarly, the use of the 'here' link may be confusing, especially when overused on a page. Figure 11.11 shows a sample page from a multimedia product where the author has overused 'here' links and so has created a page that is difficult to use.

The page could be improved by using a range of different elements to allow the user to move through the product. Many of the links could have been replaced with drop-down boxes that grouped together links dealing with common themes, or maybe a few buttons linked to themed pages.

to lack confidence with using computers and are very literal in their translation and interpretation of instructions. Such users may find it difficult to interpret elements that they do not recognise or that do not appear exactly the same as those they have seen before. Take, as an example, icons. Many people find using icons extremely straightforward, but if the target audience is unused to icons then the author of an interactive multimedia product will need to factor this into the design of the product. An inexperienced computer user will probably be able to accept that 'home' refers to the hub of a presentation,

Theory into practice

On paper, redesign the interactive multimedia page shown in Figure 11.11 so that it may be used more effectively.

As with all the elements we have considered so far, the choice of how to navigate an interactive multimedia package must be based on the needs of the target audience. When writing a product for inexperienced users, the use of buttons that change as the cursor goes over them, or control tips that appear, will make navigation clear to an inexperienced user. Perhaps the simplest and most useable link for an inexperienced user

---

The Ridgeway Pig Owners Club

To find out more about the Ridgeway Pig Owners club <u>click here</u>. You can find an application form <u>here</u>. <u>Here</u> are the minutes of the last meeting. Click <u>here</u> to download a map to our club house. An application form may be found <u>here</u>.

FIGURE 11.11 *Too many 'here' links may cause confusion*

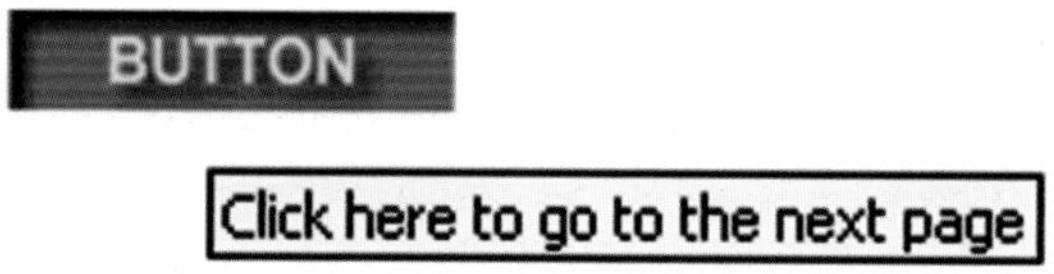

Click here to go to the next page

FIGURE 11.12 *The use of control tips may make navigation easier for the inexperienced user*

is a clearly labelled button. However, in other situations, such clarity may be exactly what the author is trying to avoid, such as when writing an interactive adventure game. Your analysis of how easy it is for the user to interact with the product must be based on a clear understanding of both the purpose of the product and the audience at whom it is aimed.

Theory into practice

Choose two interactive multimedia products that have been designed for *different* purposes. For each product, identify

* the purpose of the product

* the target audience

* the impact that the product is intended to have on the target audience.

Having identified the properties of each interactive multimedia product, write a report evaluating the effectiveness of each product in communicating its message and ensuring that the audience remembers that message.

11.2 Design considerations

Now that you have evaluated commercially produced interactive multimedia products, you are better qualified to produce your own product. However, before you do, you will need to understand some technical terms used in the construction of multimedia products.

Technical terms

Compression

Multimedia presentations may include a range of elements, including sound, images and video. Each of these elements may contain a large amount of data. When combined into a multimedia presentation, these large amounts of data will contribute to an overall file size for the presentation that is very large indeed. Larger files can take longer to download or open and take up more disk space. **Compression** is the technique for reducing the size of a file in bytes, by reducing the amount of data that the file holds. The aim of compression techniques is to reduce the data held in a multimedia file without affecting the quality of the file.

Key terms

Compression: Decreasing the file size.

Compression ratio: The ratio of the file size of the original uncompressed file to the compressed file. The higher the ratio, the greater the amount of compression.

Most multimedia packages compress the presentation by compressing elements within the presentation itself. Therefore, multimedia software will use a specific method for compressing the images included in the presentation and another method for compressing the sound. Most multimedia packages will use the Jpeg compression technique for compressing images, but, as you may come across some others, the main compression techniques are discussed below.

Compressing images

At the most basic level, images are compressed by a combination of two different techniques. The first is to look for patterns in the image data so that an image may be saved by describing the pattern and where it occurs, rather than writing the pattern out in full each time it occurs. The second is to manage the colours used in an image. This is basically achieved by reducing the amount of colours used in an image by looking where very similar colours have been used and replacing them with one main colour which is close enough to all of them. File types have been developed that use each of these techniques in different ways and each method will have a slightly different effect on the quality of the image once it is opened.

At this stage, you need to know that some of these compression schemes can be *lossy* or *lossless*. With lossless compression techniques, compression is achieved by looking for more efficient ways to store the image, and so there is no loss of information. Lossy compression techniques, however, will accept a loss of information as part of the compression process in exchange for better rates of compression.

GIF format The GIF format uses both compression and colour management to limit the size of image files. Compression is achieved by looking for patterns in the image, whilst colour management works by limiting the image to 256 colours. When the image file is saved, the software decides which 256 colours to use to best represent the original image. If a colour is used that does not appear on the list of 256, the software will then use the next best colour available. This is obviously a loss of information, as the image no longer has the original colour.

This means that the GIF can be lossless if your image uses less than 256 colours, or lossy if your image uses more than 256 colours.

PNG format PNG is a lossless format that uses compression. Compression is achieved by looking for patterns in the image, but this process is so efficient that when the image is uncompresed, the image appears identical to the original, uncompressed image.

JPG format The JPG or JPEG software format was developed by the Joint Photographic Expert Group and this format really sets the benchmark for any format intended for storing photographic images. The **compression ratios** achieved using this format can be extremely high and yet the loss of information can be minimal. Compression is achieved by discarding any information that the eye would not notice. Colours are stored in 24-bit format and so there is little colour loss. Overall, whilst this format is of the lossy type, the information lost is unlikely to have any effect on the quality of the image saved.

Compressing sound

When you record a short sound sequence on a PC, you will probably save it in the standard digital lossless format, WAVE (saved as .wav). WAVE format contains the same data about the sound as on an audio CD. If you wanted to play the sound on an audio CD player, you could save it on a CD-R or CD-RW using audio CD burning software.

A WAVE file can take up a lot of storage on a PC, so it is best to compress it before incorporating it into a multimedia presentation. You can convert it to MP3, although other formats are available. MP3 is a popular lossy compressed format that discards elements of the sound that are not noticed by the human ear. You will be familiar with this format as it has become the standard way of transmitting music on the web and for storing it on personal MP3 players.

You may also come across AIFF format, which is the standard non-compressed format used on Apple systems. Sounds recorded in AIFF format can also be compressed to MP3.

Resolution

The **resolution** is how many **pixels** are used in the image, and is either set by pixels per inch or pixels per centimetre. The higher the amount of pixels you use, the more dense any colour is, which means that more data has to be saved about any image. This has implications for printing and file saving.

When you are creating a multimedia product, you should always remember that you will be using a computer to show your finished product. It is generally recommended that you use a resolution that suits that of your monitor. Monitors typically have a resolution of between 72 and 96 dots per inch, so you should use resolution values of around this range in your work. This is important, because high-resolution images take up more file space and memory. However, you should remember that by reducing the resolution of a picture, you will also be reducing its quality, so any decision to reduce resolution is a trade-off between quality and the use of memory and file space.

Frames per second

Multimedia presentations are made up of individual **frames**. Each frame will be one very small part of the presentation. The frames per second, also known as **frame rate**, is the number of frames shown per second. By combining many frames per second, each with a slight change from the one before, a film may be created in which characters and other cast members appear to move. In reality, of course, there is no movement, only slight changes from one still image to another, which creates the illusion of movement. The more frames per second, the less each frame has to change and so the smoother the movement appears. In commercial films, a frame rate of 24 frames per second is used to create a smooth visual experience.

Multimedia packages allow you to set the **tempo** and, as with commercial films, this will be the speed at which each frame in the product is accessed. On simple multimedia products, this will be a simple flow through a series of linked frames. With more advanced multimedia products, such as the ones you are likely to produce, things are not so simple, as you will probably wish to include sound and video files. The rate at which any sound or video files play will not be controlled by the tempo of the multimedia presentation, as the rate these items play will have been determined when they were created. Therefore, when you are creating elements to include in your multimedia product, be very aware of how they will be used in the final product and take account of any timings that you may choose to use.

Figure 11.13 represents one part of a multimedia presentation. Included in the presentation is a video file that plays for two seconds. If the frame rate of the presentation is changed to suit the other elements of the presentation, the video will still play for two seconds, as this was set during the recording of the video and may not be changed using the **multimedia authoring** software.

As well as controlling the rate at which a presentation plays by controlling the rate at which frames are run, you can also choose to stop the presentation completely, or make it wait until the user clicks a button or uses a mouse. These options will be discussed later in this unit.

As well as frame rate, other factors may influence how quickly a multimedia presentation runs. Typically, these factors would slow the tempo rather than increase it. The main factors that may affect your work are discussed below.

Using a slower computer

Once you have completed your multimedia presentation, you may need to pass copies to clients or colleagues. If the computer on which they show the presentation has less processing power than the one you used to create the presentation, your presentation may run more slowly.

Using a slow Internet connection to access elements within the presentation

Some multimedia packages allow you to use elements within them that are downloaded from the Internet as they are needed, such as small

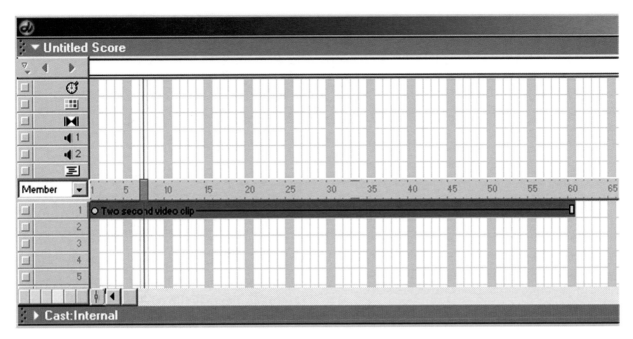

FIGURE 11.13 *Using frame rates in a product*

video clips. In other cases, you may want to give the user the option to download elements from the Internet, such as support materials. If the presentation is running on a machine with a slow Internet connection, this will make the download speeds slow and so will affect the speed at which the presentation runs. One way of avoiding this would be to download the materials at the authoring stage and include them with the multimedia package when you pass copies to other people.

The number of animations going on at the same time

Animations require processing power. The larger the element being animated, the greater the processing power required. Therefore, if you animate several large elements at the same time, the processing power of all but a very powerful machine will be stretched and so the overall tempo of the presentation would slow down.

You should try to avoid animating too many large elements, or even a large number of small elements, as even if the slow-down is not significant on the machine on which you are working, other users may watch the presentation on a slower machine, where the slow-down may be more significant.

Colour depth issues

Colour depth is the number of colours that a piece of software or hardware can show. This will depend on the bit rate of the software and hardware and it is possible that hardware being used may have a different bit rate to the software. This would happen, for example, where an older monitor or video card was being used in the machine but the software was up to date. The software would have been produced using a higher level of technology than the hardware and so would have a higher bit rate.

Due to the conflicts that different colour depths bring, there would be a slow-down in the tempo of the presentation. To avoid this, you should try to use matched equipment and software that is as powerful as possible. Not only would this avoid issues with colour depth, it would also allow multimedia presentations, which tend to require a good deal of processing power anyway, to run more smoothly.

Avoiding these issues

Most of the issues discussed above may be avoided with a little thought. Modern storage media, such as CDs and DVDs, have such high capacities that you should be able to pass copies of your completed presentation along with any linked files to a third party, such as a client, without any need for files to be downloaded from the Internet by the end user. Large elements may be reduced in size by changing their resolution. A simple statement in a user guide about the minimum system requirements for showing the presentation will at least alert the user to any issues with their own equipment. If they then choose not to update their equipment, that is their decision and they should accept any consequences. Alternatively, you could ask questions about the system at the research and planning stage. If you know that the presentation will be shown on a slower computer, you can factor this in during the authoring stage. This may mean leaving some of the more impressive elements out of the presentation. As long as you explain to the client that the decision to leave out elements is because of restrictions being placed on you by the hardware they intend to use, the end user will at least be aware that the problem is of their making.

It is important to avoid these issues, as you will have planned the tempo of your completed piece at the start. This will have been set to suit the needs of both the client and the target audience. A slight reduction in tempo throughout the presentation may be insignificant, but a drastic slow-down may change the mood of the presentation. This may affect both how your presentation is viewed by the target audience and the message you are trying to express. The basic issue here is that the tempo of a presentation is an important design consideration and one over which you should retain control, so do not let poor implementation of your plans or inferior software and hardware change the rate at which your presentation runs.

Colour depth

Colour depth, also known as *pixel depth* or *bit depth*, is the number of different colours that can be shown. The higher the colour depth of a piece of software or hardware, the greater the number of colours that may be used in each and every pixel. As we shall see, software titles based on 8-bit technology can cope with 256 colours (since 2^8=256, hence the term bit depth). This means that the colour used in each pixel on the image has to be chosen from one of 256 colours

(hence the term pixel depth). This might seem a lot, but such a narrow range of colours does not give much flexibility for shading; with 8-bit software, colour blending tends to be not very smooth. Colour depth also applies to hardware and so the number of colours that you can see is also limited by the colour depth of the monitor or the video card being used.

Key terms

Colour depth: The number of colours that may be represented by a piece of software or a piece of hardware.

The colour depth is directly linked to the bit rate of the software or hardware with which you are working. As we have already mentioned, an 8-bit display adapter will be able to show a maximum choice of 2^8 colours, which is 256 colours per pixel. As technology has advanced, so the number of colours that can be displayed has increased. Modern 24-bit video cards display 'true colour' which is 2^{24}, or at least 16 million, different colours. The colours used in 24-bit technology are so close together that the eye cannot see the minute differences, hence the name true colour.

Theory into practice

You can achieve similar effects to those in Figure 11.14 with your own images. Open a graphics software package that will allow you to save images in different formats, for example Microsoft Paint.

Use the software to open any image you have in your work area. Use the Save option to save the image in the following formats:

* True colour (Paint calls this 24-bit Bitmap)
* 256 Colour Bitmap
* 16 Colour Bitmap

You will now have three new versions of your image, along with the original. For each image, decide on the differences (if any) between the original image and the saved version.

FIGURE 11.14 *Image saved using 16 million colours; 256 colours; 16 colours*

When creating an interactive multimedia product, you will probably want to work with as wide a range of colours as possible. You need to remember that this figure will be restricted both by the software with which you are working and the hardware that you are using to display the finished product. However, this is not a new problem and most advanced multimedia packages will include features that either determine the colour depth of your system and set any multimedia product to work with this level, or will allow you to set the level for elements as you work through your authoring. Some software titles will give you both these options.

In Figure 11.15, the colour depth is being set in Macromedia Director MX for one individual bitmap cast member (*cast member* is the term used in Director to describe each element in a multimedia product).

> ✱ **Remember**
>
> The colours you can see when working with an image will be limited by the colour depth of your software *and* your hardware.

The structure of interactive multimedia products

The structure of an interactive multimedia product describes how each section of the product is linked to other sections. The three main possibilities you will need to consider are:

✱ linear

✱ hierarchical

✱ mesh.

As well as these three main structures, there are others that may be considered subtypes of these. We will deal with these as we come across them.

Linear structure

The linear structure is the simplest of the structures and describes a product where the resources are all queued up to come one after another. This means that there is only one

| Image Options for C:\Documents and Se...agnets\magnets0001 | ✕ |

Color Depth: ⦿ Image (32 bits)
○ Stage (24 bits)

Palette: ⦿ Import (Image Has No Palette)
○ Remap to   System - Win ▼

Image: ☑ Trim White Space
☐ Dither

☐ Same Settings for Remaining Images

[OK]
[Cancel]
[Help]

FIGURE 11.15 *Setting colour depth in Director MX*

possible path through the product. In this case, the interactivity would usually only be used to allow the user to proceed to the next section

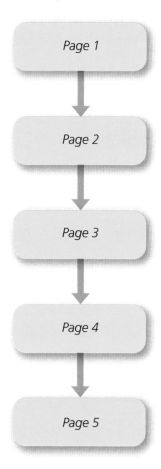

FIGURE 11.16 *A linear structure*

once they had finished with the current section. Whilst this may be described as interactive, it is unlikely that such a simple structure would satisfy the demands of the Applied GCE in ICT qualification.

Linear structures are suitable for many simple multimedia products, but it is likely that you will decide to produce a product that is structured so as to allow more than one path.

Hierarchical structure

There are two possible non-linear structures. The first of these is the hierarchical structure.

This structure is based on resources being grouped into logical sections. This organisational structure is described as hierarchical because the elements would be organised by the main group title first and then by subsequent unit titles below it. As the user navigates towards a specific resource, so they would be moving down from the overarching group name towards smaller and possibly more insignificant groups. This is rather like the organisation of a large business into different functional sections, such as marketing or human resources.

The user is able to navigate to specific sections of the product, but the choice is limited. Once the user chooses to follow a certain path, they would either need to retrace their steps or wait for a link that allowed them to access

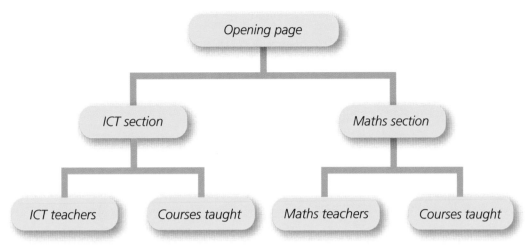

FIGURE 11.17 *A hierarchical structure*

a different path. This would be rather like following a route through a large building with many corridors. Once the explorer has chosen to go down a specific corridor, their only option is to carry on going down the corridor until a side corridor may be followed that would allow access to a different corridor, or to retrace their steps back to the start and choose a different corridor.

Hierarchical structures are very useful for displaying information that needs to be grouped and then accessed in a specific order. A school wishing to have an interactive display about different courses open to students within different departments may choose to use such a hierarchical structure. Organised around a front end, possibly with buttons that allow the user to choose which departments they want to explore, the display would give information structured in a logical manner. Within each department's areas, there may be further options, such as information about competing courses. Unless each stage of the display had a 'back' button, the user would only be able to leave the interactive display once they had completed their journey through the whole of each department's section.

Web or mesh structure

The alternative option is to organise the elements so that each is accessible from all others. This structure is known as a web or mesh structure.

As each section on a web or mesh presentation is linked to every other, it would be extremely complicated to show this structure for a presentation of more than a few sections, so Figure 11.18 shows the structure for a product with five sections.

A true mesh structure allows users to follow any available link to any resource as the whim takes them. Therefore, this structure does not impose any constraints on the user.

If you decide to set up an interactive product using a mesh or web structure, you would need to give some thought to how you would structure each frame in the interactive multimedia product. One option would be to include buttons to each and every frame, but as the product grew and more sections were included, so there would be more buttons on each frame. Soon, there would be nothing visible on the frame apart from buttons.

Alternatively, you could use a contextual link, which is the practice of using phrases or terms as hyperlinks to link to a resource that expands on the points made. For example:

'The history of the City of Bristol is linked to the development of the triangular trade between Britain, Africa and the West Indies, as well as the work of engineers such as Isambard Kingdom Brunel and the voyages of explorers such as John Cabot.'

This short passage would allow the reader to follow six links to other resources that may be of interest. The words used in the original link

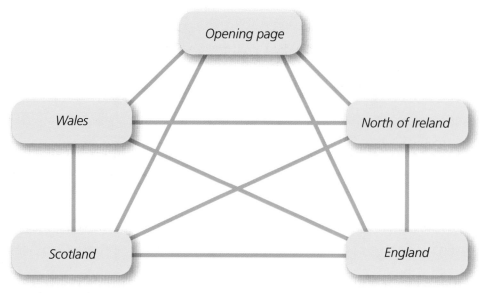

FIGURE 11.18 *Web or mesh structure*

indicate the context of the resource to which the hypertext links. As well as using the standard underline to draw attention to the hyperlink, you may consider using different-coloured or larger text to draw further attention to the link.

A structure that allowed access from all sections to all other sections within a presentation would allow the user complete control over their path through the presentation. This would mean that you would be unwise to use a web or mesh structure for a presentation where you were attempting to present a message in a preset pattern. However, if you are planning to present a range of different ideas, each presented on one distinct area of a presentation and where the order of presentation is not important, such a structure would be excellent.

Hierarchical mesh

Possibly the best structure to consider when working on your interactive multimedia product is a combination of both the hierarchical and the mesh structures. In this structure, resources are still grouped by type, as they are in a hierarchical structure, but resources of the same type are all linked. This would allow you, as author, to have some control over the pathway through the product, but would allow the users the freedom to pick their own pathway through an area once they were in that section of the interactive product.

This would be considered a hierarchical structure because there are certain set paths or routes that users must follow when they first

Theory into practice

1   Clearly explain the meaning of the following terms:

  * linear structure

  * hierarchical structure

  * mesh structure.

2   Explain the difference between a presentation that has a mesh structure and one that has a hierarchical structure.

3   The following list has been suggested for interactive multimedia productions. For each suggestion, explain which of the three possible structures would be most appropriate. Give your reasons.

  a.   An online shop

  b.   An online lecture on storage devices

  c.   A virtual tour of a school

  d.   A registration site for government benefit payments

  e.   A website showing work from all the members of an ICT class.

open an area of the product, but it would be a mesh or web structure once the users got into a certain area. This would be rather like attending a careers or trade fair, where employers or sellers working in the same area of commerce may be gathered in different sections of a building. Visitors to the fair would have to choose which sections they wished to visit once they arrived at the building, and would have to follow the pathway to the area for their chosen group of employers or sellers. This pathway may take visitors past whatever messages the organisers wished to be seen. Once in the room, the visitor could go to whichever seller or employer they wished, even going back a second or third time if there were more questions to ask or different products to check.

Different structures will suit different purposes and the decision about which structure to use is an important part of the process of designing an interactive multimedia product. The choice of which structure to use will depend on the nature of your interactive product; however, you must always be aware of the requirements of the assessment grids for this unit and be sure that whatever structure you choose to use allows you to access the highest possible grades in any work you submit.

11.3 Designing an interactive multimedia product

Once you have investigated commercially produced multimedia products, you should have some clear ideas about features you like and would want to include in your interactive multimedia product and other ideas about elements, features and effects which you would never consider using. Now begins the process of designing your product.

You will be given a commission to produce an interactive multimedia product. This commission will include a brief. We will discuss both the commission and the brief in the later section on creating elements of interactive multimedia products. At this stage, we will discuss the tools you will need to use to design your interactive multimedia product. These are standard tools and you should plan to use all of them in the planning of your interactive multimedia product. You are far more likely to produce an interactive multimedia product which achieves what it should if you follow these sections closely.

The tools are listed in the order in which they appear in the unit specifications. However, the order in which you choose to apply each tool is for you to decide. For example, you may decide to combine the fifth and second sections, so that you allow for alternative paths through your product at the planning stage. Alternatively, you may decide to plan the product in a simple linear form and then allow for alternative paths through the product at a later stage in the design phase.

Writing a script for your product

You could describe writing the script as setting out the vision for your interactive product. Whilst you do not need to share this with the client, a well-written script could be used to highlight how you think the completed product will look and operate. This is the first stage of planning your product and the script is basically the story of your product. At this stage, you are describing what will happen when the product runs and how the user will navigate through it. This may be a fairly basic picture of what happens when the multimedia product runs, which would start by discussing the first section of the product, including what elements would be visible to the user when the product first starts to run. You would then discuss how the user would move onto the second section of the product and what would be included in that section. This process would continue until all sections had been discussed.

Your script should also include some indication of how you will offer different routes through the product and how the user may follow these different routes. This does not need to be in too much detail and we will look shortly at how flowcharts may be used to represent this.

Producing structure diagrams

You will have come across structure diagrams in other units. For example, in *Unit 2: How Organisations use ICT*, you may have used structure diagrams to represent the organisation of an information system within a business. In a similar way, you can use a structure diagram to plan how an interactive multimedia product may be structured. For a business, a structure diagram shows departments as blocks and lines of communication between each department as a line on the diagram. A multimedia product, with different linked sections, may be shown in exactly the same way. Figure 11.19 shows a simple, seven-section interactive multimedia product with a hierarchical structure.

As with the business organisation chart, this structure diagram shows each of the seven sections of the multimedia product and the links between each section. Where there are two or more links leading off a section, there will be some form of interaction required, as the user is being given a choice of sections to visit. Such points are called **decision points**.

Other than showing the planned structure of the multimedia product, this diagram need not show much more detail. However, you could add notes to this diagram to indicate the nature of the link between each section, such as button or automatic link.

Using design methods

Once you have a basic structural plan completed, you can then begin to add more detail. This part of the design process is extremely important, as it will move your plan from a vague idea of how a product may be structured through to a design on paper that could be passed to an author for completion. The documents you produce as a result of using these design methods may also be used to explain your planned solution to the brief in far more detail and may be shown to the client as an indication of your plans. Showing your in-depth designs to the client is generally seen as good practice. If you choose to show these designs to the client, it is a good idea to get some form of agreement that these design plans will form the basis on which you complete the brief, as it may avoid confusion and disagreement at the end of the production process.

Storyboards

A storyboard will detail the content of a multimedia product page by page. You should

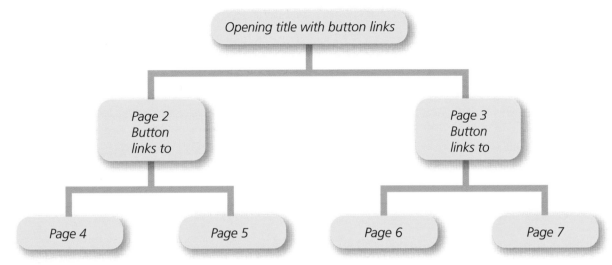

FIGURE 11.19 *A structure diagram for a multimedia product*

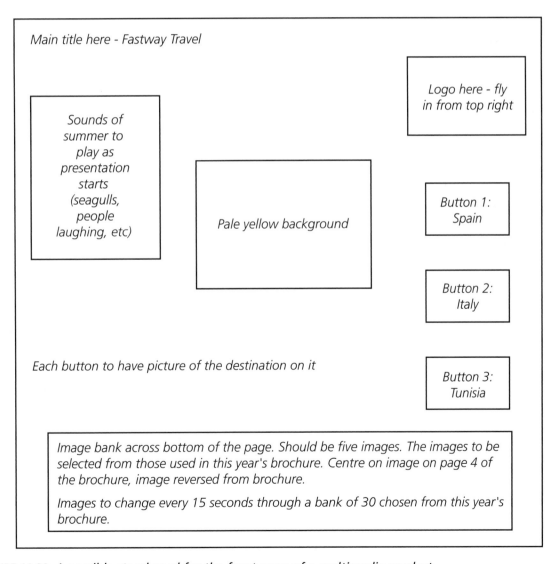

FIGURE 11.20 *A possible storyboard for the front page of a multimedia product*

include as much detail as possible at this stage: images, colour, sound and any other elements you intend to include.

If you include sufficient detail in your storyboard, it should be possible to get a very clear indication of what the completed product will look and feel like. As you move on from your storyboard, there should be few if any changes to the design of the product.

Flowcharts

Flowcharts may be used in conjunction with storyboards to show the route through a product. The flowchart will include the possible routes through the product and the different events that will happen depending on the choices the user makes at decisions points.

Producing a task list or action plan

You will be given a time-scale within which you must complete your product. To achieve this, you will have to plan your time carefully. The issue of time planning is discussed in *Unit 9: Working to a Brief*. Rather than go through every time-management technique, below we discuss a group of methods that work well together.

Identifying tasks

The first stage is to break down the production of your interactive multimedia product into

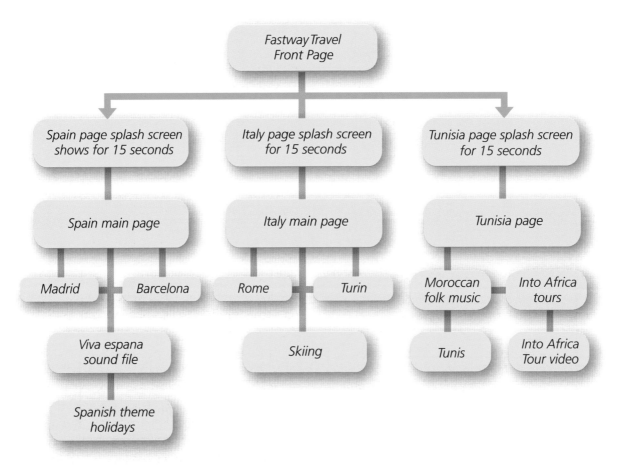

FIGURE 11.21 *A flowchart combining the previous storyboard and other elements*

manageable parts. This process is sometimes called *chunking down* and may be achieved by following a process called *top-down design*. To learn more about chunking down and top-down design, see *Unit 9: Working to a Brief*.

Your multimedia product will require the production of many different elements. As we will see, these elements may be producd in many different types of applications software and imported into the multimedia authoring package you are using to author the product. If you have created a storyboard or flowchart with sufficient detail, this will now help you to plan your time.

Go through your storyboard and list the different elements that will be combined to create the final product. Each of these elements represents at least one chunk of producing the completed product. If the element is relatively simple to create, such as a title, record it as a task or chunk. However, if the element is more complex to produce, such as editing an image once it has been created, break the production of the element down into further chunks.

Part of the chunking down of the production of an interactive multimedia product is shown in Table 11.2.

As you can see, the title for the multimedia product will be created by using the text creation tool within the multimedia software. This therefore appears as one chunk. However, the picture is four chunks, ranging from taking the picture in the first place using a digital camera, through to importing the cropped image into the multimedia authoring software.

If you follow this method of chunking down the production of all elements to be included in the multimedia product, do not forget to allow time for the creation of the multimedia product itself. As well as the various tasks that the creation of the product will require, you will also need to leave time for tasks such as the creation of support materials and testing that all aspects of the interactive multimedia product work as intended.

Deciding the order in which tasks are completed

Chunking down should result in a list of tasks that need to be completed so that the multimedia product may be created. You now need to decide the order in which these tasks need to be done. This is rather like the second stage of planning how to make a cup of tea. Your chunked down list will include boiling a kettle of water and adding water to a teapot, but unless you boil the kettle before you add water to the teapot, the result will be slightly disappointing.

One method of deciding the order is *critical path analysis*, which is based on the assumption that certain tasks have to be completed before others begin, and plots the path through these tasks so that each task is completed in the correct order. To find out more about critical path analysis and how to apply this technique to your planning, see *Unit 9: Working to a Brief*.

Making sure you complete all the tasks on time

The final technique which you could choose to employ is that of representing each task as a block on a diagram. The size of the block will depend on the time allocated for the completion of each task.

There are two main methods you could use to do this: a Gantt chart or a PERT chart. Gantt charts are probably the least complex. To find out more about this technique, see *Unit 9: Working to a Brief*.

The process of identifying all tasks, deciding on the path that must be followed and then allocating each task a slot of time should enable you to hit any deadlines you may have. However, you should

ELEMENT BEING PRODUCED	TASK
Title	Author the title using the text feature within the software
Picture of Jasmine	Take photograph using a digital camera
Picture of Jasmine	Download the picture onto the computer
Picture of Jasmine	Crop the picture as necessary within image manipulation software
Picture of Jasmine	Import the cropped image into the multimedia product

TABLE 11.2 *Part of a chunked down task list*

be realistic and allow some flexibility within your planning. This should allow for unforeseen circumstances or a failure to correctly identify how long it will take you to complete a task.

Allowing for alternative paths through your product

This topic is central to the task you have chosen to complete. You must produce an interactive multimedia product in response to the brief you will be given. If your product is interactive, the user will be given a choice of which sections of your product will be shown. Rather like the critical path analysis you carried out as part of the planning of this product, you should be aware that there are certain sections of the product that must be shown. You therefore need to plan your product so that, whichever route the user takes, all necessary sections are shown. This may be a complicated task, as the more options you allow, the more are the possible paths that become available to the user.

As well as ensuring that the users are able to visit all relevant sections of the product, you will need to ensure that they are not given options or information that are irrelevant or illogical. An example of this would be if you were plannning an interactive multimedia product about the courses available within a school's ICT department. If one of your first questions was to find out for which age group the user was gathering information, it would be illogical to then include irrelevant information about courses for other age groups. Such a mistake could occur if you were to give information about the staff teaching a particular course, but were then able to find out about other courses by following links on the individual staff member's page. Whilst it may involve you in extra work, if you want to avoid such problems, you will need to be prepared to create different versions of such pages.

Designing screen layouts

You will already have completed a storyboard or flowchart for your product. Screen layouts are the final part of this design stage and allow you to say with a good deal of detail what each frame will contain. However, you do not need to spend many hours drawing fantastic works of art that are complete in every detail, as your plan does not need to be a full mock-up of each screen. An outline plan with blocks representing elements would be sufficient, as long as it was obvious to the viewer what went where. For example, you may decide to have a video playing as an introduction to the product. Rather than spend hours drawing a perfect replica of the first frame of the video, a simple box, naming the video file and representing both the location and dimensions of the video on the opening frame, would be sufficient.

An example of a screen layout to open a presentation about a youth club is shown in Figure 11.22. The name of the youth club is shown as a banner above the video that will run as soon as the product is opened. The video is represented by the solid framed block. Also included on the screen are three buttons to other sections of the product. The screen layout has been further annotated to show design notes, such as which section of the product will open when the user clicks on each button.

Whilst you do not need to show each of these elements in detail, you should include the following in any screen layouts you produce:

* any pictures or other images you will use

* any buttons or other forms of navigation

* any text.

Your screen layouts should also include an indication of any effects that will be applied to these elements.

Incorporating navigation tools

There are several **navigation tools** available for you to use. Some of these will occur automatically, whilst others will work when the user clicks a button or other interactive element on the frame.

> **Key terms**
>
> *Navigation tools:* The range of tools that affect the order in which the frames in a multimedia product play.

As already discussed, multimedia authoring packages include many effects. The range will

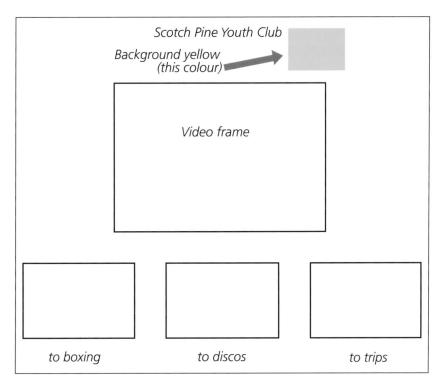

Scotch Pine Youth Club

Background yellow
(this colour)

Video frame

to boxing   to discos   to trips

FIGURE 11.22 *The youth club screen layout*

depend on the complexity of the product with which you are working. These effects include animations, which may make an element spin or stretch as it appears on the screen, or other effects that change the product to give the viewer the impression that the camera angle has changed. The order in which frames within the product are played is just another choice made from a list of possible events. For clarity, we will now use the term *button* to refer to any item which, when chosen or selected, changes what happens on the screen. This will get rid of any confusion about interactive and non-interactive effects.

Non-interactive navigation tools

You may have had the concept of disk fragmentation explained to you, or you may have had to explain to someone how you are able to find things in your bedroom despite them thinking it is a disorganised mess. The skills you use to find a matching pair of socks, or that software uses to find the relevant files on an apparently unorganised hard drive, are very much the same and both rely on navigation tools.

Your completed multimedia product will include many separate sections. You may be able to have each section saved to your product in an organised manner where each section is one after the other in the correct order (the correct term for this is sequential). However, there is actually no need for you to do this, as you can use navigation tools built into the multimedia authoring software to jump around your product from section to section. By inserting tools into your product at key areas, you can decide which sections automatically follow others, wherever these sections may be in the product.

Interactive tools

Your multimedia product will only be interactive if you give the user the opportunity to affect what is happening on the computer screen. This will either be achieved by making complete elements or parts of elements used in the product happen once the user has clicked the mouse button.

Depending on the complexity of the multimedia authoring package with which you are working, just about any element on your product may be made into a button. The choice of which element to use as a navigation tool will depend on two main considerations, both of which are linked. Your first consideration should be the general style of the interactive product and the second should be the target audience.

You will want any navigation you include to suit the general feel of your product. If this is not done, the navigation tools may spoil the overall effect of the product. So that this problem is avoided, the design considerations for the navigation, such as the colours and fonts to use, should fit the rest of the presentation. This may not be as simple as it sounds. Your user may need to find the navigation tools quickly, in which case each navigation tool will need to stand out. In this case, you should consider using colours for navigation tools that contrast with the background, or explore different sizes. Alternatively, you may want your buttons to be quite subtle, so that they do not draw the user's attention away from the main contents of the frame. You may even want

How to...

Use the navigation options available within a multimedia product

We will use the options available from Macromedia Director MX. These are similar to the options available in most multimedia authoring packages, so try to find the equivalent options within your software package.

The moving options

These are the tools that let the user move to a specific part of the product. Depending on your plan for your product, these may be applied to a clearly labelled button, which gives the user the choice of which frame plays next, or may be attached to a non-labelled element, so that the user is not sure what will happen next.

The main options are

* to go to a specific frame
* to go to a specific URL.

As you use each of these navigation options, you will be prompted to decide to which frame or URL you wish to jump. The choice of which specific frame to jump to may give you some further options, such as to jump to the next or previous marker or to go to a named frame. The advantage of choosing a specific marker as your jump target is that this marker may be dragged along as you add further elements to your product, or decide to increase the amount of frames for which an element is included in the product, whereas a link to a specific frame would have to be edited if you were planning to make these changes to your product.

Other options

Possibly two of the most useful navigation options are not really interactive options, but deserve to be included nonetheless. These options are

* to make the product wait at a frame
* to make the product loop.

The ability to make the product wait at a certain frame must be one of the most powerful tools available to the author wishing to create an interactive multimedia product. Without this ability, the product would have to run through without stopping and any interactivity would only be achieved by linking to an entirely different file. You should apply this effect to any slide where you want the product to stop playing. As long as you remember to add some form of interactivity at that point, the user will then be able to choose which frame shows next.

The option of looping a product is an extension of this stop and wait option. With this option, instead of stopping on one frame, you can choose to have a series of frames play in a loop until either the user clicks a button or a set amount of time passes. This would be particularly useful if you wanted to play a piece of introductory animation, designed to attract attention to the product. This would avoid a product reaching the end of a piece of animation and then appearing to freeze until the user clicked a button. If you were to choose to move the product on after a set period of time, it could display other general information, but would still allow the user to interact and choose to go to specific sections of the product if interested.

The other options within the Director MX navigation tools list are really specialised versions of those listed above. For example, you could choose to play a certain frame, which would occur either when the user clicked a mouse or automatically. You could then use the 'play done' facility to choose which frame played next once the chosen frame had been played. Where these tools are set to work by clicking a mouse, they are clearly interactive navigation tools.

the navigation tool to be completely hidden so that the user has to find it. In this case, you could use an element that would appear in the frame anyway, such as a book on a bookshelf or a road sign, as a hidden link. You may also consider using one part or even many parts of an image as buttons. Alternatively, you could create an area of the page or import a shape of the same colour as the background to act as a navigation tool.

Appropriateness

Whatever type of button you include in your product, it must be suitable for the general feel and aim of the product. You may choose to use different styles of button on a page, but you should be aware that some buttons, such as the home button, will need to be consistent throughout your product.

The decision about the style and type of buttons included in your product should be taken at the design stage and should be made as a result of careful consideration of what you want the button to do and how you want it to sit alongside the other elements in the frame.

Choosing where to use interactive and non-interactive navigation tools

You will want to include a range of navigation tools in your product. Some of these tools will operate automatically as the product is playing and, if applied well, the viewer should have no idea that you have used a tool at all. Other navigation tools will be set to operate once the user has made a decision. This decision will usually be recorded by selecting a button or clicking the mouse.

The choice of where to use interactive or non-interactive navigation within your product must be part of the design considerations and must suit the brief you have for your product. This will include both what the product is intended to achieve and the needs of the target audience.

> **✳ Remember**
>
> Navigation tools are the effects you choose to use to affect the order in which frames in your completed product play. Some of these tools will operate automatically, whereas others will need a choice to be made by the viewer. This choice will be registered by clicking a button.

Some of the navigation options available to you within a multimedia authoring product are discussed on the previous page (How to...).

11.4 Creating elements of an interactive multimedia product

Your client will give you a **commission** to produce an interactive multimedia product. At the same time, they will provide you with certain criteria that the work you produce will be expected to meet. For example, a business might have certain colours it wants you to use, or a school might want the school logo included in any product. Some clients may give you clear instructions about the style of the images you should use, such as all images should be black and white or photographs should be deliberately out of focus. Other clients may not give you such precise requirements but might ask you to produce a product that hits certain targets in a way you think is best.

> **Key terms**
>
> *A commission:* A task that is given to an individual or a group. Within the context of this unit, this would be the task of producing an interactive multimedia product to suit the needs of the brief.

These criteria, as well as other information, such as the submission date for the final work and the available budget, all make up what is known as the **brief**.

> **Key terms**
>
> *Brief:* The instructions given for a task.

Once you have accepted the commission, you can then set about creating the interactive multimedia product. This process may be broken into two distinct sets of tasks. The first set of tasks is to produce the items that will appear in the completed product and the second set is to combine these items into a completed product. Once you have completed the product, you will then need to make the product ready for use by the client and any other end users.

Before you create your interactive multimedia product, you will need to create the individual items that will be used. In fact, it is likely that very few, if any, of the items used in your completed product will have been created using the software you used to author your overall product. The vast majority will have been created in other pieces of software. As with this unit as a whole, the choice of which software you use to create the separate items is yours to make; however, this section will cover each of the main tasks. Whilst the software title used may not be the same as you would choose, at least the type of software should be familiar and will have tools in common with those shown here.

Creating, formatting and editing text

Text may be created in a word-processing package and copied into the multimedia authoring package and used as you wish, or may be created directly within the package using the text editing tool. Both methods are equally valid and both create elements that may be used anywhere in the multimedia product.

Creating drawings, diagrams and charts

You may want to include some graphics work that you have created yourself in your completed product. The choice of what to include will be determined by the brief, but items such as drawings, diagrams and charts are all elements that you can author yourself so that a specific target is achieved.

Drawings

Depending on your artistic prowess, you may want to create drawings to include in your completed product. You may need to create diagrams, such as plans, maps and apparatus, and include them in your completed product. You may also need to create charts to show data.

Your decision to include some drawings in your work may be made because the specific image you wanted was not available, or you wanted to create a new image to emphasise a point. For example, you could add a cartoon explaining an argument or emphasising a point made in your product.

Any graphics software will allow you to create at least simple images. As you progress onto more powerful pieces of software, so the range of facilities available to you will expand, thereby allowing you to create more complex images. However, no amount of tools are going to save you if you cannot draw. If everyone could draw, they probably would have never invented cameras in the first place, so don't worry if you do not have this particular skill. However you feel about creating your own drawings, it is probably worth at least some consideration, if only to have an item in the product that is unique and that you have produced. Even a simple stick figure may be used to great effect in multimedia products.

Diagrams

Diagrams combine images and text to give an explanation that will show or teach the viewer. If you wish to include diagrams in your completed multimedia product, you have two main choices. The first is to create the diagram by taking an image and combining it with text in a graphics package. If you choose this method, the completed image will be imported as one distinct element, rather than the text and the image appearing as separate elements. This would mean that you

FIGURE 11.23 *Diagrams combine images and text to improve the quality of an explanation*

would not be able to separate the image from the text at a later date.

Alternatively, you may decide that it suits your plan to have the image and any text as separate elements. This would allow you both to use the image independently of any text and to apply effects to either the text or the image as you wish. You could then use the image wherever else you wanted to and animate any text in a way that fitted your plan.

Charts

There are many different types of chart. Some show data in a more understandable way, in which case you might decide to use spreadsheet software to produce your chart. Other charts may show the structure of an organisation. As this type of chart is more of a graphical representation of a concept, rather than an attempt to present data, such a chart may be produced using either graphics or presentation software, although some specialist software does exist to allow you to produce organisation and other hierarchial charts more easily.

Figure 11.24 represents data on 1,000 students in a school. If this chart were not used, a table with 6,000 entries would have to be included in

the product. It should be clear that using the chart is a far better option!

Taking digital pictures, scanning images and using clip art

As well as drawings, you will want to include photographs in your product. The photographs you use may already exist, having been taken by a traditional camera, in which case you will need to use a scanner to create a digital copy of the original. Alternatively they may be ones you wish to create yourself, in which case you would be well advised to use a digital camera.

To find out more about the issues and techniques involved in using digital cameras and scanners, see *Unit 13: Artwork and Imaging*. The main issues are discussed below.

Taking digital pictures
Resolution

The first issue with using digital cameras is the quantity of pixels that can be included in the picture. This is called the resolution. Digital images are made up of tiny dots. These tiny dots are called pixels and each pixel included in a picture is a chance to record a colour, so the more

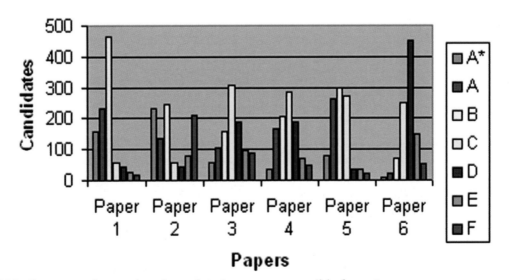

FIGURE 11.24 *Charts may be used to show data in a more accessible format*

pixels, the more coloured dots. The greater the number of coloured dots, the more information can be stored about the image. Therefore, the greater the quantity of pixels, the better the quality of the final photograph.

Effects tools

The second issue is the set of effects tools available in the camera. Some of these tools are replicated in the image manipulation software you are using and are probably best applied at that stage, whilst others will allow you to change the shooting conditions of the camera to suit the conditions at the time of taking the photograph.

Using digital cameras

If you choose to use a digital camera, you will find the user manual an invaluable document. Do not worry if you cannot find this document; many user manuals are now available on the Internet. If you simply enter your camera's name into a search engine, you should find the user manual fairly quickly. If you have already used a digital

camera of any kind, you should recognise many of the tools available, as most cameras offer the same basic facilities.

Once you have taken photographs, you will need to transfer them to your computer. This may be by the use of a cable, such as a firewire cable, in which case you are physically connecting your camera to your computer. This will require the use of specific software that must be installed on your computer.

Alternatively, you could use a card reader, which will read the data directly off the camera's memory card. Whilst this is a simpler process, you do need to take care not to touch the metal terminals on the memory card as this can affect how the card works.

Using a scanner

A scanner is an input device that scans an image or text on paper and then transfers the image to a computer. As with any other device, a scanner comes with its own operating software and, as

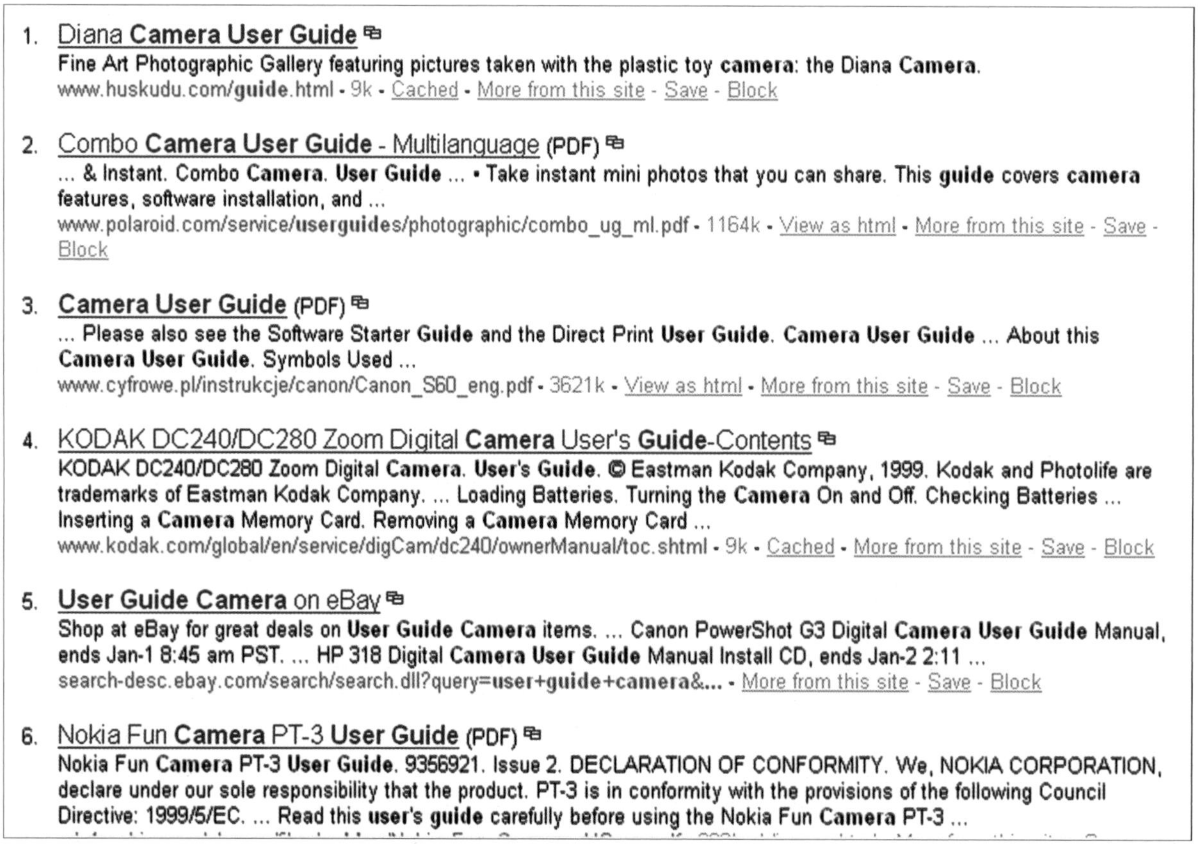

---

1. Diana **Camera User Guide** 🗃
   Fine Art Photographic Gallery featuring pictures taken with the plastic toy camera: the Diana Camera.
   www.huskudu.com/**guide**.html - 9k - <u>Cached</u> - <u>More from this site</u> - <u>Save</u> - <u>Block</u>

2. Combo **Camera User Guide** - Multilanguage (PDF) 🗃
   ... & Instant. Combo **Camera**. **User Guide** ... • Take instant mini photos that you can share. This **guide** covers **camera** features, software installation, and ...
   www.polaroid.com/service/**userguides**/photographic/combo_ug_ml.pdf - 1164k - <u>View as html</u> - <u>More from this site</u> - <u>Save</u> - <u>Block</u>

3. **Camera User Guide** (PDF) 🗃
   ... Please also see the Software Starter **Guide** and the Direct Print **User Guide**. **Camera User Guide** ... About this **Camera User Guide**. Symbols Used ...
   www.cyfrowe.pl/instrukcje/canon/Canon_S60_eng.pdf - 3621k - <u>View as html</u> - <u>More from this site</u> - <u>Save</u> - <u>Block</u>

4. KODAK DC240/DC280 Zoom Digital **Camera** User's **Guide**-Contents 🗃
   KODAK DC240/DC280 Zoom Digital **Camera**. User's **Guide**. © Eastman Kodak Company, 1999. Kodak and Photolife are trademarks of Eastman Kodak Company. ... Loading Batteries. Turning the **Camera** On and Off. Checking Batteries ... Inserting a **Camera** Memory Card. Removing a **Camera** Memory Card ...
   www.kodak.com/global/en/service/digCam/dc240/ownerManual/toc.shtml - 9k - <u>Cached</u> - <u>More from this site</u> - <u>Save</u> - <u>Block</u>

5. **User Guide Camera** on eBay 🗃
   Shop at eBay for great deals on **User Guide Camera** items. ... Canon PowerShot G3 Digital **Camera User Guide** Manual, ends Jan-1 8:45 am PST. ... HP 318 Digital **Camera User Guide** Manual Install CD, ends Jan-2 2:11 ...
   search-desc.ebay.com/search/search.dll?query=**user+guide+camera**&... - <u>More from this site</u> - <u>Save</u> - <u>Block</u>

6. Nokia Fun **Camera** PT-3 **User Guide** (PDF) 🗃
   Nokia Fun **Camera** PT-3 **User Guide**. 9356921. Issue 2. DECLARATION OF CONFORMITY. We, NOKIA CORPORATION, declare under our sole responsibility that the product. PT-3 is in conformity with the provisions of the following Council Directive: 1999/5/EC. ... Read this **user's guide** carefully before using the Nokia Fun **Camera** PT-3 ...

FIGURE 11.25 *Many user manuals are now available on the Internet*

FIGURE 11.26 *The Microsoft Word drawing tools*

you would expect, the software for one model of scanner is unlikely to work with another model. Whilst this is true, the main choices available with a scanner are fairly constant. These choices are all to do with the digial image you create:

* image size

* image type

* image resolution.

Image size and type are important. The size may be set by typing dimensions directly into the scanning software or by creating a window around the area you wish to capture once you have done a preview scan. The type of digital image you create is important because this will limit what you can do with the image once it is scanned. You will be offered a range of options, from black and white through to full colour. As you add more colour to the scan, so you are adding more detail and, ultimately, creating a file that requires more storage space.

As with digital images, the number of pixels per inch is an important consideration. However, you will remember from the section on resolution in this unit that, whilst it is useful to have a high resolution for graphics that you wish to print out, with images that are to be shown on a screen only, the resolution of the screen itself is a important factor. Before you take hundreds of high-resolution images, or create high-resolution scans, check out the resolution of your client's monitor.

Using clip art

How you use clip art will depend on the software package you are using. Some packages will allow you to paste any clip art item into the software package as an element, whereas other software packages will require you to import any piece of clip art into a graphics package before you then import it into the package itself. Whichever method you use, the clip art will then behave just like any other image.

Editing images, including clip art

Whichever images you choose to use, you will probably need to edit them. Except for clip art, which may be edited within its host software and will be discussed below, you will need to import an image file, including photographs, into a piece of graphics software. It is worth choosing one of the more complex pieces of graphics software for this purpose, as the editing tools open to you will be greater. You should also avoid the software that came with your camera, as the editing options may be restricted and the software may force you to save the edited image in a format that works with that software only.

For advice on how you may edit any images using graphics manipulation software, see *Unit 13: Artwork and Imaging* (but beware, this is a multimedia unit, so do not get too carried away working with graphics manipulation software and forget to complete your multimedia project).

Clip art is embedded in other software and you are therefore able to edit clip art within the host software before it is exported into the multimedia authoring package. There are some advantages to this. Firstly, there are some specialised tools available. Secondly, because clip art is a piece of vector graphics rather than a bitmap, you can change the size of any piece of clip art whilst it is still in the host package, and it will not pixellate (this is where it gets all lumpy and curves appear less smooth as you zoom in on the image). Once you copy and paste a piece of clip art into a bitmap package, it becomes a bitmap image and so will pixellate if you increase the size of the image.

Figure 11.26 shows the drawing editing tools available within Microsoft Word.

When working with clip art, the most useful tool is the Ungroup option. This will break any piece of clip art down into all the blocks and other shapes that make up the image. Once the clip art has been ungrouped, you can then use the Fill Color tool to change the colour of these shapes. This all sounds great, but with complicated pieces of clip art, made up of many different blocks, it can be very difficult to regroup the whole of the clip art.

How to...

Edit clip art

1 Select a piece of clip art and insert it into your document.

2 Make your image as large as you can. This will let you work on the image more closely.

3 Right-click on the clip art and select Format Picture. Click on the Layout tab and select Tight from the Wrapping style options.

4 On the Drawing toolbar, click on Draw and select Ungroup. Your image will now no longer be one whole image, but all of the different shapes that were combined to create the piece of clip art.

5 Now use the Fill Color tool to change the colour of blocks used in the image.

6 Once you have edited the clip art, you should regroup the separate shapes and blocks. To do this, hold down the Shift key and right click on all of the separate elements. Once you have selected all the elements, click on Draw in the Drawing toolbar and use the Group tool to regroup the separate shapes into one piece of clip art.

Importing and converting text and graphic files

As we have already seen, most of the elements you include in your product will have been created on other pieces of software. These elements will then have to be imported into your multimedia authoring software. Some packages call this adding to the library, whilst others call it adding to the cast. Whatever term is used for where the elements go, it is nearly always achieved by using the Import tool, which is part of the File drop-down menu.

When you import elements, you may be asked to convert them to suit the authoring software with which you are working. Generally, this will be when importing graphics files, where you may be expected to set the colour depth to suit that of the rest of the product being created. In Figure 11.27 the Macromedia Director software is asking the author of the product to choose whether to set the colour depth to 32 bits, which is the current setting for the image being imported, or reduce it to 24 bits, which is the colour depth of the stage onto which it is being imported. The author is also being asked whether any white space around the image should be removed or kept and whether the image should be dithered (for an explanation of dithering, see *Unit 13: Artwork and Imaging*). If you choose to remove white space, you will

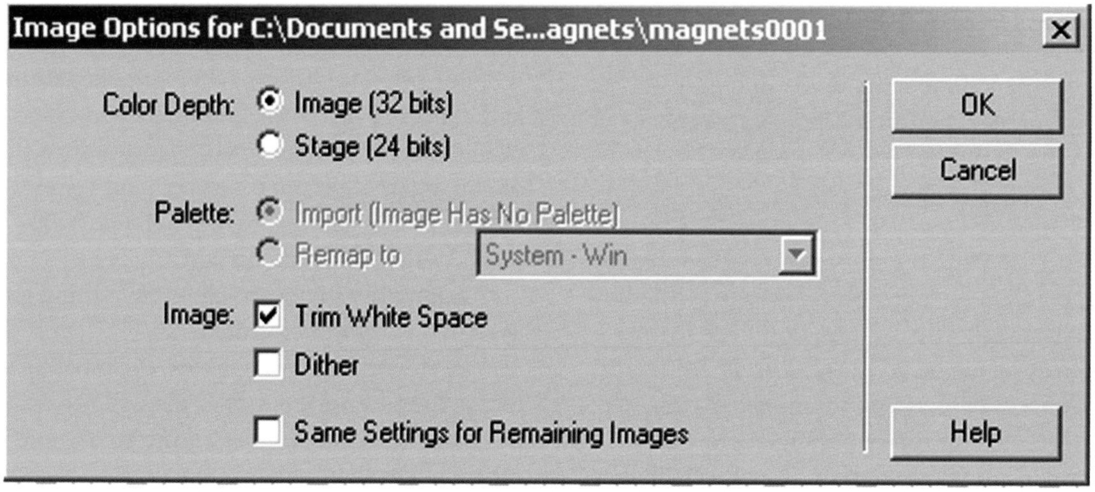

FIGURE 11.27 *Import options within Macromedia Director*

cut any white pixels around the edge. If your image has a white border, this option should be deselected.

Creating animation

When working with multimedia authoring software, animation simply means to make something move. This may be applied to elements on the stage, which move around the stage using motion paths, or other predetermined effects. We will look at these sort of animations in the section on authoring an interactive multimedia product below. At this stage, we are mainly concerned with the other sort of animations, the moving gifs, cartoons and other elements, which you may want to include in your product.

Firstly, you will need to decide whether to include or create animations to appear in your product. If you wish to include animations, such as animated gifs you find on the Internet, you will need to be aware of copyright issues, although there are many gifs and animations

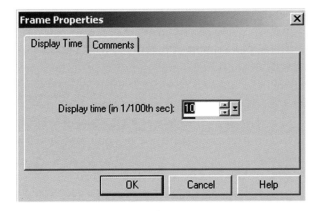

FIGURE 11.28 *Frame properties within Animation Pro*

that are copyright-free. However, if you wish to create your own, then your choice of how and what you animate will very much depend on the software available to you. Some very powerful software is now becoming available to schools and colleges and will allow you to create some very impressive animations. With these more advanced software packages, you can produce animations that will seriously enhance the quality of your product.

How to...

Create simple animations

This can be completed in any piece of animation software. The images are created in a graphics manipulation package and imported into the animation package, but, with some packages, you will be able to create the image directly in the animation software. Follow each step to create a traffic light system.

Step 1: Using any graphics software package, draw a traffic light, with background colour white and three circles where the lights will be. Do not add the red, green or amber at this stage. Save your file as 'Traffic light', but do not close it.

Step 2: Use the fill tool to make the top circle on your traffic light red. Save the file as 'red'.

Step 3: Either undo your fill, or close the file and reopen 'Traffic light'. All three circles should now be white again. Fill in the middle circle with orange and save as 'amber'. Repeat the process for 'green' and 'red amber'.

Step 4: Import all four images into your animation software. Having checked with others in the room about what is the correct sequence for traffic lights (ask someone who is just about to do their theory test!), put your images in the correct order and you will have a traffic light system.

Step 5: Review your product. How realistic is it? Does it do what it is meant to do? You may have created a superb piece of animation straight away, but it is more likely that your animation will have problems, such as how long each frame is shown on the screen. Figure 11.28 shows a properties dialogue box from Animation Pro, which has a default setting for each image to be on the screen for a tenth of a second. This may be all right for animations that are animating animals or people, but we do not need such a fast frame rate, so this time should be extended. If you are using software with a timeline, you may have to lengthen the time that an element is on the stage for, or slow down the speed at which the animation plays.

Even if you do not have some of the more advanced packages, there are many examples of frame-based animation packages, which allow you to create simple animations that can then be included in your product. Whilst you could download animations from the Internet, you will find it rewarding to create at least a few of your own animations for inclusion in your completed product.

Recording and editing sounds

You will want to include sounds in your completed product. These may be speech, such as commentary or the results of an interview, or may be musical, which includes effects. Along with creating your own animations, this can be one of the really fun parts of working on this unit.

It has never been so straightforward to create digital sound files. Most MP3 players have a record function, so you may record someone or something away from your computer. Most computer operating systems include a sound recorder as part of the package. Windows, for example, includes the Sound Recorder facility as part of its entertainment tools. This may be used to record directly into your computer.

However you record your sounds, you will want to edit them once you have them on a computer. This editing will probably involve one of the following tasks:

* cropping the sound file
* combining the sound file with another
* adding effects.

Editing a sound file is a relatively simple process and, as with all other areas we have considered, you can buy any one of a number of different software titles that will be more than capable of creating edited sound files of the quality you require. You may also find that some sound cards now include sound editing software as part of the bundle of software distributed with the hardware.

Figure 11.29 shows a sound file opened in Creative WaveStudio. The red line represents the sound in the file. If you wished to get rid of part of the file, such as the bit at the start where you ask if the microphone is working, then you simply

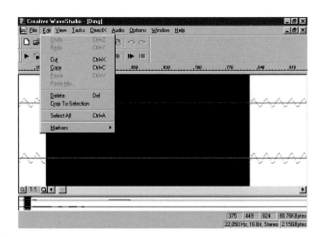

FIGURE 11.29 *A sound file being edited in Creative WaveStudio*

select it by dragging over it with the mouse and then press Delete. Similarly, you can lift out sections that you may want to use in other files, or even in other places in this file. This all sounds straightforward, but you will need to listen to your sound file a few times before you recognise which peaks and troughs are the sections you want to keep or discard.

This software will also allow you to apply certain effects, such as adding echo or fading in and out. More complex software will give you more control over how you edit your sound file.

Recording and editing video clips

You will also want to include video files in your work. These are best recorded using a digital video camera; you can also make digital copies of videos recorded on video tape, but this will need video capture software. If you are capturing video from tape, you have the advantage that you will be able to select which scenes you wish to use at this stage, rather than edit any files you have created using the digital video recorder.

These files will also need editing. The tasks you may want to perform will include:

* removing any scenes you do not want
* cropping scenes
* adding effects, such as fade in and fade out
* adding text.

As you will expect by now, the range of software available is vast. It is likely that you will have been given some software with your digital video camera; if not, software such as Windows Movie Maker is relatively straightforward to use.

The process of editing a piece of digital video is not unlike the process of editing sound files, and relies on you selecting sections to delete or save. Text is usually added as part of a set effect.

11.5 Authoring an interactive multimedia product

Now that you have created all the elements for inclusion in your interactive multimedia package, the time has come to put them all together in your product. Your initial designs will be invaluable here, so keep them close.

You will start by importing all the elements into the software package. As we saw, this is achieved by using the Import tool. Once you have all the elements imported, they can be included as part of the **cast**. The cast is all those elements that will be in the completed product. This is a bit like the list of all the stars of a film, which scrolls past as a film closes.

Key terms

Cast: Anything, other than effects, that will appear in the completed product. This includes sound files as well as images.

Once you have assembled your cast, you can now create your product. Look back at your design and pull out the very first cast member to be shown. This will probably be an image that is shown as a background or a sound file that runs as the product opens. Whatever it is, can you see how excited it is? Fame at last, after all these months of waiting!

Depending on your software, you will probably be working with a timeline. This represents the product from the beginning (at the left) to the end (at the right). The timeline in Figure 11.30 is from Macromedia Flash. Each section represents an individual frame. If you set a frame rate of 12 frames per second, you will need to ensure that your cast member covers 60 frames if it is to stay on for five seconds. Carry on building your product until you have the product set up as you intended.

Cast members will usually appear in layers. If your most important cast member is obscured by a lesser cast member, either bring your star forwards or send the offending cast member backwards. You will find this happens quite a lot as you begin to build your product; as you become used to how the software works, you will learn to build each frame from the back.

Transitions

Think carefully about transitions. Transitions are the way that one scene moves into another. You may just want a scene to disappear and be immediately replaced by another, as though it was part of one film. This is useful. However, making

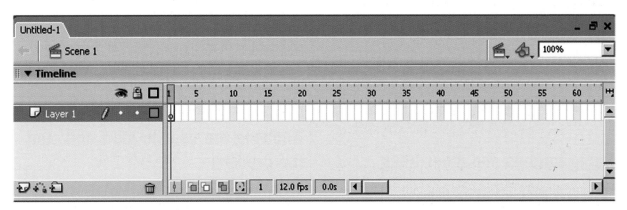

FIGURE 11.30 *The Macromedia Flash timeline*

one scene gradually fade out and another appear may also be useful. Your choice of software will limit the transitions available to you. If you wish to create a professional looking presentation, you should probably stick to using only a few transitions, maybe using one to close a scene and another to open the next.

Using frames

You will remember that a frame is the smallest part of a completed multimedia product and that a competed product will be made up of lots of frames. When you plan a multimedia product, you will decide how long an element needs to be on the screen. The amount of frames needed to achieve this will depend on the frame rate.

Frames also act as a defined point on your product and may be used with buttons to allow the user to move through the product. This would be achieved by using a simple Go To application, which would be applied to a button. When the button is clicked, the viewer will then see that part of the presentation which follows on from the frame to which the multimedia product has jumped.

Allowing text and numeric input

You may want to collect certain data from the user and then use this data later in the product. To do so, you will need to create an area for the data to be entered into. This is called making an element editable. To make an element editable is simply a case of changing the element's properties and, depending on the software you are using, defining the number of frames for which the element is editable.

You should use this facility to collect the user's name, for example. This data can then be included in the product from then on. This would be a great way to make the product more personal.

Using buttons and other links

We have already discussed using buttons to add navigation to your product. This is the simplest way to include interactivity with your product.

Include buttons of any type – make your own using a graphics package, or include an obvious text link, whatever suits you.

Creating interactive images

Interactive images are another way of allowing the user to control the flow through your product. These were also discussed in the section on interactivity above.

You can choose to make the whole of an image interactive, or maybe just a section of it. If, for example, you were showing a map or plan of a building, you could create a hotspot link from each room to a section about that room. This is a relatively easy task to achieve. Software such as Macromedia Fireworks allows you to create either square, circular or irregular hotspots from the Web tools menu.

One further bit of interactivity you could use is to add a rollover. This is the effect where an image or part of an image changes when the cursor moves over it. This is achieved by applying a specific piece of code (the rollover code) to an image or part of an image and stipulating which image will appear to replace what is currently shown.

Using drag and drop features

Drag and drop is a great bit of interactivity, but is not available in all packages. What drag and drop does is to allow the viewer of your completed product to move an element from one area into another. This would be a great way of allowing the viewer to cast a vote or to make some other decision when viewing your product.

It is not necessary to include a drag and drop feature in your product. If you wish to do so, you will need to check the help files for the software you are using, as each product deals with the procedure differently. Alternatively, a quick Internet search will bring up many tutorials on this.

Allowing the user to start and stop the product

The interactivity we have discussed above is mainly to do with moving to areas of the product. One further piece of interactivity you could add would be to allow the user to start and stop the product. When we talk about starting and stopping a product, we are not actually talking about opening or closing the product, but controlling how it plays.

If you wish to allow the user to start or stop a product playing, you will need to add a command to an element. In Macromedia Director, there are specific codes for pausing, stopping or restarting a product. Other authoring packages will have similar options.

Your product is just about ready to play. All you need now is to add the navigation tools and any animation effects that you have planned. These will usually be called behaviours and held in a library within the multimedia editing software. They are either added directly to the timeline or added to the cast list and then applied to a cast member.

The last remaining task is to add the navigation instructions to the navigation elements. We have discussed the range of behaviours available to you above, so review that section if you need to revise how to do this.

Congratulations, you have now created your first interactive multimedia product!

11.6 Testing and documentation

Once you have completed your interactive multimedia product, there are two further tasks that you must complete. The first of these is testing, which is vitally important, as it is unlikely that your completed product will work as you intended it to straight away. The second task is to produce the supporting documentation to go with your product. This section will look at both of these tasks in turn.

Testing

Before you send your completed interactive multimedia product to your client, you must test it to check whether it works as you intended. There are five main areas you should check:

* testing all links and pathways
* testing all effects
* proof-reading text

* checking the layout and alignment of all elements
* checking the timings.

You should develop a **test plan** to test each of these areas.

Testing all links and pathways

Plan to click on each link in your product. The expected result for these tests is that you should go to the planned area of your product.

A sub-section of this test is to test other events that will be run by clicking on buttons or other areas within your product. For these tests, the expected result is that the planned event will happen. For example, this may be a video or sound file playing.

Testing all effects

Effects will be applied to different elements in your product. You should test that each and every effect you have applied to your product works as intended. This may be a long list, but you included these effects for a reason; you should now make sure that the effect you planned to include does actually work as you intended.

Proof-reading text

One test that is often missed out is to simply read the text. This is one of the most simple of all tests, but is possibly the most effective. Your spell checker will probably pick up some spelling mistakes if you import text from a word-processing package, but you will need to create some text elements directly in the product, so check spelling as well as other errors. Look out for the standard errors, such as 'there' and 'their' or words repeated at the end and beginning of lines.

Checking the layout and alignment of all elements

This test is self-explanatory. You should simply go through and test that images, boxes and other set shapes line up as you intended at the start. You will want your product to appear as professional as possible, and alignment, as well as spelling, are both areas that can make a product look unprofessional if not completed with care.

Checking the timings

As well as checking the layout of all the elements in your product, you will need to check that the timings work as you had intended. This may be a physical check to see whether a video plays for as long as it should, or whether an element is shown for sufficient time. It may also be a check to see whether a text item has been displayed long enough for the reader to take in the information.

We have already stated that you should do your testing once you have completed your product. However, with more complicated products, you may want to create your test plan as you go along. By creating the test plan in this way, you will be able to enter elements for testing into the plan as they are created or added to the product. This will help to make sure that everything that needs to be tested is tested. Trying to create a test plan once the product is complete is a very painstaking task, but it need not be if you use a bit of time and thought as you are going along.

If any of these tests highlights problems with your product, you must go back and edit your work. Once you have completed this editing process, you must then retest those aspects that did not behave as you had intended. You must carry on this process until all of these issues have been fixed.

Your testing needs to be both planned and clear. The best way to show a test plan is to list the items that will be tested, as well as

ELEMENT TO TEST	TEST DESCRIPTION	EXPECTED RESULT
Button to boxing section	Click on button	Boxing section title page will open
Button to discos section	Click on button	Discos section title page will open
Button to trips section	Click on button	Trips section title page will open

TABLE 11.3 *A test plan for the Youth Club interactive product*

the planned tests and the expected result of each test. This may be shown in table format. An example of a test plan for the youth club interactive multimedia product is shown in Table 11.3.

It needs to be stressed that the test plan shows the tests that you will carry out. If your test plan includes the results from actual tests, then it is not actually a plan, but a report on the testing that was carried out. You will need to include the results of any testing in your work and so you should also produce a report on any testing you carried out. As well as listing the tests you completed from your test plan, you should show the results of your testing and any actions that you had to take as a result of your testing. This may include an explanation of a piece of code that needed changing, or a link that needed redirecting. Remember to retest any changes you make. The results of these tests may be shown in a supplementary test report.

An example of a section from a completed test report is shown in Table 11.4.

ELEMENT TO TEST	TEST DESCRIPTION	EXPECTED RESULT	ACTUAL RESULT	ACTION
Button to boxing section	Click on button	Boxing section title page will open	Title page opened	None
Button to discos section	Click on button	Discos section title page will open	No page opened	Examined and repaired link

TABLE 11.4 *A section of the completed test report for the Youth Club interactive product*

A test plan is completed before you start testing the product. Do not include results of testing in your test plan, as this will make it a test report, rather than a plan.

The questions below are based on the ICT Department Interactive Multimedia presentation and the test plan in Table 11.5 (overleaf).

1   What is the difference between a test plan and a test report? Comment on the structure of the test plan for the ICT Department presentation.

2   Look at the test plan. What is the expected result of test 1? Is there any other way this element could have been tested?

3   When the product is sent to the client, the animation runs for too long. This item was tested by the programmer, but this fault was not identified. Explain how this fault was missed.

Extension

Think about your favourite soap or other programme. At the end of every programme, there will be a big ending, and then a closing sequence. This sequence will include some music, the credits (the names of the people who made the programme) and a standard bit of film.

Create a test plan that could be used to test that all elements of the closing sequence are present.

Documentation

You will need to include documents with your completed product when you submit it to your client. These documents should include:

* the purpose of the product

* the system requirements

* how to install and use the product.

The purpose of the product

This will simply explain what the product is for. If the aim is educational, you should explain what subjects or skills are covered and to what level.

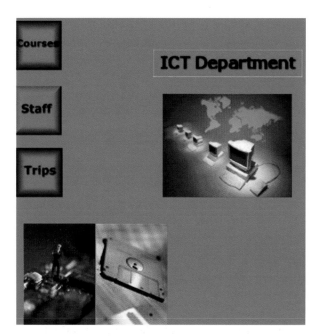

FIGURE 11.31 *The ICT Department interactive multimedia presentation opening frame*

You should also explain what the educational goals are. These goals may be to introduce the topic to the target audience or to increase their understanding of the topic. You may also decide to explain some of the techniques used in the multimedia product to achieve the educational goals of the product.

If the product is to give general information, your explanation of the purpose will include some of the same issues as you would have covered if the product was educational. This will include an explanation of the content and the goals of the product, as well as the techniques used.

The last option is if the product is to entertain. There are many different ways in which an interactive multimedia product could be used to entertain. The first would be to create an adventure game, where the user has to pick their way through different options. The second may be an online story, where the user can influence what happens during the course of the story.

If your product is intended to entertain, your explanation of the purpose of the product will differ slightly from the first two options. In this case, you should explain the aim of the product closely and make it clear who the product is aimed at. You may still explain how the product achieves

WHAT WILL BE TESTED	HOW WILL THIS BE TESTED	EXPECTED RESULT	ACTUAL RESULT
Link to staff appears	Watch	Link appears	Link appeared
Animation element	Watch	Animation will progress through three separate frames	All three frames shown
ICT logo flies into position	Watch	Logo appears	Logo appeared
ICT logo on screen for enough time	Watch. Allow product to run on a loop	Logo stays on the screen	Logo disappeared after 17 seconds. Reappears as product loops
Link to trips	Click on the trips button	Trips section begins to play	Section played

TABLE 11.5 *Section of the test plan for the front page of the ICT Department interactive multimedia presentation*

the goals, but you will not necessarily include the same amount of detail. This would be especially true if you were creating a multimedia product that included elements that were intended as a surprise, as you would not want to give the game away.

The system requirements

Your interactive multimedia product has been created on a specific package and, usually, on a specific machine. When you have completed authoring your product, you should make it ready for viewing by the client and the target audience. This process should save the finished product in a format which means that the completed product does not need to be opened on the same software as was used to create the product. For example, when you use the 'publish' command in Macromedia Director, the software automatically saves your work in html and Shockwave formats. Other multimedia packages will include similar features.

By saving your completed product using a more universal format, your authoring software has removed a good deal of the system restrictions that could apply. In the example above, as long as the client has a copy of Shockwave software (which they can download for free) as well as browser software installed on the machine they intend to use with the multimedia product, they should be able to run the product. However, as your product will include sound, you may wish to include some comment about the quality of any sound cards or other associated hardware that would suit your completed product.

How to install and use the product

This information is usually included in the **user documentation**. There are specific requirements for what should be included in user documentation.

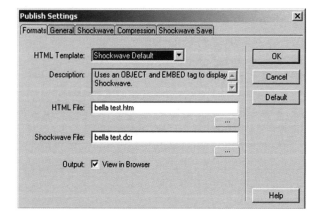

FIGURE 11.32 *The publish command in Macromedia Director*

User documentation is any documentation included with a program to help the user to run the package. Another term for user documentation is a user guide. Your user guide should fully explain to the user how to install and run all aspects of the package. It should also have a trouble-shooting section, dealing with common problems and explaining the importance of any error messages which may appear and how they may be dealt with or avoided. Increasingly, a user guide would include a 'frequently asked questions' (FAQ) section.

The section on how to install the product should give the user enough information so that the product will run, as intended, once installed. This might include instructions about specific folders that need copying or creating. You may also decide to include software with your product. This will, typically, be software that is available free, but without which your product would not function.

The section on how to use the product should cover all aspects of using the product. Your work should explain at least the following:

* how to start the product
* how to access different areas or sections of the product.

You may decide to include other areas that the person installing the product needs to be aware of, but these will depend on any special features you include in your completed interactive multimedia product.

11.7 Reviewing your final product

In the section on reviewing a commercially produced product, we discussed what makes a product either successful or unsuccessful. Once you have completed your product, you will need to be as critical of your product as you were of others.

The exam board requires you to complete a review of your interactive multimedia product. This report must include:

* a full analysis of the completed product
* a full analysis of your own performance in producing the completed product.

This report will also be used to assess the quality of your written communication.

A full analysis of the completed product

As stated above, you will need to re-use all the skills and techniques you used to criticise commercially produced multimedia products to criticise your own. You will need to comment on how well your completed product meets the original brief. This analysis will be based on your interpretation of your completed product, for which you may want to refer back to your original designs, as well as the original brief itself. However, as well as your opinion, you should ask others their opinions of your completed product and any supporting materials, such as user guides, and use these comments to inform your general overall opinion of your completed product.

Once you have completed your analysis of the strengths and weaknesses of your product, you should be able to identify how the product may be improved in the future. These comments should be included in with your overall analysis of the completed product.

A full analysis of your performance

By the time you have completed your product, you will have developed a range of new skills. As well as software skills, these may include other skills, such as time management or interpersonal skills developed whilst working with your client as part of the initial negotiation and subsequent development of your product. The contribution you have made to producing the final product will therefore be central to the success or failure of that product.

As part of your analysis of the final product, you will need to comment on the quality of your performance. This should be a comment on what you did well, as well as what you did less well. You may decide that you took too long to learn to use specialist software or that you are very proud of how you interpreted the needs of the client. You may decide that you did not leave enough time to produce high-quality user documents or that your testing was extremely well planned and helped you to test and finally produce a product that worked extremely well.

Whatever conclusions you come to, you will need to include them in your review of the final product. Once you have listed those good and bad issues, you will be in a position to explain how you would be more effective in the future. It may well be that your testing was excellent, in which case you can explain that you will ensure you follow the same testing regime on any subsequent product; it may be that you did not leave enough time to complete a quality user document, in which case you should explain how you will either allow more time in any future plan for this task or employ better time management techniques so that a plan is kept to.

It is important that you do not just list successes in this section. As well as learning how to use new software, this unit allows you to learn more about how well you work. Your analysis of your performance can discuss what went wrong, as well as what went well.

Knowledge check

1 Explain the difference between slide show and multimedia software.

2 Name the four main elements that may be combined to create a multimedia product.

3 What is meant by the term *target audience*?

4 Explain the following terms used in multimedia authoring:

   * the cast

   * a frame

   * behaviours

   * compression

   * frame rate.

5 'When creating multimedia products, you must set a frame rate fast enough to make sure that your product has smooth movement.' Explain this statement.

6 Why is it important to allow different paths through an interactive multimedia product?

7 A multimedia author may use a range of 'tricks of the trade' to influence the viewer's opinion. Explain how each of the following may be used to do this:

   * music

   * pace

   * colour

   * fonts.

8 What is the difference between a mesh structure and a hierarchical structure? State one application for each of these structures.

9 Explain why it is important to test your product once it has been completed.

10 Explain why it is important to get the client's acceptance of any design plans before you continue to produce your multimedia product.

UNIT ASSESSMENT

You have been asked to produce an interactive multimedia product for Fastway Travel. The completed product will give information on a range of popular holiday destinations. Fastway has been experiencing increased bookings from families but would like to increase the bookings received from young couples and single people. As well as general information about resorts, Fastway would like you to incude specialist information that would appeal to these two target groups.

Task A

This task is in two parts. The second part wil be completed after you have planned your interactive multimedia product.

Choose two interactive multimedia products with elements you may wish to include in your own product. Write a report discussing the good and bad points of each product.

Note: Because you cannot complete this task until you have designed your product, the mark bands for this task are shown after task D. You should have a look at the parts that refer to researching into interactive multimedia products for advice here.

Task B

Now that you have researched into interactive multimedia products, you should have a clearer view about the features you want to include in the interactive multimedia product for Fastway Travel.

For this task, you should produce detailed designs for your interactive multimedia product. Your designs should show where you plan to include different elements, as well as any animation and other behaviours you plan to include.

Remember that Fastway wants to appeal to different target audiences and wishes to include materials aimed at different groups. You should plan to include a range of materials and give the user different paths to follow, so that they may access the materials which are relevant to them.

Mark Band 1
The minimum requirement for this task is that you produce one simple design for an interactive multimedia product. Your design will be lacking in detail and will probably only give an outline of what you are planning to produce.

Mark Band 2
You should produce more than one design plan. Your plans do not have to be in great detail, but should give sufficient detail that they may be counted as designs, rather than just outline drawings with little detail.

Mark Band 3
You will produce more than two designs, all of which are in some depth. Typically, your designs will be of sufficient quality and include enough detail that they could be passed to someone else for completion.

Task C

You now need to decide which of your designs you will develop.

For this task, write a report evaluating each of your designs. Your report should identify the strengths and weaknesses of each design. You should use this evaluation to decide which of the designs you will develop.

Mark Band 1

Your report will comment on the effectiveness of your designs, but will not discuss the strengths and weaknesses, and will not explain how you chose which design to develop.

Mark Band 2

Your report should list the strengths and weaknesses of your designs. You should use this list of strengths and weaknesses to explain which design you chose to develop.

Mark Band 3

You must submit a report that fully discusses the strengths and weakneses of each of your designs and fully explains how you reached your decision about which design to produce.

Task D

This task is the follow-on task from task A

Now that you have completed your designs, you will have a clear idea about how the features you found in the two commercially produced products influenced your design.

Finish the report you started in task A.

Mark Band 1

As a minimum, you should decribe *both* products.

Mark Band 2

There should be some comparison of the two multimedia products as well as a description of both products. Your comparison should focus on comparing similar features in each product.

Mark Band 3

Your report should fully decribe and evaluate both products and must discuss the good and bad points of each multimedia product in full. Your report will fully explain how each commercially produced interactive multimedia product has influenced the design of your product. This part of your report should discuss each of the features you have commented on and explain what you liked and did not like and what you decided to include in your completed product, and why. You may also have made some design decisions based on elements that you found in the commercially produced products but did not necessarily like, but which with improvement could be used. These should also be discussed.

Task E

Now that you have completed the design process, you should produce your interactive multimedia product. As you work, you should take note of how your skills have developed. You will use these notes to write a report on how your skills have developed as you worked on the multimedia product.

The following is an explanation of how marks will be allocated within assessment objective AO1 for this task.

Mark Band 1

Your starting point for this assessment objective is that you must produce a product that meets the needs of Fastway Travel. Mark Band 1 is achieved by doing this and then writing a report that identifies some of the skills you have used to produce the product. You will use your knowledge and skills to produce a solution to the client's brief. Your solution will not necessarily be effective and there may be some sections of the client's brief that are not fully met.

Mark Band 2

You must produce an interactive multimedia product that meets the client's demands and, in doing so, develops your own range of skills. Your report into how your skills have developed should identify the full range of skills you have used to produce the interactive multimedia product. You will be awarded marks from within this mark band if you produce work that is well designed and effective.

Mark Band 3

You will need to produce an interactive multimedia product that meets the client's demands and, in doing so, you should identify skills areas that need developing and ensure that your skills develop sufficiently to perform all the tasks you have identified in your plan. Your report into your skills will identify the full range of skills that you have used to produce the interactive multimedia product. You will need to produce a solution that covers all aspects of the brief and which is well designed and includes a range of different interactive features.

Task F

When you have completed your interactive multimedia product, you will need to test that your product works as you have intended. You will now produce a test plan to check your product and then carry out testing, making changes to your product as issues arise.

Mark Band 1

At the very least, you will need to produce a test plan. This test plan will check that the product covers what was shown in the design specification. Your test plan should show what tests you intend to carry out.

Mark Band 2

Your test plan must be more detailed than for Mark Band 1. It should not only test that the product covers the brief but also that all aspects of the product actually work. You must also use your test plan to test the product.

Mark Band 3

Your test plan must cover all aspects of the product, including checking both the content and the functionality. You will then use the test plan to test your product and make any changes to the product that the testing shows is necessary.

Task G

Your user will need some help to run and install the product. You should produce clear user documentation for your product, which includes graphic images and fully explains how to use the product and also explains the technical aspects of the product.

Mark Band 1

Any user documentation must include the system requirements and instructions on how to install the product. This is the basic standard required for this task. Make sure that your user guide also includes a statement about the purpose of your interactive multimedia product. It may be obvious to you and to your client, but the product and guide may be passed on to someone else, and they will need to know what the product is trying to achieve.

Mark Band 2

Your explanation must include an explanation of what the product is trying to achieve as well as the system requirements and how to install and use the product. You should also include some technical details in your guide, which will outline aspects such as the software used to produce the product.

Mark Band 3

Your user documentation must be of a high quality, with graphic images used to aid the explanation of points. Your guide must include a full explanation of the purpose of the product and how to use all aspects of it. Your technical section will fully detail the system requirements, as well as providing a full guide to installation and other technical aspects of the product.

Task H

Your final task is to review both the product and the role you played in producing it. The review should fully discuss how effective the product is in meeting the initial brief and should include some feedback from the user. There should also be some indication about how the product could be improved in the future.

Your review of your own effectiveness in producing the product will identify strengths and weaknesses and will include a discussion of how you would overcome any shortcomings in the future.

Your review should be written in Standard English and contain few, if any, spelling mistakes.

Mark Band 1

You must include some comment about how good the product is in meeting the brief. This may be a basic statement, with some examples from the product. Your self-review will include a few comments about how well you did and give areas in which you could have done better. Your report may contain errors in spelling, punctuation and grammar.

Mark Band 2

You will need to get feedback from the user. You will then use this feedback to help you review your completed product and to identify the strengths and weaknesses of your product. Once you have identified these strengths and weaknesses, you will make suggestions for how the product may be improved in the future.

Your report into your effectiveness will identify what you did well, and what you failed to do well, and will give some suggestions for how you could do better in the future. Your report will contain few spelling, punctuation and grammar errors.

Mark Band 3

Your review of the completed product will need to be full and critical. You must gather feedback from the client and use this along with your own analysis to discuss how well your product has met the brief and how it could be improved in the future. This will include a full discussion of the strengths and weaknesses of your solution.

Your analysis of your own performance starts by identifying the strengths and weaknesses of your performance and uses these points to fully explain how you would do better if you were to do this project again. Your report will be consistently well-structured and will have few, if any, spelling, punctuation and grammar errors.

Publishing

By studying this unit, you will

* appreciate the uses of desktop publishing (DTP) and word-processing packages and their capabilities, and apply them to a variety of tasks

* recognise the variety of documents produced using DTP facilities and the range of hardware and software available for this purpose

* sample the work undertaken by designers, illustrators, newspaper artists and draughtspersons.

As you work through this unit, you will need to apply the knowledge and skills you gained from *Unit 1: Using ICT to Communicate.*

Introduction

Publishing is the process of making information available to people, especially in a book, magazine or newspaper, or the production of books, magazines, newspapers and other documents, usually for sale. The advent of desktop publishing (DTP) software has revolutionised the publishing process and made it accessible to anyone with a computer and the appropriate software. However, to create publications of a professional standard, many of the traditional publishing processes still need to be followed. In this unit, you will learn about different types of publications, the facilities DTP software offers and the publishing processes that need to be followed.

How you will be assessed

This unit will be assessed on a portfolio of evidence that you will produce. The assignment at the end of this unit will provide you with the evidence to complete the portfolio.

What you need to learn

In this unit, you will create a **camera-ready copy (CRC)** of a document to meet a client's brief. To do this, you need to learn about

* document types and presentation styles
* combining information
* researching a brief, planning your response and presenting your solutions
* the final printed output.

> **Key terms**
>
> *Camera-ready copy (CRC):* The final copy of a document exactly as it will appear when it is printed, i.e. it is ready to be photographed to create the printing plates.

FIGURE 12.1 *Different types of publication*

12.1 Document types and presentation styles

Publishing techniques can be applied to create a variety of different types of documents, not just books, magazines and newspapers. Each type of document can be created in a number of different presentation styles. The presentation style of each document will need to match the document type and the audience for which it is intended.

Billboards and posters

A billboard or poster is essentially an advertising tool. The subject may be a product, an event or an important message. The essential feature of this type of document is, therefore, that it is eye-catching to grab the attention of people passing it. One way that this is achieved is through size – the bigger the better. If someone has to get up close to a billboard or poster to read the information, the main purpose has been lost. Most billboards and posters will be a minimum of A3 in size and many are much larger, sometimes covering the side of a building. Billboards and posters are, therefore, often produced in sections that are fitted together when the billboard or poster is displayed. DTP software may provide an option to design a poster that is printed out on several sheets of paper with overlaps so it can be assembled after printing (Figure 12.3).

The design of the content of a billboard or poster is also important. Most billboards and posters make use of graphic images to help get their message across. Text will be in a large font size so that it can be read from a distance. The quantity of text will also be kept to a minimum and will aim to get the point across. The poster shown in Figure 12.2, which was designed to encourage people to join the armed forces during the First World War, was effective because it included these design features.

FIGURE 12.2 *Billboards need to be eye-catching*

> **Think it over...**
>
> Locate and take photographs of as many different billboards and posters as you can find. In a group, for each billboard or poster, discuss the following:
>
> * What is its purpose?
> * Who is the audience?
> * What presentation techniques have been used?
> * How well does it meet its purpose and audience?

Books and manuals

Books come in many different forms. A manual is simply a particular type of book that gives you practical instructions on how to do something or how to use something, such as a piece of software.

Manuals

Most manuals will include illustrations to demonstrate the actions that are being described in the text. In the case of a software manual, this may take the form of screen shots. A manual for a television set or a printer, for example, is likely to include pictures of the item with important parts, such as the controls, clearly identified. The text needs to be clear and easy to follow, and technical terms and jargon should be avoided. The use of bullets and numbered lists helps to break the instructions into steps that can be easily followed. Most manuals use numbered headings and subheadings that are included in a detailed contents list so that the reader can find the information they need. An index is also likely to be included.

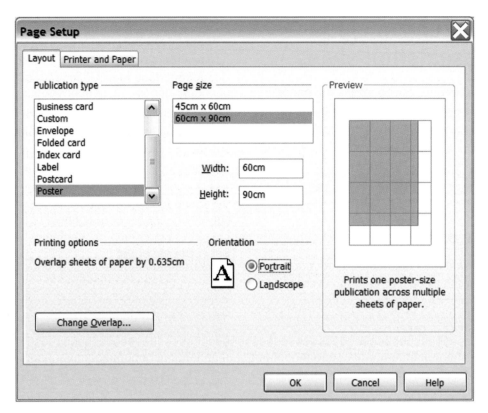

FIGURE 12.3 *Printing a poster on several sheets of paper*

Books

The format of other types of book will depend very much on their purpose, topic and audience. A fiction book for an adult audience is likely to consist entirely of text. This text may be divided into sections and will almost certainly be divided into chapters and paragraphs. Non-fiction books are more likely to include illustrations of one sort or another. A biography, for example, may include photographs. These are sometimes collected together in separate sections so that they can be printed on glossy paper. Textbooks may include diagrams and other images, depending on the subject. Books on art or photography may consist almost entirely of pictures, but, on the whole, books for adults will contain more text than pictures. On the other hand, books for very young children will consist almost entirely of pictures with limited text. What text there is will be in a large font size using simple words and sentence structures and often using repetition to encourage word recognition. Such books will have only a small number of pages and may be printed on card or even fabric so that they stand up to the rough handling they might receive.

Books also come in many different sizes, both in terms of the size of each page and the number of pages – some are not even the normal rectangular shape! The smallest book on my bookshelf has a page size of just 7 cm by 10 cm and is designed to fit in a pocket, whilst the largest has a page size of approximately 27 cm by 39 cm. So-called 'coffee table' books can be even larger than this.

Brochures/leaflets and newsletters

The *Compact Oxford English Dictionary* defines a brochure as a magazine containing pictures and information about a product or service, and a leaflet as a printed sheet of paper containing information or advertising and usually distributed free.

Brochures

On this basis, brochures by definition include pictures and text, but the way these are organised will vary depending on the type of brochure. Most brochures will consist of a number of pages depending on the range of products or services included. Where an organisation wants to impress, its brochures will be printed in high-quality colour on glossy paper. Your school or college prospectus, or ones you have been sent by universities, may well fall into this category.

Leaflets

A leaflet, on the other hand, by definition consists of a single sheet of paper. However, many people also use the term for a short document consisting of two or three sheets of paper that are stapled together or folded inside one another. There are a number of different ways that the piece of paper can be folded. Figure 12.4 shows examples of common ways of folding a leaflet. The piece of paper itself can also be different sizes, for example A3 or A4. You should note, however, that if you select a brochure layout in Microsoft Publisher, it is actually a three-section leaflet.

Leaflets can include graphics or consist entirely of text and can be printed in full colour on glossy paper, in a single colour on white or coloured paper, or anything in between. To convey the maximum amount of information in the available space, leaflets will almost always be printed on both sides of the paper.

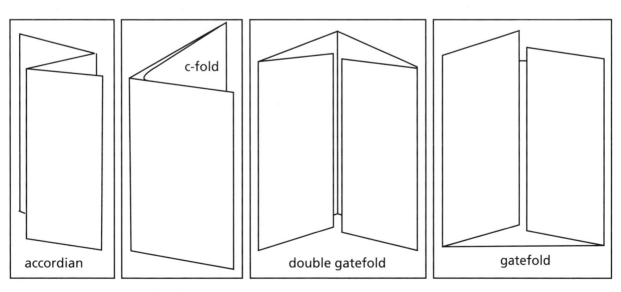

accordian   c-fold   double gatefold   gatefold

FIGURE 12.4 *Common leaflet folds*

Newsletters

A newsletter is simply a document that contains information about the recent activities of an organisation and that is produced and distributed regularly to members of the organisation and sometimes to the general public. Most newsletters are printed, but online newsletters are distributed by email.

The presentation style of a newsletter will depend on a number of factors. Large organisations may produce multiple-page newsletters printed in full colour on glossy paper, illustrated with many photographs. A small club, on the other hand, may produce a text-only newsletter printed on a single sheet of standard paper. Most, but by no means all, newsletters have the text arranged in columns. The name of the organisation is likely to appear in a prominent position. As newsletters are produced regularly, an important feature on any newsletter is the date it was produced. All newsletters are likely to contain a number of different stories or articles, each with a headline or heading. Some may use **banner headlines** to draw attention to important stories.

Think it over...

Your school or college probably produces and distributes a newsletter. What presentation techniques does it use?

Try to collect other examples of newsletters.

✱ What, if anything, do they have in common?

✱ What is different about them?

✱ What factors have influenced the presentation techniques used in each newsletter?

Forms and mailshots

Forms

Forms are a means of collecting information. You will probably have filled in an application form for a driving licence, passport, job or a sixth-form or college place. Once every ten years, every household in the country has to fill in a census form. During your time at school, your parents will almost certainly have completed forms to give permission for you to take part in trips or other activities. Other types of form include tax forms, loan application forms, order forms and product registration forms. Figure 12.5 shows an example of an order form.

Forms should be designed to make them as easy as possible to complete. Where something has to be written in, there needs to be enough space for someone to do so. To reduce the amount of writing and to speed up the completion of the form, options with tick boxes or other means of indicating choice should be provided.

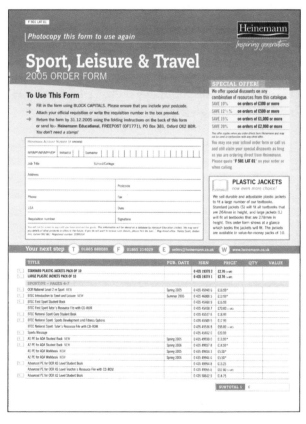

FIGURE 12.5 *Forms are used to collect information*

The questions on a form should be in a logical order and possibly divided into sections. Where the information is to be entered into a computer, the order of items on the form and on the data input screen should be the same. Where this is the case, the space for writing in text is often divided up so there is a box for each letter, matching the number of characters that can be input. Similarly, a space to write in a date will be divided up to show the format required. More and more forms are now available online so that they can be completed and submitted electronically, removing the need for data to be keyed in from a paper form.

An important aspect of any form is that it includes instructions for completing it. Some important forms, such as a passport application, have separate instruction booklets on how to fill them in. However, any form should include instructions such as 'Use capital letters' or 'Tick one box only'.

for responding within a certain time. Mailshots frequently include forms for the recipient to place an order or apply for membership, for example.

Microsoft Publisher provides the option of adding a mailing address to a three-part leaflet that could then be used as a mailshot. A name and address could be added to the back of a brochure so that it can be posted as a mailshot. Another type of mailshot is a personalised letter, often sent in a window envelope with other materials.

Key terms

Mail merge: The process of combining a standard document with a database, usually of names and addresses. Multiple copies of the document are created, each with the details from one record in the database.

Think it over...

Collect different types of forms and find examples of online forms.

* What features do they all have in common?

* What is different about them?

* What is the purpose of each form?

* Does the purpose of the form affect the features included?

* How easy is each form to complete?

* How do online forms differ from paper forms?

Think it over...

As a group, collect all the mailshots that your families receive, i.e. 'junk' mail that is specifically addressed to someone. For each consider

* format

* purpose

* audience (you, parents, grandparents)

* techniques used

* any common features

* effectiveness.

Mailshots

The variety of 'junk' mail that lands on your doormat will tell you that there is no single standard format for mailshots. However, the production of mailshots is likely to involve **mail merging** a standard document with a database of names and addresses. This might simply involve adding each individual name and address for mailing purposes, or it might involve inserting each individual's name or other details at various points throughout the document to personalise it. This is one method of persuading the recipient to act on the contents of the mailshot. Other methods might include 'free' offers and prizes

Magazines and newspapers

Magazines

A visit to a newsagent shop will provide an insight into the vast range of magazines available, but this is only part of the story. Some organisations, such as supermarkets, now produce magazines that are distributed to their customers; supporters' clubs and fan clubs produce magazines – sometimes called fanzines – for members; newspapers often include magazines, particularly in weekend editions, and so on. All magazines will be aimed at a specific audience. In some cases, this might be quite broad, for example *The Sunday Times Magazine* will be aimed at anyone who reads the newspaper. The audience for other magazines may be much more specific. Bridal magazines, for example, are aimed specifically at women who are about to get married and others involved in organising a wedding. A model aircraft magazine is aimed only at those who are interested in that particular hobby. The audience for a magazine will largely determine its layout and content.

Most professionally produced magazines are printed in colour on glossy paper. They make extensive use of photographs and other images. Almost every magazine will include a contents page that lists the main stories or articles it contains. This is sometimes divided into regular articles that appear in every issue and special features. Text in magazines is often presented in columns, but these may be broken up by photographs or significant quotes from the text that spread across more than one column. Magazines may also use frames to position smaller articles on a page.

Nearly all magazines include advertisements. Even a small community magazine will include advertisements for local businesses who have provided funds so that the magazine can be distributed free or at low cost. Large glossy magazines would be much more expensive were it not for the revenue generated by the advertisements they carry. In the case of 'free' magazines included with newspapers, the publication is totally funded by advertising. In this case, it is the positions of the advertisements that is paramount and the articles are fitted round them.

Newspapers

Like magazines, newspapers are produced for different audiences. These might be national or local.

Broadsheets and tabloids

National newspapers tend to be divided into two categories – broadsheet and tabloid – reflecting the size of the page as well as the audience for the paper. The tabloid page is half the size of the broadsheet page, meaning that the same printing presses could be used for both. Until recently there was a clear division between broadsheet and tabloid. The broadsheet papers included the more serious titles such as *The Times*, *The Guardian*, *The Daily Telegraph* and *The Independent*, aimed at an educated, professional audience. The tabloids included the *The Sun*, *The Daily Mail* and *The Daily Express*, amongst others, aimed at a more general audience.

Recently, nearly all broadsheet national daily newspapers have reduced in size, mostly to tabloid size, as they are easier to handle and read on buses and trains on the way to work. This has not, however, changed the audience or the style of the

FIGURE 12.6 *Most newspapers are broadsheet or tabloid*

headlines and content, and the terms broadsheet and tabloid still tend to be used to distinguish between the two types of newspaper. At the time of writing, of the national daily newspapers, only *The Daily Telegraph* has kept its broadsheet size. However, the size reduction has not extended to the Sunday papers – most people can read these at home with room to open them out.

Layout and style

As with magazines, newspapers arrange their text in columns with frames and rules used to separate stories. Newspapers also include photographs and other images. The ratio of pictures to text will vary from paper to paper depending on the audience. Broadsheet newspapers have more text than pictures, whilst a tabloid newspaper like *The Sun* has a much higher proportion of pictures. In all newspapers, the use of photographs is significant, as they can make visual statements that can express an idea more clearly than any number of words.

The text itself also varies depending on the audience. Broadsheet papers will use longer sentences and a more extensive vocabulary than some of the tabloids. Another major difference is in the headlines, which tend to be more sensationalist in the tabloids than in the broadsheet papers. It is worth mentioning here that it is the **subeditor**, not the journalist, who composes the headlines. Even in the more serious papers, subeditors try to inject some humour into the headlines they compose.

Content

The first page of a newspaper is the most important. It is the page that contains the most up-to-date and important news stories – in the editor's view. It is often the last page to be composed, especially if there is a breaking story, and it is not unusual for the front page to change from one **edition** of the paper to the next. The front page also depends on the audience for the paper. Unless there is a major story, such as the threat of a flu pandemic or the effects of an earthquake or hurricane, the front page of some tabloid newspapers is more likely to include stories about film, pop or sports stars than politics or world news.

The vast majority of the revenue for a newspaper comes from advertising, rather than the cover price. It is, therefore, the amount of advertising sold that determines the number of pages in a particular edition. Most newspapers now include some pages printed in colour. Again, it is the advertisements on the page that determine whether or not that page is printed in colour or black and white. With the possible exception of the front page, it is the advertising space sold that determines the layout of each page, with the space for advertisements being positioned first and the pictures and stories being fitted round them.

If you read a story in a newspaper, you will notice that all the main points of the story appear in the first few lines. The rest of the article then gives more details about these points. This makes it easy for the stories to be cut if there is not enough space for it all to be included. Before computer-based publishing, newspaper pages were made up on pasting boards. Artwork and advertising would be literally pasted onto the board and the text typed up and pasted into position. If a story was too long, the excess would be simply cut off. Nowadays, more sophisticated editing is possible to ensure a story fits the space available, but it is still quicker, in the hectic environment of getting a paper to print, to simply remove additional detail from the end.

Local newspapers

Local papers, as their name suggests, are aimed at the people living in a particular locality and will include stories and articles of local interest. These vary in size and style but tend to be less extreme than some of the national daily papers. Although some local papers are published daily, especially in cities such as London or Manchester, many are only published once a week. To encourage people to buy the paper, some publishers of local papers distribute free papers to people's homes in the area; these papers consist mainly of advertisements, but include some of the stories that will appear in the main paper along with details of offers that the reader will have access to if they buy the paper.

Think it over...

Compare a broadsheet newspaper with a tabloid and a copy of your local paper, preferably published on the same day.

* What presentation techniques do they all use?

* What is different?

* What is the proportion of pictures to text?

* What is the proportion of advertisements to stories?

* Do they all cover the same stories?

* Where the broadsheet and tabloid cover the same story, is there a different approach?

* What sort of headlines are used?

Reports

The *Compact Oxford English Dictionary* describes a report as an account given of a matter after investigation or consideration, or a piece of information about an event or situation.

There are, therefore, many situations when a report will be produced. This might be to present the results of a scientific investigation or a statistical survey. If there are proposals for the development of a new airport, shopping complex or leisure centre, a report will be produced that details why it is needed and the investigations that have been carried out to confirm its feasibility. Companies produce annual reports for shareholders that detail what has happened in the previous year and the current financial position of the company.

Reports are formal documents, so they need to be written clearly, in a formal style, with correct grammar, punctuation and spelling. They will use headings and subheadings to divide the text, often with multi-level numbering so that each section can be easily referred to. In longer reports, the text might be divided into chapters for the different topics covered. All reports should have a **contents page** and most will also have an **index** so that specific items can be located. Other features frequently included in reports are **appendices** and a **bibliography** to list any information sources used. Depending on the purpose of the report, photographs, diagrams, tables of figures or graphs and charts may be used to illustrate the text. Annual reports for large public companies may be very glossy publications aimed at impressing their shareholders and potential investors.

Key terms

Contents page/table of contents: Lists the main sections of a document in the order they appear, with page numbers for the start of each section.

Index: Alphabetical list of key words that appear in a document, with the page number(s) on which each word can be found.

Appendices (singular: appendix): Separate numbered or lettered sections at the end of the document that contain additional information that the author refers to but does not want to include in the main text.

Bibliography: Detailed list of all information sources used in compiling a document. It should enable someone else to locate the same information.

Think it over...

Try to obtain examples of different types of reports and study them to identify their format and layout and the presentation techniques used.

FIGURE 12.7 *A suite of stationery*

Suites of stationery

A somewhat different publishing task is the creation of suites of stationery. As part of your work for *Unit 1: Using ICT to Communicate*, you might have created a letterhead for an imaginary organisation. You will have then used it as part of a template to create a letter. Most organisations will have pre-printed headed notepaper, business cards, compliments slips, fax header sheets, and so on. These will all be created to follow the house style or corporate image of the company.

To create the stationery shown in Figure 12.7, a photograph was scanned and converted to grey scale. The image transparency was then reduced to 25 per cent and a rectangle removed from the bottom right corner to give a design element. Finally, the dark green text was added – the address and telephone numbers have been deliberately obscured. A camera-ready copy of the letterhead, compliment slip

and business card were produced and sent to a printing firm to be printed in bulk.

Suites of stationery will be designed and produced when an organisation first starts up or when an organisation undergoes a change of image.

✳ Remember

Publishing techniques are used to create

- ✳ billboards and posters
- ✳ books and manuals
- ✳ brochures/leaflets and newsletters
- ✳ forms and mailshots
- ✳ magazines and newspapers
- ✳ reports
- ✳ suites of stationery.

Each type of document has standard features, but the presentation styles used will depend on the audience and purpose.

12.2 Combining information

In this section, you will learn about the different tools and techniques for combining information in a publication. There are many different software packages available that provide these tools. These range from relatively inexpensive packages for the 'home' user, to expensive, sophisticated software used by commercial publishers. Examples in the first category are Microsoft Publisher and Serif PagePlus. A package such as Adobe PageMaker offers more facilities, but most commercial publishers will use a professional package such as QuarkXpress or InDesign.

Although modern word-processing software offers more and more DTP-like facilities, one of the main benefits of using DTP software, rather than word-processing software, is its greater ability to combine and organise different types of information. DTP software uses frames to contain the different types of information. These frames can be accurately positioned so that the designer has complete control over where each type of information will appear on the page. It is also possible to link text frames so that an article can continue in another frame when the first becomes full.

Each of the different types of information may be saved as a different file type. Sometimes it may be necessary to convert one file type to another before it can be imported into the document you are creating.

Combining and converting information

Image files

There are many different types of image file. These fall into two main categories – vector and bitmap – which describes the way the image is represented. Vector images are stored using the coordinates and mathematical properties of the elements that make up the image. Bitmap images are stored using the colour of each pixel of the image. You will find more details about these two types of image in *Unit 13: Artwork and Imaging*.

Vector graphic images

There is no standard file format for vector graphic images. Each vector graphics software package creates its own file type. For example, CorelDRAW vector graphics software creates files with a .cdr extension, while Micrografx Draw creates files with a .drw extension. Both of these file types can be imported into Microsoft Publisher, but other vector graphics file types may need to be converted. Also, other DTP packages may accept different vector graphics file types, again requiring files to be converted. This will involve using another graphics package that can import the vector graphics file and save it with a different file type that the DTP software can import.

Bitmap image files (.bmp)

There are several bitmap graphic file types that are standard in most bitmap graphics software packages. The main difference between them is the size of the file and the quality of the image. The standard bitmap file type has the extension .bmp. This file type gives the best quality image, but file sizes can be very large. The file size of the image in Figure 12.7 is approximately 30 MB.

Bitmap image files (.jpg)

Another standard file type for bitmap images is JPEG, which has the extension .jpg. This considerably reduces the file size, but it does so by reducing the quality of the image. When saving an image in this format, you can select the quality of the saved image as a percentage of the original. Saving the image in Figure 12.7 as a JPEG at 90 per cent quality reduces the file size to approximately 2.5 MB. Providing you start with a full bitmap, compressing a JPEG file to 75 per cent has little noticeable effect on the clarity of the image. However, the editor of a publication must finally make a subjective decision on the level of compression that is acceptable. One thing you should not do is try to enlarge a JPEG image. Doing so exposes the fact that detail has been lost, resulting in **pixelation** and jagged lines.

Bitmap image files (.gif)

Graphic Interchange Format (GIF) – extension .gif – is another standard file type that reduces the file size of bitmap images. In this case, the reduction in file size is achieved by reducing the number of colours used from true colour to 256, 128 or 64. Saving the image in Figure 12.7 as a 256-colour GIF file gives a file size of just under 5 MB. GIF files are often used on websites, as they provide smaller files, which are faster to download, without a reduction in quality.

Importing graphic files

It is likely that any DTP package will be able to import any of the three bitmap file types. There are also other common bitmap graphic file types that are compatible with many DTP packages. Different packages do, however, have their own file types and it may be necessary to convert them to a different format that can be imported. This should be relatively straightforward, as the majority of packages will give the option of saving as .bmp, .jpg or .gif files.

As the facilities for manipulating images are limited in DTP packages, it makes sense to crop or resize them to the required dimensions in a graphics software package before you import them into your publication. This may also have the benefit of reducing the file size. You should also ensure that the shape of the image matches that of the frame you want to import it into (that is, it has the same **aspect ratio**). If you do not, the image will be distorted.

Word-processed files

Whilst it is possible to enter text directly into a text frame in a DTP package, word-processing software provides better facilities for entering large quantities of text. Using word-processing software for text entry also means that articles can be produced by different people and then imported, requiring only one copy of the DTP software. Also, articles that already exist as word-processed files may be used. The thing to bear in mind is that extensive formatting of the word-processed document should be avoided. The formatting tools within the DTP software should be used to ensure consistency. The most common type of word-processed file ends in .doc and is created by Microsoft Word. This type of file can be imported into most, if not all, DTP packages. However, different versions of the software may cause problems and there are other word-processing packages whose file types are less universally accepted. The easiest way to ensure that a word-processed file can be imported is to convert it to a text file.

Text files

There are two types of text file: plain text (.txt) and rich text format (.rtf). A plain text file contains virtually no formatting, although bullets and numbered lists are kept. Rich text format keeps some of the formatting of the original document, such as the font style and size, bold, italic and underline and paragraph formatting such as

justification. If only standard formatting tools are used, the document saved as a .rtf file will appear very similar to the original document saved as a word-processed file. Figure 12.8 shows the same document saved as a plain text file (top) and a rich text file (bottom). The latter is very similar to the original .doc version.

Databases

Database file types depend on the software used to create them. Microsoft Access uses the file type .mdb, whilst dBase uses .dbf. These files contain all aspects of the database, including tables, queries and reports. It is not possible to import a whole database into a DTP package, nor are you likely to want to. There are, however, several ways that you might want to combine part of a database in a DTP document. The most obvious of these is to use a table or the results of a query as the data file for a mail merge. To do this you will need to export the table as a separate file. Microsoft Access provides a Microsoft Word merge file type, but you could also export the table as a spreadsheet file or a **comma-separated variables (.csv) file**.

Another way that you might want to combine part of a database in a DTP document is to incorporate the results of a query, either in table format or as a report. Again, you will need to export these with an appropriate file type. The most appropriate file type

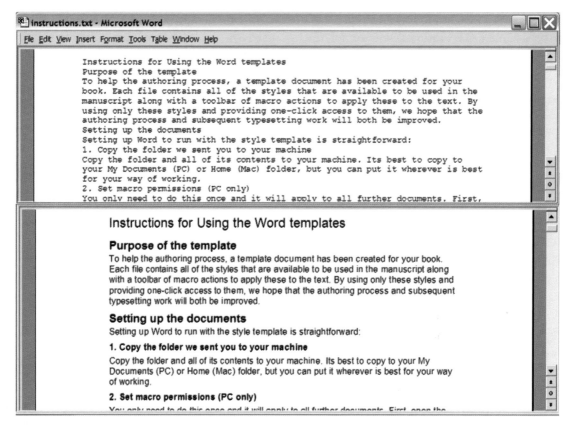

FIGURE 12.8 *A document saved as .txt (top) and .rtf (bottom) file types*

in both cases is likely to be .rtf. This will lose some features in the report, such as **horizontal rules**, but will keep most of the formatting. When exporting a table of data, .rtf will keep the table format.

Chart and graph files

As with database software, modern spreadsheet software, such as Microsoft Excel, does not save charts and graphs as a separate file but as part of a workbook (.xls). To combine a chart or graph in a DTP package, you could copy and paste the chart into a graphics package that can then be imported. The other option is to import the workbook into the DTP document as an embedded object. Double clicking on the object will allow you to select the sheet containing the chart so that this will be displayed.

How to...

Embed an Excel chart in a DTP document in Microsoft Publisher.

1 Select Object from the Insert menu.

2 Select Create from file in the dialogue box.

3 Click on the Browse button and locate the .xls file.

4 Open the file and click OK.

5 Double-click on the object to edit it.

6 Select the sheet tab for the chart so that it is visible.

7 Click outside of the object to exit the spreadsheet file.

8 Resize and position the object as necessary.

Objects can be embedded in the same way from other software that supports **OLE**.

OLE: Stands for object linking and embedding, a facility that allows one type of file (A) to be accessed within another (B). Linking means that only a link to file A is included in the file B. Any changes made to the file A will automatically appear in file B, but both files must be available. Embedding means that file A is actually part of file B but can be edited in the original software by double-clicking on it.

Compressed files

As you have already discovered, some graphics files can be very large. There are two different ways of compressing files. One method that we discussed earlier is changing the file type. Converting a .bmp file to .jpg will reduce its size, but with some reduction in quality; converting a .bmp file to .gif reduces the file size by reducing the number of colours but not the quality. Graphics files that are compressed in this way can be imported directly into a publication.

Another way of reducing file size is to use compression software. However, before this type of compressed file can be included in a DTP document, it must be decompressed to its original file type. This means that you will need a copy of the appropriate decompression software.

Probably the most common compression/decompression software is WinZip. If you locate and select the compressed (zipped) folder in My Computer, selecting Extract all from the File menu will activate the extraction wizard to decompress the file(s).

Editing and formatting tools and techniques

There are many different editing and formatting tools available in DTP and word-processing software to help you to achieve the required result. The tools available will depend on the software package you are using. The screen shots and examples in the following sections use Microsoft Publisher and Microsoft Word as appropriate, but similar features will be available in other packages and you will need to find out how to use these tools and techniques in the software you are using.

Headings and subheadings

Headings and subheadings divide up text, making it easier to refer to specific sections of the text and improving readability. There needs to be different levels of heading and subheading, each with its own style so that the reader can identify it. In this unit, there are four different heading styles, apart from the main unit title.

This is heading style A

This is heading style B

This is heading style C

This is heading style D

Set up and apply styles for each heading level

In Microsoft Publisher, to set up styles for each heading level, select Styles and Formatting from the Format menu and then click on Create new style.

Enter a name for the new style, such as heading1, to indicate how it will be used. You can then select the font and other attributes you want that style to have. You can also select which style will follow the heading. This will usually be body text. Click OK to add the new style to the list of available styles.

You can now apply the appropriate style to existing headings and subheadings by selecting the heading and then the style. Alternatively, you can add headings and subheadings by selecting the appropriate style and then typing in the heading.

Body text

Body text is the font style that will be used for the main body of the text. It can be set up in the same way as a heading style. Unless you are creating a publication in a fancy style, body text should be a standard, easy-to-read font, such as Arial, Helvetica or Times New Roman. The font size should normally be between 10 and 12 point and the style regular (not bold or italic).

Footnotes and endnotes

Footnotes are notes that appear at the bottom of the page, while endnotes are notes that appear at the end of the document. In either case, a superscript number or other character is placed in the text where the reference is required – see Figure 12.9. Footnotes and endnotes allow you to provide important information that you do not want to include in the main body of the text. An example of using a footnote would be to provide details of the source of a quotation.

Not all DTP packages support the use of footnotes and endnotes, but word-processing packages, such as Word, do. Selecting Footnote from the Insert menu will open the dialogue box shown in Figure 12.9. Here you can select whether a footnote or endnote is needed and whether the references will be automatically numbered or identified by some other character. Clicking OK will insert the reference number in the text and a horizontal rule at the bottom of the page (if footnote is selected). The cursor also moves to the bottom of the page so that you can type in the note.

Bullets and lists

The use of bullets can improve the readability of a document and draw attention to important points. Rather than having a list of points in a long sentence separated by commas, it is much clearer to the reader if the points are in a bulleted list. As well as the standard round bullets, many different characters can be used as bullets to suit the document being produced. Selecting Bullets and Numbering from the Format menu in Word or Publisher will allow you to customise the

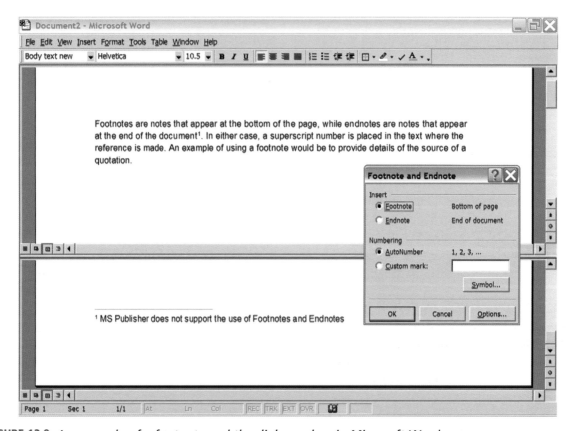

FIGURE 12.9 *An example of a footnote and the dialogue box in Microsoft Word*

bullets used. As well as the symbol to be used, you will also be able to set the indentation of the bullet from the left margin and the indent of the text from the bullet.

Bullets are usually used when there is no order to the points in the list. Where the list is of instructions to be completed in a particular order, or the points are in order of importance, a numbered list is usually used. Selecting Bullets and Numbering from the Format menu will allow you to select the numbering system to be used and how the numbers will appear. There is more flexibility in the formatting of bullets and numbering in Word than there is in Publisher. Word also allows the use of multi-level numbering.

Tabs

Tab stops allow you to align text at different distances from the left margin, in much the same way as in a table. The default tab stop is left-aligned, but tab stops can also be set to be centre-, right-, or decimal-aligned. The last of these is useful for a column of decimal numbers. It means that the decimal point will always be in the same position, so units, tens, hundreds, and so on, will each be in a vertical line. Another benefit of using tabs rather than a table is the facility to include a **leader**. A leader is a line, either solid or dotted, that leads up to the tab stop, for example:

..........................Tab

Selecting Tabs from the Format menu in Word or Publisher allows you to set the position, alignment and any leader for each tab stop required.

Key terms

Leader: A line, either solid or dotted, that leads up to a tab stop.

Drawing more complex shapes using grouping, layers and filters

Both DTP and word-processing software provide drawing tools so that shapes can be drawn directly onto the document, rather than importing them from a graphics package. As well as lines and arrows, there are a number of different autoshapes that can be selected and used. By combining these shapes and using the tools available, it is possible to create quite complex shapes. The tools that assist in this are grouping, layers and filters.

Grouping

Grouping allows separate graphic elements to be combined so that they can be treated as one. To group a number of objects, either drag a box round them using the selection tool, or select each one with the mouse while holding the Shift key down. Next select Group – this is in the Arrange menu in Publisher. Any resizing, rotation or movement will apply to the group, rather than individual objects within it. Some filter effects can also be applied to the whole group.

Layers

If you draw a number of filled shapes that overlap, the most recently added will cover parts of previous objects. You can alter this by changing the layer on which the objects appear. By selecting Order, you can send an object to the back, bring it to the front, send it backwards one layer or bring it forwards one layer. Figure 12.10 shows the

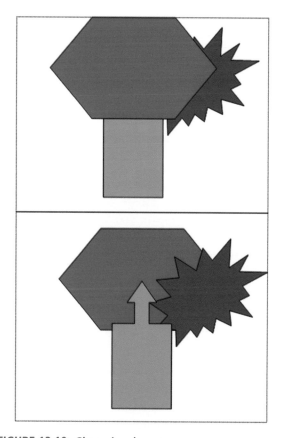

FIGURE 12.10 *Changing layers*

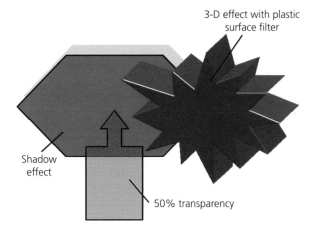

FIGURE 12.11 *Using filters and effects*

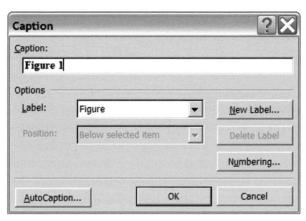

FIGURE 12.12 *The Caption dialogue box in Microsoft Word*

effect of changing layers on a shape made of three objects. You need to adjust the layers before you group objects, as the layers cannot be changed once the objects are grouped.

Filters

Filters allow you to apply effects to the shapes you have drawn. However, not all effects tools are strictly filters. The range of filters and effects tools available will vary depending on the package you are using. The shapes in Figure 12.11 show the use of three of the filters and effects tools available in Publisher. The red hexagon has a shadow effect applied, the green block arrow has a transparency of 50 per cent and the purple explosion has a 3-D effect with a plastic surface filter.

Figure captions and figure numbers

Figure captions and figure numbers relate images to the text that they are illustrating. Each image or figure is given a number that indicates its position relative to other figures. The chapter number may also be included, as in this book. The figure caption indicates what the figure shows.

Figure captions and numbers are particularly important when the figure is not immediately next to the text, as is often the case. The figure number can be used in the text to direct the reader to the figure. Figure 12.12 shows the dialogue box for inserting figure captions and numbers in Word.

As well as figures, tables and equations can also be numbered in the same way, as they too are not always immediately next to the text that refers to them.

Headers and footers

A header is text that appears on every page of a document within the top margin, whilst a footer appears on every page within the bottom margin. Depending on the software being used, you can set different margins for odd and even pages, for the first page and for different sections within the document. In Word, for example, you can set all of these options from the Header/Footer dialogue box. In Publisher you will need to create different **master pages** for each section and add the relevant headers and footers to each. To achieve different headers or footers on odd and even pages, you will need to use the two-page option and add the appropriate header or footer to each page.

Tables

Tables are a means of organising information. The information may already exist in table format, such as a spreadsheet or database table, or it may need to be entered into a table. Existing tables can be imported into a document either as a text file or as an OLE object. To create a table, word-processing and DTP software provides options to insert and format tables. There may be a number of automatic formatting options, or you will be able to add borders, shading and other formatting as required. Once a table is created, depending on the software, you can insert or delete rows or columns, merge or split cells and carry out other functions such as sorting the data, using formulae or replicating data from one cell into a column or row.

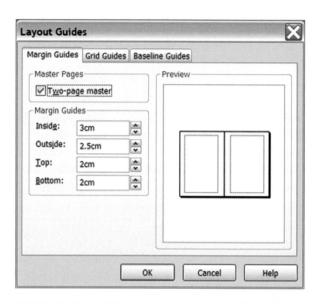

FIGURE 12.13 *Setting margins in Microsoft Publisher*

Theory into practice

Find out how to use the following tools and techniques in the software to which you have access:

* headings, subheadings and body text styles

* footnotes and endnotes

* bullets and lists

* tabs

* figure captions and numbers

* headers and footers

* tables.

Document editing

DTP and word-processing software provide editing tools to control the layout and appearance of documents and to improve the accuracy of the content. In DTP software, some of these features will need to be set in the master page so that they apply to all pages. The tools available will depend on the software you are using.

Setting margins

A margin is the area at the top, bottom, left or right edge of a page that does not normally contain text or other data. There are obviously exceptions to this, as headers and footers appear within the top and bottom margins and some documents include marginal comments in the left or right margins.

The width of the margins will depend on the type of document being created. Some documents, such as leaflets, may have no margins or very small margins to maximise the available space. A book that is to include marginal comments may have an extra-wide margin to allow for this. Any multi-page document that is to be bound or held together in some way will need to have a margin on the hinge side so that information is not lost in the binding. Where such a document is to be printed on both sides of the paper, this margin will be on the left side of odd pages and the right side of even pages.

Figure 12.13 shows how the margins can be set up to alternate for odd and even pages using a two-page master in Publisher. The inside margin is wider than the outside margin to allow for the binding.

Formatting

Formatting tools allow you to change the appearance of the text in a document. This includes setting text attributes, selecting fonts and changing case from capital letters (upper case) to small letters (lower case). Formatting text will be covered in more detail in the section on text attributes later in this unit.

Justification

Justification determines how text appears on the page in relation to the left and right margins or column edges. Text that is left-justified is aligned with the left margin and has a jagged right edge. This text is left-justified.

Right-justified text is aligned with the right margin and has a jagged left edge. Right-justification is only used in certain circumstances, such as to align an address on the right side of the page or for effect.

Text that is fully justified is aligned with both the left and right margins. The software inserts additional space between words to achieve this. Text in newspapers is usually fully justified. However, using full justification with narrow columns when the text contains a number of long words can lead to problems. This can result in 'rivers' of white space through the text and, occasionally, one word at the beginning of the line and one at the end with white space in between.

The final form of justification is centre-justified. The centre point of the text is aligned with a point halfway between the left and right margins and both edges are jagged. Centre justification is usually used for headings or in flyers and posters.

Justification can be set via the Format Paragraph dialogue box or using the buttons displayed on the Formatting toolbar.

Tabulation, columns and gutters

Earlier in this unit we discussed the use of tabs and tables to arrange text in columns. This is known as **tabulation**. Tabulation is usually used to arrange some of the text on a page into columns, usually individual words or short phrases, or columns of figures. There is no link between items in separate lines of text or separate cells in a table. If all the text on a page is to be arranged in columns, as in this book, the column tool is used. Text is entered, or imported, into the first column and, when this is full, automatically continues in the next. Columns can be applied to the whole page, or to the text in a frame. The space between columns is called the **gutter**.

Where columns are to be used on all pages, the column guides should be set on the master page, as shown in Figure 12.14. You can then align the text frames to the column guides and flow the text from one frame to the next. The spacing or gutter between the two columns can

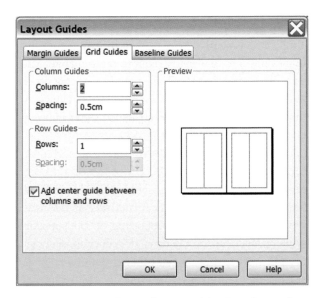

FIGURE 12.14 *Setting column guides in Microsoft Publisher*

be adjusted to suit the document. When column guides are set on the master page, text or graphic frames can be positioned within the columns or overlapping them. For example, a picture could be positioned in the centre of the page overlapping two columns, or a text box could be made the full width of the page and arranged in three columns when the rest of the page is arranged in two.

Leading and kerning

Leading (pronounced *ledding*) and kerning are two terms that have survived from the time when text was printed by positioning individual letters on lead blocks – known as type – in a frame. Strips of lead were put between the rows of type to create space between the rows of text on the page, hence the term leading. In DTP software, leading also allows you to adjust the space between the rows of text. In Publisher you need to adjust the line spacing, which is the distance between the bottom of one line and the bottom of the next line. This is done by adjusting the between lines spacing in the Format Paragraph dialogue box.

Kerning allows you to adjust the spacing between letters. The more kerning there is, the more the letters will be spaced out. Figure 12.15 shows the dialogue box to apply kerning in Publisher. It can be accessed from the Format menu. The sample shows how the letter spacing is affected.

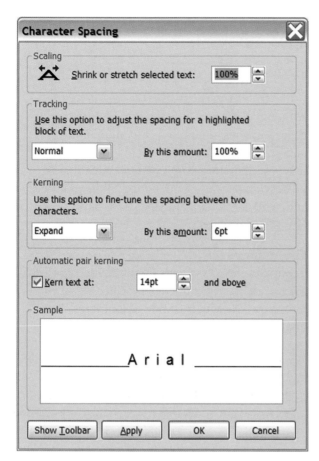

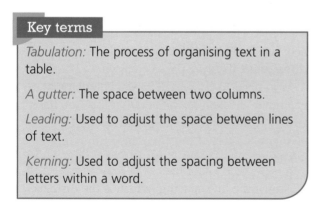

FIGURE 12.15 *The character spacing dialogue box in Microsoft Publisher*

Alignment

Alignment allows you to position objects and frames as well as text relative to each other on the page. Alignment can be vertical or horizontal and text can also be indented in various ways.

Vertical alignment

This can apply to both text and the alignment of frames and other objects. Text within a frame can be aligned to the top, middle or bottom. Top is the normal alignment where text fills down from the top of a frame. With bottom-alignment, the text fills up from the bottom of the frame. If a text box has middle-alignment, the text will be arranged equally either side of the vertical midpoint of the frame. These options can be changed in the Format Text Box dialogue box in Publisher.

The same three options are available when aligning objects or frames, but they behave differently. To align objects or frames with each other, all must be selected. Align top adjusts the positions so that the top of each object is in line with the top of the highest one. Align bottom adjusts the positions so that the bottom of each object is in line with the bottom of the lowest one. Align middle lines up the vertical midpoints of each object. These options are used by selecting Align or Distribute from the Arrange menu in Publisher. In Word, select the same option from the Draw menu on the Drawing toolbar.

Horizontal alignment

Horizontal alignment of text is the same as justification. Objects and frames can be aligned left, right or centre. As with vertical alignment, align left moves the objects to line up the left edges of all selected objects with the one that is furthest to the left. Right-alignment lines up the right edges with the one that is furthest to the right and centre lines up the horizontal midpoints of all the objects. This is not necessarily the horizontal centre of the page. These options are selected in the same way as vertical alignment.

Indentation

Indentation is when text starts or finishes some distance from the left or right margin. A whole paragraph may be indented, often from both left and right margins, to make it stand out from the rest of the text. For example, a quote may be treated in this way. A first line indent is mainly used to signify a new paragraph, rather than a blank line. Hanging indents are usually only used with bullets or numbered paragraphs so that all the text starts at the same point as the text on the first line. You can change the indentation by selecting Paragraph from the Format menu.

Pagination, avoiding widows and orphans

Pagination determines where page breaks occur. In word-processing software, a new page is automatically started when the previous one is full. However, you can force a page break before a page is full by selecting Break and then Page from the Insert menu. In DTP software, text is imported or entered in frames. When a frame is full, the software asks whether you want to flow the text into a new frame. You can then select the frame the text should flow into or allow the software to do so automatically. In this case, a new frame will be created on a new page. You can create a new page by selecting Page from the Insert menu.

Widows and **orphans** occur when the last line of a paragraph is forced onto the top of a new page or the first line of a paragraph is left at the bottom of a page. Widows and orphans also occur at the end of a frame or column. Widows and orphans control prevents this. If there is only room for one line, it will be moved onto the next page. If you end a paragraph on the first line of a new page, the last line on the previous page will be moved onto the new page to join it.

Key terms

Widow: Where the last line of a paragraph ends up on its own at the top of a new page.

Orphan: Where the first line of a paragraph is left on its own at the bottom of a page.

Another aspect of pagination is keeping a heading with the text to which it refers. Having a heading at the bottom of one page and the body text at the top of the next is not good practice. When you set up heading styles, you can check the 'Keep with next' box so that the heading stays with the paragraph that follows it. This will not work if you leave a blank line between the heading and the paragraph. To avoid the need for this, make sure you include some 'space after' when setting up the heading style.

Grammar check, spell check and hyphenation control

Although DTP packages do provide some spell check facilities, the options are more limited and grammar checking is not always provided. It is best, therefore, to prepare text in a word-processing package, making use of the grammar and spell checking facilities, before importing it into DTP software.

Grammar check

Grammar checkers compare what you type with a set of rules. You can choose which set of rules to use by selecting the style of language that you want to use, such as formal or technical. A grammar checker will help you make sure that there is a capital letter to start a sentence and only one full stop at the end of it. It will also indicate if you have a single subject but a plural verb, for example 'they is', or vice versa.

Grammar checkers will also indicate where you have used the passive rather than the active voice. The passive voice is where the object of the sentence comes first, for example: 'The play was enjoyed by the audience.' The active voice is when the subject of the sentence comes first, for example: 'The audience enjoyed the play.' The active voice is much easier to read and has a more direct effect than the passive voice.

You need to take great care when using a grammar checker, however. Do not be too hasty to accept the changes suggested. Not all the changes suggested improve the grammar of a sentence – some might change the meaning or make it meaningless.

Spell check

A spell checker will help you to check and correct the spelling of words and will also pick up repeated words, such as 'the the'. However, a spell checker only compares the words you type with an inbuilt dictionary. If you type 'form' when you mean 'from' or 'manger' when you mean 'manager', the spell checker will not identify these as errors. On the other hand, you

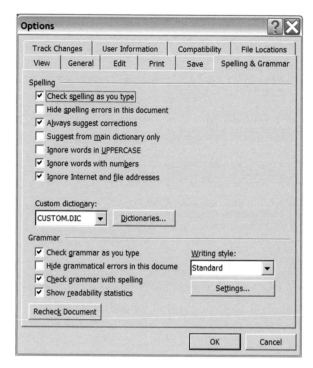

FIGURE 12.16 *Spelling and grammar options in Microsoft Word*

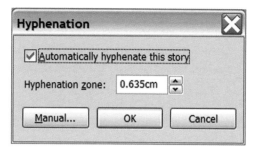

FIGURE 12.17 *Hyphenation control in Microsoft Publisher*

Set the hyphenation control

To access the Hyphenation dialogue box, click on Language in the Tools menu and select Hyphenation from the drop-down menu that appears.

With the Automatically hyphenate this story box checked, long words that will not fit on a line will be split automatically. The Hyphenation zone determines how frequently this can occur – in this case, once every 0.635 cm. Making the hyphenation zone smaller will give a more even right edge or fewer white gaps in the text. A larger hyphenation zone means there will be fewer hyphens and fewer short syllables before or after a hyphen.

Hyphenation can be changed manually by unchecking the Automatically hyphenate this story box and then clicking on the Manual button. This takes you through the text, suggesting words that could be hyphenated, and allowing you to add a hyphen by clicking Yes, and identifying words that are hyphenated so you can remove them if required by clicking No.

may type a name, such as 'Agnew', which you know is correct, but the spell checker identifies it as an error. This is because 'Agnew' is not in the dictionary. If you use a lot of unusual words or proper names, you can create your own personal dictionary containing these words.

You should not become reliant on the spell checker to spell for you. The spell checker will often provide a list of alternative spellings – you will need to know which one to select. Sometimes the correct word may not be in the list or the spell checker cannot offer any suggestions, so you will need to correct the word yourself. Remember also that the spell checker may be configured not to check certain words, such as those in capital letters. The Options dialogue box that can be selected from the Tools menu in Word allows you to configure the grammar and spelling options (Figure 12.16).

Hyphenation

Hyphenation control determines whether long words will be split by a hyphen if they do not fit on a line. Figure 12.17 shows the Hyphenation dialogue box in Publisher.

Text attributes

Text attributes are the different tools available for controlling how text appears. You need to know how and when to apply these text attributes.

Bold, underline and italics

Bold and *italic* are mostly used as part of a heading style or to highlight particular words or phrases within the body text. These attributes should only be used sparingly. Whole paragraphs in bold or italics lose their impact. However, a quote, for example, may all be shown in italics to differentiate it from the rest of the text. Underline is rarely used in printed documents other than to indicate a web page or email address. Bold, italic and underline can be applied from the Font dialogue box, using the buttons on the Format toolbar or using shortcut keys: CTRL+B for bold, CTRL+I for italic and CTRL+U for underline. Pressing the same key combination again switches the attribute off.

Superscript and subscript

Superscript and subscript are used for specific purposes. Superscript is text that appears near the top of standard text, while subscript appears below the line of standard text. Superscript is used for ordinal numbers, such as 1st, 2nd and 3rd. Word does this automatically. Another use for superscript is to show powers of numbers, for example 3^2. Subscript is used in chemical formulae such as H_2O.

> ### How to...
>
> **Change a character to superscript or subscript**
>
> Select the character, access the Font dialogue box from the Format menu and then check the appropriate box.

Overscore

Overscore is where a line appears above the word rather than below it (underscore).

Upper and lower case

Most body text will be a mixture of upper and lower case. Upper case will be used at the start of sentences and for the first letter of the names of people and places, months and days of the week and other proper nouns. You need to ensure that your use of capital letters is consistent. Some headings may be all in upper case. If so, it is a good idea to set this in the heading style. That way, if you forget and enter the heading as lower-case letters, it will automatically appear in upper case.

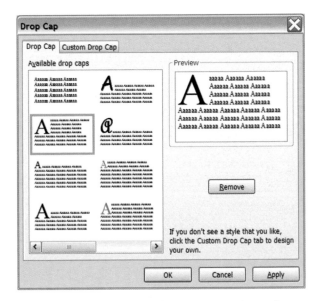

FIGURE 12.18 *Drop capital options in Microsoft Publisher*

Text in all capitals should be kept to a minimum, as it is not as easy to read as lower-case text. You will also need to proof-read such text carefully to check for errors, or ensure the spell checker is configured to check words in upper case.

As well as standard-height capitals, you can use small caps. THIS USES CAPITAL LETTERS THE SAME SIZE AS LOWER CASE. THE SHIFT KEY GIVES A STANDARD CAPITAL LETTER.

Another option for upper-case letters in DTP software is **drop capitals**. These can be used at the beginning of paragraphs and are where the first letter is enlarged and covers several rows of text. Figure 12.18 shows some of the options available in Publisher.

> ### Key terms
>
> *Drop capitals:* A feature used in publications where the first letter of a paragraph is enlarged and covers several lines of normal text.

Font size and style

Word-processing and DTP software now provide a huge range of font styles, most available in font sizes from 4 to 72 points and beyond. The trick when creating publications is not how to apply these font sizes and styles, but how to apply them appropriately.

It goes without saying that the font styles and sizes you use should match the purpose and the audience for the publication. You may get away with using an 18-point font in a picture book for a young child, but not for the body text in a newsletter for your school or college. A fancy handwriting style font may be suitable for an invitation to a wedding and the order of service, but not for an instruction manual for a spreadsheet. The other watchword when deciding which font styles and sizes to use, is *consistency*. Decide on a *small* set of font styles and sizes and use each for the same purpose throughout the publication. The fonts you use may be determined for you by the house style of your client's organisation.

Page layout techniques

There are several techniques for page layout that you need to understand and be able to apply. Some of these have already been mentioned but we will draw them together in this section.

Structures and styles for sections of a document

The assessment evidence for this unit requires you to create a camera-ready copy (CRC) document of at least ten pages. Within those ten pages, there are likely to be different sections that require different structures and styles. Each section may require a different header or footer. For example, each unit (chapter) in this book has the unit title in the odd page footer. A magazine that includes articles each covering several pages may use a different structure for each article, for example a different number of columns or a different gutter width between them. Such a magazine might also include pages of small advertisements arranged in a table structure as well as advertisements and pictures that fill the page with no margins.

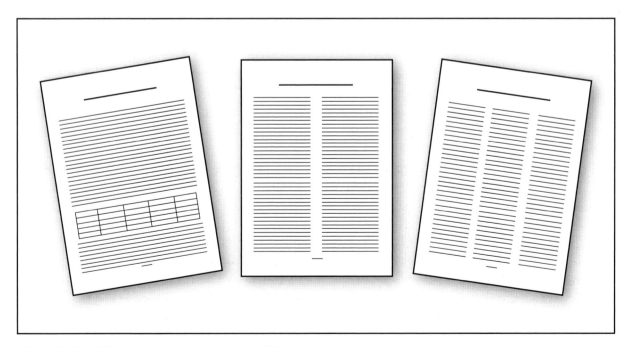

FIGURE 12.19 *Different sections may need different styles and structures*

When designing a publication, you will need to consider whether it needs to be divided into sections. If it does, you should decide how each section needs to be structured and what style should be used. The trick here will be to ensure that the structure and style matches the content of that section whilst you maintain the consistency of the publication as a whole. Once the design of each section has been decided, separate master page layouts can be set up for each.

Techniques for text boxes

Text boxes introduce enormous flexibility in how text is organised on a page. You can place a text box anywhere on the page and move it around at any time. You can make a text box any size and change the size at any time. You can format text in each text box differently and you can format the text boxes themselves differently, with different borders and backgrounds. You can divide the text in a text box into columns and you can connect text boxes so that text can flow automatically from one to another. Connected text boxes do not have to be on the same page – Publisher even provides an option to add 'Continued on page…' at the bottom of a text box.

Figure 12.20 shows a page that uses a number of text boxes (containing dummy text called *greeking*). The headline is in a text box with a thick black border around it. Below that, the main story is in a text box in a single-column format. The story at the bottom is in a text box organised in three columns, with a thin black border. It uses a slightly smaller font and a smaller first-line indent. The story heading is in a separate text box that overlaps the first two columns. The story text is wrapped around this text box. The vertical text has been achieved by rotating the text box through 90 degrees. The text is centre-aligned and the text box has then been given a light-green background with no border. The final text box contains the date. This overlaps the top edge of the green filled text box and has no border.

To format the text in a text box, you select it and then select Font or Paragraph from the Format menu. To format the text box itself, select Text box from the Format menu. Figure 12.21

FIGURE 12.20 *Using frames*

shows the options for colours and lines. The other tabs provide different formatting options.

Layering

We discussed the concept of layering in relation to drawing objects earlier in this unit. Layering can also be used with text boxes, picture frames and any other object on a page. The word Date in Figure 12.20 is only visible because the text box containing it is in front of the one with the green background. Similarly, the text box containing the story heading is in front of the one containing the story. If the story heading text box is sent to back (or the story text box brought to front), the word wrapping will no longer apply and the story text will appear over the story heading. Working with layers is, therefore, an important aspect of page layout.

Borders

Figure 12.20 also demonstrates the use of borders. In this case, borders have been used around

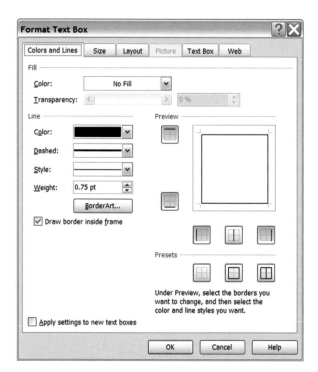

FIGURE 12.21 *The Format Text Box dialogue box in Microsoft Publisher*

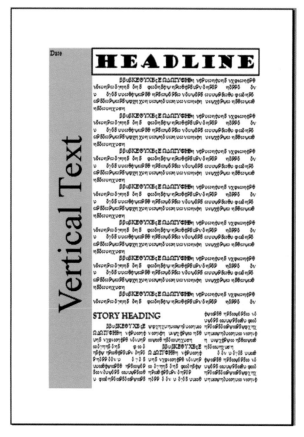

FIGURE 12.22 *This page lacks borders*

individual text boxes – the main heading and the three-column story. In the case of the headline, a thicker border has been used to match the heavy font and make the heading stand out. The three-column story uses a thinner border to show that this is separate from the main story.

Figure 12.22 shows what the page would look like without the border round the three-column story. Despite the story heading, it is difficult to differentiate one story from the other.

There are several options for the type of border that can be used and also where the border will appear – all around or just on selected edges of the text box. You can also apply borders around picture frames and other objects and around the whole page. DTP packages provide numerous options for border art, from simple lines to repeating patterns of all sorts of images. You should use great care when selecting the border to use. Suitability for purpose and audience should be your first consideration.

Shading

Figures 12.20 and 12.22 show a simple use of shading. The vertical text box has been filled with a single plain colour. This serves to separate the vertical text from the rest of the page and to create a design feature that could be carried through onto subsequent pages of the publication. Shading can also be used to add emphasis to particular items or to provide a background to the whole page.

The options available for shading are almost endless. As well as a full palette of colours, different gradients, patterns and textures can be used and a picture can even be used as a background to a text box or page.

How to...

Use the Fill Effects facility

Figure 12.23 shows the Fill Effects dialogue box in Publisher. This can be accessed from the Fill Colour drop-down list in the Format Text Box dialogue box. Each of the tabs provides different fill options. Selecting Background from the Format menu and then More backgrounds provides access to the same dialogue box, but applied to the whole page.

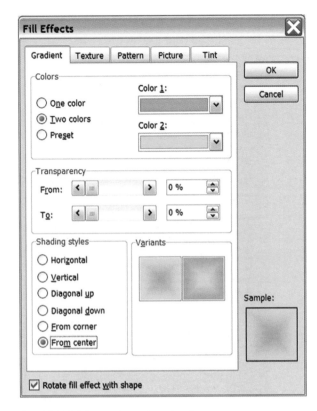

FIGURE 12.23 *Options for shading*

A word of warning here: if the shading is to appear behind text, it is vital that it does not overwhelm the text. Using a dark or highly patterned background to a page may be effective for some publications, but use white or light-coloured backgrounds for any text boxes so that the text can be read. Remember also that any shading used must match the purpose and audience for the publication.

Headers and footers

Headers and footers are important features of multi-page documents. At the very least, the page number should appear on each page. Other items that may be included in a header or footer are:

* the title of the publication
* the author's name
* the chapter number and title
* the filename
* the date
* the version number
* copyright information
* the name of the company or organisation.

There may be different headers and footers for different sections of the publication and for the first page. Publications that are to be printed on both sides of the paper and bound will need to have mirrored headers and footers, so that the same item, such as the page number, appears on the outside edge of each page. Look at the footers on the pages of this book, for example.

When you are designing a publication, you will need to consider:

* whether to use a header, a footer or both
* what should be included
* where each item should be positioned
* what font style and size to use
* whether to separate the header and footer from the rest of the page with a rule or border
* how headers and footers will change from page to page or section to section.

Indexes, tables of contents and cross references

Indexes

An index is an alphabetical list of important words or phrases that appear in a publication, along with the page numbers where each appears. An index usually appears at the end of the publication, as in this book. Depending on the software being used, you can identify words that you want to appear in the index and the software will create the index for you. This feature is available in Word but not in Publisher. If the pagination of the publication changes, the software will update the index to correspond. You will need to decide whether an index is appropriate for the publication you are creating and, if so, which words need to be included. Obviously, the words included in the index need to be relevant to the topic of the publication. Look at the index in this book. Publishers like Heinemann employ professional indexers to compile the indexes for the books they publish.

Tables of contents

A table of contents is a list of the main topics or chapters in a publication in the order they appear. The page number where each topic starts is listed alongside the topic title. This is usually organised in a table format, hence 'table of contents'. As with indexes, depending on the software you are using, the table of contents can be created automatically by the software. This is usually linked to the different heading styles used in the publication. If you have to create a contents list manually, for example in Publisher, it should be the last thing you do, so that the correct page numbers are included.

Cross-referencing

In a complex document or report, you may want to refer the reader to something covered on another page of the document and vice versa. This is called **cross-referencing**. You could just type in 'see Figure 9 on page 10', for example. This would direct the reader to the right place until the pagination of the document changes. If you use this manual method, it means that you will need to check that every cross-reference is correct before the final version is printed – an arduous task if there are more than a few cross-references. Some software, such as Word, will allow you to insert automatic cross-references so that if the pagination changes the cross-referencing is still correct.

Theory into practice

Use Microsoft Office Help to find out how to create indexes, tables of contents and cross-references.

Watermarks

A **watermark** is any picture or text, such as a logo or the word 'DRAFT', that appears on top of or, more usually, behind existing document text. The term watermark comes from papermaking, where patterns or words worked in wire are placed on the surface of a roller under which the wet paper passes. This design is transferred into the structure of the paper. It can only normally be seen when the paper is held up to the light, when the pattern is more transparent than the rest of the paper.

Any text, WordArt or drawing objects that are going to be used as a watermark must first be saved as a picture.

How to...

Create a watermark on your documents

These instructions are for Microsoft Publisher, but the technique for Word is similar.

1 Create the text, WordArt or drawing object that you want to use as a watermark.

2 Right-click on the object and select Save as picture, then select the options you want and click Save.

3 Delete the original text, WordArt or drawing object and then insert the picture you saved.

4 Right-click on the picture and select Format Picture. Change to the Picture tab.

5 Under Image Control, select Washout in the Colour list and then click Recolour.

6 Select the colour you want for the watermark and then click OK.

7 Click OK again in the Format Picture dialogue box.

8 On the Arrange menu, point to Order and select Send to back.

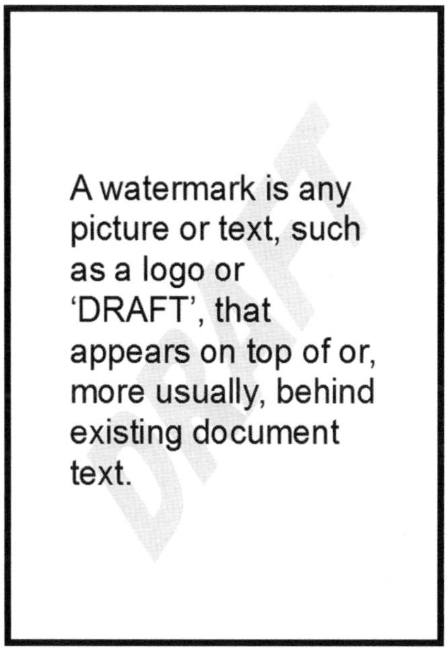

A watermark is any picture or text, such as a logo or 'DRAFT', that appears on top of or, more usually, behind existing document text.

FIGURE 12.24 *A watermark*

Watermarks may be used to give a corporate identity to a document by using the company logo, for example. Watermarks can also be used to identify an important point about the document, for example that it is a draft or is confidential. Some care is needed, when using watermarks, that they are not too intrusive. Choosing lighter colours will result in a fainter watermark, making it less obvious. Remember, genuine watermarks can only be seen clearly when they are held up to the light.

✷ Remember

Publishing is about combining different types of information into a coherent publication. These different types of information may use a number of different file types. Some file types may need to be converted before they can be combined in a publication. Find out which file types can be imported into the software you have access to, and which you will need to convert.

DTP and word-processing software provide a range of editing, formatting and page layout tools and techniques that you need to be able to use appropriately to create publications of a professional standard. Make sure you know which tools and techniques can be used in which software package and how to use and apply them.

Theory into practice

Create an information booklet of at least four pages on a topic that interests you. Try to use existing word-processed, text and graphics files and possibly other types of file. Use as many of the different editing, formatting and page layout tools and techniques you have learned about in this section, as appropriate.

12.3 Researching a brief, planning your response and presenting your solutions

So far we have looked at the different types of publication that publishing techniques can be applied to and the tools and techniques available in DTP and word-processing software to combine, edit and format information. In this section, we will consider the procedures that you need to follow to gain approval for a publication that you create to meet a given brief. These procedures are the ones followed in the publishing industry to create professional publications on a large scale.

Publishing-industry procedures

The four stages of publishing-industry procedures that you need to learn about and follow are:

✷ the draft/design stage

✷ the enhancement of presentation of text

✷ the final production stages

✷ procedures for coping with external factors.

Draft/design stage

This is the first stage once the brief has been received and all the information required for the publication has been collected. The draft/design stage will include all of the following activities, although not necessarily in the order in which they appear below.

Following house style

If the brief is for an existing organisation, the likelihood is that they will have a **house style**. The new publication will need to follow this house style if it is to meet the client's requirements. You will need to find out what the house style is. Some organisations may provide detailed guidance on the rules that must be followed. This might include:

✷ details of the position, size and colours of their logo

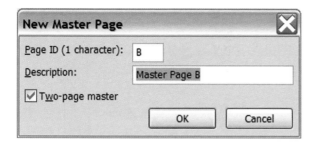

FIGURE 12.25 *The New Master Page dialogue box*

* the font styles, sizes and colours of headings and body text for different types of document

* whether paragraphs should have an indented first line or be separated by a blank line

* whether text should be fully justified or left-aligned (unjustified)

* the style of bullets or numbers in lists

* whether numbers should be in figures or words.

If no such guidance is available, you will need to collect examples of documents from the client's organisation so that you can study them to determine the house style rules. Then you will need to ensure you follow the rules that apply to the type of publication you are designing.

If your client does not have a house style, you may be required to create one. Looking at publications for similar purposes and audiences will help you to create a set of house style rules. These can be followed when designing the publication and for other documents the client may require.

Creating master page layouts

We have mentioned master page layouts at various points in this unit. They are an important step in the design/development stage of the publishing process. Depending on the publication, there may be one master page layout or there may be a number. Each master page layout must include all the elements that will appear in the same position on every page in that section of the document. This may include margins and column guides, headers and footers, text boxes, picture frames, watermarks and drawing objects.

How to...

Create a master page layout in Publisher

1 Select Master Page from the View menu.

2 Click on New Master Page to open the dialogue box shown in Figure 12.25.

3 Accept the Page ID but change the description if you wish.

4 If you want a two-page master, make sure the box is checked – leave it unchecked for a single page.

5 Click OK.

6 Access the Layout Guides dialogue box by clicking on the button on the Edit Master Pages toolbar or from the drop-down list associated with the master page name in the Task pane.

7 Change the layout guides and click OK.

8 Add headers and footers, text boxes, watermarks or drawing objects as required as shown in Figure 12.26.

9 Click Close Master View.

To apply the master page layout, select Apply Master Page from the Format menu. You can then select the master page layout you require and which pages it will be applied to.

Presenting page proofs for reading

Page proofs are required to check the layout and content of the publication so that errors can be corrected. Page proofs may be produced at different stages. For example, if a publisher is waiting for artwork to be produced, page proofs may be produced with just the text in place, with frames to show where the artwork will be positioned. A further set of page proofs would then be needed once the artwork had been added.

Page proofs are usually printed in black and white on paper larger than the final page size. The edge of the final page is indicated by **crop marks** at each corner (see Figure 12.27). The space around the page can be used to indicate any changes or corrections that need to be made. Further page proofs may be required to check that any changes have been made correctly.

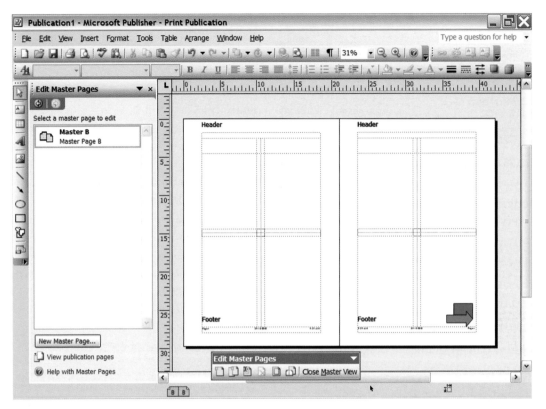

FIGURE 12.26 *Creating a two-page master page layout*

Depending on the size of each page in your publication and the printing facilities you have available, you might not be able to print page proofs on paper larger than the final page size. You should, however, still print proof copies of each page so that they can be read and checked for errors.

Key terms

House style: Determines the style that an organisation uses for all the documents it produces, so that the documents can be recognised as coming from that organisation.

Page proofs: Printed copies of the pages of a publication that can be read and checked for errors.

Crop marks: Marks on page proofs that show where the edges of the final printed page will be, i.e. where the paper will be cropped. They consist of a short horizontal and a short vertical line that cross precisely at each corner of the page.

Using white space

White space is an area of a page or other printed surface where no text or pictures appear. It may not actually be white. If the document is printed on yellow paper, it would actually be yellow. White space is more correctly empty space.

A document with little or no white space appears crowded and is difficult to read; see Figure 12.28 for example. White space gives text and graphics 'breathing room'. There are several

FIGURE 12.27 *A page proof of a label showing crop marks*

FIGURE 12.28 *This page lacks white space*

There are some instances when white space is bad, for example trapped 'rivers of white space' within the text that sometimes occur when text in narrow columns is justified. Another instance of bad white space is when there is too much space between bullets or numbers and the text in lists.

There are no hard and fast rules about the correct amount of white space to include. You need to achieve a balance of ink and white space to suit your design. Generally, if a page looks or feels crowded, it probably needs more white space. The more white space you use, the more professional and up-market the page will feel; cramming as much as you can on the page will make it look cheap and amateurish.

Think it over...

Look at how white space is used in a range of different publications.

Does what you see bear out the statement above about the relationship between the amount of white space and the 'feel' of the document?

ways that you can add white space to a page. The most obvious of these is to increase the size of the margins. Generous margins give a more formal and up-market feel to a design. Tight margins suggest a more 'mass produced' design where cost constraints require the maximum information in the space available.

Other ways of adding white space include:

* increasing paragraph spacing by using a line space or a deep indent (but not both)

* increasing the space between columns

* putting space at the end of lines of text by leaving text unjustified – as in this book

* leaving more space around graphics – don't wrap text too tightly

* increasing the space before and after headlines

* increasing the space between lines of type (leading) and between individual characters (kerning).

Producing artwork sketches

In professional publishing, artwork for a publication is usually created by graphic artists, rather than the author or the designer of a publication. So that the artist can create exactly what is needed, artwork sketches will need to be provided. These will usually be hand-drawn sketches to show what the author or designer wants to convey, possibly with annotations to add any details that are not clear. Figure 12.29 shows a form that is used for artwork sketches. It allows the author or designer to include all the information that is needed about the artwork. This includes the title of the publication it is for, the figure number, the chapter number and the type of artwork required. There is a request to circle any instructions to the artist so that they do not get treated as labels.

The likelihood is that you will create any artwork that is needed in the publication you produce, but you should still create artwork

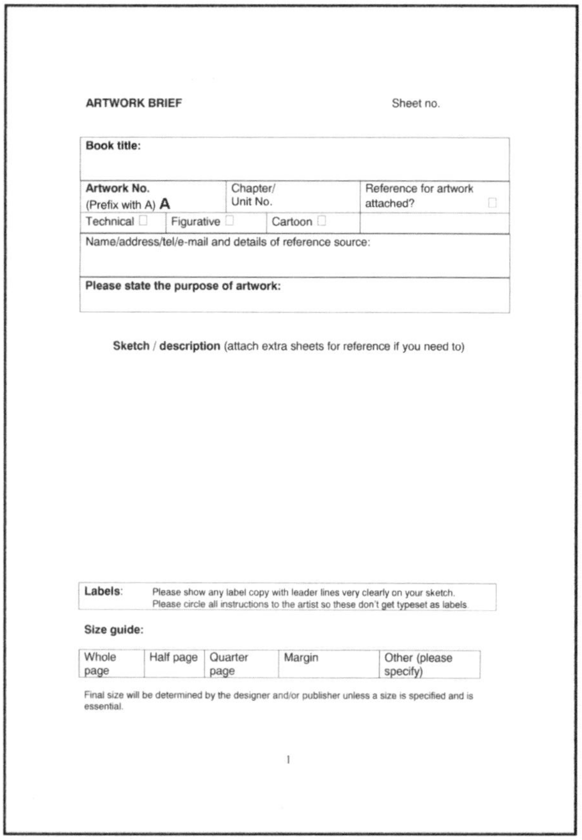

FIGURE 12.29 caption form content:

ARTWORK BRIEF   Sheet no.

Book title:

| Artwork No.
(Prefix with A) **A** | Chapter/
Unit No. | Reference for artwork
attached? ☐ |

Technical ☐   Figurative ☐   Cartoon ☐

Name/address/tel/e-mail and details of reference source:

Please state the purpose of artwork:

Sketch / description (attach extra sheets for reference if you need to)

Labels: Please show any label copy with leader lines very clearly on your sketch.
Please circle all instructions to the artist so these don't get typeset as labels.

Size guide:

| Whole
page | Half page | Quarter
page | Margin | Other (please
specify) |

Final size will be determined by the designer and/or publisher unless a size is specified and is essential.

FIGURE 12.29 *A brief for artwork sketches*

sketches. This will allow you to check with your client that the artwork meets the requirements of the brief. Your client may also provide you with artwork sketches to show exactly what artwork they require.

Setting text orientation

In most documents, the text has horizontal orientation. In English and most other European languages, we read from left to right along each line of text. However, different effects can be achieved by changing the orientation of text. Earlier in this unit we showed how a text box could be rotated through 90 degrees so that the text had a vertical orientation (see Figure 12.20 on page 178). The watermark in Figures 12.24 (page 181) and 12.28 uses a diagonal orientation so that it fills most of the page. Text boxes can be rotated to any angle. Using WordArt creates another possibility: letters one under the other in a vertical line. All of these changes in text orientation should be used sparingly.

Creating style sheets

Early in this unit we discussed the need to set styles for headings, subheadings and body text. When you create a style, you are creating a style sheet that includes all the attributes and formatting for that particular style. You will need to do this for all the styles you intend to use in your presentation. To apply a style, you either select the style and then start typing, or select the text and then select the style. In Publisher, you can only create styles for paragraphs, so if you apply a style it will affect the whole paragraph. Some DTP software allows you to create character styles that can be applied to only specific words, even when they appear within another paragraph style.

There are several reasons for creating and using style sheets. Firstly, it allows you to maintain consistency throughout a publication. Secondly, it allows you to make quick changes to the text throughout a document. Suppose you had used a main heading style that used an 18-point Times New Roman font in Red with 6 points of spacing before and 3 points after. When you show your client the page proofs, they decide that they would prefer a different font in a slightly larger size and a darker colour. Without styles you would need to go through the document selecting each heading and reformatting each one. With styles, you would simply need to modify the style sheet as required and all the main headings would change.

A style sheet can also be a document that lists all the styles to be used, along with their features and what they will be used for.

Enhancement of text presentation

The next stage of the publication process is the enhancement of presentation of text. Some of these techniques have already been covered in other parts of this unit, but they are mentioned here for completeness.

Watermarks

A watermark is any picture or text that appears on top of or, more usually, behind existing document text. You should refer to the earlier section on watermarks to find out how to create them and how they might be used.

'Greeking' and 'latining'

If you want to demonstrate a font or fill a space that will take proper content later, one technique you can use is called 'greeking', although 'latining' is a more appropriate name, as you will see. This technique uses a nonsense paragraph that looks like Latin but actually means nothing. Part of this is shown below.

'Lorem ipsum dolor sit amet, consectetaur adipisicing elit, sed do eiusmod tempor incididunt ut labore et dolore magna aliqua. Ut enim ad minim veniam, quis nostrud exercitation ullamco laboris nisi ut aliquip ex ea commodo consequat. Duis aute irure dolor in reprehenderit in voluptate velit esse cillum dolore eu fugiat nulla pariatur.'

If you write real text as a sample, people will spend more time reading the text than looking at the font. This text is sufficiently like ordinary text to demonstrate a font without distracting the reader. Letters occur with approximately the same frequency as they occur in English, which is why at first glance it looks realistic. The letters and letter spacing in this text display the weight, design, and other important features of a font. The amazing thing is that this same fake Latin text has been used by the printing and publishing industry for over 500 years!

Repeating elements

Repetition means that you should repeat some aspects of your design throughout the entire publication. Repetition acts as a visual key that ties your publication together, and readers will gain comfort from having the same elements repeat themselves at consistent intervals or in the same position on each page. Repetition also controls the reader's eye and helps to keep their attention as long as possible. Some possibilities are:

* using the same font for all your headlines
* using the same graphic rule in the same position on all the pages
* putting repeated elements, such as page numbers, in the same position on every page.

Think it over...

What repeating elements have been used in this book?

Special characters

There are some special characters that you may need to use in publications. If you are producing mathematical material, you may need to use Greek characters such as π or Σ. You can access these by selecting Symbol from the Insert menu. The dialogue box shown in Figure 12.30 will appear in Publisher.

Select Basic Greek from the Subset list and the letters of the Greek alphabet will be shown. Select the one you need and then click the Insert button.

Selecting the Special Characters tab gives access to other special characters you may need to use. For example, a dash between words is usually longer than the standard hyphen on the keyboard. This longer character is called an **en rule**, because it takes up the same space as the letter n. If you are typing text in, an en rule will be used automatically if there is a space before and after it, although you can turn this feature off. However, if you want to insert a dash in text that already exists, you will need to use the Special Character dialogue box to do so. Alternatively, you can use the shortcut key: CTRL and the minus key on the numeric keypad.

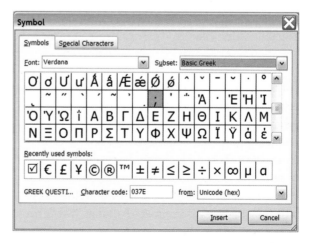

FIGURE 12.30 *The Symbol dialogue box*

Another character you might need to use is called an **ellipsis**. This is used to indicate when something has been omitted, for example from a quote. You may also need to use the copyright, registered and trade mark symbols. A quick way of entering © is to type (c) – both Word and Publisher will automatically convert this. Similarly, (R) will give ®.

> **Key terms**
>
> *En rule (–):* Used as a dash. It takes up the same space as a letter n.
>
> *Ellipsis (…):* Used to show that something has been omitted.

Ruler grid lines

Ruler grid lines help to ensure that text boxes and other objects are positioned accurately. It is also possible to apply baseline guides so that the text in different text boxes is on the same horizontal line.

Text boxes and other objects can be made to snap to ruler lines and layout guides such as page and column margins. In Publisher, pointing to Ruler Guides in the Arrange menu provides options for adding and formatting ruler guides. Pointing to Snap in the same menu will allow you to control what text boxes and other objects snap to.

You can adjust the baseline guides using the Layout Guides dialogue box. When defining styles, you then need to check the Align text to baseline guides box in the Format Paragraph dialogue box.

Callouts and labels

There are two different publishing devices called callouts. The first of these is a label, similar to a photo caption, that is used to identify parts of an illustration. This may simply be text around the edge of the illustration with or without a line or arrow to the section of the illustration it refers to, or it may be framed in boxes, balloons, use arrows or other features – look at the callout AutoShapes in Word or Publisher.

FIGURE 12.31 *Using a text callout or pull-quote*

The other device known as a callout relates to text and is also known as a pull-quote. This is an extract from an article that is set apart in a larger or contrasting font to attract the reader's attention, especially in long articles (see Figure 12.31). This type of callout may be framed by rules, placed within the article, span multiple columns or be placed in an empty column near the article. Look at magazines to see examples of how this type of callout is used.

Automatic generation

As we have discussed previously, there are some features of documents that can be generated automatically in some software. These include notes (footnotes and endnotes), an index and a contents list.

Final production stages

The publication you create may or may not go on to be printed in bulk. In either case, there are terms relating to the final production stages that you need to understand and be able to use.

Colours of print and paper

To reproduce full-colour photographic images, typical printing presses use four colours of ink. The four inks are placed on the paper in layers of dots that combine to create the illusion of many more colours. CMYK refers to the four ink colours used by the printing press. C is cyan, M is magenta, Y is yellow, and K is black, the key plate or keyline colour – see Figure 12.32.

For printing, images must be separated into these four colours so that a separate printing plate can be produced for each one. Most DTP software allows you to output your publication as a CMYK composite Postscript file that could be used by a printer to create the four separate plates.

The colours that appear on paper may not be exactly the same as they appear on screen. This is because of the different ways our eyes perceive colour. On screen, red, green and blue light combines to create the colours we see. On paper, we see the colour of the light that is reflected by the ink; that is, the light that is not absorbed. If it is vital that your printed publication uses particular colours, you will need to use printed colour charts to select the shades you use.

Paper as well as ink is available in different colours and shades. Even white paper, like white paint, comes in different shades, from a yellowish white to a bluish white. Yellowish white or cream paper will give a warm feel to a publication, while a brilliant or bluish white will give a cleaner, crisper feel. The colour of

FIGURE 12.33 *Paper colour affects the appearance of images*

the paper will affect how ink colours appear, as well as the overall impact of the publication. Figure 12.33 shows the effect of printing the same image on green and white paper. For this reason, coloured paper is best used with monochrome documents (when a single ink colour is used). This may be black or a darker shade of the same colour – dark green ink on light green paper, for example.

Paper weights and sizes

As well as different colours, paper comes in many different sizes. In North America – USA and Canada – the printing industry uses paper sizes based on the letter size (8.5 × 11 inches, 216 × 279 mm). Tabloid is twice this size (11 × 17 inches, 279 × 432 mm) and broadsheet is twice as big again (17 × 22 inches, 432 × 558 mm). *Note:* These are not the same as the sizes of broadsheet and tabloid newspapers in the UK.

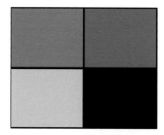

FIGURE 12.32 *The four ink colours used for printing*

Elsewhere, the ISO (International Standards Organisation) paper sizes are mainly used. There are two main series, A and B, with a third, C, that is used for envelopes – an A4 page will fit unfolded into a C4 envelope. In each series, each size is exactly half the previous one, so A4 is half A3 and A5 is half A4. The A series is the most commonly used, with A4 (210 × 297 mm) being the standard for most desktop printers.

The other consideration when selecting paper is its weight. This is measured in grams and is the weight of one square metre of paper. From this, you should be able to work out that the higher the stated weight of the paper, the thicker it will be. The thickness of the paper will not affect the printed image quality, but heavier paper will give a more substantial feel to a publication. Standard paper for photocopiers and printers is usually 80 g/m^2. High-quality paper used for letterheads may be 90 g/m^2 or 100 g/m^2, while 120 g/m^2 is thin card.

CRC – the final layout

As we defined at the beginning of this unit, camera-ready copy (CRC) is a final copy of the document exactly as it will appear when it is printed; that is, it is ready to be photographed to create the printing plates.

Binding and folding

Once a document is printed, the pages must be folded and bound to create the final publication. Although this is the final stage in the process, the method to be used will need to be considered at an early stage of design, as it may affect the layout of the pages.

Folding

There are many different ways that a single sheet of paper, such as a leaflet, can be folded. These have names such as a C fold, a gate fold and an accordion or zigzag fold. Some of these were shown in Figure 12.4 (page 157).

Many multiple-page documents are printed with two pages on one sheet of paper and then folded – creating an A5 booklet by folding A4 paper, for example. Look closely at the top of the spine of this book. You will see that it is made up of several folded booklets.

There are two issues when folding multi-page documents. Firstly, the pages will need to be organised so that they appear in the correct order

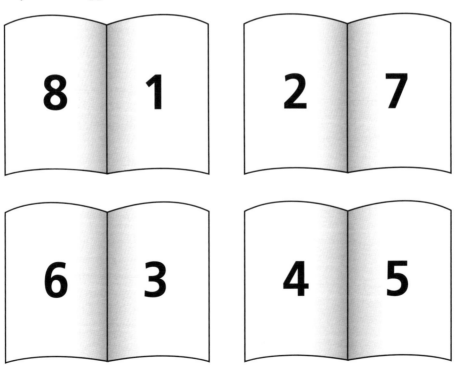

FIGURE 12.34 *Page layout for an 8-page folded booklet on two sheets of paper (the spreads on the right are printed on the back of the spreads on the left)*

when folded. For example, if a booklet has eight pages, page 8 and page 1 will need to be printed side by side with pages 2 and 7 on the other side of the paper. Next, pages 6 and 3 with pages 4 and 5 on the other side (see Figure 12.34).

The other issue is known as creep. If you fold a number of sheets of paper in this way, the outside edges will not be exactly even because of the thickness of the paper. Try folding eight or ten sheets of A4 paper in half like a booklet. Professional publications are trimmed after folding but this means that the outside margin would be slightly narrower on the middle pages than the outside ones – the text creeps towards the outer edge. Because of this, the inner and outer margins may need to be adjusted very slightly from page to page to take account of creep.

Binding

There are several different ways that the pages of a publication can be bound together. The choice will depend on the purpose of the publication, how hardwearing it needs to be, the appearance and the cost. You will also need to consider whether the publication needs to lay flat when it is open. Some of the options for binding a publication (Figure 12.35) are:

* ring binding – possibly the simplest method, it only requires holes to be punched, and sufficient margin provided to do so

* comb binding – plastic teeth fit through rectangular holes in the edge of the paper

* spiral binding – a continuous coil of plastic or wire passes through holes in the edge of the paper

* thermal binding – tape or plastic strips are fused to the edge of the document using heat

* saddle-stitching – two or more staples are placed along the fold of a folded booklet

* side-stitching – staples are placed about 5 mm from the edge and a cover may be glued on.

Given the right equipment, you could use any of these binding methods. There are other binding methods that are only used in the publishing

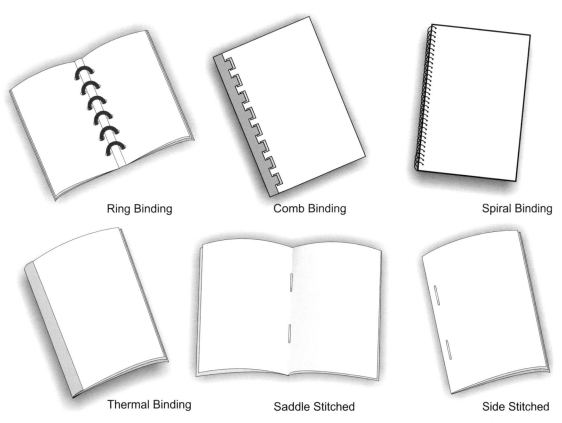

Ring Binding   Comb Binding   Spiral Binding

Thermal Binding   Saddle Stitched   Side Stitched

FIGURE 12.35 *Different binding methods*

industry. Paperbacks, booklets, telephone directories and some magazines use a method called perfect binding, while hardcover books use a process called case binding.

Printing devices and services

Small quantities of publications can be produced using desktop printing devices. The most commonly used are inkjet and laser printers. Inkjet printers spray the four ink colours (CMYK) onto the paper to create the image. The type of paper used is crucial in the final quality of the image. As the ink is wet, it soaks into ordinary paper, even that designed for inkjet printers, resulting in a poor-quality image. Using photo-quality or glossy paper reduces the amount of ink absorbed, resulting in greater definition in the final image. However, photo-quality paper is much more expensive than standard inkjet paper. Laser printers use dry toner, which is transferred to the paper from an electrically charged drum and then fused to the paper using heat. High-quality images can, therefore, be produced on ordinary paper. A colour laser has four toner cartridges and four print drums to provide the four CMYK colours. The paper passes over all four drums, picking up the separate colours from each. Although colour lasers are becoming much cheaper to buy, the running costs are still high, as replacing all four toner cartridges can cost almost as much as the printer.

For larger volumes of printing, the services of a commercial printer will be required. In some cases, the commercial printer may use a process called digital printing, which is essentially the same as a high-volume laser printer. This tends to be used for relatively short print runs, as it is comparatively slow compared with other methods. One advantage of this method is that variable data can be incorporated, so it is ideal for mail merge applications.

The most common commercial printing method is offset lithography. This works on the principle that oil and water do not mix. Four plates are created for the CMYK colour separations. This can now be done using computer-to-plate (CTP) technology. This uses electronic files to create the plates, rather than having to develop large film negatives to create them. Each plate is wrapped

around a cylinder and water is applied to the non-image areas. The ink, which is oil based, is applied to the image areas. The inked plate comes into contact with a rubber blanket wrapped round another cylinder and transfers the image onto it. The paper passes between the rubber blanket and a third cylinder, where the image is transferred to the paper. This is repeated for the remaining three colours. The paper never actually touches the plates, which is why it is known as offset.

Presses can be sheet fed, where individual sheets pass through the press, or web fed, which uses very large rolls of paper, as in newspaper printing. Commercial presses are very fast and have very high-quality output. Other commercial printing processes include silk screen, gravure and flexography.

> **Think it over...**
>
> Use the Internet, encyclopaedias or the library to find out what is involved in the silk screen, gravure and flexography printing processes.

Proof-reading

You will have, hopefully, been proof-reading your work since you produced communications in *Unit 1: Using ICT to Communicate*. Proof-reading is the careful checking of the content and layout of a document to eliminate any errors. In professional publishing, specialist proof-readers are employed to check page proofs before they are published.

Proof-reading is more than simply reading the text. If you do so, it is easy to miss errors as your mind reads what it thinks is on the page, rather than what actually is. Proof-readers focus on each word as well as the grammar and punctuation of the text. Other aspects that are checked include the consistency of capitalisation, figure captions and numbers, references to figures, tables and appendices and so on.

Proof-reading symbols

Proof-reading symbols are a form of shorthand that tell the typesetter what changes need to be made to proof copies. Typesetters do not read the text, so proof-reading symbols have two parts, a mark in the margin and one in the text where the change is needed. The typesetter will scan down the margin looking for marginal symbols; only when one is found will the typesetter look along the line of text to locate the change required.

Without some sort of standard, different proof-readers could use all sorts of different symbols. Typesetters then might not know what the proof-reader meant by each symbol. To overcome this, a British Standard was devised. Most proof-readers

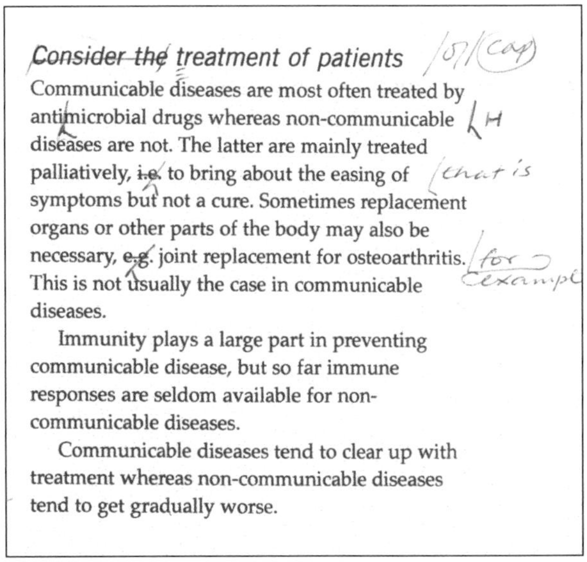

CORRECTION	MARGINAL SYMBOL	SYMBOL IN TEXT
Insert in text the characters or words shown in the margin	new text ⋏	⋏
Delete	⸆	⊢——⊣
Leave unchanged	⊘	··········
Change to italic type	⊔⊔	———
Change to bold type	∿∿	∿∿
Change capital letters to lower-case letters	≢	encircle characters
Change lower-case letters to capital letters	≡	≡≡≡
Start new paragraph	⌐	⌐
Run on (no new paragraph)	⌒	⌒
Transpose characters or words	⊔⊓	⊔⊓
Indent text	⊏	⊏
Insert space between lines or paragraphs	mark starts in the margin and extends between the lines	——c or ⌐

TABLE 12.1 *Some common proof-reading symbols (BS 5261 Part 2 (1976))*

FIGURE 12.36 *A proof copy marked up with BS 5261 Part 2 (1976) proof-reading symbols*

use symbols according to BS5261 Part 2 (1976). Some of these are shown in Table 12.1, while Figure 12.36 shows how they are used.

After the syllabus for this course was finalised, an updated British Standard (BS5261C:2005) was introduced.

External factors affecting the production process

In any production process there will be factors outside of your control that affect the process. You need to understand the impact these factors may have and how to cope with them.

Problems that might arise

Deadlines are important in the publishing industry. A programme for a concert is of little use if it is not completed before the concert takes place. Magazines have a specific publication date each week, month or quarter, and money will be lost if they are not published on time. Teachers and students want a textbook like this one before the course starts. Exam papers must be printed and distributed before the date of the exam. When you are producing a publication, you need to start at the required publication date and work backwards, allowing time for each process and setting deadlines for each stage in the process. You also need to build in some extra time, if possible, to allow for tasks overrunning the specified time. That way, even if some interim deadlines are missed because someone is ill or equipment is not working, you should still be able to meet the final publication date.

Setting up a timetable is also useful, as many of the people working on a publication, such as copy editors, graphic artists and proof-readers may be freelancers. This means that they do not work for a single publishing company, but sell their time and expertise to the company (and others) for particular projects. These people will not be required for the whole process, so it is important that the publishing company knows when they will be required, so their time can be booked. If one stage goes over deadline, it may mean that another freelancer may have booked time but have no work to do, losing them money. When the work is required, the freelancer may have already moved onto another job, so someone else may have to be found at short notice, often costing the company more money.

Legislation and copyright material

You will have learnt about the Copyright, Designs and Patents Act (1988) in *Unit 2: How Organisations Use ICT*. This act essentially gives the creator of a piece of work ownership of it. For example, I own the copyright to this unit of the book because I have written it. If you look in the front of the book, you will see the symbol © with my name after it. As well as written work like books, the act applies to many different types of work including computer programs, drama, music, art, sound recordings, films and radio and television broadcasts. Even the way the pages of this book are arranged and the different font styles used are covered by this act.

The act makes the copyright owner the only person who can, for example, copy or adapt the work or issue copies to the public. Other people can only do these things with the permission of the copyright owner. For example, where I have used work that other people have created, I have had to obtain permission to use it and, in some cases, the publisher will have had to pay the owner of the copyright to use the work.

There is a widely held assumption that information and, in particular, graphics that are downloaded from the Internet are copyright-free.

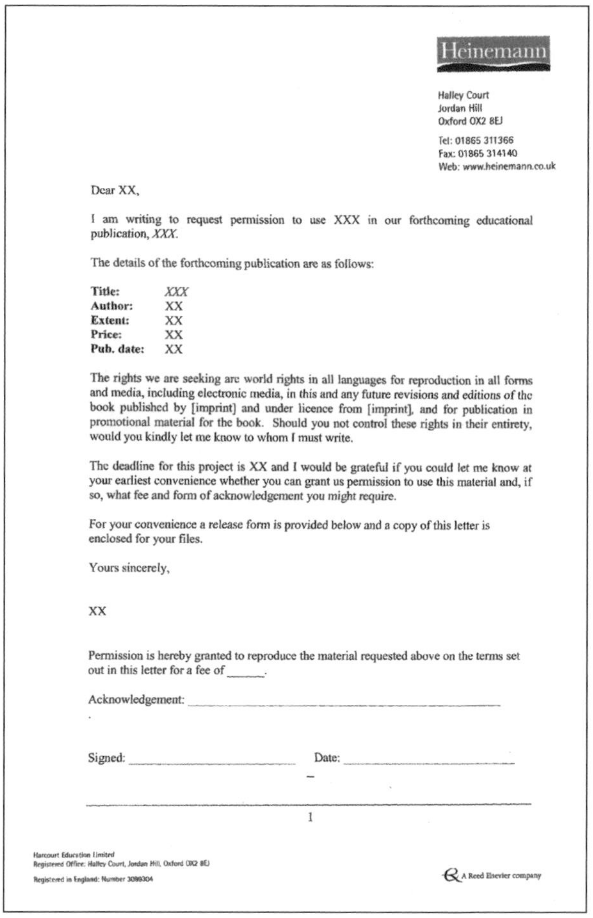

FIGURE 12.37 *A letter requesting copyright clearance*

This is not the case – you should assume that anything that has been created has copyright unless there is a specific statement to the contrary. However, the Copyright, Designs and Patents Act (1988) is very complex and does allow some copyrighted material to be used for educational purposes. On this basis, you are unlikely to be breaking the law if you use a downloaded image in one of your assignments. However, if you are creating a publication that will be distributed, you will need to obtain permission to use it.

To obtain permission, you will first need to find out who owns the copyright. This is not always as straightforward as it seems. For example, it is not the subject of a photograph who owns the copyright, but the person behind the camera. Once you have found the copyright owner, you will need to write to them explaining exactly what you want to use and how you want to use it. You will also need to say how the publication will be distributed and to whom. Will it be for educational purposes? Will it be free or will people have to pay for it? Will it be sold for commercial gain, to raise money for charity or simply to cover costs? The more information you can give, the greater your chance of a favourable response. Figure 12.37 shows a letter that Heinemann use to request copyright clearance. If the response is negative or the copyright owner asks for payment that you choose not to make, you must not use the material in your publication. To do so would break the law.

CASE STUDY

Francefilez is a UK-based company that produces brochures advertising holiday homes in France and Spain. You have produced a CRC of a new 20-page brochure for them. The brochure will be saddle stitched and 10,000 copies are required.

Write a letter to Francefilez to accompany the CRC that gives a full breakdown of the final production stages that the brochure will need to go through and any external factors that may affect production.

Completing a commission

The assessment evidence for this unit requires you to produce materials for a client. This will involve:

* negotiating the brief with the client
* considering the ICT tools available
* choosing a suitable solution in consultation with your client
* planning the presentation of your portfolio of ideas to your client
* getting product approval from your client.

Negotiating a brief

You will need to interview your client thoroughly to ensure that you have all the information

you require to design and produce the material required. If possible, the interview should be carried out face to face, as it will allow the client to give you copies of material to be included and examples of existing documents. It will also be easier for you to ask supplementary questions to ensure you have all the information you need. If a face-to-face meeting is not possible, you will need to conduct the meeting by telephone, email or letter.

In any event, you will need to prepare a list of questions to ask your client. The exact questions will depend on the material you are to produce, but the following questions will almost certainly need to be on the list:

* What type of material is required?
* What will its purpose be?
* Who will be its audience?
* When is the material required?
* Is there a house style that must be followed?
* What content is required?
* Does it already exist and, if so, in what format?
* If the materials relate to an event, what are the details – date, time, venue, etc?
* How many copies will be required eventually?

This list is not exhaustive but will give you a starting point. Further questions will almost certainly arise during the interview. You will also need to agree a deadline with your client for the final submission of the CRC. You may in addition agree dates for further meetings so that you can present your portfolio of ideas and check that your chosen solution meets the client's needs.

Think it over...

In a group, consider what other questions you might need to ask your client when negotiating a brief.

You will need to make detailed notes of your client's responses. You may want to record the interview so that you can refer back to it.

However, if you do, you will still need to make written notes of the interview to submit in your portfolio. You may find that you have not got all the information you need. In this case, you will need to contact your client to arrange another meeting, or ask additional questions over the telephone or by email. Make sure you keep a careful record of all contacts with your client and the outcomes of those discussions.

ICT tools available

As part of your discussions with your client, you will need to consider the possible software and hardware that could be used to produce the materials. For example, you might discuss whether word-processing or DTP software would provide the best solution, or which particular DTP package would be most suitable. You should consider the implications of choosing different packages, such as the tools available or the ability to position items accurately. You may also need to consider the types of files used for graphic images, perhaps trading quality for smaller file sizes. Hardware considerations may include the type of printer to be used, the availability of disk space or the method used to transfer files.

Inevitably, the hardware and software chosen will depend on what you have access to, but you will need to consider other possibilities not available to you.

Choosing a solution

You will need to choose the final solution in negotiation with your client. You will need to sketch a number of different ideas for the design and layout of the material that you can present to your client. The final solution will need to meet the purpose of the brief, match the intended audience and meet with your client's approval.

Presenting ideas

In order to choose a final solution, you will need to present your initial ideas to your client. You will need to set up a meeting to do this. Before the meeting you will need to plan how you will present your ideas. This should be done in a professional way. You will need to present your design and layout sketches in a portfolio along with explanations as to why you feel each meets the purpose of the brief and matches the intended audience.

Getting product approval

When your client has agreed on the final solution, you will need to follow the design-stage procedures to create the CRC. This may involve the client at certain points, such as the presentation of page proofs, when any required changes can be made. The final stage will be presenting the CRC to the client for approval. You will need to include a letter with the CRC, presenting it to the client and requesting approval. You should also explain in the letter the further stages required to produce the final published document.

> **✱ Remember**
>
> When you are researching into a brief, planning your response and presenting your solution, you will need to know about and follow, as far as possible, publishing industry procedures. These will include
>
> ✱ the drafts/design stage
>
> ✱ the enhancement of presentation of text
>
> ✱ the final production stages
>
> ✱ procedures for coping with external factors.
>
> You will need to be able to
>
> ✱ negotiate a brief
>
> ✱ consider ICT tools available
>
> ✱ choose a suitable solution
>
> ✱ plan your presentation of your portfolio of ideas
>
> ✱ get product approval.

12.4 Final printed output

The effects achieved in the final printed output will depend on the type of printer, the type of media and the printer resolution. We have touched on some aspects of this in previous sections but will bring it together here.

Types of printer and media

Three of the main types of printer in common use are:

* laser

* dot-matrix

* bubble-jet or ink-jet.

Each uses a different method to transfer the image onto paper or other media.

In a laser printer, electric charge is used to attract dry toner onto a drum. The toner is transferred from the drum onto the paper and fused to it using heat. Both monochrome (black and white) and colour laser printers are available. In a colour laser, the paper picks up toner from four separate drums to add the four colour separations of cyan, magenta, yellow and black (CMYK) and combine them to produce the final image. As dry toner, rather than liquid ink is used, laser printers produce high-quality output on any quality of paper. However, since heat is used in the process, it is important that any acetate used is produced for use in laser printers.

A dot-matrix printer is a type of printer known as an impact printer. The image is transferred to the paper by a set of pins that push an inked ribbon onto the paper. Although it is possible to use a dot-matrix printer to print graphics, they are usually used to print text. The quality of the print will depend on the number of pins used to create each character. Both 9-pin and 24-pin printers are available: 9-pin printers produce very low-quality output with rough edges to the characters; 24-pin printers produce better-quality output but still not as good as other types of printer.

Most dot-matrix printers are monochrome. Colour dot-matrix printers are possible – a four-colour ribbon moves up and down to give each colour, and each row is printed four times to combine them. However, such printers are extremely slow and very noisy. Dot-matrix printers used to be the cheapest available, but this is no longer the case. The economics of scale and demand has lead to ink-jet and even some laser printers being cheaper to buy than dot-matrix printers. The main reason that dot-matrix printers are still used is that, because they use

impact, they can transfer the output to the second and subsequent copies of **multi-part carbonised paper**. Dot-matrix printers also have sprockets to move the paper through the printer, so that they can be used with continuous **fan-fold paper**.

Key terms

Multi-part carbonised paper: Sometimes called NCR paper. Paper that has two or more sheets attached on top of one another. The paper is treated so that anything written or typed on the top sheet is transferred to those beneath it. This is due to the pressure applied, so does not work with non-impact printers such as lasers or ink-jets. Multi-part paper is often used for invoices and order forms so that one copy can be sent to the customer or supplier and the other kept as a record.

Fan-fold paper: Paper that comes in a continuous strip, rather than separate sheets. There are perforations between each sheet so that they can be separated after printing, and the paper is folded along the perforations, like a concertina. A series of holes along each edge of the paper fit on the printer sprockets to move the paper through the printer. Depending on the application, there may be perforations between the holes and the printing area so that the strip of holes can be removed.

Bubble-jet and ink-jet printers transfer the image to paper or other media by spraying microscopic jets of liquid ink. Chemicals within the ink ensure that it dries very quickly once on the paper, but if you print a photograph or other dense image on a sheet of ordinary paper, you will see and feel how wet the paper can become. For this reason, bubble-jet and ink-jet printers are most susceptible to the quality of paper and other media used.

Ordinary paper designated as being for ink-jet printers produces acceptable results in monochrome. However, if used for colour printing, some of the ink is absorbed and bleeds into adjacent colours resulting in poorer print quality. Various qualities of paper can be bought that are coated to reduce this ink absorption. Generally speaking, the better the paper quality, the higher the quality of the printed output will be. To achieve the photo-quality images advertised by printer manufacturers, you would need to use photographic-quality paper, either glossy or matt. It is also possible to achieve high-quality images on acetate, either for use as overhead transparencies or for other purposes. However, the correct type of acetate sheets must be used and you must print on the correct side of the sheet. Acetate sheets for use with ink-jet printers have a slightly roughened printing surface so that the ink can stick to it.

The quality of the paper will have some impact on the quality of the image obtained from laser printers. High-quality, glossy paper will produce images that have even more vibrant colours than those printed on standard paper. We have already seen in Figure 12.33 (page 189) how the colour of the paper used affects the final printed output.

As well as paper and acetate, fabric can be used as a medium for printed output. However, in most cases, the image is not printed directly onto the fabric, but onto a heat-sensitive transfer that is then ironed onto the fabric. As fabric has more texture than most paper, this texture will affect the appearance of the image.

Printer resolution

Printer resolution is measured in dots per inch (dpi). The specification for a printer will usually quote both the horizontal and vertical resolution, as these are not always the same. This is the maximum possible resolution. In general terms, the higher the number of dots per inch, the higher the quality of the printed output will be. However, the resolution of the image will also have an impact. For example, if an image is scanned at a resolution of only 300×300 dpi, printing it at 600×600 will not improve its quality.

✳ Remember

Different effects can be achieved in the final printed output depending on

* the type of printer
* the print medium.

The printer resolution will also affect the quality of the printed output.

UNIT ASSESSMENT

For the assessment of this unit, you will need to negotiate a brief for and produce a CRC document of at least ten pages. The best way to achieve this is to find a real client that needs a suitable document produced. Failing this, your teacher will need to give you the brief and act as the client so that you can carry out the negotiation process.

You must *not* pretend that you have a client and make up the discussions. This unit is all about the process of producing material to meet a brief, not just using DTP software.

The following list would provide suitable briefs but there will be many more:

* a magazine for your school or college
* a sixth-form prospectus
* a programme for a concert or play
* a set of leaflets for local tourist attractions
* an instruction booklet for a database or spreadsheet solution
* a brochure for a local business
* a newsletter for a local community or club.

Whichever brief you are working to, you will need to carry out and produce evidence for the following tasks.

Task A

Take notes during an initial meeting (and any subsequent meetings) with your client, negotiating and amending a brief for the production of a CRC document.

Mark Band 1

You will produce notes taken during the negotiation of a brief with the client. These notes will evidence discussions of possible software solutions together with some discussion of alternative solutions. You do not consider deadlines.

Mark Band 2

You will also take notes during subsequent meetings with the client. Your notes evidence a full discussion of possible software solutions and a full discussion of alternative solutions. You agree deadlines.

Mark Band 3

In addition, your notes will fully evidence all discussions of all possible software solutions together with the implications of each of these solutions.

Task B

Draft and produce a CRC of your final document to meet the brief and, in doing so, show that you can create and capture images, as well as import material from other packages, utilise object libraries such as clip art, and select and develop images to meet the style and content of the final copy as negotiated with the client.

Mark Band 1

You will produce different types of information to be used in the final copy, and will follow the design-stage processes including most of the following: sketching different initial document designs, following house style, creating master page layouts, presenting page proofs, producing artwork sketches, setting text orientation and creating style sheets.

Mark Band 2

Some of the information you produce needs to show evidence of information having been manipulated to explore different styles of presentation. You will follow, and demonstrate through annotation, all of the design-stage processes listed under Mark Band 1.

Mark Band 3

You will produce, edit and use a variety of types of information for inclusion in the final copy, and will show clear evidence of using a range of editing and manipulation tools available within the appropriate applications package in order to explore different means of presenting the same information. You will follow and demonstrate through identification and explanation all design-stage processes listed under Mark Band 1.

Task C

Produce a CRC document, of at least ten pages, that combines different types of information, presented to the client for approval, together with a letter which correctly describes the final production stages and external factors that may affect the completion of the final published document.

Mark Band 1

You will produce a CRC of the agreed design that combines information. The document should be appropriate for the audience and free of errors. There will be little evidence of the use of editing and formatting techniques. You will produce a final letter that presents the CRC to the client for their approval with little or no consideration of how the project could be broken down into a series of stages.

Mark Band 2

The combined information in your CRC will be used in an appropriate manner. The document will show clear evidence that you have used more than four text styles and more than two text attributes and that you have edited a piece of imported text. Your final letter to the client will include a full breakdown of the further stages required in the production of the final published document.

Mark Band 3

In addition to the requirements of Mark Band 2, your CRC will need to show clear evidence of the effective use of advanced editing and formatting techniques. Your final letter to the client should explain how the final product can be altered at a later stage.

Task D

Evaluate both the layout and content of the final copy and your performance.

Mark Band 1

You will comment on the effectiveness of your CRC, with some overall indication of how your work might be improved in the future. You will describe how the CRC was produced, with some suggestion as to how your methods could be more efficient in future. Your report may contain errors in spelling, punctuation and grammar. You will comment on your actions and role in solving the problem and identify areas for improvement.

Mark Band 2

You will provide an analysis of your CRC, identifying the strengths and weaknesses in order to refine the solution, and will take into account client's feedback and describe how you produced the CRC document. Your report will contain few spelling, punctuation and grammar errors. You will include an analysis of your own performance by identifying your strengths and weaknesses, with some suggestions for improvement to the overall process.

Mark Band 3

You will provide a full critical analysis of your CRC, identifying how well it meets the initial brief and any subsequent refinements, taking account of user feedback. You will include a discussion of how you produced the CRC document following the negotiation of the brief through to the submission of the document for approval. Your report will be consistently well structured with few, if any, spelling, punctuation and grammar errors. You will use the analysis of your own performance to show how you will address any weaknesses to be more effective in the future.

Artwork and imaging

By studying this unit, you will

* develop skills needed when producing artwork for inclusion in publications

* improve your skills in creating and modifying artwork and images for display

* understand the kind of work undertaken by designers, illustrators, newspaper artists and draughtspersons

* understand the laws and guidelines that relate to the use of ICT

* extend previous ICT graphics work

* cover the skills and techniques used in the creation of more complex artwork and images

* work alongside a client whose needs you must meet

* research a brief, plan a response, and produce a quality solution.

As you work through this unit, you will need to apply the knowledge and skills you gained from *Unit 1: Using ICT to Communicate*. The knowledge and skills gained whilst working on this unit may be applied to other units within this qualification.

Introduction

This unit is about creating final images in response to a request from a client. In producing these images, you will use a range of techniques and learn new skills. Some of the work you produce will have been created from scratch using different packages, whilst other work will show how you can edit an already existing digital image. The digital images you edit and manipulate will have been captured using a range of different sources, such as digital cameras, scanners or (with permission) the Internet.

This unit encourages you to be imaginative and to use a wide range of techniques and tools, as well as giving you the opportunity to reflect on what you have learned. If you enjoy the work you do, experiment with some of the wide range of different effects and tools, and keep a diary of what you have learned, you should find this unit both interesting and rewarding.

How this unit will be assessed

This unit will be assessed on a portfolio of evidence that you will produce. The assignment at the end of this unit will provide you with the evidence to complete the portfolio.

What you need to learn

You need to learn about
* developing artwork and images
* editing artwork and images
* file formats
* final printed output
* laws and guidelines
* researching a brief, planning your response and presenting your solutions.

13.1 Developing artwork and images

Whilst working through this unit, you will produce a range of different images. Some of these images will be drawn freehand, whilst others will be from existing sources. So that you can use images from different sources, you will need to learn how to capture images from different sources. These sources will generally be:

* digital cameras
* video cameras and players
* scanners
* online resources.

Once you have created your images, you will then need to develop them further. This may be by adding text or shapes to an image, combining the image with another to create a new image or using different software tools and techniques.

Before you start

Artwork and images may be developed using any graphics manipulation software you choose. You may even decide to complete some tasks using other software, such as merging different elements into a new graphic which may be completed in some word-processing packages. In order to complete this unit, you will need to work with a range of graphics tools. Basic tools include the selection, eraser, freehand draw, text and flood fill tools. More complex tools, such as masks, layers, filters and effects, are generally only available when using more advanced graphics manipulation software.

However, if we do not have any artwork with which to work, there is not much that we can do in this unit. We will start by looking at creating a new image of our own and then go on to look at capturing an image that already exists.

Creating an image file

Strictly speaking, there are many ways in which we can create image files. When we take a digital photograph, we are creating an image file. The same is true when we scan an image into a computer using a scanner. So that we avoid any confusion, this section will begin by looking at creating a new image from scratch. We will then go on to consider how we might add other elements to an image to create a unique image of our own. We will also consider using digital cameras and scanners to capture an image of something that already exists.

Before we start, we need to consider some basics that apply to all digital images. Because you will come across these as soon as you create a new file, we will start at this point.

All data held on a computer system is held in different files. Images are no different to this and so when you create a new image, you are creating a new file. To create a new file, either click on the New option on the File menu, or use the New icon. This will bring up the New Image dialogue box.

The New Image dialogue box lets you set the fundamental characteristics of your image before you carry on. Most software packages will let you set the dimensions of your image, the resolution and the background colour. We shall discuss each of these in turn.

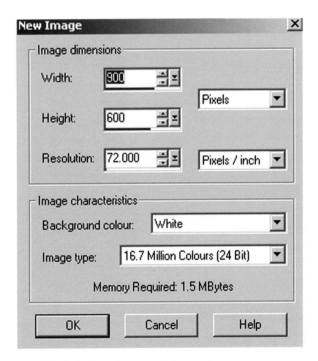

FIGURE 13.1 *New Image dialogue box*

Dimensions

The dimensions are the width and height of your image. This can be set by **pixels**, which are the individual dots of colour that make up your image, or by inches or centimetres. You may decide to have a large image, but remember that the larger the image, the greater will be the file size for the image. Therefore, you may need to think about your storage capacity, especially as you are likely to be working with a few different images during your work on this unit.

Resolution

Resolution is how many pixels are used in the image and is set by either pixels per inch or pixels per centimetre. The higher the number of pixels you use, the denser any colour is, which has implications for printing and file saving. It is probably best if you work with the default setting at this stage.

Key terms

Pixel: A small dot of an image; the smallest part of an image that can be displayed. Images are made up of many pixels.

Resolution: Describes how clear the image will be and is based on how many pixels are in a fixed area of an image. This may be described as pixels per inch or pixels per centimetre.

Background colour

The background colour is the colour of the background. This is a simple concept, but one which can have big effects. The choice of background will depend on how you will use the final image. For an image that will be used as part of an animation, and so will need to move across a screen, you would usually choose a transparent background. For all other images, you would usually use white, unless you have a very clear idea about the final image you will produce, in which case you may choose a specific colour.

Other possibilities

You may be given the option of changing the image type. This usually refers to the bit depth of an image. As you increase the bit depth, so you increase the amount of colour you can use in your image. Most software packages will give you some indication of the amount of RAM memory that you will need on your computer to create a new image. If the indicated RAM is more than your computer has, you should decrease either the colour depth or the image size.

Finding the properties of images that already exist

It is all very well knowing how to set the dimensions and resolution of new files, but you may need to work with images that already exist. Luckily, this is a simple process and is a case of accessing the image information. Figure 13.2 shows how this information is presented when using Paint Shop Pro.

There is a lot included here, but the main items of information that interest us are those grouped under Image. Specifically, we are interested to know that the image measures 291 pixels by 327 pixels and, secondly, the resolution is set at 72 pixels per inch.

We have now considered how to set up a very basic image. In fact, if you have followed the explanations and created an image as you have read through the unit, you will have an image which is completely one colour with no detail at all. You could consider such an image a canvas on which you are going to work later to create a far more complex finished product.

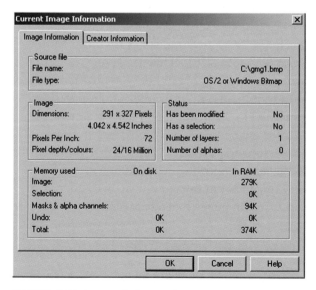

FIGURE 13.2 *Image information*

We shall now go on to look at other ways in which you could create an image file. The image files you create using the following techniques can all be edited to create far more complex images.

Capturing an image

When you capture an image, you are creating an image file based on an existing source. This existing source may be an image that you have found, in which case you would probably use a scanner to capture it, or it may be that you want to create an original image based on something that physically exists, in which case you would use some form of camera. The final option is that you may choose to capture an image from a piece of film or a DVD, in which case you would connect the player to your computer via a video card or use your computer's DVD drive. We will look at each of these methods in this section. As we move through, you will see that (other than the method of capture) the basic principles are the same for each method.

Using a digital camera

You will probably have used a digital camera already and be well aware of the advantages it offers compared to using a traditional camera.

In the same way that digital cameras attached to mobile phones are trying to become more like standard digital cameras, so digital cameras are trying to offer at least the same as a traditional camera. As technology has improved, digital cameras have developed in two main ways. The first of these is the amount of pixels that can be included in the picture, which affects the quality of the final photograph. The second is the effects tools which are available. Some of these tools are replicated in the image manipulation software you are using and are probably best applied once the image file has been transferred to your computer, whilst others will allow you to change the shooting conditions of the camera to suit the conditions at the time of taking the photograph.

You should refer to your camera's user manual for a complete breakdown of the possibilities offered by your camera, but, as a basic skill, you should be able to set the resolution of any photographs you take.

The beauty of a digital camera is the flexibility it offers. Modern digital cameras are very light and are small enough to fit into a pocket, yet offer you a range of facilities which would require a good deal of specialist equipment if you were using a non-digital camera. For example, if you were not using a digital camera, you would need a large bag just to carry the peripheral lenses and other items that come as standard with a digital camera.

Transferring photographs to your computer
Once you have taken photographs, you will need to transfer them to your computer. You could use a cable, such as a firewire cable, in which case you are physically connecting your camera to your computer. This will require the use of specific software that must be installed on your computer.

Alternatively, you could use a card reader, which will read the data directly off the camera's memory card. This is a simpler process, but you do need to take care not to touch the metal terminals on the memory card as this can affect how well the card works.

Theory into practice

If you have used a digital camera before, you may want to skip this section.

You have been asked to take some photographs for inclusion in a yearbook for your class. These photographs should include some of people around you and others who will remind you of your time in education. The photos may be of anything you choose, but at least one should be a panoramic shot of your school or college taken from a distance.

Use your digital camera to take up to ten photographs that suit this brief. You should experiment with the different settings available to you on the camera to suit the conditions and the subject matter.

When you have taken these photographs, transfer them to your computer using the most appropriate method.

Write a report explaining how the different settings on your camera helped you to take effective photographs. You should include the photographs you have taken in your report.

Capturing an image from a video or DVD player

Still images can be captured from videos and DVDs, but you will need to take some care over copyright before you capture images from shop-bought videos or DVDs. Most DVD playing software will allow you to capture what is effectively a screen dump by simply pressing a button, although the quality of the image may not be very good.

You can also purchase specialist software that will allow you to capture images from a video or DVD player connected to your computer via a video card. Images produced in this way can be of a high quality. The software used to capture these images will allow you to make some changes to the image before you work on it further in your chosen image manipulation software.

Using a scanner

A scanner is an input device that scans an image or text on paper and then transfers the image to a computer. There are different forms of scanner, but the one you will most likely use is a flatbed scanner, where the piece of paper with the object to be scanned is placed face down on the glass surface. The scanner then shines a strong light onto the piece of paper and measures the light that is reflected back. This information is then used to create a digital version of the original image.

As with any other device, a scanner comes with its own operating software and, as you would expect, each model of scanner's software is different to any other model of scanner. However, as time has gone by, the software which operates scanners has become more similar, so you can usually expect all scanning software to have just about the same features. Of these features, the ability to preview your image before it is finally scanned is probably the most convenient.

The main features available when you choose to scan an image are:

* image size

* image type

* image resolution.

The image size is usually set by drawing a box around the area of the previewed image that you want to capture. This will then limit the area captured, thereby removing the need for the image to be cropped at a later date. The larger the dimensions of the scanned image, the larger will be the file size of the scanned image.

The image type is a choice of what format you want the scanned image to take. At the most basic level, this may be black and white or colour. However, if the scanner you are using is not a colour scanner, this option will be unavailable to you. A colour image will result in a larger file size, whilst a black and white image of the same size and resolution will have a smaller file size, simply because a colour image needs to save more data than a black and white version of the same photograph.

The file size of the scanned image will depend on its resolution. The more pixels per centimetre or inch, the more data will need to be stored about the image and so the file size will be larger.

As your scanner is already attached to your computer, the image will automatically be transferred to your hard drive once the scan has been completed.

✱ Remember

The image size, type and resolution will all affect the final file size of your scanned image.

Using images in online information systems

The most important online information system, and the one you will probably use most frequently, is the Internet. However, any resource that is available to you because your computer is connected to another computer is considered an online resource. If you are working on a network, you may find image libraries that you can use. These will either have been purchased by the person responsible for maintaining the network or will be images that other users of the network have taken and put onto the network for others to use. You may also have access to clip art libraries, which are full of professionally drawn images that you can use and edit to suit your needs. Use of these images is effectively free at the point of use, which means you can use them as you wish, but some bought resources may require you to acknowledge the source. As this is a legal issue, make sure you understand the implications of using any images you find on your network before you proceed.

If you do find images available on your network, these may be opened in the usual way, as long as you are able to find the image library, from the Open dialogue box accessed via the File menu.

The Internet is full of useful images that you could use in your work. However, these images will generally be covered by copyright restrictions. It is possible to use images found on the Internet, but this is generally only possible with the copyright owner's permission. However, it is also possible to subscribe to an online image library, which will let you use images in return for a fee.

Capturing images from the Internet

Images found on the Internet are made up of data and, just like any other form of file, can be large. The speed of download will depend on the Internet connection you are using and, even with a broadband connection, the time taken can be significant.

There are three main methods of acquiring images found on the Internet. The first is to download the image to your computer as you would any file. This is the standard way of downloading images contained in emails, for example.

The second and third methods are available to you as options within the right-click menu of your Internet browser software. If you are using a computer on a network, your network manager might have removed this facility, as the right mouse button is a very powerful tool that allows the user greater control and access to the computer system than the network manager may choose to give.

If this facility is available to you, you can either copy or save the selected image.

FIGURE 13.3 *The right-click menu options within Internet Explorer*

If you choose to copy the image, you can then paste it. Some graphics manipulation packages, such as Paint Shop Pro, give you the choice of pasting as a wholly new image or as a new layer. We will discuss layers later on in the unit. Other graphics manipulation packages are not quite as flexible and you will need to have set up an image file in preparation for the copied image to go into. Once it is pasted, the newly created image file needs to be given a suitable filename and saved.

Alternatively, you can choose just to save the image directly from the right-click menu. The advantage of this is that you will be able to use the image at a later date. If you do choose to save the file, it will be saved using the filename it was given at the time it was created.

✱ Remember

Downloading from the Internet does not come without some risks. You should be aware of copyright issues and the possibility that the downloaded file might contain a virus.

Developing images

You will need to use a range of techniques to develop the images you create or capture. Some of the more complex tools will be explained later in this unit, but for the present we will focus on some of the more straightforward tools. We will not look at them in any great depth, as you will probably have used most of them before.

Before we carry on, it is important to highlight the very great difference between bitmap and vector graphics.

Bitmap graphics are sometimes called raster images. These images are digital images made up of many coloured pixels. Because each pixel used in the image has to have a colour assigned to it, the file size of bitmap images can be very large. Scanners, for example, create bitmap images.

Vector graphics software, however, are saved as a series of instructions that make up shapes within an image. These instructions are basically mathematical formulae that control the location and characteristics of these shapes.

So how does this affect the work you will be doing? In the simplest terms, images created using bitmap software are usually more realistic, but as each pixel in the image has a set colour, the image will distort and edges will appear jagged if the image is resized by any significant amount. However, images created using vector graphics software are not created pixel by pixel and so, as an image is resized, the instructions about the shapes that make up the vector image are reapplied, so that the image is effectively redrawn. This removes the possibility of any distortion.

As vector graphic images are stored as a series of instructions, rather than information on each pixel in the image, they have a far smaller file size than bitmap images.

Some of the tools we will now look at are only used with bitmap software, whilst others are for use on vector software. It should be clear as you work through which is which.

Drawing basic shapes

The specifications for this unit ask you to include polygons. A polygon is a shape with at least three sides. Therefore, a triangle, a square and a pentagon are all examples of polygons. A circle, however, is not. When you work with basic

FIGURE 13.4 *Basic shapes available in Microsoft Paint*

shapes, it would be a good idea to make sure that you include at least a few with at least three sides.

Any image manipulation software will include the ability to draw basic shapes. Even the simplest packages include basic shapes such as squares and circles, and allow you to choose the style you want for each shape.

Figure 13.4 shows the basic shapes available in Microsoft Paint.

You can find out more about how to set the style of a line in the next section. More complex software packages will come with a range of shapes, some of which are quite complex.

FIGURE 13.5 *Images created by combining basic shapes in Microsoft Paint*

You will also be able to create your own shapes by using lines and curves.

As well as creating images from scratch, it is also possible to edit images by adding basic shapes, such as squares and circles, to them.

How to...

Create a complex shape by combining basic shapes

Figure 13.6 is a combination of circles and rectangles.

For most software packages, simple shapes such as circles and rectangles are drawn by clicking where you want the shape to start and dragging to where you want the shape to finish. A circle, for example, would be drawn by clicking at one spot and dragging towards the bottom left or right until a complete circle has been drawn. If you were to drag immediately to the left or right, you would create a flatter, more eliptical shape. Depending on the software package you use, the colour of any shape may be set before it is created or may be added later as a fill.

1　Open a graphic manipulation program of your choice. Create a new file of 500 pixels width and height. Choose a white background.

2　Start by drawing two circles to represent the wheels of the train.

3　Add the main body of the train. This is a rectangle that sits just above the wheels. The rectangle should be just wider than the distance between the two outside edges of the wheels.

4　Continue to add circles and rectangles to create the side-on view of the train shown in Figure 13.6.

FIGURE 13.6 *Basic shapes train*

Creating artwork by combining text, pictures and basic shapes

So far, we have looked at creating simple images. We will now look at combining text, pictures and basic shapes to create a complex image.

Figure 13.7 combines the three main elements – text, pictures and shapes. The original image started as a simple digital photograph. A blue square and a red circle were then added. Finally, the text was added.

Tools and techniques for creating artwork and images

Figure 13.7 is a simple image, but it gives you an impression of what may be created by combining a very basic understanding of the facilities available to you with any graphics manipulation package. Now is the time to start looking at some of the more complex facilities and how they may be used to create far more complex images.

Layers

Layers are an extremely useful tool when working with digital images and definitely come into the group of tools that are associated with the more in-depth software packages. Software packages such as JASC's Paint Shop Pro and Serif's PhotoPlus allow you to achieve good effects when working with this particular tool. Unfortunately, more readily available software, such as Microsoft's Paint software, does not include this facility.

Imagine that you have two sheets of clear plastic. The first sheet has a background image on it,

FIGURE 13.7 *A combination of text, pictures and shapes*

such as a range of hills, whilst the second sheet has a castle or a far-off town on it. By laying these sheets on top of each other, you will create the illusion that they are one image of a castle on a hill. If you now move the sheet with the castle on it, you can place the castle in a completely different location and, again, there is the illusion of a complete image.

As you work with these two sheets, you may want to add other items to the picture. You could add these items to one of the two sheets you have already and therefore fix the relative position of the new image to any that was already on the sheet. Alternatively, you could create a new slide altogether and combine this sheet with the other two to create new images, where each item may be moved around as much as you wish. Assuming that the sheets you are using are perfectly transparent, you could continue adding more and more sheets with more and more items on them until you have a complete picture.

This is exactly how layers are used in image manipulation software. Layers are added to an image to carry extra items and, until the layers are merged into one new image, each layer is effectively a different sheet lying across the other layers. Just like the plastic sheets, layers can be moved or edited as is necessary. However, one advantage that using software has over using plastic sheets is that we can position the layer where we want it to be and then switch the layer off so that we can work on the other layers. This saves us having to reposition the layers when we return to the completed image.

Creating a layer Typically, you will be working with images that you have created elsewhere. These may be images that you have scanned in or used a digital camera to capture. These images will have one layer. This is called the background layer. However, you will probably want to add other elements, just as if you were working with clear plastic sheets.

A layer may be created in many ways. The simplest is to create a new layer from the layer menu. If you choose this option, you will usually be able to set various options at this stage. You can then add elements, such as text or shapes, to this layer.

The next section looks at adding all or part of an image to another image. So that this does not get too complicated, we will call the image you are working on image 1 and the image you want to import image 2. As this is likely to be how you use layers, it is best to read this section carefully before you continue.

You may want to combine another image, or selection from an image, with the image on which you are working. When you first try this, you may be surprised by the results, especially when what you thought was a small selection, taking up only a small part of image 2, appears huge once it is pasted into image 1. This is because the imported image keeps the properties it had before it was copied across. This may seem complicated at first. Basically, before you start to combine images or parts of images, it is a good idea to check on their dimensions. Keep in mind the transparent plastic sheet example. If you were to cut a picture out of a transparent plastic sheet and stick it onto another sheet, the cut-out bit would stay the same size it was in the original picture. If you wanted to make

it appear smaller, you would have to recreate the plastic sheet smaller and then cut it out.

This may be an onerous task with a transparent plastic sheet. With image manipulation software, it is simply a case of changing the dimensions of the image before you make your selection. This was discussed in the section on scale, but most software packages include an image resize button. However, once you have resized your image, you may need to zoom in to see enough detail. If you do have to resize your images, it is best to have both images set at the same zoom level so that you can compare the relative sizes.

Once you have made your selection from image 2, you will then use the Copy option on the Edit menu to capture the selection. If you now open image 1 and try to paste your selection, you will be given the option of pasting as a new image or as a new layer. As you want to add the selection to image 1, you should choose the layer option. Once this is completed, you now have a new layer which you can manipulate as you wish.

Working with layers Figure 13.8 shows a typical layers options box and gives us a good deal of control over how our layers perform. We will concentrate on four aspects in this section:

* switching a layer on and off
* changing a layer's position in the stack
* the merge properties
* opacity.

As you work with layers, you will find other tools that are as useful, such as the ability to group layers so that you can work with more than one at a time, but we have a lot to get through here, so we need to be selective!

Switching a layer on and off In this case, the dialogue box shows that we are creating an image with three layers. The layer named 'trees' is currently invisible (it has been switched off). This means that it is still there, but that we just cannot see it. This makes it easier for us to work with the remaining layers. The layer named 'child' is highlighted, which shows that it is the active layer. As you create layers in your work, it becomes increasingly easy to change one layer when you think you are working on another.

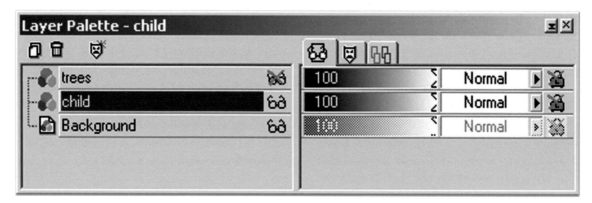

FIGURE 13.8 *A layer dialogue box*

As a general guide, before working on a layer, just check that it is the active layer before you waste time applying changes to the wrong layer.

In this example, the first (bottom) layer is the background whilst other layers are laid on top. The background is created automatically and the best way to think of it is that it is like the canvas on which a painting is created.

Because the layer named 'trees' is currently switched off, this allows us to work on the other layers without the distraction of the 'trees' layer. This is an extremely useful option when you are working with many layers. In this case, to switch the layer on and off, you simply click on the Glasses icon. A layer that is switched off has a red cross through the icon. Other software packages may use an icon of an eye or something similar, but, fundamentally, this option is always there and the icon is going to be something that represents being able to see. If you cannot find this option at your first attempt, look again – it is there.

Changing a layer's position in the stack The dialogue box shown in Figure 13.8 also shows the layers in the order they appear in the image. In this case, the layer called 'child' is behind the layer called 'trees'. This will mean that areas of the 'child' layer will be hidden by areas of the 'trees' layer. We would like to position the 'child' layer in front of the 'trees' layer, so we need to bring the 'child' layer to the very front. This is a simple process and is usually achieved by clicking on the layer you wish to promote and dragging to the new position in the stack of layers. As layers at the top of the stack are in front of those below them in

the stack, this will be achieved by dragging a layer higher up the stack.

The merge properties It is also possible to change how layers merge into each other. This can be changed by accessing the drop-down menu in the dialogue box or by accessing the Layer Properties dialogue box. Most software packages have a similar range of merge types and it is worth working through a few options before you carry on much further with this unit, but for now it is probably best to leave the merge option set to 'normal'.

Setting opacity The opacity option is usually set using a slider or a spinner. However opacity is set, the range is from 100 per cent to 0 per cent. At 100 per cent opacity, the image is totally opaque and obscures everything that is below it. As the

FIGURE 13.9 *The child layer*

FIGURE 13.10 *The final image composed of three separate layers*

opacity decreases, more of the underlying layers show through. A 50 per cent opacity shows 50 per cent of the active layer and 50 per cent of the lower layer, whilst a 25 per cent opacity will show 25 per cent of the active layer.

And finally... Remember the example of the clear plastic sheets at the beginning of this section? The problem with these is that they can be disturbed; despite the illusion of being one image when they are all laid on top of each other, they always remain separate sheets. When we have finished working with our layers, we will need to merge them all into one background layer. This is sometimes called 'flattening' an image. We must do this at the end of our work for two simple reasons. Firstly, computer-generated images that contain layers require a good deal of memory and, secondly, as we will see later in the unit, many file formats cannot cope with layers. The problem is that, once we have merged our layers, the layers are lost and the image becomes far more difficult to edit; so, if you are working with layers, make sure that you only merge layers when you are ready.

To merge layers, select the 'merge all' option from your layers drop-down list. Some software packages give you the option of only merging visible layers, and leaving the invisible layers unmerged. This is because invisible layers are usually changed to white at the merging stage,

which is probably not what you wanted to happen. However, if you want to use the image in other formats, you will have to merge all layers at some time, so try to avoid leaving layers that are transparent unless you want them to appear white at the end of your work. Take care because, once you have merged your layers, the action can only be undone if the image file has not been closed.

> ✳ **Remember**
>
> Only new layers can be added to a background image. Remember that not all graphics formats can cope with layers. If you save using one of these formats, such as JPEG, the image will be created as a background image. It is extremely difficult, if not impossible, to split a background image into the original layers.

Object overlay

You may wish to create complicated graphics by combining two or more elements. As you add elements, you may find that more recently added elements obscure those that already existed on the page. This is fine if you have planned your work and are adding elements from the bottom first. However, this is unlikely. What is far more likely is that you will suddenly realise that an image that you had hoped to be in the front of a graphic will disappear or that an image you had hoped to shine through from underneath will effectively be lost.

There are two possible remedies to this problem, both of which may be dealt with by manipulating the layers included in your graphic. The first lies in the order in which layers are displayed. As explained above, if you want a layer (or the object on that layer) to be displayed on top, make it the topmost layer. If you wish to have a layer appear with elements of other layers bleeding through – which means you can see them through the other layer – then make your topmost layer less than 100 per cent opaque.

Using different styles

So far, the only images you have created have used a solid colour fill. However, many graphics manipulation packages allow you not only to add a solid colour fill but also to add different style of fill. You may also use different styles for other elements used on your image, such as lines and text. A good example to use here would be adding a line to an image. The line could be dotted, dashed, dotted and dashed, solid, have arrows at either or both ends, or even throughout. Similar options exist when working with the fill tool. Once a shape has been created, you can decide whether or not to fill it in with a simple colour, a simple or repeated pattern or even, in some cases, with an image.

There are many options and you will undoubtedly have come across some already. If you have not, spend a few moments now trying out the different styles of line, fill colour or text that your software package lets you use.

Shading and rendering

Shading and rendering are great techniques to learn, and may both be applied to graphics that you create. Both techniques are the process of adding colour and shadow to an image, either to exaggerate an image and emphasise the dark and light sections, or to add a 3D feel to a graphic.

In Figure 13.11, the original graphic is shown with no shading. The graphic in Figure 13.12 does have shading, which has been applied to emphasise the shape of the glass. Because this shading runs in the same direction and is sympathetic to the general shape of the glass, the glass appears far more three dimensional than the original graphic.

This effect was achieved using an airbrush. The opacity and density of the tool were then reduced

so that any lines added were gradually more subtle than the main graphic.

This technique of using an airbrush to add a light fill to a graphic may also be used to add shadows to graphics and to hide or add elements that are included in a graphic. This technique, for example, may be used to add leaves to trees in a digital photograph, despite the original photograph having been taken in the depth of winter!

Rendering is the effect gained by adding colour *and* shade so that the object looks solid and real.

Importing images

The decision about which image to use and how it should be captured is an important one. We have already discussed the many ways in which you can capture images for use in a project. As you plan your project, you must decide how to acquire any images you need. For example, you may decide you need to include an image of a local landmark. Should you use an image from the Internet or should you take the photograph yourself using a digital camera? The image on the Internet will probably look more professional than yours, but, as you will be aware, may be protected by copyright.

The process of importing images into graphics software is quite straightforward. By far the simplest way in which a graphic created using one piece of graphics manipulation software may be opened in another is to simply use the Open command on the File menu. Many modern graphics manipulation software packages will work with graphics created in other packages

FIGURE 13.11 *A basic graphic of a glass*

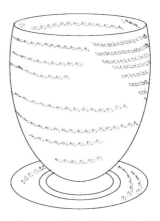

FIGURE 13.12 *The graphic with added shading*

and the list of supported file types, including those associated with specific models and manufacturers of digital cameras, keeps growing.

The second-simplest method is to use copy and paste. Using this approach, the image you want to use is simply pasted into a graphic, either as a wholly new graphic or as an addition to a graphic that already exists. However, there is some confusion here, as some packages will ask you whether you wish to paste your image as a new layer or as a new image. This is where an understanding of layers is useful. If you choose to add the image as a new layer, you may edit the imported image as a layer in its own right. Once you have completed any editing, you may merge or flatten the image to create an image with only one layer.

As well as copying and pasting images that already exist, it is possible to capture directly from an input device, such as a scanner. In many graphics manipulation packages, there is the facility to import directly, from either a scanner or a digital camera. When working with scanners, this can be a very useful tool, as it is frequently the case that it is easier to use the import function with a graphics package than it is to use the scanner's own software.

Adding borders
A border is an area around an element or the whole of a graphic. Adding a border is usually a process of setting a border within a dialogue box and then applying the border to the graphic. You should remember that any border will increase the width and height of your graphic by twice the width of the border. The border will usually be given the background colour currently in use by the software, so remember to change the colour to one which suits before you begin adding your border.

Controlling grid spacing and snap to grid
A grid can be a useful tool and is probably one that you have not yet used. When you work by combining images, you may have some problems aligning any new images properly. By using the grid, you are able to more accurately place new images onto your graphic. The grid is usually off by default, but you can turn it on from the View menu.

FIGURE 13.13 *An image with grid lines shown*

You can change the spacing of the grid to suit your needs. These changes are usually made in the Preferences tab. For more accurate work, you may choose to decrease the space between the grid lines so that, as you zoom in, you can align objects more easily. You may also choose to change the colour of the grid if you find the default colour hard to work with.

To make things even easier, most software packages will let you choose the snap to grid option. If this option is selected then, when a newly moved image is released, the software will automatically align an edge along the nearest grid line.

Scaling
Whenever you create a new image, you will be asked to set the dimensions for that image. This will involve you setting the width and height for your image. Similarly, you should now know that it is possible to set the dimensions when you acquire an image from an existing source.

Once you have created or captured an image, it may be useful to scale that image. You can do this using the Image Resize button (or equivalent), which, as you may expect, will let you change the width and height of the image.

There are a few extra options available to you when you use the image resize tool. Firstly, you can choose whether or not to change the size of one layer or all layers. Secondly, and possibly most importantly, you can choose whether or not to maintain the aspect ratio. With the Maintain aspect ratio option ticked, the ratio between the width and the height of the image is kept constant. This means that if you make the image twice as wide, it will become twice as high. By maintaining the aspect ratio, you will have made the dimensions of the image bigger but will not have distorted the image in any way.

If you untick the Maintain aspect ratio option, you will be able to change both the width and the height of the image independently and so will be able to distort the image. This can be a useful tool, but remember that, by distorting the image, you are changing the relationship between elements of the image. This may be a useful effect, but a stretched image may not look quite right and you may find that it is better to make a selection from an image and resize the selection rather than to distort the original image.

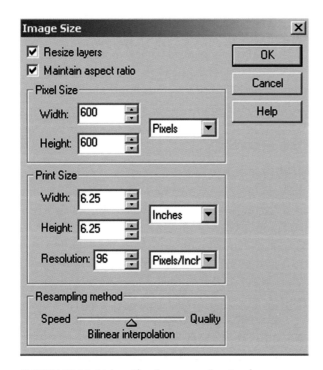

FIGURE 13.14 *Using the image resize tool*

As well as resizing the image, you can also resize the canvas. The canvas is the area available for the image to fit in. This might seem a bit complicated at first, but try to think what would happen if you had a bigger desk. If your desk doubled in size, the books, magazines, articles and CDs on it would not change in size; you would merely have more space in which to store more books, magazines, articles and CDs. The same applies to changing an image size.

The option to resize a canvas is a useful one. If you choose to increase the size of your canvas, you have more area with which to work and so you can fit more images into your final piece. However, if you choose to decrease the size of your canvas, you will lose detail from the edge of any work you have currently done. This detail can only be recovered by undoing the last action, so be careful not to resize an image and then close it immediately afterwards.

Using object libraries, including clip art

We have already discussed using online resources in the section on using images in online information system. **Object libraries** are collections of different objects that you may use in your work. Some graphics manipulation software packages include object libraries. Paint Shop Pro, for example, includes many objects in the 'picture tube'. This collection of objects ranges from the useful to the bizarre, and some excellent results and hours of fun can result from playing with the different images and effects available.

Clip art is a more complex object library and may be regarded as a resource in its own right, rather than an aspect of, or tool included with, a specific software title. Clip art comes free with many packages and it is possible to buy specialist clip art that gives the technical report writer a wealth of images that may be used to enhance a report or other document.

The beauty of object libraries is that most objects included are vector-based. This means that, whatever the size of the image into which these objects are imported, the object may be expanded to suit, without any fear of distortion or pixelation.

Sharpening

Sharpening is the process of making objects included in an image stand out more by exaggerating the colour differences between these objects. Because this changes the graphic, sharpening is treated as being a distortion tool. The distortion options, including sharpening, are dealt with in Section 13.2: Editing artwork and images.

Removing scratches and blemishes

Most graphics manipulation packages include a tool to remove scratches and blemishes. In each case, you simply choose the tool, highlight the area that you wish to remove, and then use the tool. The scratch tool will look for areas outside of the highlighted area that match with those inside and copy pixels in to replace those that have been obscured by the scratch. The blemish removal tool will look for areas of colour that stand out from the others in the selected area and will replace his 'rogue' colour with the majority colour and then generally blur the whole area.

Both tools can be extremely useful. The scratch tool may be used to remove evidence of damage to an original image from a scanned version, whilst the blemish removal tool may do more for the confidence of a person than any cream or lotion could ever achieve!

Darkening/lightening shadows

Anyone who has ever taken a photograph with a traditional camera has taken at least one photograph that is superbly grouped, with a brilliant background and where everyone is smiling, but that is either too light or too dark. If you had taken this photograph with a digital camera, you would probably just delete it and take another. However, how would you be sure that the perfect group with the perfect smiles all at the same time will be willing or able to pose in exactly the same way?

If you were a professional photographer working in a changing situation, or where time is important, such as at a wedding or major sporting event, you may never get the same photograph again. You would probably not delete the image, but would use the brightness/contrast effect to change the light levels in the image.

This is a simple task and can save the most underexposed or overexposed photograph. This effect allows you to change two properties of the image. Firstly, you can change how dark or light an image is. Secondly, you can change the contrast in the image. The contrast is the spread between darkest and lightest values and can be used to emphasise the darker or lighter regions within your image.

Dodging and burning

Dodging and burning are two further options that some software packages, such as Adobe PhotoShop, offer. The dodge tool is used to lighten pixels, whilst the burn tool darkens pixels. How this differs from the brightness tool discussed above is that the dodge and burn tools may be applied to areas of an image, whilst the brightness settings apply to the image as a whole. This means that if you have an image where the face is underexposed, for example, or you want to add emphasis to one area only, you are able to use the dodge tool to lighten that part.

Alternatively, if you had an image that was well exposed, but the background distracted the viewer from the subject of the image, you could use the burn tool to darken the background, thereby getting the effect of an overexposed background, combined with a well-exposed foreground.

Controlling page size and orientation

If you have come straight to this section from the importing graphics section, you have missed some great bits and should go back later to have a look. If you have worked through all sections in order, you are probably desperate to learn how important this section is.

The most important lesson to learn here is to do with zooming. The outcome of this lesson is that you will be able to copy and paste elements of one image into another and have the pasted elements appear at the size you intended. This outcome is achieved by stressing to you that it is possible to have two graphics open at the same time, and that both graphics may be shown at different levels of zoom. As any element cut from a graphic will be pasted at the same *real* size (as opposed to the on-screen or zoomed size), pasted elements cut from images at different zooms will often be either smaller or larger than you intended. When working with different graphics, a rule of thumb is to have both images set at a 1:1 zoom. This will allow you to check the relative size of each graphic and gauge how large a copied element will appear once pasted. Once you have seen both graphics, you can resize either so that the elements may be combined at the correct size.

Using the cut, paste, copy, crop and mask tools

One of these tools (mask) is quite complex and will need some in-depth explanation. It is included with the other four because it basically does the same thing, in that it obscures part of an image in the same way as the crop tool cuts bits

away or the copy tool selects areas, but there the similarity ends. The other four tools are common to just about every graphics software package you are ever likely to use.

The cut and paste tools are used together. The term *cut and paste* refers to moving a section of an image and pasting it to another location in the same or another image. This is an easy way of adding parts of one image to another and is one we will look at later when we learn about using layers.

The copy tool is equally straightforward; it copies a selection of an image if one has been made or the whole of an image if one has not.

The crop tool is used to select an area of an image that you want to keep. The area outside the selected area is discarded.

When working with graphics manipulation software, a mask does to a graphic exactly what it does to a face, in that it hides some bits and lets other bits be seen. Masks are applied to layers to obscure parts of the layers below.

Creating a mask Depending on your software, a mask can be created from selections, images, values within an image or from scratch. A mask

FIGURE 13.15 *Masks obscure what you want to hide and let the viewer see what you want to show*

can be set up so that it is transparent, which reveals the whole layer, or opaque, which hides the whole layer, or you can set the transparency at some level in between these extremes. Where a mask is created from a selection, some of the mask will be transparent and the rest opaque. The choice of how you create a mask will depend on how you want to work with what is in the layer.

How you create a mask will depend on the software packages you choose. As you create your mask, you may be asked how your software will use different values within the layer, such as its opacity. Some software packages will allow you to save your mask so that it may be applied to other images. This is particularly useful if you are creating a standard mask you want to use on many images.

Theory into practice

You have been asked to produce an image representing the separate cultures and traditions within Britain. This image will be presented within a mask created from the outline of Britain.

You should research into the cultures and traditions of England, Wales, Scotland and Northern Ireland and choose images that represent these cultures and traditions.

When you have chosen your images, create a merged image that shows these traditions, which will vary geographically within each separate country within Britain as well as across the different countries.

You should place each image so that it fits the geographical area or region to which it relates within the mask of the map of Britain.

Repeating patterns

There are many examples of repeating patterns in art. If your software allows, you may want to create an image that repeats a simple pattern so as to create a far larger graphic. This final graphic may be created by rotating the original pattern along lines of symmetry or may be a simple case of copying and pasting into a basic grid. This grid can be used to line all of the cells in your graphic so that each instance of the repeated pattern is lined up with those above, below and to the left and right – rather like the squares on a chess board.

Alternatively, the grid may be set up like the bricks on a wall, where individual bricks do not sit directly below their neighbours, but are offset by half of the width of the brick. This is called a half drop.

Some graphics manipulation packages include a repeated pattern tool. The explanation below shows how you may create a simple repeated pattern mosaic using the copy and paste tools.

How to…

Create a simple repeated pattern using copy and paste

This task is an application of copy and paste, but may be extended by rotating your image so that the final graphic is symmetrical.

1 Create a new file with a white background. A suitable size would be 500 pixels by 500 pixels. Using a line tool, grid this image into 50 by 50 pixel squares.

2 Create a second file with a white background. Make this file 50 pixels by 50 pixels. You may need to zoom in to work with this graphic.

3 Draw a simple shape on the 50 by 50 canvas. This will be the basis of your pattern.

4 Copy this simple pattern and paste it into the top left-hand square of your 500 by 500 pixels graphic.

5 Continue to build up the image by pasting your simple shape into the squares on your 500 by 500 pixels graphic.

Extension

1 Use the rotate tool to turn each pasted cell so that your graphic becomes more complex.

2 Instead of drawing a simple pattern, scan an image onto the computer and use this to create your pattern.

Working with colours

We have now discussed a wide range of tools, techiques and applications which can be used to create and enhance graphics. The final section looks at working with colour.

You may have come across the term CMYK when working with digital images. You may also

FIGURE 13.16 *A half drop repeating pattern*

have seen colours represented as being different amounts of red, green and blue (RGB).

The CMYK combination (cyan, magenta, yellow and black – referred to as 'key', hence the 'k') of colours refer to a printing process, where each colour is printed separately as a series of tiny dots, which when combined produces a huge array of colours. The RGB combination refers to the colours (red, green and blue) included in light that combines to make up the colours we see all around us. Many graphics manipulation packages will report a colour in terms of how much red, green and blue it contains. Therefore, a very strong blue may be described as being red 48, green 1 and blue 221, whilst a strong green may be described as being red 116, green 167 and blue 5. In each case, the numbers, which are up to a maximum of 255, represent how much of the three basic colours are included in the colour itself.

Both groups of colours may combine to make up the colours we see. Graphics manipulation packages allow you to work with these sets of colours to change how your images appear.

Colour balance

Colour balance is the balance between the cyan, magenta and yellow colours. As you adjust the colour balance, you change the levels of these three basic colours as they appear in your image. Try working with your software to explore the effect that changing the colour balance can have.

Colour correction

As well as working with the CMYK colours, you may need to further manipulate your graphics by using the colour correction tools. These tools work with the green, red and blue channels to control how these three colours balance against the cyan, magenta and yellow in your graphic. For example, if you are working with the red channel, you would be controlling the balance of red and cyan. As you reduced the red in your image, you would be replacing it with more cyan. Similarly, blue and yellow are matched, as are magenta and green.

Colour inversion

Colour inversion is the process of swapping a colour for its opposite colour. This is achieved by taking 255 away from each RGB value and wrapping around. The effect is to produce an image which is very much like a colour negative.

Working with levels

How you use the colour levels tool will depend on the software you are using. At the most basic, the amount of red, green and blue as well as luminance in your image can be displayed. This may simply allow you to analyse your image to compare different images. However, some software packages let you change the levels of red, green and blue, as well as how light appears on your image, so that you may draw attention to some features and enhance the overall effect.

Tones

To understand what can be achieved by using this tool, you need to know that light is made up of many different tones and that if these tones are changed, the quality of light itself will change. The spread of tones within your image can be shown on a histogram. In some software packages, these tones can then be manipulated by changing various values. The range of values open to being changed and how this may be achieved will also depend on the software package being used.

FIGURE 13.17 *Compressing the range of light*

Using the histogram tool to change levels

If you explore your software, you will find a histogram tool. This tool will, at least, allow you to explore the distribution of the main colours and light within your image. With more advanced software packages, you should be able to manipulate the distribution of tones to affect either the quality of the light or of colours used within an image.

Using the histogram tool can achieve some dramatic effects by changing the range of light or colour within an image. In Figure 13.17, the levels have been changed to make the image appear far more dramatic than the original. This was achieved by suppressing the range of light within the image so that there are far narrower light tones within the image, which gets rid of the softer tones in the middle ranges and creates an image in which there is strong contrast between light and dark. As the image is of a building, the contrast between light and dark is mainly around the windows and the shape of the building itself. These have now been emphasised.

Theory into practice

This activity will explore the effects of changing the tonal quality of images using the histogram tool. You should be aware that not all software packages allow you to manipulate this tool. Find the histogram tool in your software package and check whether you can manipulate your image from this dialogue box.

We will now compress the light tones in your practice file to make it appear more dramatic.

1 Open your practice file.

2 Open the histogram tool within your software package and choose Luminosity from the drop-down menu. Your histogram should have peaks to show the distribution of tones within your image and should also have a straight line from bottom left to top right. This shows that no distortions have yet been applied to the tones in the image. If you do not have a smooth line from bottom left to top right, you will need to reset this tool. There is usually an icon for this on the histogram dialogue box.

3 We need to narrow the range of tones available to us in our image. In the example above, this is achieved by dragging the arrowheads at the bottom left and bottom right of the histogram closer together.

4 As you narrow the range of light tones in the image, watch how the image in the preview screen changes. Keep changing the levels until you have a really dramatic effect.

Extension
Either undo your changes or reopen the practice image file. Try changing the red, green and blue levels.

Applying colour separation

Colour separation is an important concept if you are producing work that will be printed using an offset printing press. These printing machines use a separate plate for each of the CMYK colours and will, by a process of combining plates, create the colours that are used in each image. If your image is eventually going to be printed in this manner, you will need to print it

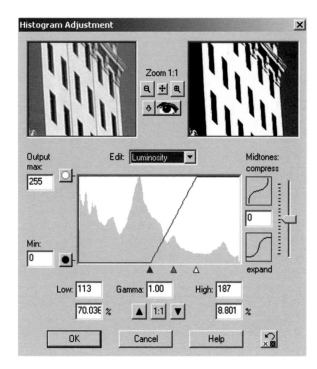

FIGURE 13.18 *Histogram for the image in Figure 13.17*

out with each colour separated so that each plate can be created.

Technical terms

As well as being able to use different tools and techniques, you should be able to understand and use technical terms such as washing, dithering, pixelation and posterisation. This section will explain these terms. The section on editing artwork and images will explain how each of these technical terms and the tools to which they apply may be used in your work.

Output format

And finally, what are you outputting to? You will spend many hours working on your solution to the brief. You do not want to find that your final output, which looked great on the screen, is not as good when it comes to be printed out.

We have already explained that if you work with RGB colours, there may be some difference between the way colours are represented on a monitor and when printed. The same may be true for resolution. It is highly likely that the monitor you use will be, by default, set to a higher resolution than the printer you use. As we

shall see, printers work by transferring ink onto paper. The amount of dots per inch of colour is the resolution of the printer. Most printers work at around 600 dots by 600 dots per square inch. At the minimum, your monitor is probably set to 800 dots by 600 dots in total, which usually works out as 72 or 96 dots per inch. This means that at the minimum default settings, your monitor is showing your work at a much lower resolution than your completed work will be printed.

13.2 Editing artwork and images

Now is the time to apply all that you have just learned. As well as understanding how different tools work, you should be able to use technical terms correctly. You will have come across some of these terms in the previous section, but, as you work through this section, certain of these technical terms will be highlighted in the Key terms boxes. You should make every effort to ensure that you understand these terms and know when to use them.

There are several tools with which you need to be familiar if you are to edit images to meet the needs of your client. You will have used some of these tools before, whilst others will have been explained in the previous section. Where you have used tools before, this does not mean that you will not have to use them again – remember that your client wants the overall impression to suit the needs of the project, and this may be achieved with more simple techniques as well as some of the more complex.

The tasks at the end of each section will let you practise using the tools studied here, but you may find it helpful to open the software you intend to use for this unit now.

Some of these tools may be applied to a selection within an image, whilst others may usually only be applied to the whole image.

Using basic tools and techniques

We have now looked at a very wide range of tools. When you work on your solution to the brief, you will need to apply these tools to your work. This section will explore some of the tools that we have already discussed and will introduce a few more that you may wish to use.

Transforming images

This is the process of transforming images from one state to another. Rotation, scaling and mirroring are all examples of how images may be transformed.

Working with scale

We have already discussed scaling and also looked at the importance of knowing at which level of zoom you are working. In this activity, we will look at combining two versions of an image. The second version will be an enlarged version of the first.

FIGURE 13.19 *A row of steadily shrinking Don Quixotes*

Work with scale

This activity works best if you have an object that you can easily cut around so that you get a smooth shape. An image of a building is useful, athough a person could also work.

1   Open a graphic file from your computer. Note the dimensions of this image.

2   Select and copy an area on the image. Open a new file the same dimensions as your original graphics file. Save this as **file 2**.

3   Paste your selection onto file 2.

4   Resize your original graphic so that it is about three-quarters of its original size. You could use the percentage resize tool here (set percentage to 75% for three-quarters).

5   Reselect and copy the selection. Paste it onto file 2.

You could now continue to rescale your graphics and paste in new objects, so that you have a row of steadily shrinking people or objects, as in Figure 13.19.

FIGURE 13.20 *The original image*

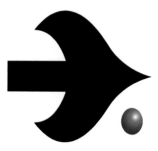

FIGURE 13.21 *90-degree rotation*

Rotate

This tool may be applied to the whole of an image, or just to a selection or layer of an image. The description of this tool will refer to an image, but it could as easily refer to a selection or a layer of an image.

If an image is rotated, it is spun around its centre point. Having decided to **rotate** an image, you need to decide by how much. This will involve a bit of basic maths. Remember that if an image is turned through a circle, so that it ends up facing the same way as it did before (which would be pretty much a waste of time), it will have gone through 360°; if it ends up on its head, facing in the opposite direction to before, it will have gone through 180°.

Some students become confused about the difference between the **mirror** tool and the rotate tool. These are two very different tools and you need to be sure of the difference. The mirror tool will reverse the image so that the left becomes the right and the right becomes the left.

FIGURE 13.22 *270-degree rotation*

FIGURE 13.23 *Mirror versus rotate*

The image in Figure 13.23 is a mirror of the original from Figure 13.20. Notice that the sphere has changed side and is now to the left of the arrow. If this image were to be rotated, the sphere would stay in this position relative to the arrow.

Distortion filters

There are many different types of **distortion** filters available and the choice open to you will depend on the particular software package that you are using. In the simplest software, you may only have the choice of a few filters; as the software you use becomes more complex, the options increase. Filters are usually found in the Image or Effects menu on your software.

As a basic guide, you should be able to blur, sharpen and add noise. The blur filter removes definition from an image by softening any hard images, whilst the sharpen effect does the opposite by finding adjacent pixels within the image and increasing the difference between them. Adding noise is basically the same as if you were adding noise interference to a radio show, but, instead of adding sound, you are adding random pixels with random colours. This will increase the graininess of

the image, which can be a useful effect for making an image look like it comes from a newspaper.

The blur filter will probably come with many different settings, such as blur, Gaussian blur, motion blur and soften. These all achieve a similar effect but work in slightly different ways.

Using filters

Many filters will have options within them, so that you may customise how the effect works on your image. As a simple rule of thumb, the higher the number you dial into the option box or the further along you move the slider, the greater will be the effect. For example, if you decide to blur an image, you may be asked for the intensity of the blurring. If you choose a low intensity, the image will be only slightly blurred; if you choose a high intensity, the image will be so blurred that you will be unlikely to make out any detail other than basic shapes. This can be useful if you want to remove detail from the background of an image so that the viewer's attention is drawn to what is going on in the front.

The motion blur lets you make an image appear as if it is moving. If you use this tool, you will be asked to decide on two options. One will be the direction in which you want the image to appear to be moving and the other is the speed. You will usually set the speed by changing the intensity.

In the Motion Blur dialogue box in Figure 13.24, the Direction (Angle) box has been set to 270°

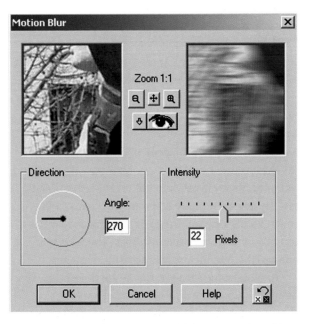

FIGURE 13.24 *Setting options within the motion filter*

and the Intensity box to 22 pixels. This software uses an intensity range of 0 to 40 and so the effect will be to make the image look as if it is going at a medium speed. Because the direction is 270°, the image will appear to move from right to left.

Filters are great fun and can really change how an image looks. However, when you come to produce your final assessment, remember that your client may not want you to use every filter available. Try to choose filters that add to the overall effect of an image, but that fit the needs of your client and the intended audience.

As you work through the activity below, keep notes of the effect of each distortion filter. This will help you with the final submission for this unit, as you will be able to show that you have explored different options and made informed decisions.

Theory into practice

Open your practice file.

Now go to the filters list in your software and explore how each of them changes your image. As you work through, you will find some distortion filters that may be useful to you when you are working on your final assignment.

Key terms

Distortion: Changing how an image looks without changing the basic content of an image.

Effects

Most software packages will include effects. These are commands which apply special effects to the layer, selection or image on which you are working. Some of these effects, like the brightness or contrast effect present in many software packages, will improve the original image. Others allow you to add items to the image, whilst others let you change the overall appearance of the image.

As you move through the range of effects available, you may discover that the results they achieve become more and more specialised or maybe even bizarre. Some effects let you make

your work look like an old newspaper, or as if it has been coated in hot wax. You may find effects that allow you to twist an image of a friend's face, or stretch it as if it were in a hall of mirrors. Not all software packages will have the same effects, but most will have many similarities between their effects and those included in another package. In some cases, different software packages might have the same effect but call it by a different name. The message here is to explore the package with which you are working and find out what it can do.

You can really have fun working with these effects, but remember that, as well as being creative, you need to meet your client's brief. You may find that using a distortion tool which pinches in the centre of an image and drags out the top and bottom is just what your client needs, but be ready to accept criticism if it is not.

Posterisation

This effect is standard in most advanced image manipulation packages and can be applied to a whole image or a selection. The effect is to reduce the amount of colours and levels of brightness in the image. This gives a flatter-looking image with bands of solid colour rather than smooth changes from one colour to another in an image.

This filter can achieve some good effects, especially when it is used on an image with few distinct colours but with many shades of the same colour, such as a face or an image made up of a lot of sky. A further option within this effect is to set the number of levels. The lower the number of levels, the greater will be the **posterisation** effect.

Key terms

Posterisation: Decreasing the levels of colour and light in an image to create bands of colour.

Other effects

Another simple effect is to render an image by adding a light source to it. The light source will depend on the software package you are using. Typical options include adding the sun or a spotlight or a candle. Again, this is a simple task and one which can have great effects, especially when used just above a building.

Use the illumination tool in Paint Shop Pro

Many other software packages include this feature.

To use this effect, open the Illumination dialogue box and choose one of the effects listed. The two options in Paint Shop Pro are sunburst and lights. You will then be asked to decide where to place the light source.

Different software packages will do this in different ways. When using Paint Shop Pro, you start by positioning a cross-hair on an image where you want the light source to be. When working with lights, you will also have to set the direction in which the light is pointing and the arc of the light (imagine the light like the cross-section of an upside-down ice-cream cone, with the light source at the pointed end. As you change the arc of the light, so you change the width of the open end of the cross section). Once you have decided on where the source should be, set the intensity if you need to, and you will have added your light source.

There are many more effects available to you. The skills you will have used whilst applying these effects will help you when you use the other effects that are available.

Theory into practice

Open your practice file.

Now go to the effects list in your software and explore how each of them changes your final image. As you work through, you will find some effects that may be useful to you when you are working on your final assignment. You will also find other effects which, whilst not directly useful at the moment, are full of potential.

Working with layers

You will come across layers in your work. Whenever you paste an object onto a graphic you will be asked whether you want to paste as a new image or a new layer. If you are adding the pasted element to another, you will paste as a layer.

CASE STUDY

Images for a wildlife park
You have been asked to apply for a commission to produce images for a wildlife park. As well as many wild and exotic animals, the park has a funfair for younger visitors. The manager of the wildlife park is aware that attendance at the park suffers both because it is totally outdoors and also because it has a quiet image. The application for this commission should include a list of some of the images you would plan to include and any effects and filters you would choose to use with these images. You should also include a justification for your choice of effects and filters with your application.

You decide to apply for the commission and submit a list of ten sample images.

Images for a nightclub
The owner of a local nightclub wants to relaunch the venue and attract a younger group of customers. She already has images for use on the poster for the relaunch, but needs some advice on how she can make the final poster more exciting.

The images are of people enjoying a party at the club, the resident DJs at the mixing desk and the inside of the club. Suggest and justify a range of possible effects and filters that could be applied to these images to make the club appear more exciting.

Once you have completed the task, compare your thoughts with the others in your group. You should be prepared to defend your choices if called upon to do so! If others in the group have different suggestions, make a note of the effect or distortion filter they have suggested and try to find out why they think it is better.

Extension
Look back over the suggestions that have been made. There may be some that you had not considered.

Spend some time looking at these other effects or filters. If you are keeping notes, update them now to include these extra effects or filters.

By following the steps below, you will be able to create an image that combines elements of different images in layers to create a new image.

You are going to produce a simple advertising poster for London which is intended to increase the number of tourists who visit the city. This will combine some very simple text and an image.

1 Open your software and create a new image. Your image needs to be reasonably large, but should let you work on other parts of your desktop. Something like 400 pixels by 600 pixels should be fine. Make a note of the dimensions you choose. Give your image a red background colour.

2 Add another layer to your work. Call this layer 'text', as it will hold the text 'London', and set it to 50% opacity. Use your text tool to type in the words 'London'. The choice of font is yours, but you need to use a large font size. If your software package gives you the choice, create the text as a vector so that you can change the size of the text if you need to, without losing any image quality.

3 Add a final layer to your work. This will hold an image of London. Try to choose one that suits the brief.

Open your image and check the dimensions. Remember that the image you are creating is 400 pixels by 600 pixels, so, as you want your image of London to fit on that image, you may need to change the dimensions of your London image. Depending on the image you choose, you may need to change the dimensions so that your selection fits. A bit of thought and planning at this stage will save you a great deal of time later.

Decide on how much of the image you want to use and either select the whole of the image or a selection. When you are ready to proceed, copy your selection.

Select the image you are creating and paste in your selection as a new layer.

If you want to work on the extension tasks for this activity, leave step 4 until you have finished working on your image. If you do follow this step and then decide you want to work on the extension task, you can undo the merge command as long as you have not closed the image file.

4 Merge or flatten your layers to create one background layer.

You have now completed this task and created a simple merged graphic using three separate layers.

Extension
This is a pretty simple image and you may decide that you need to include a few more details.

Use the add layer tool to add some more detail to your image. Possible additions could include an address for a tourist board, a logo, or a strap line aimed at enhancing the image's message. The choice is yours, but be imaginative.

Grouping

Grouping is where otherwise independent elements work together, rather like a group of individual fish all deciding to swim in one direction and then turning at exactly the same time.

When you work with graphics, there are many times when you will want to group objects into a new graphic which combines other elements. It is possible to combine text and graphics when working with word-processing software and you may well have done so to create logos.

Graphics manipulation software allows you to group layers. This is simply a case of adding a marker to each layer in a group, which defines it as part of the group. Paint Shop Pro does this by making layers part of the same numbered group, for example. Once grouped, each layer operates as if it were no longer an individual, but is happy to follow every other member of the group. This means that when you drag one member of the group, the rest will follow and will maintain their position relative to each other. This is extremely powerful and allows you to manipulate groups of objects far more easily.

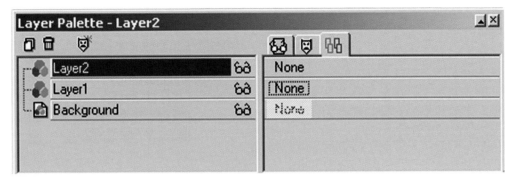

FIGURE 13.25 *No layers are grouped in this selection (Paint Shop Pro)*

The screen shots in Figures 13.25 and 13.26 are both from Paint Shop Pro and show an ungrouped layering and a grouped layering.

You should note that it is impossible for the background layer to become part of a group.

How to...

Group objects in Paint Shop Pro

The method of grouping layers is very much the same in other software packages.

To check whether a layer is part of a group, open the Layer Groups tab. Each layer's group button is initially set to the None button (Figure 13.25). To group layers, simply click on the None button. A '1' will appear (Figure 13.26). This layer will now be grouped with all other layers that are in this '1' group.

3D objects and tracing

You will probably want to include some graphics that look as though they have three, rather than two, dimensions in your work. You can either create these graphics or use an image library to find ones that suit your needs. If you wish to create your own 3D graphic, the earlier section on rendering and shading explains the process of creating the illusion of shape and depth by adding lines that fit the body of an object.

Tracing, also known as ray tracing, is the process of adding depth to 3D graphics by working out where the rays of light from a light source may end up once they bounce off an object. Because this is a potentially huge number of rays of light, we only really work with those rays of light that are going to bounce off and then hit our eye. By working with these rays, we are able to simulate what happens to real light hitting a real object and, by taking account of issues such as refraction, are able to create a graphic that creates a very realistic 3D feel.

Ray tracing is a complicated concept to discuss in any depth here and is unlikely to be available to you within the software with which you are working. However, there are lots of websites that deal with the topic and many include links to software that may be used to render shapes to create very lifelike images indeed.

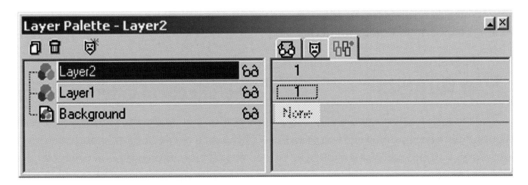

FIGURE 13.26 *Layers 1 and 2 are now grouped*

Suiting the needs of different users

The term *target audience* for a piece of artwork is the audience for which the artwork is produced. This audience may be very wide, made up of many different types of people, very narrow, focusing on a very distinct group, or somewhere between these two extremes.

Each target audience will have different needs, tastes and interests. The better able you are to identify these and to interpret them in your work, the more successful you are likely to be.

The term can also be applied to other forms of published material, such as music, newspapers and magazines.

You are required to make changes to your work to suit the needs of different target audiences. The changes you should make are to:

* resolution
* colour depth
* file formats.

In each case, the changes you make must be linked to the needs of the target audience.

Compatibility issues

In the next section, we will look at different file formats. You will learn that some formats are more suited to different software packages than others. For example, web browsers will only support certain types of graphics files. Similarly, as we have learnt, graphics that use the RGB colour palette do not produce faithful reproductions when printed; so, if you were working towards creating a printed product, you would be better to use the CMYK colour palette.

As you work through your project, you must be aware of the needs of your target audience and ensure that the work you produce meets these needs.

13.3 File formats

As you have been working through the activities in this unit, you will have been saving your work. As you did so, you will probably have noticed that you could save your file as one of any number of file types.

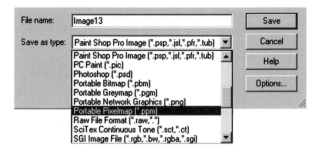

FIGURE 13.27 *Just some of the file types available in Paint Shop Pro*

You need to understand what these different file types offer and the effect that choosing different types will have on your image. Below we will look at the main options available to you.

Why do different file formats exist?

As mentioned earlier in this unit, computer images are made up of data. Some of these file sizes can be very large, especially with bitmap image files. As larger files can take longer to open, and take up more disk space, there is the need to compress image files to try to get over this problem. Different file types have been developed that deal with compression in different ways. At this stage, you need to know that some of these compression schemes can be lossy and others are lossless (for an explanation of these terms, see *Unit 11: Interactive Multimedia Products*, page 117).

As well as dealing with **compression**, different file types treat colours differently. As we shall see, an image that uses many colours will be saved differently from a file that has few.

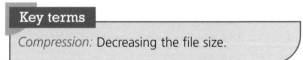

Key terms

Compression: Decreasing the file size.

The effects of different file formats

The first big issue with graphics files is the difference between bitmap and vector graphics. We will look at the range of file types available in the bitmap format and then go on to look at vector graphics.

Working with bitmap graphics

As you should be aware by now, bitmap graphics files include a great deal more data than do vector graphics files. For this reason, a lot of work goes into keeping the benefits of bitmap graphics types, but trying to cope with the issues to do with file types. Different file types deal with the issue in different ways and some ignore it altogether, which we will see as we work through our list of file types. This is, effectively, the key difference between bitmap file types. Before we carry on, we should start by explaining a few terms.

Compression

Compression is a term used for the process of making a file size smaller. With lossless compression techniques, this compression is achieved by looking for more efficient ways to store the image, and so there is no loss of information. Lossy compression techniques, however, will accept a loss of information as part of the compression process.

Colours

Different file types cope differently with colours. A simple black and white image will use only two colours and so the image would be saved as a list of simple yes/no options, one per pixel. This image would have an extremely small file size and would be quick to open. However, as technology has increased, so the amount of colours which **video cards** can display has increased and, alongside this, how colours are treated has had to change. Modern 24-bit video cards will display what is known as true colour. These cards can show at least 16 million different colours. When you have finished trying to name more than one hundred different colours, you will realise that if a card is showing 16 million, the difference between colours as you move through the range is extremely small! The colours used in 24-bit technology are so close together that the eye cannot see the minute differences, hence the name true colour. Not all file types will utilise all of the possibilities afforded by modern video cards and some, such as the .gif format (see below) will use 256 colours or fewer.

The implications and limitations of different file formats

We have already discussed the difference between bitmap and vector graphics. Now is the time to return to these graphics types and look at the importance of some of the different file types which you may use when working with these very different forms of graphics. We will start with bitmap graphics file types.

Bitmap file types

TIFF, PNG, GIF, JPG, RAW and BMP may be considered the 'big six' image file types and these are certainly the types which you will probably have come across before. It is more than likely that you will have saved any work you have already created in this chapter as one of these file types. If you have not, you will have saved your work as the default file type for your software package, which will be a proprietary format particular to the software you are using. We will come on to these proprietary file types later.

We will discuss each of the big six. We shall start with a format you have probably used already.

GIF format

The GIF format uses both compression and colour management to limit the size of image files. Compression is achieved by looking for patterns in the image, whilst colour management works by limiting the image to 256 colours. When the image file is saved, the software decides which are the best 256 colours to use to best represent the original image. If a colour is used which does not appear on the list of 256, the software will then use the next best colour available. This is, obviously, a loss of information, as the image no longer has the original colour, but one which the software considers is close enough.

The upshot of this is that the GIF can be lossless if your image uses less than 256 colours, or lossy if your image uses more than 256 colours.

BMP format

BMP is another format you will probably have come across. This format was developed by Microsoft and is the default format type for use in software such as Microsoft Paint. This format is uncompressed and so any images saved using this format will be very large.

JPG format

The JPG or JPEG software format was developed by the Joint Photographic Expert Group and this format really sets the benchmark for any format intended for storing photographic images. The **compression ratios** achieved using this format can be extremely high and yet the loss of information can be minimal. Compression is achieved by discarding any information which the eye would not notice. Colours are stored in 24-bit format and so there is little colour loss when using this format. Overall, whilst this format is of the lossy type, the information lost is unlikely to have any effect on the quality of the image saved.

TIFF format

TIFF files are usually very large, as the TIFF format normally uses no compression at all, therefore no information is lost. Some software does support TIFF files with lossless compression.

RAW format

RAW is a format used by some digital cameras. Reasonably good compression ratios can be achieved using this format, but, as each manufacturer uses a slightly different version of this format, unless you have an advanced software package which can deal with all the different commercial versions of this format, you will need the manufacturer's software to view your photographs.

PNG format

PNG is a format that uses lossless compression. It is a true-colour successor to GIF, but less widely supported.

Vector file types

There are two vector file types mentioned within the specifications for this unit. These are SVG and EPS.

SVG format

SVG stands for Scalable Vector Graphics. This format has been produced as an open standard by many different software manufacturers working together and so is very widely used in a range of applications, including mobile phones, global information systems devices and on the World Wide Web.

Because this format allows for the combination of vector graphics shapes with images and text, it offers an extremely flexible format with which you may work.

EPS format

EPS stands for Encapsulated PostScript and is actually a format used to send files to printers. However, it can be considered a vector format, because the files include the mathematical information which make up the vector files. Strictly speaking, files of this type are not always vector graphics files, as bitmap files may also be saved in EPS format.

EPS files are supported by a very wide range of graphics software and so this is a format recommended when moving vector graphics from one application to another.

Other formats

As you use image manipulation software, you will come across different file formats from those discussed above. It is likely that you will already have saved image files using different file formats. These will be the proprietary formats that have been developed by different software manufacturers to go with their software. Paint Shop Pro images are saved as .psp, whilst Photoplus images are saved as .spp and Photoshop image files are saved as .psd.

Each of these formats has been developed to make the most of the specific software to which it belongs and it can therefore offer more flexibility than the formats discussed above. Proprietary formats are more able to deal with layers, for example, and it is possible to save images with unmerged layers if you choose the proprietary format. Whilst it is probably best to use the manufacturer's format for saving whilst working on your images, you should save any completed files using one of the formats discussed above.

Effective use of file formats

So, which format should you use? Each format brings its own advantages and it is probably a good idea to save using a lossless format when you are still working on an image, but to save using one of the lossy formats at the end. The choice will depend on a number of factors, one of which is the amount of file storage space available to you on your computer. If space is not a problem, then you will not need to worry about compressing files as you are working on them. However, if you have a limited amount of space available to you, then uncompressed image files may be a luxury you have to do without.

As well as the advantages and disadvantages discussed in Table 13.1, you should be aware that not all image formats are viewable on the web. If you are creating images that you ultimately wish to use in a website, it is best to save them using either the JPG or GIF format, although more browsers are now supporting the PNG format. As this format is both lossless and produces relatively small files, this will probably be used more and more as web browser technology develops.

Saving in JPG format

Because of the ability to set compression ratios via the quality setting when saving in JPG format, this issue needs some thought. As we have discussed, when images are saved in JPG format, information which the eye will not notice is discarded. As the quality setting decreases, the compression ratio increases, so the amount of information discarded increases. At lower compression ratios, this will, indeed, be invisible to the naked eye. However, at higher compression ratios, the amount of information discarded may become significant. This effect is then amplified, as information is discarded every time a JPG graphic is saved.

As with many things in life, JPG compression is a trade-off between two choices: file size versus quality of image. The decision about where you set your quality setting will depend on the purpose of your image. If you are creating an image for use on the web, file size is important. In this case, a quality setting of about 75 is considered the industry standard. If, however, you are producing an image that will be used in a printed format, then quality becomes your most important factor. However, if you were producing an image for printing only, it is likely that you would be using a format other than JPG anyway.

FORMAT TYPE	PLUS POINTS	MINUS POINTS
.gif	Small file type. Great for images using less than 256 colours.	Photographs use more than 256 colours, so you will lose information.
.bmp	Few, if any, except that it is widely supported.	Large file size.
.jpg	Small file size with excellent picture quality.	Each time you edit and then save a .jpg image, quality is lost.
.tiff	No loss of information, so great for use whilst working on an image.	Large file size.
.raw	Proprietary software comes free with your digital camera. Reasonably good compression ratios.	Can only be opened using proprietary software.
.png	Allows a large number of colours. Great for images that have large banks of one colour, as good compression ratios can be achieved. Lossless.	Achieves lower compression ratios than .jpg format and so produces medium file size images.

TABLE 13.1 *Advantages and disadvantages of format types*

Set JPG compression rates

This is a straightforward process in most of the more advanced packages. However, this facility is not offered in all packages.

The following explanation is for Paint Shop Pro, but the process is similar for other packages.

1   In your software package, click Save as. From the drop-down menu, choose the JPEG format.

2   If you now click the option button, you will be presented with a slider and two radio buttons. The slider is used to set the quality. Choose a value between 1 and 99.

3   The two radio buttons govern how the image builds when seen on the Internet. When saved in standard encoding, the image builds top to bottom. With progressive encoding, the image starts as a rough image, but becomes sharper as the image builds. Choose whichever is appropriate.

13.4 Final printed output

For a full discussion on final printed output, turn to *Unit 12: Publishing*, page 196.

13.5 Laws and guidelines

You will already have learned about guidelines and laws that affect the day-to-day use of ICT. These guidelines and laws also govern how images may be used. Laws such as the Data Protection Act and the Copyright, Design and Patents Act affect which images you may use, what those images can show and also what you need to do to get permission to use other people's images.

The Data Protection Act 1998

The Data Protection Act 1984 (updated 1998) was introduced to control the use and storage of data about living people. The Act places the following restrictions on the use of data by registered data users:

* Data must be fairly and lawfully collected and processed.

* Once collected, data must be held or disclosed only for the purpose given at the time of collection, and this purpose must be lawful.

* Data held must be adequate, relevant and not excessive for the stated purpose.

* Data must be accurate and up to date.

* Data should not be kept any longer than is necessary.

* People who have data held about them have the right to see that data and, where decisions have been based on this data, they have the right to have the decisions explained.

* All data should be held securely so that it cannot be accessed or changed without authorisation.

* Data cannot be moved outside of the European Union unless the country where the data is being held has adequate data protection laws.

You may have heard stories about people who have not been able to take photographs of their children at the school play, or that schools are not permitted to use pictures of a class involved in an ICT lesson because this contravenes the Data Protection Act. You may even have been to events where you have been banned from taking photographs unless you asked for permission from everyone present. Section 36 of the Act explains that where images are being used 'by an individual only for the purposes of that individual's personal, family or household affairs (including recreational purposes)', they are exempt from the Act, so it seems that stories about parents being banned from taking photographs are more to do with over reaction than the application of the law!

To find out more about the Act, visit the Information Commissioner's website (via www.heinemann.co.uk/hotlinks, express code 2148P).

CASE STUDY

You work as a reporter for the *Ridgeway Times*. The following letter appeared in the letters section.

Dear Sir
I am writing to express my concern about the disregard for the law shown by members of the public at the recent sports competition at the Ridgeway Sports Fields. During one of the races, I noticed that a gentleman was filming from the side of the track. When I asked him to stop filming, he told me that his son was in the race and that, as his wife was unable to attend, he was filming it for her to watch later.

Whilst I have every sympathy for him and his wife, I pointed out to him that his actions were illegal and asked him to stop. He replied that he would not stop as he was only filming the race for his wife to see at home. I was disgusted and went to get a steward. By the time we returned, the filming had ceased.

Is the writer of the letter correct? Has the Data Protection Act been broken by the parent filming his son and his classmates?

Your editor thinks that this would make an interesting subject for a story and has asked you to research into the Data Protection Act and write a short article of about 400 words explaining what the Data Protection Act covers and how it applies to the incident at the Sports Fields.

The Copyright, Design and Patents Act 1988

You are probably aware that you cannot just photocopy articles from magazines and books without permission from the author and you should be aware that you must not use software without a licence. You may have read about online file sharing sites where music is swapped and downloaded to people's hard drives without any payment to the bands and artists who originally recorded the music. If you have, you may also be aware that many of these sites have had to be closed down because the artists took legal action against the sites. The Copyright, Design and Patents Act 1988 (amended 2003) protects the right of the author of any piece of work to be identified as the author and stops the unauthorised copying and use of work without the permission of the copyright holder.

Many people believe, wrongly, that these restrictions do not apply to the Internet and that images included on websites can be used without permission from the author or copyright holder. As many of the file sharing sites have found, the law is as applicable to the Internet as it is to any other medium.

Health and Safety at Work Act 1974

This Act covers the duties which employers have to employees and the general public, and employees have to themselves and to other employees. The Act covers issues such as eye strain, radiation from VDU screens, stress and avoiding accidents which may arise due to the layout of rooms and other dangers.

Other legislation

Two major pieces of legislation exist to avoid discrimination and negative representation of groups within society. Both the Equal Opportunities Act and the Disability Act make it illegal to discriminate against people on grounds such as race, gender, sexual orientation and differing levels of ability.

When working with graphics, you need to ensure that the way that people are presented in your graphics does not contravene these Acts. As a general rule of thumb, positive images are always better than negative.

CASE STUDY

A bad day at Trallong Coaches

Trallong Coaches is a small coach travel company operating in the south-west of England. It specialises in day trips to beauty spots on the Cornish coast and other areas of local interest. Every April, the company produces a pamphlet explaining the tours. Included in the pamphlet is information about day trips, as well as photographs of each location.

When planning this year's trips, one of the directors of the company found a website about the Roseland Peninsula. Included in the website were some excellent photographs of beaches and wildlife in the area. Rather than employ a photographer to take the photographs this year, the director decided to use photographs he found on the website.

The new pamphlet was published in early April. A week later, Trallong Tours received a letter from Jones, Small and Hings, solicitors for Mr A. Hansford, explaining that

Mr Hansford was threatening Trallong Tours with court action for using photographs he had taken for his website about beaches in Cornwall.

1 How could Trallong Coaches have used Mr Hansford's images of beaches on the Roseland Peninsula and not broken the law?

2 Mr Hansford has insisted that his name is shown beside any of his photographs that Trallong Tours uses. Does he have the right to insist on this?

In a group, discuss whether it is right that images, music and text are protected on the Internet. Should the Internet, as some people think, be an area where everything is shared without restriction? How would you feel if you had produced a piece of art and found it was being sold by other people, but you were not receiving any payment? Would it matter to you if the artwork was being distributed in a book or electronically?

13.6 Researching a brief, planning your response and presenting your solutions

Applying for the commission

If you were trying to book a band for a party, you would probably be faced with a wide range of options. To help you make that choice, you would probably book a band you had used before or one that had been recommended to you. However, if you or your friends did not know of a good band, you would probably contact a few different bands and ask each of them for a demo tape. You would then base your decision about which band to book on the songs which the band had played on the tape. It is therefore important for bands to have demo tapes that represent both the range of music they play and also how good the band is.

So, if you wanted to employ someone to create artwork for you, how would you do it? Well, you would ask to see a graphic artist's portfolio. Designers, illustrators, newspaper artists and draughtspersons all have a portfolio of work that shows the style and quality of work they do. This allows potential customers to decide whether or not the style and quality of work suits their project, in much the same way that the band's demo tape lets you decide if the style of music played suits the event you are planning.

Creating a portfolio

You will need to create a **portfolio** of work before you are able to compete for a commission. Most work in the portfolio should be produced using ICT tools but some may be produced freehand. Your portfolio may include the following:

* Simple line drawings. These may be diagrams of room layouts, plans for a design or just a picture. Whatever you choose, you should combine squares, circles and other shapes to create the final image.

* Simple statistical charts that show the use of scale so that the viewer can see any patterns in the original data.

* Flow charts that show a sequence of events, such as step-by-step instructions on how to bake a cake.

* Icons that can be used to express an emotion or to add emphasis to a piece of text.

* Different background styles that may be used to add clarity or emphasis, such as making an instruction look like it is from a school by making the background look like an interactive whiteboard.

* Specialist diagrams, such as specific apparatus you might use, or more complex diagrams, such as showing how a Trebuchet works.

* Hand-drawn cartoon or sketches designed to go alongside text so that the meaning of the text is clearer.

* The use of a variety of different styles to meet the needs and interests of different audiences, such as young adults or motorbike riders.

Key terms

Portfolio: Samples of work. Usually used as evidence of the artist's or designer's imagination, ability and skill.

---

* Remember

Your portfolio is a separate part of the final assessment in this unit and it is as important to include a range of images that show your skills as it is to produce excellent images in response to your client's brief.

Whichever software you choose to use, your portfolio should show a range of different skills being used, as well as different manipulation tools. Whilst your portfolio does not need to include examples of the use of every single tool, effect and filter covered in this unit, it is clear that if you want to achieve a good grade in this particular task, your portfolio will need to include evidence that you have used a comprehensive range of editing tools. The specifications clearly indicate that as a basic requirement you should include evidence of the use of colour inversion and colour separation of your images.

The process of negotiating a brief

When you are given a **commission** to produce any type of artwork for a client, you will be given certain criteria which the work you produce will be expected to meet. For example, a business might have certain colours it wants you to use, or a school might want the school logo included in any images. Other clients may give you clear instructions about the style of the images you should use, such as all images should be black and white, or photographs should be deliberately out of focus. Other clients may not give you such precise requirements, but could ask you to produce final images that appeal to a target audience. These criteria, as

well as other information – such as how many images are required, the submission date for the final work and the available budget – all make up the **brief**.

Once you have accepted a commission, your client will expect you to produce draft proposals. These will be your initial ideas about how the client's needs may be met. These initial ideas may be produced using ICT or non-ICT methods and will cover a range of possible responses. This is an important stage of producing the work required, because you will be able to explore your ideas with the client and discuss in more depth what is expected from you. Whilst you will be able to go back to the client for further meetings as you progress, the better you discuss the brief and any possible solutions you have

STAGE	ACTIVITY
Apply for a commission	This would usually involve an initial communication by letter, phone or email.
Submit portfolio	This stage may be combined with the previous stage, but needs emphasising.
Submit initial ideas in response to the brief	You should submit a range of different ideas, all of which potentially meet the requirements of the brief, but in different ways.
Meet with the client to discuss the initial ideas	At this meeting, you should gain a clear idea about which, if any, of the initial ideas will be developed into the final product. It may be that you have to go away to think some more at this stage.
Interim meeting with the client to discuss progress	It is a good idea to keep the client informed of the progress you are making and to show some of the ideas that are being developed. You may come away from this meeting with more feedback from the client and you should be prepared to change your plans if necessary.
Final submission and acceptance of the final product	If you have kept your client fully informed of the work you have been doing, this should go smoothly. You do not want to be giving the client any nasty surprises at this stage.

TABLE 13.2 *The stages involved in liaising with the client*

in mind at this stage, the easier will be your progress to a final product that meets the client's needs.

Liaising with the client

Without a client, a graphic artist would have no work. Without work, the graphic artist would earn no money.

If a graphic artist does not keep clients happy, he or she will soon run out of work and then would not be a graphic artist any more. It is all a matter of economics really.

The only way to keep a client happy is to produce a finished product that fully meets the requirements of the brief.

It is important that you have the final meeting and that the client signs off the final product, as this will mark the end of your relationship with the client to produce these images. Without this formal agreement that the needs of the brief have been met, your client may continue to plague you with small requests, all of which may be beyond what was included in the initial commission.

Knowledge check

1 What is meant by the term *target audience*?

2 What is meant by the following technical terms:

   * posterisation

   * distortion

   * compression ratio?

3 What is the difference between a layer and a mask?

4 What is the difference between a GIF and a JPG?

5 What is the difference between a commission and a brief?

6 (a) Give two reasons why you would save an image file in a proprietary format.

   (b) Give two reasons why you would not.

7 Explain the increased flexibility that using layers brings when creating images.

8 (a) What factors affect which type of printer an office manager would buy?

   (b) Which type of printer would you buy if you were concerned about the level of noise produced? Explain your answer.

9 Explain why it is important to maintain contact with a client whilst producing work to meet a brief.

10 (a) Outline the contact you should have with a client during the process of applying for a commission and submitting the final product.

   (b) Explain the importance of each meeting.

You are aware that Fastway Travel, an independent travel agency, has opened in a nearby town and is trying to recruit someone to produce images for use in its catalogue. You decide to apply for the commission to produce these images.

Task A

Refer to the list of images that need to be included in your portfolio. Using software of your choice, as well as other methods as required by the task, build up a portfolio of images.

Mark Band 1

As a minimum, you should produce a portfolio that includes examples of simple line drawings, simple statistical charts, flow charts (referred to as boxed charts in the specifications), icons, background styles and repeated patterns, and scientific and technical diagrams. You should also show some evidence of colour manipulation in your work.

Mark Band 2

Your portfolio must show some evidence that you have used some of the different editing tools available in your software to develop some of these images.

Mark Band 3

Your portfolio will need to include evidence of the use of a comprehensive range of the editing and manipulation tools available in your software. You should include examples of different tools having been applied to the same image so that your client can then be clear about the different effects that may be achieved by using these different tools. As well as using these tools, you should include titles and labels which make it clear which tool was used to achieve the effect.

The brief

Your application is successful and you have been awarded the commission. The travel agency specialises in adventure holidays and would like images to be included in its new brochure. It specifically wants to target people in the 18 to 30 age range.

The brief is to produce 16 different images. Some of these may be photographs, but there should be some images that you create yourself. These images must meet the following criteria:

* All images should be in colour.

* All images should appeal to our target audience.

* All images should capture the excitement that an adventure holiday offers.

* A wide range of different adventure activities should be portrayed.

Tasks B–E tasks will be completed as you produce the images to meet the brief. As you work through each task, you should keep a record, maybe in the form of a diary, of how your skills in using image manipulation software develop as you progress.

As you work, you will use some effects or create some images that you later reject. You should keep these rejections, as they will show that you have been selective in your choice of images and effects. Your client may also suggest certain amendments as you are working, and you should keep these suggestions, as well as evidence of how they have affected your work.

Task B

Read the brief and produce initial ideas about how the client's needs may be met.

This planning stage is important, as it will allow you to explore your ideas. Spend time thinking about different ideas, as your first idea may not be the best. The more time you spend planning, the more likely you are to produce an excellent final result.

Mark Band 1
As a minimum, you should produce some sketches of images that will meet the brief. These need not be produced using ICT methods, but your response should, at least, discuss how you could use different software packages to meet the brief.

Mark Band 2
You must produce several initial ideas for your client (who in this case may be your teacher or lecturer) and then develop one idea based on the feedback you get from your client. This idea may be a development of a specific idea you submitted or an amalgam of ideas based on your initial thoughts as well as the client's response.

Mark Band 3
You will need to submit several initial ideas, developing an idea based on the feedback you receive and writing a report on the implications of the solution that has been chosen. This report may focus on your choice of software package, the time it will take to complete the project or any other resource or knowledge implication which you feel will result because of the decision that has been made.

Task C

Comment on the effectiveness of your designs. Your report should be written in Standard English and contain few, if any, spelling mistakes.

If you are keeping a record or diary of your work, you could comment on your designs in this record. If you are not, you should write a short report, which you should attach to your initial designs.

Mark Band 1
At its simplest, you should comment on the effectiveness of your designs. This could be a simple statement saying that your designs are good ones and would meet the brief, and you could then go on to give reasons for your views.

Mark Band 2
You will need to identify the strengths and weaknesses of each of your initial designs and use this analysis, along with feedback from the client, to decide on which design you will develop further.

Mark Band 3
Your report should be in-depth and, as well as identifying good and bad points, should make it clear how the designs could be improved. Your criticism of each of your initial designs, along with feedback from the client, should be used to decide which design you will develop further.

Task D

Produce a final product to meet the needs of your client.

This is the production task and is where you can really show the skills you have developed whilst working through this unit. As you are creating images, try to use as wide a range of tools, effects and filters as you can, but remember that you must satisfy the brief, so maybe you should not include every distortion filter in your final submission. There is nothing to stop you applying different distortions to an image and then rejecting the idea though; if you look at Mark Band 3 below, you will see that by doing this you might just get more marks for this section.

Mark Band 1

You will produce a final product which will include images that you have created, captured and developed. You must also use material created in more than one package, as well as pre-prepared materials, such as clip art.

Mark Band 2

You must satisfy the criteria for Mark Band 1 as well as take account of feedback from the client.

Mark Band 3

The work you produce must be of a professional standard and show real imagination and flair. You must also use a comprehensive range of the ICT tools available to you in your software package. As you are working, you should keep any images that you reject as being unsuitable, as these will show that you are able to be selective and have not just thrown all the images you create into your final product, irrespective of their quality and the extent to which they meet the requirements of the client.

> **✳ Remember**
>
> Although working with your image manipulation software can be great fun, this task is only worth 12 marks out of the 500 available for this unit. Do not spend all your time producing the images you need and neglect the other aspects of this assignment!

Task E

Comment on the ICT skills you have used to produce the finished product.

This task is best completed as you are going along and the diary makes a great form of evidence here. As you work through the tasks, you should comment on how well equipped you are to deal with the different requirements. It may be that you need to review your understanding of the application of a particular tool, or that you do not know how a particular input device may be used. A good way of doing this would be to have a section called 'What have I learnt today' or 'Targets for tomorrow'.

As you progress, you will be explaining how your skills have improved and it should be clear to any reader of the diary just what software skills you have gained and the actions you have taken to increase these skills.

Alternatively, you could use a table for this; but a diary seems more natural and you are more likely to achieve higher marks, as you are more likely to discuss all aspects of your skills development. A diary would seem a more intuitive way of providing evidence that you have used your initiative to develop and extend your skills.

Mark Band 1

You will identify some of the ICT skills you have used.

Mark Band 2

You will identify the full range of ICT skills you have used.

Mark Band 3

As well as identifying the full range of ICT skills you have used, you must show that you have used your initiative to develop and extend your skills. This could be by providing evidence of the list of different information and advice you have used, maybe with some useful URLs for websites that you have used. Another form of evidence for this could be witness statements from a range of people you have asked for help and advice.

Task F

This task is in three parts:

1 Comment on how well your final product met the requirements of the brief.

2 Give advice about the best printer to use to produce a hard copy of the images you have produced.

3 Analyse your performance in producing the images.

This final task brings together all the issues to do with producing your images and gives you the opportunity to reflect on how well you have worked and how successful you have been. It is not often appreciated, but you can get as many marks for explaining how and why you were not successful as you can for explaining how and why you were, so even if you have had a complete disaster with this unit, you can still gain marks in this area. When you are discussing your performance, remember that this part of the task is about showing what you have learnt about yourself and how you work as much as anything else, so be honest! This will probably give you more scope for discussion and give you greater opportunity of gaining higher marks.

The discussion of different printer types should take account of the advantages and disadvantages of different printer types.

There are several different tasks that combine to make up the mark bands descriptors for this task, but they combine together well, so we should look at them as a group.

Mark Band 1

Your work should, at least, include a written discussion of the images you have created. Your report may contain errors in spelling, punctuation and grammar. This discussion should include a short discussion of whether you have met the brief, as well as some indication about how the overall finished product may be improved.

You should also state which printer you recommend for printing out the final product, but you will probably not include any discussion of alternatives.

You should give some brief comments on how well you worked to produce the images and suggest how you would improve your performance if you were to do the activity again.

Mark Band 2

Your analysis of the finished product should be in more detail and should identify the strengths and weaknesses. It should be possible to use this list of strengths and weaknesses to further develop the images to better meet the requirements of the brief.

You should discuss printers in general and suggest a suitable printer and resolution for producing the hard copy. You should show some awareness of alternative printers and resolutions that may also be suitable. Your report will contain few spelling, punctuation and grammar errors.

Your reflections on your own performance should include an identification of your strengths and weaknesses, as well as giving some suggestions for future improvement.

Mark Band 3

Your analysis of your final product will discuss all elements of your work and compare it to the initial brief to show how well your work meets the client's requirements. Your report will be consistently well-structured and there will be few, if any, spelling, punctuation and grammar errors.

As well as identifying the strengths and weaknesses of your performance, you should discuss how you could address any weaknesses identified and explain how you would change your method of working to avoid these issues in the future. This may be a discussion about the quality of your initial planning and how this may be improved, or about how well you kept to deadlines. The range of items under discussion will depend on the weaknesses you highlight, but, again, the more honest you are at this stage, the more likely you will be to achieve higher marks for this section. You may also find that you work more efficiently when you are working on other tasks!

Choice of software

The choice of which software package to use will, obviously, be limited by the range of titles you have available. The choice of which software package to use is yours, but you should be aware that you should choose a software package that gives you access to a wide range of tools and effects. The assessment grid refers to using a comprehensive range of advanced editing and manipulation tools and it is unlikely that the more basic image manipulation packages will offer sufficient tools to meet the requirements of this unit.

Responding to feedback from clients

You will probably have noticed that you need to show that you have responded to feedback from clients during the production of these images. There are different ways you could show this, but, again, the diary is a possible source of support here. If, following feedback from your client, you comment in your diary that a certain change in style has been made or you have decided not to use a particular effect or other tool, this would go some way to showing that you have responded to feedback. You may also decide to have a section which shows plans and images that you abandoned following feedback.

You should also keep written evidence from your meetings with your client, such as minutes signed by both of you as being correct or any letters you receive in response to submissions to your client.

Whichever method you choose to evidence this, it is clear that you should have regular meetings with your client to get feedback on your work. Without these meetings, you will not be able to get the feedback which you need to ensure that you meet the client's needs.

Developing and creating websites

By studying this unit, you will

* learn the requirements for setting up a website

* understand the terminology relating to the Internet

* discover the differences in the range of web programming languages available for developing web pages

* learn the differences between Internet and intranet sites and the network security implications of running web servers.

This unit is about planning, creating and publishing multi-page websites in response to a brief from a client.

The first stage of creating your website will be to evaluate commercial websites and identify features which you then choose to include in your own website or dismiss altogether. Once you have completed your research, you will then design your website. You should use a range of tools and techniques to help you with this design process. These tools and techniques will be explained to you during this unit. Having designed your website, you will then justify your design decisions.

You will then create your functioning website. This website should be a multiple-page website which includes a range of interactive features and multimedia elements. The structure of your completed website should both fit your initial designs and suit the requirements of the brief.

You will need to test your website to ensure that everything works as it should. In order to do this testing, you will need to produce a thorough test plan for your website and provide evidence that this testing has been carried out.

You will need to publish your completed website on the World Wide Web. In order to do so, you will need to choose a suitable domain name and location. Once your website is published, you will need to ensure that it may be accessed in the correct sequence.

Having published and tested your website, you will need to evaluate its effectiveness. You will need to gather the views of others to help you with this evaluation. Your evaluation should include a full justification of all elements you included in your website, as well as an indication of the strengths and weaknesses of your website as a whole and any suggestions for future improvements.

Your final task will be to evaluate your approach to designing, producing and testing the website and to suggest ways in which your approach might be improved in the future.

How this unit will be assessed

This unit will be assessed on a portfolio of evidence that you will produce. The assignment at the end of this unit will provide you with the evidence to complete the portfolio.

What you need to learn

You need to learn about

* web server requirements
* planning a website
* designing and documenting a website
* creating a website
* testing a website
* uploading a website
* evaluating a website
* laws and guidelines.

14.1 Web server requirements

A web page is the basic unit of the web. A web page may contain text, graphics (which here means drawings as well as things that are generally treated as photographs), sound, video and a whole range of interactive elements, such as forms and guest books. A website is a collection of web pages.

Creating and viewing websites

It is important to differentiate between creating a website and viewing a website. A website is created using **web development tools**, but viewed in **web browsing software**.

Key terms

Web development tools: The tools used to create websites.

Web browsing software: The software you use to view a website.

Web creation software

As we shall see, websites in their simplest form are created using **HTML code**. With even basic knowledge of HTML, you can create a web page by entering text into a word-processor or text-editing software, adding a few bits of HTML code, and saving your file as a web page. This all sounds pretty simple and the great thing is that it pretty much is, if you know the code. At this stage, if you have never created a web page you may be thinking of choosing another unit; actually, not only is it easy to create a web page once you know the code, the code itself is also very easy to work with, so stick with the unit for a bit longer at least!

Instead of editing the HTML code, it is also possible to use a **web authoring package** to create a website. These work by effectively turning web page creation into a version of desktop publishing. You create a web page by viewing it in a version that looks very much like your completed view as seen when using a web browser. FrontPage calls this the normal view, whilst Dreamweaver calls it the design view. Elements are then laid out on the page and formatted as you go along.

Once you have learned how to use a piece of web authoring software, creating new pages can be an incredibly easy process. Recent versions of some of the more advanced WYSIWYG authoring programs allow you to create some very complex websites packed with some of the more complex features.

The main focus in this unit is on the creation of websites using WYSIWYG software packages. Therefore, when we describe how to create elements of a website, we will concentrate on using these packages. However, you are also required to have sufficient understanding of HTML to be able to make changes to the structure of your website by altering HTML code. We will therefore also look at HTML code as we go through the unit.

Web browsing software

Web browsing software is the software you use to access your website. There are two main brands: Internet Explorer and Netscape Navigator. A web browser will interpret the instructions included in the HTML code and present the viewer with a web page. Because a web page is really a set of instructions that a web browser does its best to follow, if the instructions are followed correctly then the web page will look as the author intended.

Web server definition

When you come to publishing your website to the World Wide Web, you will need a web server. If you search for a definition of a web server on the Internet, you may become slightly confused. This will be because some sites suggest that a web server is the hardware which serves out your website, whilst other sites will make it very clear that the web server is the software that does the serving. In the purest sense of the term, and to the level you are working, a web server is the program that sits on a machine and serves up the website to web users. However, because, in networking terms, a server is an actual computer, the hardware and software elements have become blurred for most people over recent years.

Internet protocols

Websites are basically files that are held on one computer and that are transferred to a viewer's computer. Although it is a bit more complicated than that, it is true to say that when you open a web page, you are asking for data to be sent to you from someone else's computer. Because of the range of manufacturers, there is a need for some common standards, so that data sent by one type of computer may be opened on another type of computer. These rules are called protocols. Protocols define how the data within resources should be organised and transferred.

TCP/IP

TCP/IP stands for Transmission Control Protocol/Internet Protocol. TCP/IP sets out the rules for how individual signals are sent across the Internet and is designed to allow communication across the Internet for all computers, whatever their make.

HTTP and FTP protocols

There are two main ways that this data may be transferred from one computer to another:

✳ Hypertext Transfer Protocol

✳ File Transfer Protocol

You will have come across website addresses which begin with http://. These are websites which use the Hypertext Transfer Protocol to serve up the data which makes up the website. You may also have come across websites which have names which begin with ftp://. These are sites which use the File Transfer Protocol to serve up the website.

Key terms

Hypertext Transfer Protocol: The protocol created to allow the transfer of HTML pages between web servers and clients.

File Transfer Protocol (FTP): The protocol created to allow the transfer of files across the Internet.

The major difference between the two protocols is that FTP may be used to transfer whole directories as well as individual files. It is therefore the protocol used to upload your website to the web server. Each of these protocols need different servers to be installed, with HTTP requiring the installation of a web server and FTP requiring the installation of an FTP server.

By far the most popular form of file transfer protocol on the web is the HTTP protocol and the vast majority of websites will have URLs which signify that they are HTTP websites, rather than FTP ones. We will therefore concentrate on websites of this nature for the rest of this chapter.

Web server software

Web server software sits on a machine and serves up pages, via HTTP, in response to a request for a specific page from an HTTP client. Your browser is acting as the HTTP client and, when you choose to open a link to a web page, you are sending a request for a transfer of data from someone else's machine to yours. Once that data is received on your machine, your web browsing software then shows it in the form of a web page.

The request for a page is usually for the home page of a website, especially if the web user has been given the web address by another website or by a search engine. However, the request may be for a page within the website, especially if the web user has bookmarked that specific page. It is worth remembering that users may enter your website from pages other than your home page, and you should allow provision for this in the design of your web pages, maybe by making it easy to navigate to the home page from any page in the site.

Two of the most popular web servers are produced by Apache and Microsoft. Indeed, it is more than likely that Microsoft's IIS server will be the web server used in your school or college.

Internet naming and addressing systems

Finding data on the web is a bit like finding a house. If every house did not have its own address, it would be impossible to deliver mail, visit friends or have services delivered. Similarly, if data did not have its own address, it would be impossible for web users to find a specific website or any other resource. So that we can find specific data on the web, each item of data has its own unique address. An address on the web is known as a **uniform resource locator (URL)**.

Key terms

Uniform resource locator (URL): The address for an item of data on the Internet.

Uniform resource locators (URLs)

As you will now know, the first section of the URL tells us that the website uses the HTTP protocol to serve up the website. The second section is the host name, which is the computer on which the file is stored. The final part gives the location of the specific file. This is a bit like giving an address in a block of flats: first of all the building is given and then the address of the flat.

The structure of a URL is shown in Figure 14.1.

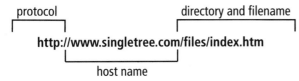

protocol | directory and filename

http://www.singletree.com/files/index.htm

host name

FIGURE 14.1 *Parts of a URL*

Domain names

Your website will need a unique **domain name**. This will be the web address that anyone who wants to visit your site will use to navigate to your site when using web browsing software. Examples are www.bbc.co.uk or www.yahoo.co.uk. To most web users, this domain name will refer to the location of the website itself, but, as we have seen, websites are hosted by web server software located on a specific computer. This specific computer will have a unique **IP address**, which the **domain name server** will link to the domain name in its database. Effectively, thanks to the link between the domain name and the IP address of your computer established by the domain name server, your domain name is a written version of the IP address of your computer.

Domain name structure

A domain name is made up of three distinct sections: the organisation name, the domain type and the country code. In both of the examples shown above, the country where the website is based is the United Kingdom. The domain type *co* tells us that the organisation that the website represents is a company or a commercial organisation. The bit of the domain name left over once these two separate items have

CODE	COUNTRY
au	Australia
de	Germany
fr	France
nl	Netherlands
uk	United Kingdom

TABLE 14.1 *The main country codes*

been considered is the organisation name. The organisation names are therefore *bbc* and *yahoo*.

All countries in the world have their own code. The main ones you may come across are shown in Table 14.1.

Websites do not have to use these codes, but many do. The United States does not use a country code, so, if you find a website with no country code, it is reasonable to assume that it is based in the United States.

The list of domain types is always expanding, but a representative sample is shown in Table 14.2.

Internet protocol address

Every computer that is linked to the Internet has an Internet protocol (IP) address. This is the actual address of the machine itself. Domain name servers

CODE	DOMAIN TYPE
ac	Academic institution – mainly used in the UK
com	A commercial organisation (mainly non-UK)
co	A commercial organisation (mainly UK)
edu	Educational institution
gov	Government
org	A charitable or not-for-profit organisation

TABLE 14.2 *Examples of domain types*

link domain names to IP addresses, so that, when a web user types in a domain name for a website, they are directed to the machine that is hosting the website to which the domain name refers.

Security

There are three main Internet security considerations:

* the security of the computer hosting the site
* the security of the website
* the security of transferring data.

The security of the computer

As we have discussed, websites are published by web servers. These web servers are pieces of software that serve up the necessary code for web browsers to use. Therefore, it follows that, for your website to be available, a web user needs to be able to contact the machine that holds your web server. This means that you have to have a link – usually called a port – to the outside world permanently open. This is, therefore, a security issue. Whilst this may be seen as a problem for an individual hosting a website from their computer at home, it is a security risk that brings the risk of complete disaster for an organisation that includes a web server as part of its network of machines.

Having a link to your computer permanently open may be seen as an invitation to others to explore your computer. Whilst most web users will not take up this perceived invitation, there are

some that will, and various attempts have been made to ensure that such unauthorised access to your computer system is prevented.

Installing a **firewall** has become the method used to prevent unauthorised access to sections of a computer system (see *Unit 16: Networking Solutions*, page 375).

The security of the website

Your data will be published on a website. As we shall see, it is a simple process to look at the code behind a website. This code is the source code for the website and is used by the web browser software to display the website. So, if you change this code on your machine, you change the website. Seems logical and simple (and dangerous), doesn't it?

Fortunately, this is not the case. The only way in which a website may be changed is to edit the file to which the URL refers, and this is held on a remote computer. What you get on your machine is effectively a copy of the code, sent by the web server to your computer, which your web browsing software then shows you. If you change this code, you will only change the way that the web page looks on your computer.

The files that are used to serve out your website are called the source files and access to these is protected by a password. As long as you do not choose a password that is easy to guess or hack, your website should be secure.

Proxy servers

The idea of a **proxy server** is a bit like going into the least user-friendly library in the world and having to ask a librarian to get a book for you. All access to books and other resources is therefore controlled by the librarian. In a library such as this, there might even be a librarian who is excellent at predicting what books people want, maybe by analysing records and other data, and

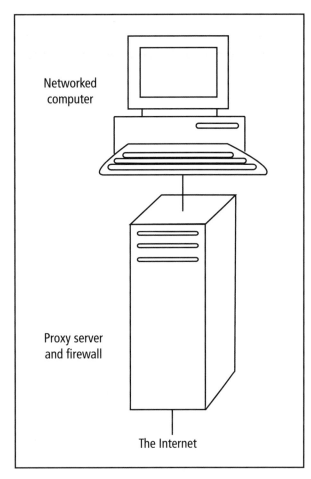

FIGURE 14.2 *A combined firewall and proxy server security system*

this person might store popular titles under the desk, just waiting for the request that, according to the statistics, will come very soon.

A proxy server behaves in the same way. Access to resources is controlled by the proxy server, so that web users actually make a request for data from a proxy server. The proxy server verifies that the request is a valid one and then, if it is, checks whether the data is ready to hand (but not under a desk) or goes and gets it from the shelves, which in this case is the web server.

> **Key terms**
>
> *Proxy server:* A server that appears to serve up the website or any other data requested, but which is actually serving the website on behalf of another machine.

As should be quite clear, a proxy server, by not allowing access to the main computer system, provides another layer of security. Many organisations will combine a firewall and a proxy server to provide security for their systems (see Figure 14.2).

The security of transferring data

It is unlikely that you will be using your website to transfer out or receive in any payments. However, should you choose to do so, you would need to have a system that protects sensitive data, such as credit card numbers and other account information, from being accessed by others.

The standard method chosen to achieve this security is to employ a secure socket layer. This is another protocol and it has two distinct features. The first is to encrypt any data that is being sent and the second is to allow the computer to identify any server to which data is being sent.

14.2 Planning a website

Planning is central to the success of your website. If you are going to create a website which appeals to the **target audience** and communicates effectively, you will need to plan the structure and content of the website closely.

> **Key terms**
>
> *Target audience:* The audience for which a piece of work has been produced. Each target audience will have different needs, tastes and interests.

Reviewing existing websites

The best way to start planning a website is to look at others. You will probably already have a few favourites that you use all the time, as well as some others you use reasonably often. Start by thinking what makes a site your favourite. Each of the sites you visit will have features that you like, as well as a few you may not. Is this what makes a site your favourite? Is your favourite site the one which has least features that annoy you, or are you prepared to put up with some annoying features because the content is so good? Many websites carry adverts. Do these distract you and make you wish they were not there, or do you accept them as a necessary part of the Internet?

Probably the one site you use more than any other will be your favourite **search engine**. There are many search engines and you have probably tried a few but always come back to the same one. We will start by considering what it is about our favourite search engine that attracts us.

The activity on search engines is a good place to start thinking about websites, because just about anyone who uses the Internet will have used a search engine to find something on the web. However, you will not be creating a search engine, so you now need to move your thoughts on a bit further.

The exam board specifications require you to comment on the design and structure of at least two existing websites and to identify the features that you may or may not include in your website.

Website features

We will look at the features included on a website in the section on planning a website. However,

you will need to have a basic understanding at this stage so that you know what you are looking for.

Websites may combine the following features:

* graphics
* text
* video
* animation
* interactive elements
* navigation aids
* sound.

Graphics and text should need no explanation. Video and animation should not be confused. Video is fundamentally a film and will play as a film. Animation is altogether different and is the action of making something move on the web page itself. This may be achieved in many ways, but by far the simplest is to include a marquee, which will make text scroll across the page. 'Interactive elements' is here used to mean those elements that need some input from the user, such as searching or completing a form. Navigation aids are those parts of the website that allow the user to get to other parts of the website itself or beyond the website and into the World Wide Web. Finally, sound is any sound file that plays whilst the website is being viewed. This may be sound that plays throughout the time that the website is open or may be sound that plays when something occurs, such as the user clicking a button.

Reviewing structure

Your first analysis of a website will be to analyse the overall structure. This will be an analysis of

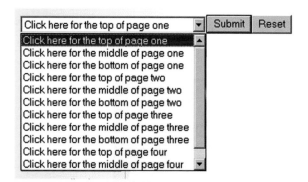

FIGURE 14.3 *A useful drop-down menu, or overcomplicated?*

how the pages of a website flow together and is basically a report into the map of the website itself. Different website structures are explained in the section on designing and documenting a website below and it is worth jumping ahead slightly to read this section before you write your report.

The report you write should explain what you thought was good about the structure of the website and does not need to include an in-depth site map. However, you may want to comment on the following issues:

* How easy was it to find your way around the website?

* How easy was it to find specific pages on the website?

* Could you easily find your way back to the home page?

The answers to these questions will form a good basis from which you can criticise the structure of your target website.

Remember that you are commenting on the structure of the website and how easily you can move from one part of the site to another. If the site you are viewing has a navigation bar on every page, with all pages accessible from that navigation bar, then the structure may appear

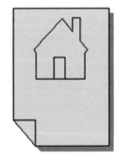

FIGURE 14.4 *Spot the home button*

excellent. However, such a navigation aid may cause more problems, especially as the navigation bar may be overcomplicated, or require huge drop-down lists. The best thing to remember is that it is sometimes as hard to see something that is there as it is to see something that is not, especially when there is so much other detail that what is there is lost amongst all the other items. The old saying 'You can't see the wood for the trees' is something some web designers may want to bear in mind.

Reviewing the design

The design of the site is as important as the structure. You should comment on the colours, the use of fonts and how easy it is to find elements. You may decide that the home button is not at all clear.

However, you may find some designs that are excellent and that you would like to use in your own website. Look at the section on checking out HTML code below for how you can do this.

One final consideration will be the target audience. As you are reviewing a website, always be aware of the needs of the target audience. If the target audience is a highly computer-literate group then maybe the website can afford to be a little more complicated than a website for young children. This may explain more technical language or the choice of which elements to include. However, this would not explain poor design, which makes it hard to find the home button, or poor structure, which makes navigating through the site a nightmare. The website you are reviewing must work, and for it to work the users must be able to access those sections that hold the information that they need or that the web designer wants them to see.

How did they do that? Finding out the programmer's tricks

It is generally possible to see the code for the websites you visit. This is a useful way of teaching yourself the skills of HTML authoring. However, do not forget that the Internet is covered by the Copyright, Design and Patents Act 1988 (amended 2003) and so you may not just copy and reuse sections of any website you admire.

Checking out the HTML code

If your website does not use frames, the source code can be seen by selecting Source from the View menu within Internet Explorer. If your website does use frames the source code can be seen by right-clicking within the frame.

The first time you look at the source code for a professionally produced website, you will probably find it very difficult to locate the section of code that refers to the particular feature you admire. As your skills and understanding develop, you will become better at finding the bits of code you want to examine.

As we work through this unit, we will discuss how different elements of web pages may be created using HTML. HTML uses tags to instruct web browsers how to present web pages. There are many different tags, but each works in basically the same way, which is to indicate to the browser that a particular effect needs to be switched on and then switched off. For example, in the section below, the word 'lounge' would appear in bold:

```
In my house there are many rooms.
Personally, I prefer the
<b>lounge</b>.
```

The <b>...</b> parts of this code are the tags that instruct the web browsing software to present the word 'lounge' in bold. The first part of the tag, the <b> part, tells the browser to start presenting in bold, whilst the </b> part tells the browser to stop doing so. In this way, the first part of the tag may be considered to have switched the tag on, whilst the second part switches it off.

What should you include in your plan?

We will discuss this issue in more depth as we work through this unit, but, at this stage, you need to be realistic when planning your website. A basic rule of web design and authoring is to keep it simple. Just because you can do something, it does not mean you have to! The website you produce for this unit should suit the needs of the brief you are given and not just be an opportunity for you to show your web development skills.

Increasing hits

The World Wide Web is a collection of many millions of different websites. Your website will be just one of them. Are web users going to be able to find your website? If you are going to rely on search engines, how many other websites will be listed alongside yours? You could test this. Think of how web users might search for your website using a search engine. Think of a phrase or a few words they might use. Open your favourite search engine and enter your search criteria. Whichever search engine you use, you should be given the total number of websites that the search engine has found and which it considers match your search criteria.

This is a good exercise because it points out to you how much competition you face. If your website is one of a relatively small number found by the search engine (say 1,500) would it be looked at? When you do a search on the web, how far down the list do you work before you assume that there will be nothing relevant? Your answer is probably two or three pages, which is probably about 30 websites, and that list may include the same website more than once. In truth, unless your website comes in the top 30 hits, it is unlikely to be accessed from a search engine site. However, do not despair; there are strategies you could use which can move you closer to the top of the search engine list.

Using metatags

Search engines collect data on websites and use this data to respond to searches. This information is usually collected automatically by what are known as spiders or robots. These are programs that work through the Internet, following links between websites. When they find a website, they work through the code and analyse the content of the website. Metatags are used to give the search engine a further bit of help with deciding what your website is about.

Metatags are one more form of HTML tag that goes at the top of your HTML code. The first part of the tag sets the tag up as a metatag and the second part, the content part, includes key words that will give search engines a clue about what your website is about. The search engines will then store this information, along with the web address, in its database. This database will be used to list websites in response to a search.

The code below is a metatag for a website about radiators.

```
<META NAME="keywords"
CONTENT="radiator,heat,heating,
central heating">
```

Okay, so this is not a long list, but how many words can you associate with radiators? Any web user who uses any of these words as search criteria will get your website in the list produced by the search engine. The position of your website on the list will be determined by how relevant your website is. Different search engines have different criteria for deciding the relevance of a website, but the more terms you can insert into the contents list, the more likely the search engine will be to list your website high on the list.

Link to other websites

As well as using metatags, you can use the Internet equivalent of asking a friend to introduce you. This is done by asking other websites to link to yours. You, in turn, will then link to theirs.

Not only does this increase the chances of a search engine spider finding your website in the first place but it also uses another measure that search engines use to decide relevance, which is measuring how often a search engine spider is directed to your website. To keep with the theme of invitations, if enough people mention you to someone else, you get a certain reputation. Search engines work in the same way and assume that if there are loads of websites with links to yours then your website must be relevant.

Ask the search engine to come and find you

Waiting for a search engine spider to come and find your website can be a long process. One alternative is to announce yourself to the search engine and ask them politely if they would not mind coming to have a look at your website.

Most search engines will have a 'submit your site' option. This is a form you complete with details about your site. This service is free and relatively straightforward.

Figure 14.6 is from Yahoo!, but the process is the same for most search engines. As Yahoo! states on its submission form, the Yahoo! Search index is 99 per cent populated from the free search index.

Downloading graphics and information

As you browse the Internet in search of inspiration, you will come across graphics and information that you may want to use in your own website. As has already been said, you will need to be aware of the restrictions placed on you by the Copyright, Design and Patents Act. In some cases, a quick email to the owner of an image asking for permission to include a graphic in your web page will receive a positive response.

If you are given permission to use graphics and other elements, such as downloadable documents, they will need to be saved so that you may use them later on. This is one of the range of tools available to you when you right-click.

Saving pictures

If you wish to save a graphic, right-click on the graphic and then select Save picture as. You should then navigate to where you want the graphic saved. If you already have a folder structure set up for your website, you will usually save to a folder called Images.

Saving documents

If you wish to save a document, you have two options. You can either open the document and

FIGURE 14.5 *Come into my parlour, said the fly to the spider*

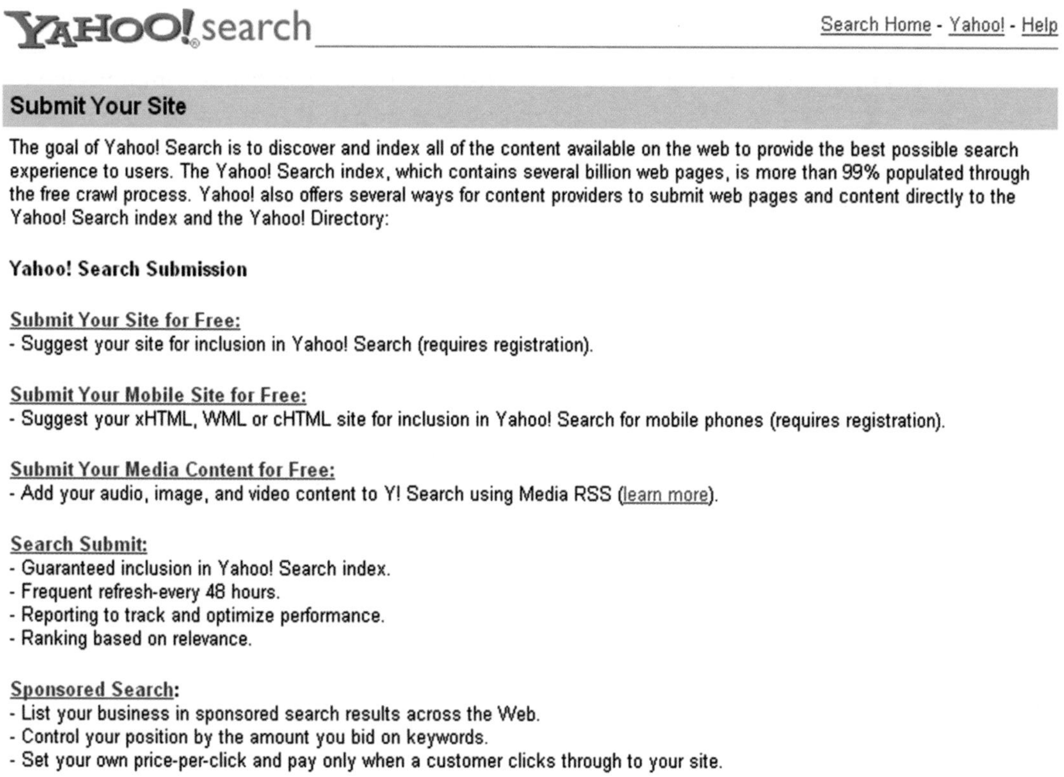

Submit Your Site

The goal of Yahoo! Search is to discover and index all of the content available on the web to provide the best possible search experience to users. The Yahoo! Search index, which contains several billion web pages, is more than 99% populated through the free crawl process. Yahoo! also offers several ways for content providers to submit web pages and content directly to the Yahoo! Search index and the Yahoo! Directory:

Yahoo! Search Submission

Submit Your Site for Free:
- Suggest your site for inclusion in Yahoo! Search (requires registration).

Submit Your Mobile Site for Free:
- Suggest your xHTML, WML or cHTML site for inclusion in Yahoo! Search for mobile phones (requires registration).

Submit Your Media Content for Free:
- Add your audio, image, and video content to Y! Search using Media RSS (learn more).

Search Submit:
- Guaranteed inclusion in Yahoo! Search index.
- Frequent refresh-every 48 hours.
- Reporting to track and optimize performance.
- Ranking based on relevance.

Sponsored Search:
- List your business in sponsored search results across the Web.
- Control your position by the amount you bid on keywords.
- Set your own price-per-click and pay only when a customer clicks through to your site.

FIGURE 14.6 *The Yahoo! submit a website option*

save it in the usual way, or you can right-click on the **hyperlink** to the document and then choose Save target as. This method may be used to save any element that you may click on to download.

> **Key terms**
>
> *Hyperlink:* A link to another web page location. Hyperlinks may be attached to text, images or other interactive elements on a web page. Clicking the hyperlink takes you to the new location.

Website structures

The structure of a website describes how each page in the website is linked to the rest. This therefore determines how the user may navigate through the website.

The three possible structures you could use are:

* linear
* hierarchical
* web or mesh.

You will probably have come across many different examples of each of these structures as you have browsed the web.

Linear structure

This is the simplest of all the possible structures and is best used where there is only one possible route from one web page to another. A linear structure is a relatively simple layout for a website and you really should be considering a more complex structure at this level.

Hierarchical structure

In a hierarchical structure, resources are grouped into logical sections. This organisational structure is termed hierarchical because the web pages are organised by the main group title first and then by subsequent titles below, forming a hierarchy.

This structure does allow the user to choose the path through the website, but the choice is limited so that once the user chooses to follow a certain path, they would either need to retrace their steps or to wait for a link allowing them to access a different path.

FIGURE 14.7 *A linear structure*

Hierarchical structures are very useful for displaying information that needs to be grouped and then accessed in a specific order. A website selling music may allow the user to choose the band or artist whose music they wish to purchase, but, once this choice has been made, only information related to this band will be displayed.

Web or mesh structure

The alternative option is for the user to be able to move to any other area of the website from anywhere in the website. This structure is known as a web or mesh structure.

As each section on a web or mesh website is linked to every other, it would be extremely complicated to show this structure for a website of more than a few sections, so Figure 14.9 shows the structure for a website with five sections.

A true mesh structure allows users to follow any available link to any resource as the whim took them. Therefore, this structure does not impose any constraints on the user. Because of this, you would be unwise to use a web or mesh structure for a website where you were attempting to present a message in a preset pattern. However, where you were presenting a range of different

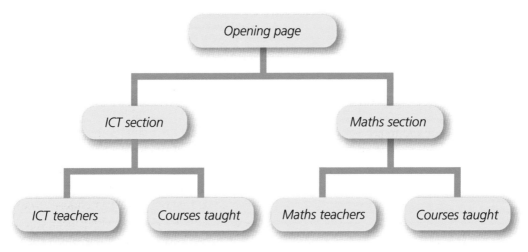

FIGURE 14.8 *A hierarchical structure*

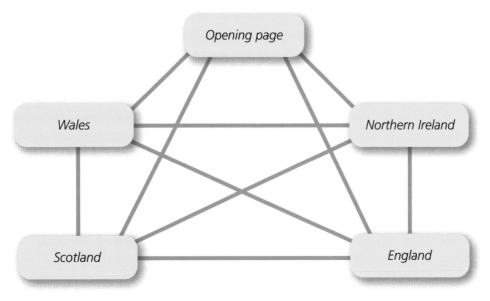

FIGURE 14.9 *Web or mesh structure*

ideas and where the order of presentation was not important, such a structure would be excellent.

Hybrid structures

In practice, most large websites have a combination of a hierarchical and a web or mesh structure. These websites will have large sections organised into logical groups but will allow free movement from one web page to another within the section. This would be rather like going to a shopping centre dealing only with sports equipment. Once you were in the shopping centre, you could then go to any shop you wished.

Planning and designing a website

Your research into commercially produced websites will have given you some ideas about the features and layouts of websites in general. The design stage is where you will apply these ideas.

You will be given a commission to produce a website. This commission will include a brief. In its simplest form, a brief will explain what your completed website should achieve. This may be as simple as 'publicise our band' or 'tell people about our school'. However, you may be given a more complex brief, which will not only tell you what your website should achieve, but will give you some indication of how this should be achieved.

The client may, for example, tell you a particular style to use or suggest a range of images that would be appropriate. There may be a group of corporate colours that needs to be included, or a requirement that each page include a quote from a well-known person.

Page layout

Page layout is vitally important and is to do with what elements are on the page and where each element goes. To some extent, you could consider this either at the end of the design process or at the beginning. By considering the page layout at the beginning of the design process, you can decide what your page will contain, without being distracted by specific elements.

The process of designing your page should begin with some thought being given to the effect you wish to achieve and the target audience to which you are planning to appeal. These two considerations will run through the whole of this design process, but it is well worth stressing them at every opportunity. You must consider how the structure of a page may affect how your target audience will use the page or, even, if the target audience will use the page. You must remember that all the elements of your page are important and all will contribute to the effect of the page. White space used well, for example, may be as effective as an image or a piece of text. If you practise seeing the web page as a whole as the important issue, rather than individual elements, your web page will be more effective.

As you continue through this section, keep in mind that you are considering the relative merits of different candidates for inclusion. In a basic way, you should include all of the features that will be discussed, but how often and how prominently is your decision, albeit within the constraints of the brief.

Consistency of design

One further thing to consider before we look at the different elements you could include is consistency. As you have browsed different websites, you will have come across many different designs, but what you will also have seen is that for virtually all websites, each page on the website will be structured in the same way. This does not mean that all the pages are identical, but that each page on the website is recognisable as being from the same website as the other pages. This will usually mean that there will be images in just about the same place on every page, or that the text is always in the same font, or that a banner or heading is prominent on every page. Other possibilities would include the type of picture used, or the colours.

You will need to plan a website that achieves at least some consistency. Where you choose to change the structure of a page or a section, there should be a good reason why you make that decision. If you have looked at some very big websites, you will have realised that there are some differences in page layout and structure. There may be many reasons why this is the case and it may be true that, in some cases, pages have not been created using the same design specifications. This would include a site that is being constantly revised, but some pages have not yet been revamped. However, differences in page layout and structure could be deliberate for other reasons, which would include the need to give a different feel to a specific section of a very large website.

Your website is unlikely to be very large and will be not be in the process of being revised, so your aim should be that all pages on your website should have the same layout and structure. If you choose to include pages that have a different layout, this

should be reflected in the designs for the site and it would be appropriate to provide some basic reasons for your decisions as part of the design process.

Theory into practice

This activity will enable you to practise the skills involved with planning the layout of the pages of your website. You will begin by reviewing the layout of two websites and use this analysis to help you create the first designs for a website of your own. You will need to review two websites that are trying to achieve the same sort of thing. You could, for example, look at two television websites, or two websites for bands.

Choose a website that has a consistent layout for each page. On a clear sheet of paper, draw the design plan for the layout of the standard page used in this website. You do not need to draw the elements in any great detail; blocks representing the location of elements on the page will be fine.

Comment on the extent to which the standard layout of the site suits the purpose of the website.

Repeat these tasks for one further website of your choice.

You have now considered the design for two websites that are both trying to achieve the same basic aim. Use your analysis to help you develop a layout for a standard page for one of the following projects.

1 A website for a band of your choice.

2 A website for your town.

3 An information website giving advice about the weather.

Once you have completed your design, write a report justifying your design decisions.

Using text

Whilst it is possible to create a website with only images, it is likely that, at this level, you will need to include a combination of text and graphics, with text probably making up the majority of your website. However, this is not a rule and there may be plenty of reasons for you to create a website where the content is largely graphical. Even if this is the case, you will still need to include some text.

Text needs to convey some of the message of your website. You must decide how much text you will use and how it will be laid out on the page. You will also need to think about the tone of your text. This will need to be read and understood by your target audience. One way of ensuring that your explanations are suitable is to check the readability statistics of your text. This is a fairly easy task, as most word-processing packages will produce these statistics for you.

Assessing readability

Figure 14.10 shows the readability statistics for a document created in Microsoft Word. The section at the bottom of the report gives you the feedback you need to assess how easy your document or section of text is to read.

Passive sentences are listed in readability statistics because they are generally considered to be difficult to understand. Most advice on passive sentences is that you should not use them unless you have to.

The Flesch Reading Ease statistic gives you another indication of the readability of your document. The statistic is given in a range from 0, which is just about impossible to understand, through to 100, which is easy to read. A score of 60 is considered to be plain English and should be considered the minimum acceptable level for most text you would write.

The Flesch-Kincaid Grade Level is an attempt to match readability with age. The test uses a combination of the average sentence length and the average syllables per word to produce a score that equates to a US school grade level. For example, a score of 9.0 means a child in the 9th grade should be able to understand the document. A general target for your work is that it should be between 7.0 and 8.0.

If the Flesch Reading Ease or Flesch-Kincaid score for your piece of writing is not within the acceptable range, the solution in both cases is to reduce the number of words in your sentences and also to avoid using long words.

One final point about text has to be the importance of the use of correct spelling and grammar. It might suit your target audience to use text that is deliberately misspelt, or that follows the spelling conventions created by those who regularly use SMS text messaging services, but, if you choose to use this technique, you run the risk of making your text extremely difficult to read and understand. The correct use of grammar and punctuation can, for example, avoid problems of interpretation. The correct use of spelling not only ensures that the reader is presented with the correct word correctly spelt, but also suggests a level of attention to detail that may be missing, or appear to be missing, from the work of a candidate who produces a website with misspelt words, whether those words are misspelt deliberately or not.

Large blocks of text written using SMS texting conventions are extremely hard to read. If your website really needs such text, then use some, but keep it to a minimum.

Using graphics

You will need to understand how to use graphics in your site. Graphics may perform different functions. A graphic can explain a point far more clearly than text: it can convey a feeling or atmosphere, it can emphasise a point, or it can simply be decorative.

Loading speeds

It is vital that you realise the effect that graphics files can have on how long it takes to load your

Readability Statistics	
Counts	
Words	609
Characters	2762
Paragraphs	19
Sentences	40
Averages	
Sentences per Paragraph	2.8
Words per Sentence	15.0
Characters per Word	4.3
Readability	
Passive Sentences	5%
Flesch Reading Ease	65.7
Flesch-Kincaid Grade Level	7.8

FIGURE 14.10 *Usability statistics for a Microsoft Word document*

website. If you use only a few small images on your web page, it will be small in bytes and quick to load. However, if you use a few larger images, or even one very large image, the web page can take some time to load fully. You may consider that this is less of a problem now that so many people have broadband Internet connections. However, you should not assume that all your users will have this facility and, even with a broadband connection, a large file can still take some time to download. If you are not careful, as you add more features to your web pages, the web page you create may become larger and larger and the time taken to download can increase considerably.

There are other techniques for reducing the time it takes your browser to download your page. Firstly, you should try to use one graphic as often as possible. You may, for example, want to use a graphic to take you back to the home page, or use graphics as buttons generally. You could choose to use a different home page image on each page or use a range of different images for buttons. However, if you choose to use only one image for your hyperlink to the home page and another for buttons in general, not only will you bring consistency to your site but you will also reduce the time it takes to download your website. This is because each image will only have to be downloaded once, however many times it is used.

It is possible to give each graphic used in your website an **alt** attribute. **Alternative text** was initially used to represent graphics on web pages when a web page was viewed using a text-only browser, or where graphics had been turned off.

> ### Key terms
>
> *Alternative text (alt):* Text that appears in place of graphics when a website using graphics is viewed using a text-only browser.

In the example in Figure 14.11, the user has chosen to turn off graphics in their browser. The browser has been used to view a web page including an

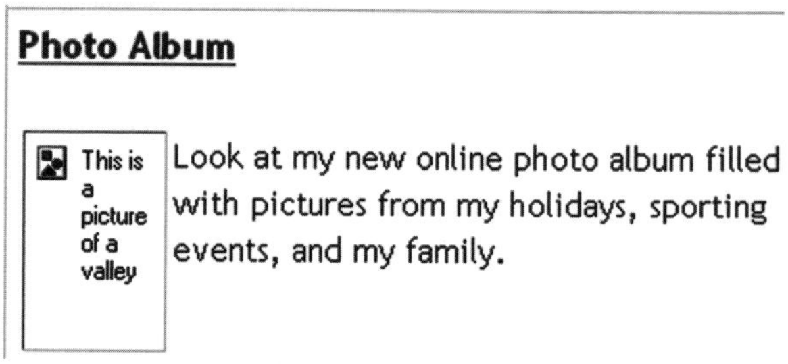

Photo Album

 Look at my new online photo album filled with pictures from my holidays, sporting events, and my family.

FIGURE 14.11 *Alternative text is used to represent an image when a web page is viewed using a text-only browser.*

image of a valley. The image has been replaced by the alternative text.

If a user has a slow web link, it is possible that they may turn off graphics in this way. You should include alternative text as a matter of course in case this option is chosen.

Another option is to resize the graphic in a graphics package to make it smaller. This is a simple process and not only reduces the physical size of the graphic, which is the amount of pixels it covers, but also reduces the amount of data that is required to store the graphic. This therefore reduces the amount of time taken to download the graphic when a browser is attempting to display a web page containing it.

When you change the size of an image, try to maintain the aspect ratio, which is the ratio of the height to the width. Basically, if you divide the height by two, for example, make sure you divide the length by two. If you did not, the image would distort, which may actually be something you want to happen. As with so many things in this unit, if it suits your brief, then do it if you want to, but be prepared to comment on your decision when asked to do so.

Finally, ask yourself if all the images you are planning to include in your website are really necessary. For each graphic, consider whether the graphic adds to the page. Does it give information or is it there because it looks good? A basic rule of thumb is 'no fluffy bunnies'.

Graphic types

As you will be aware, there are many different graphic types available for you to use when creating images. However, there are only three

FORMAT TYPE	ADVANTAGES	DISADVANTAGES
.gif	Small file type. Great for images using less than 256 colours	Photographs use more than 256 colours, so you will lose information
.png	Excellent compression rates with little or no loss of detail	Will not support animations (unlike animated gifs)
.jpg	Small file size with excellent picture quality	Each time you edit and then save a .jpg image, quality is lost

TABLE 14.3 *Advantages and disadvantages of graphics types*

main types that may be relied upon to be supported by all of the major web browsers:

* gif
* png
* jpg.

Each of these file types brings benefits and problems. Table 14.3 summarises these.

If you are about to create images to go on your website by drawing them freehand, you should consider using the .gif format to do so, especially if the image will only use a few colours. If you intend to use photographs, you could choose to use either .jpg or .png format. If you intend to use graphics that are saved in any format other than those listed above, you should use image manipulation software to convert them to one of the universally supported graphic formats. This process is explained in the section on creating a website below.

If you wish to explore further the differences between each of these file types, you should refer to *Unit 13: Artwork and Imaging*.

Choosing graphics for your website

Your choice of graphics is as important as your choice of text. The images you choose should suit the task given to them. If you are looking for an image to explain something then the image needs to be clear and the meaning unambiguous, which means that it should be clear to the majority of your target audience what the message of the image is. If the meaning of the image is not clear, you should consider not using it. You should also remember that just because a meaning is clear to you, it may not be to the target audience. It is worth giving some time to testing any images with members of the target audience. It is worth doing this with all images, but is especially true of images on which you are relying to convey an important message.

Similarly, images used as decoration should be very much in the background of the viewer's attention. These images have been chosen to break up the page and perhaps could be replaced by an area of white space. These images have definitely not been chosen because they make a point or further emphasise the message and so should not distract the viewer from that central message. These decorative images should not be bold and should not be the first thing that the viewer notices.

The decision to include images only for decoration brings its own challenges. However, if used well, such images can really enhance the website you create and can mean the difference between a viewer being enthused to read a page, and a viewer deciding that this is too much to read and moving on.

As well as deciding which images to use, you will need to consider the size of any image on a page. If your image is too large, it can swamp the web page and detract from your message. Conversely, if your image is too small, it may be lost amongst text or be so small that any detail cannot be seen. As you plan which graphics to use on your website, you will need to show awareness of the balance between elements on your page. However, one final feature of which you need to be aware is the issue of screen resolution.

Screen resolution

Screen resolution is set by individual users and controls how much may be seen on a screen.

As the screen resolution is increased, so the space available on the desktop increases.

However, as this space increases, so the relative size of images or other elements on the page decreases.

Most people tend to have their monitors set to 1024 by 768 pixels, but you should not rely on this being the case. It may be that you prefer to use a lower resolution and had not considered this as an issue. However, as screen resolution settings will affect how your website is viewed, you need to be aware of the effects that different resolutions can have on your completed website. If you do choose to use a resolution that differs greatly from the standard screen resolution, you may be surprised by some strange effects that may occur, so it is probably better if you aim to work with a fairly standard resolution, rather than one that the majority of users are unlikely to use.

There is little you can do to force users to choose a specific screen resolution, other than to include a statement indicating the best resolution to use to view a website, and hope that the user follows your instructions. A statement such as 'This website is best viewed in 1024 by 768 pixels' is probably your best hope.

Working with speech synthesisers

You will spend a good deal of time planning your website and the images that it will include. Images are fundamentally a visual experience, but, as we have discussed, they can serve many purposes on your website. Many people who use the web are visually impaired and will use speech synthesisers to read aloud the text included on a web page. However, there is an obvious difficulty when such synthesisers come to images. One response to get around this problem would be to use alternative text.

If a visually impaired user is using a speech synthesiser to read aloud the text on a web page, as the speech synthesiser software comes to the image, it reads the alternative text. If the alternative text is sufficiently descriptive, this will allow a visually impaired viewer to better access all the information, visual and textual, that you have on your web page.

Using hyperlinks

Hyperlinks are the code that moves the viewer from one area to another. This area may be within the page on which the hyperlink is inserted, in which case it will link to a bookmark within the page. Alternatively, the link may be to another page within the website or to a website on the World Wide Web.

The jump to another area is achieved by clicking on an interactive element, which then runs the code. An interactive element is one that requires some action from the user in order for something else to happen. For example, you may click on a button which will then open another page of a website. However, you do not have to use buttons with hyperlinks. For example, you could attach a hyperlink to a graphic or to a piece of text.

Buttons

The buttons will appear as formal elements in your website and may be grouped together into a toolbar that is present on each web page.

Buttons can show text or images. You can also create buttons that change as they are selected or clicked, or as the mouse moves over them.

There are many ways to create a button that you may use on your web page. The simplest is to create a button using a graphics package. The process is explained below. This can be a good idea, because you can quickly and easily create series of buttons that all follow the same design principles.

Theory into practice

1 Use the How to create buttons instructions to create the following text buttons for a website. Each button should be 150 pixels wide by 60 pixels high. The text should be dark blue and the background yellow. You may use a font type of your choice.

Button a: A **home** button

Button b: A **submit** button

Button c: A **next** button

Button d: A **back** button

2 Recreate each of the four buttons you made in 1 above, but create them as graphical buttons, rather than text buttons. It should be clear what the purpose of each button is.

Create buttons in a graphics package

This is a straightforward activity but is one that will allow you to create simple buttons that are, as a group, unique to you and that all follow the same design principles.

1 Decide on what you want your buttons to look like and how large they need to be.

2 Open a graphics package. You will be able to create some reasonable buttons in a simple package, but, in order to create something that actually looks like a button, you will need to be able to raise the image so that it appears as a button on a page. In Paint Shop Pro, this is achieved by using the Buttonise option; in Serif Photoplus, it is possible to emboss an image to achieve a similar effect or to apply effects such as bevelling to the text.

3 Open a blank canvas. Remember to set the canvas size, background colour and font colour and type to suit the button you need.

4 Create your image. This may be drawn freehand or may be a piece of text.

5 Use the tools in your graphics package to make the image look like a button. There may be a range of tools you could use, such as Buttonise, but this will depend on the software package you are using.

Graphical links

A graphical link is usually used with a thumbnail image that, when clicked on, opens a larger version of the graphic. However, this sort of link has other uses. You may decide to use obvious images, such as the home icon or a logo, or less obvious graphics, which would require the user to find the link. You may also decide to use a part of

FIGURE 14.12 *A textual button*

FIGURE 14.13 *A graphical button*

a graphic as a link, or break a graphic into sections, with each section linking to a different site. This is particularly powerful if you want to have data linked to a map but wish to be able to present regional data. A map divided into sections, with each section being a geographical area, would be a very powerful device to use in your website.

Textual link

The text link is useful because it can link a phrase or individual word to further information about the subject. For example:

'The history of the <u>City of Bristol</u> is linked to the development of the <u>triangular trade</u> between <u>Britain</u>, <u>Africa</u> and the <u>West Indies</u>, as well as the work of engineers such as <u>Isambard Kingdom Brunel</u> and the voyages of explorers such as <u>John Cabot</u>.'

This short passage includes contextual links to seven other items of information that might be of interest.

We will discuss how to create each of these elements in the section on creating a website.

Drop-down lists

You will have come across drop-down lists in a range of different software titles. These are the lists of tools and applications that become available when you click on the name of the drop-down list in the toolbar.

Drop-down lists can be an extremely useful way of organising hyperlinks into sensible groups. For example, the drop-down list in Figure 14.14 has been used to allow the user to jump quickly to a page on the world tour website.

Navigation bars

Navigation bars are buttons or drop-down lists that are organised into a group. This group is then included on all web pages in the website.

Drop-down lists and navigation bars are extremely useful for navigating more complex websites. You could also decide to use navigation

Welcome to my world tour web site!

This is my site about my recent travels. The drop down menu on the right shows where I have been recently.

Click on the place name which interests you.

| Madrid ▼ | Go to selected page |

Madrid
Morocco
Turkey
Llandudno
San Marino

FIGURE 14.14 *A drop-down list of hyperlinks*

bars to contain links to the major areas of your website but use contextual links within each web page to allow the user to visit other areas which may be of interest.

Other links

As well as links to other areas, you may choose to include two further links within your website. These are links to email and links to FTP server documents, which may then be saved to the viewer's computer.

Using navigation aids

Navigation is the process by which a visitor to your website accesses the web pages in your site. It is therefore vital that any links you have on your website are easy to find. This is a simple concept but is one that is often ignored.

There are a few simple tips you can follow to help your visitor find their way around your website more easily.

* Start with a link to the home page on every page of your website.

* Use a structure that groups together pages covering materials that sit together. These web pages can be accessed via a common front page, if that suits your needs.

* Use contextual links to other areas from within your web page.

* Include navigation at the top of the page, so that casual viewers of the web page can move on easily and quickly, and also at the bottom of the page, so that those people who read your web page may also move on easily.

Welcome to my Madrid page

[history.htm] [geography.htm] [people.htm]

FIGURE 14.15 *Screen dump of a navigation bar*

* Keep to standard accepted settings for links. Textual links should be underlined and in blue, unless they have been followed, in which case they should become purple. Do not use underlining for anything other than links.

* Keep to a standard design and layout. This allows users to become used to finding their way around the website.

If your website is easy to navigate, it will be easier for visitors to find the information they require. This will therefore increase the probability of users visiting your website again.

Hints and prompts

The final issue to consider here is that of hints and prompts. One further advantage of using alternative text is that most browsers will show the alternative text when the mouse is over the image. This can be an extremely useful way of adding instructions to an image that you choose to use with a hyperlink. The advantage of using alternative text in this way is that the information is given as the mouse is over the graphic being used as link, but disappears when the mouse

Click here to follow this link to more information about music

FIGURE 14.16 *Alternative text can be used to give clear instructions*

moves away from the graphic. This means that the user is only given instructions when they are needed; the instructions are not usually on the page and therefore do not clutter up the page.

Style of font

The style of font for a website is specified within the HTML code. However, unless the font is available on the user's machine, the font will not appear as the author intended. For this reason, websites tend to be written in the more common fonts, such as Arial, Times New Roman and Verdana. The choice of which of these to use will depend on the target audience and intended message of the website. If you want to convey a serious message, then you should use a serious font, such as Times New Roman or Arial, both of which are seen as part of the strong, silent group of fonts. However, some font styles have been developed specifically for use on websites. Verdana, Tahoma and Bookman are all examples of these.

If you wanted to use other fonts then it would be something of a gamble whether the font was available for all visitors. To avoid this issue, you should create any piece of text that uses a non-standard font as a graphics file.

Theory into practice

This activity will give you the opportunity to explore different fonts and how they may be used.

You have been asked to produce a wall display and teacher's notes to explain how different fonts may be used for different effects. You have been asked to suggest fonts for the following uses on your poster:

1 Present a serious message.

2 Present a fun message.

3 Create a poster with a historic feel.

4 Create a poster that includes text that looks like handwriting.

5 Create a poster with an arty feel.

The teacher's notes will be used to explain why each font has been chosen as the most suitable. Make sure that you include good reasons for your choice of each font.

As well as thinking about the fonts used, you should be considering the number of different fonts that have been used. It is important that the font does not become more important than the words and the message that they convey. If you start to use a different font on each section of your website, the audience will soon start to notice the font more than the message. Also, whilst the range of fonts specifically intended for use on a website is quite narrow, each font does have a different feel and you may give the audience the wrong message by changing the font for each section, as the audience may interpret the message in a different way because of the use of a different font.

Using colour

Colour may be used in three main ways on a website: text, background and buttons.

The obvious use of colour is when setting the colour of text. The default colour for any text used on a website, other than textual hyperlinks, is black. This is great if you want black. However, you may want to use some other colours to brighten things up. A bit of red here, just to make people notice, or some purple there, to draw attention to a special quote, will make your website appear that bit more dynamic.

Colour may also be used for backgrounds. By default, any website has a white background. However, you can, in theory, have any colour background you wish. You should not confuse the use of a background image with the use of colour. A background image can be used to create a complex background for a web page. This can be highly effective. Colour, however, tends to be one wash with no texture. The final point to make here about colour is that some WYSIWYG packages do allow you to use a textured background with a colour. This usually takes the form of a repeating pattern, such as a tartan. Unless you have a very good reason for using such a background, the advice is simple: do not use such a background if you want people to visit your website more than once!

Finally, colour may be used when you are creating buttons. As you are designing your buttons, think about how you want them to be noticed. If you want your buttons to stand out then use a colour that contrasts with any background colour or any colours that are immediately around the button. Contrasting colours are discussed below.

We will discuss adding colour to your website later in this unit. However, before you go ahead and create a website with a mauve background and yellow text, there are a few things of which you need to be aware. The first is the psychological effect of colour and the second is fitness for purpose.

Contrasting colours

Some people may find it difficult to read the text on your web pages if there is not sufficient contrast between any background colour and the colour used for any text. This can be especially true when you use a background image for your web page, especially one with many colours. Luckily, this is a simple problem to avoid with a bit of thought.

There are three main things you should avoid:

* Do not use dark-coloured text on dark backgrounds, such as blue on green.

* Do not use light-coloured text on light backgrounds, such as yellow on white.

* Do not use multi-coloured images as backgrounds.

The psychological effects of colour

A quick search of the Internet will bring up many websites that explain the psychological effects of colour. You will need to be aware of the significance of colours when designing your website. Turn to *Unit 11: Interactive Multimedia Products*, page 109, for a discussion on the uses of colour.

Fitness for purpose

You will already have browsed many websites and you may now be considered something of an expert on different designs, so ask yourself the following questions:

* Were you aware of the background colour of each and every website?

* What colour, if any, is most frequently used as a background colour?

* How does colour affect how you view a website?

The answer to some of these questions may surprise you. Over the past few years, most websites have tended to abandon using background colour on their websites and it is now quite difficult to find a professionally produced website that uses background colour at all. Similarly, text tends to be in one or two colours and is quite often black. It seems that despite having all these great tools to use when creating a website, most programmers, or maybe it is most clients, choose to have websites that avoid using a great deal of colour, either as backgrounds or with text. This is not to say that you must not use colour. You will find some websites that make excellent use of colour and, if you choose to make a statement with the use of a strong background colour, or to highlight sections of text, this can be very effective.

As with so many other aspects of your website, you must be guided by your brief. If you are not sure about how your client wants colour used in the finished website, you must ask. However, if you feel that a combination of colours will not work, then you need to express your concern to your client.

Use of interactive features

The final part of planning a website is to decide which interactive features you will include. These interactive features are usually called **forms** and are used to provide you with feedback from the people who use your website.

A form is made up of special elements with which the user interacts. They include:

* buttons – used to start procedures

* text fields – used to enter text

* check boxes – used to gather answers based on simple binary options (e.g. yes/no)

* submit buttons – used to send the contents of a form

* reset buttons – used to return a form to the default setting

* menus – used to give further interactivity.

These elements may then be combined with graphics or other text to improve how the form looks.

For most forms, once completed, all data collected is sent to your web server. Once there, it is analysed by special scripts created for the purpose. These scripts are called **Common Gateway Interface (CGI) scripts**. If these scripts do not exist on your server, your data cannot be analysed.

The exception is for forms that send an email. In this case, there is no data to collect as the message is in normal text and not direct responses to questions.

You should plan to use at least two forms in your website. When you come to create your forms, remember to include the Submit and Reset buttons. Some web page creation packages, such as FrontPage, include this by default; others, such as Dreamweaver, do not.

Each of the interactive features listed below will bring different benefits to your website.

Full text search

This allows the viewer to search your website for a specific word or phrase. This can be extremely useful if you create a large website or one with a lot of text, as it allows the user to find the part of the website that interests them.

If you plan to include a full text search facility, give clear thought to where in your website you want this element to appear. It would seem sensible to have it on the first page, and most commercially produced sites tend to place theirs on the top right-hand side of the index or home page. Whilst this is not a rule, most people feel comfortable with what is familiar to them, and web users are no different.

Table of contents

This is another great element to include in a large website, as it lists the pages in the website and presents each web page as a hyperlink to that web page. As with text searches, think about where the page needs to be in your website.

Many web page creation packages ask you for the first page on the website to list. When you first use this feature, you may ignore it as irrelevant. However, if the first page of your list is the same page as where the table of contents is included, the first link on the table will be a link to that page. This may seem like a small issue, but it gives an unprofessional feel to the website.

When you create a table of contents for your website, some web creation packages, such as FrontPage, will ask you how you wish to organise your table. The simplest option is to organise it based on the navigation structure of your website. However, it is also possible to organise your table by page type. To do this, you will need to have assigned each page to a category. This is a setting within the properties for each page and, for FrontPage, is set up within the folders view.

Guest books

This feature allows people who visit your site to leave some feedback. The feedback may simply be their name with a few lines of text, or could be the answers to a few questions you set.

Guest books are a great interactive feature and can build into a huge resource. Many people enjoy having the opportunity to leave some feedback about a site, especially if you have made some contentious points. If you are building a site to advertise a product or a service, this is an invaluable feature, as it will allow web users to contact you to ask for further information.

Message boards

These are intended to be part of an ongoing conversation. A visitor may therefore start a topic or add a comment to a conversation that has already taken place.

Feedback forms

These are messages that are sent to a preset email address. Typically, they are used to collect visitors' opinions on a topic.

Sending a message

As well as including forms for visitors to use, you may also wish to allow them simply to email you.

One Tree Publications

We hope you have enjoyed our website.

We would value your opinion of our website. Please use the space below to make any

comments which you feel would help us to improve.

Submit | Reset

FIGURE 14.17 *A feedback form to collect suggestions in response to a direct question*

When a user clicks the email link, it will open the default email service defined for the computer on which they are working.

When using web page authoring software, emails are added by inserting an email hyperlink into your document. This is basically the same as inserting any other hyperlink into a document, but, when prompted, you choose to add an email address rather than a URL. By default, an email link will appear in the form:

mailto:myemailaddress

where myemailaddress is, strangely enough, the email address. However, as with other hyperlinks, emails may be textual links or attached to buttons and graphics.

14.3 Designing and documenting a website

Why do you need to plan? Hopefully, this is not a difficult question to answer. Planning is not only a requirement of the specifications for this unit, but is also part of the negotiation process with your client and may be used for further development of your website at a later date. By following any of the planning techniques explained below, you will be creating an organised record of what will go into your website. If your plans are stored in a logical manner, the ability to dip into them at any stage, without having to work through the website, will save time and will allow both the end user and whoever is working on the site to be able to have conversations about any work that is required, safe in the knowledge that they are definitely both talking about the same page.

Structure diagrams

You will have come across structure diagrams in other units you have studied for this qualification. For example, in *Unit 2: How Organisations use ICT* you may have used structure diagrams to represent the organisation of an information system within a business. In a similar way, you can use a structure diagram to plan how a website may be structured.

For a business, a structure diagram shows departments as blocks, and lines of communication between each department as lines on the diagram. A website, with different linked sections, may be shown in exactly the same way. Figure 14.18 shows a structure diagram for a hierarchical, seven-page website.

Each page of the website is represented as a block and the links between the pages are shown as lines. As you can see, the plan is that this website will have a hierarchical structure.

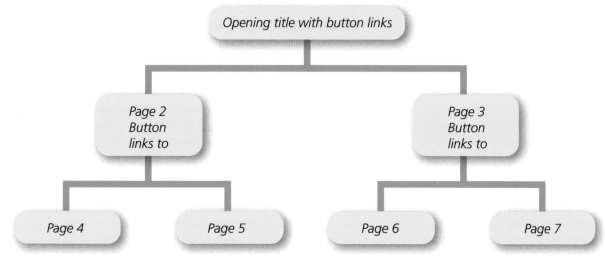

FIGURE 14.18 *A structure diagram for a website*

It is also possible to plan both mesh and hybrid websites using this technique. Figure 14.19 shows a hybrid website of 11 pages.

Theory into practice

Choose one relatively small website with which you are familiar. Your school or college's website would be ideal, unless it is large and very complicated, in which you may want to concentrate on a particular department or faculty's website.

Produce a structure diagram for this website.

Storyboards

A storyboard lays out what will happen as the viewer progresses through your planned website. It does this by explaining, in some depth, what will be on each page. Each element of every page should be considered and explained. For example, for a piece of text, you could consider the following issues:

* What do you want the text to say?

* Is the piece of text a quote? If it is, you should explain who it will be from.

* What font size do you want the text to be?

* What colour will the text be?

* What font will you use for the piece of text?

Your answer to these and any other questions you may think of will set targets for you to meet when creating your text item. The importance of this process is that you can plan all text items by answering the same questions. If you then set yourself similar questions to answer for all other web page elements, you will have a procedure for planning the whole of your website.

Theory into practice

We have already seen that you may use set questions to decide which elements may be included in a website. This activity gives you the opportunity to plan questions for all elements of a website and then compare your suggestions with others working on this unit.

Individually, plan questions that will help you decide on the following elements for your website:

* images and photographs

* videos

* buttons and other navigation tools

* background images and colours.

In a group, compare your suggestions with those made by others in your group. Discuss each of the suggestions made and try to come up with a list of questions that you will all use for planning websites.

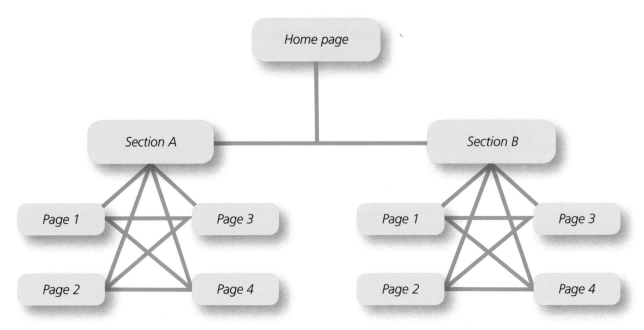

FIGURE 14.19 *A structure diagram for a hybrid website*

Index of pages in the site

This is simply a list of all the pages that will be used on the website. It is used by the web designer and the end user to ensure that the website covers the full range of topics. It may also help with progress checking.

Task list or action plan for development

You will be given a time scale within which you must complete the planning and creation of your website. If you intend to meet this timescale, you will have to plan your time carefully. The issue of time-planning is discussed elsewhere in this book (see *Unit 9: Working to a Brief* for further information). Rather than go through every time-management technique, we will discuss a group of methods that work well together and suggest that you follow it when producing your solution.

Choosing a domain name

Suppose you run a business called 'Mega Dogs'. It is reasonable that you will want the address of your website to be based around the name of your business and so you would try to register a website

with the organisation name **mega dogs**. Therefore, you will want a website address along the lines of www.megadogs.com or www.megadogs.co.uk. These sorts of names are easy to remember, look great on adverts and attract attention. A web hosting service such as GeoCities would give you a website with an address something like www.geocities.com/.../megadogs/megadogs.htm.

This address is based on the GeoCities domain name and would work as a link but is virtually impossible to remember. If you want people to access your website regularly, you will need to find a simple and effective domain name.

Your first decision is to decide on the domain name you want to use. Having done this, your next port of call must be any one of the number of websites that allow you to check if a domain name is available. Many of the sites that allow you to purchase a web address will include a function that enables you to check whether the web address has already been purchased. Alternatively, a web search for 'domain name' will bring up many sites where you can both search for a specific domain name and then buy it if it is available.

When you find a domain name you like that is available, you will need to register the right to use it. You will be able to do this using the site you used to check whether the domain name was available. You will be charged a fee to do this and your registration will last for one or two years.

Legal considerations

Cyber squatting is the practice of people registering and using a domain name that clearly should belong to someone else. This practice has led to legal actions. As you search through available domain names, you may find a variation on a well-known business name available. It is best to ignore it and move on to choose a domain name with less risk attached.

Who will host your site?

To some extent, the answer to this question will depend on the software you use to create your website. Not every web server will work with every website. Microsoft FrontPage, for example, requires that a web server has the FrontPage Server Extensions installed.

Before you go too far down the path of choosing who will host your website, take a browse through the help files that explain the process of publishing the website. If there are any special requirements associated with the web page authoring software you are using, the help files will make this clear and suggest that you contact any website hosts before you try to publish to their web server.

Hosting internally

As we have discussed, you will need access to a web server if you are to host your site. If your school or college already has a web server, you may be able to negotiate with them for your website to be hosted by the school or college's web server. If you are able to do this, you will need to be very clear about the security in place within the school or college's network.

ISP

If you pay for web access via an Internet service provider (ISP), you will probably have been given a limited amount of file space for a website of your own as part of the deal. This can be an excellent solution, as the ISP will not only host your website for you, but will also have security set up to protect your website. Again, as with hosting your website

within your school or college, you must be fully aware of these security arrangements.

Web hosting

The final option is to host your website with an organisation that will host your website in return for a fee. Unlike websites hosted by ISPs, you are more likely to be able to use your own domain name with a site hosted by a web hosting service.

14.4 Creating a website

The specifications for this unit require you to create a website using WYSIWYG software. You will then make changes to the HTML code to change the page layout. This section will therefore concentrate on using web authoring software, but with some indications about how changes may be made to HTML code.

Web page development software

There is a range of web page development software available. Whilst creating your website, you should use the full range of tools available within your chosen package and be prepared to explain how using the software affected the quality of your completed website.

Most of the web page development software available uses the concept of WYSIWYG to create a website. This effectively means that you are creating a web page as if you were working on a desktop publishing task. Using such a programme, if you drag an image onto an area of the web page you are creating, the software will create the necessary HTML code for you. Similarly, more complex elements, such as interactive online forms or elements requiring plug-ins, may be created by a few clicks of the mouse.

Templates and colour schemes

Most packages now include wizards that lead you through a series of questions to produce a web page for you. These questions will then feed into a template that is used to set up your web page or website. Whilst using wizards on their own may result in web pages and websites that look very much like those created by other people, they do provide you with a basic canvas to which you may add your own individuality and the specific items requested by your client.

Templates are basically just groups of HTML code set up to define a basic page. You can then add to this basic page by working on the WYSIWYG view or the HTML view of the page.

Similarly, you can choose to use a pre-set colour scheme if your software allows. As you may have guessed, this will be a scheme that applies a set of colours to different elements on your web page.

We will now begin the process of creating a website. We will add features to this website as we work through this unit. This website will be created using Microsoft FrontPage, but many of the features and techniques used are common to all web page development software packages.

Now that you have created a basic structure for your website, you can create your first web page.

Checking the source code

As well as displaying web pages in the Normal View, WYSIWYG software allows you take a look at the source code. This is called the HTML View. The Normal, HTML and Split Views (see Figure 14.22) refer to how you see pages and should not be confused with the Page, Folders and other views available within FrontPage, which refer to how you see the website as a whole.

If you now double-click on the index.htm page, and then go to the Page View, you should see index.htm as a blank page. If you select the HTML View, you should see the code behind the web page you have just created.

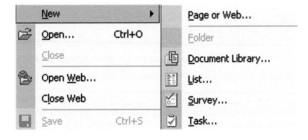

FIGURE 14.20 *New File options available within Microsoft FrontPage*

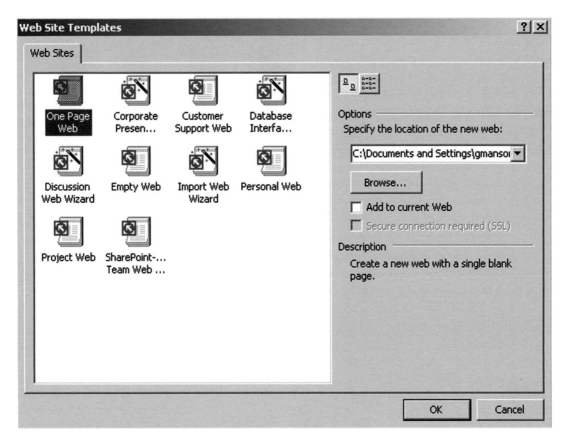

FIGURE 14.21 *Website template options available within FrontPage*

HTML uses **tags** to give instructions to web browsers about how the page should look. We are interested in three of these tags at the moment:

<html> and </html>

<head> and </head>

<body> and </body>

These three tags are called structure tags.

Simply, the <html>…</html> tag is the first structure. It tells a web browser that the page is a web page, and should enclose the whole document. The <head>…</head> tag is used to define basic information, such as the title. Finally, the <body>…</body> tag holds the content of your page.

At the moment, the only other code on your index.htm page is within the header area. Ignore this code for now; we will come back to it later on.

FIGURE 14.22 *Web browser, HTML and split tabs in Microsoft FrontPage*

Web programming languages

The main web programming language with which you will deal is HTML. There are, however, other programming languages you need to be aware of:

✳ Java

✳ JavaScript

✳ VBScript

✳ ActiveX

✳ Perl

✳ VRML (virtual reality markup language).

An introduction to using JavaScript or any of the other web programming languages would expand beyond both the space allocated here and the time you have for the course. However, you are required to have a basic understanding of what each of the programming languages is.

Understanding web programming languages

Table 14.4 explains the main features of the web programming languages listed. This is not an exhaustive list, but an introduction.

With the exception of HTML, without which you probably would not be able to create a website at this level, each of these languages gives you some opportunity to enhance your website rather than create one from scratch. It is unlikely that you would use every one of these languages in your website and some are more likely candidates than others. A good suggestion would be to include some elements of JavaScript within your website.

How to...

Add JavaScript to your website

There are many websites that give you free JavaScripts. To find them, you should either do a search for JavaScript, or, if you know what you are looking for, you could type a description of the task into your search engine.

Figure 14.23 shows the results of a search for 'disable right click'.

We will now add the script to disable right-click to viewers of our website.

1 Once you have found the script you want to use, highlight the script with your cursor, and copy it (using the CTRL+C).

2 Paste the script onto those web pages to which you wish to apply it, following the instructions in the code. For example, the disable right-click JavaScript has a section that goes into the head section of your web page, as well as a section which goes into the body.

Theory into practice

Search for the JavaScript required to disable right-click on your website. Insert this JavaScript on all four pages on your site.

WEB LANGUAGE	MAIN FEATURES
Hypertext markup language (HTML)	The web authoring language. Despite recent changes in web creation techniques, HTML remains the most frequently used language for creating websites.
Java	Java is used to create applets, which may then be downloaded from a web server and run on the computer being used to view the web page.
JavaScript	Allows a far more dynamic experience over what was offered by HTML on its own. JavaScript may be added to HTML documents to create elements that wish the viewer a pleasant afternoon or good night, based on the time on the viewer's computer, rather than the time at the web server, or can be used to mark a series of questions and give a mark out of ten.
VBScript	VBScript is based on Visual Basic. VBScript will typically be an instruction for an event to be carried out. Web browsers will interpret the VBScript alongside the HTML.
ActiveX	This may be considered to be Microsoft's equivalent of Java and may be used to create small applications that are transferred to the viewer's computer.
Perl	A text processing language used to create CGI scripts.
Virtual reality markup language (VRML)	VRML allows you to create 3D images on a web page.

TABLE 14.4 *Main features of web programming languages*

Web | Images | Video | Audio | Directory | Local | News | Shopping | More »

`disable right click`   Search

My Web   Answers BETA   Search Services   Ac

Search Results   Results 1 - 10 of about **7,430,000** for **disable right click**

Also try: **disable right click** html, **disable right click** on myspace   More...

SPONSOR RESULTS

- HTML Protector - Block Web Site Thieves
  www.antssoft.com   Software to **disable** the View Source function and the **right-clicks** in your Web pages.
- Cancel **Right Clicks**, New Software
  www.html-protector.com   Encrypt your HTML, hide your PayPal links, add password protection, lock to your URL, **disable** printing/clipboard, and more.

1. Dynamic Drive DHTML Scripts- **Disable right** mouse **click** script
   Categories. Other Sections. Compatibility. IE5+: IE 5 and above. FF1+: Firefox 1.0+. NS6+ and FF beta are assumed as well. Opr7+: Opera 7 and above. FF1+ IE5+ **Disable right** mouse **click** script ... browser DHTML script that will prevent the default **right** menu from popping up when the **right** mouse is clicked on the web ...
   www.dynamicdrive.com/dynamicindex9/no**right**.htm - 0 - Cached - More from this site - Save - Block

2. osCommerce: **Disable right click**
   ... **Disable right click**. This contribution **disables** the **right click** on your website ... captures event.button 2 & 3. **Disable right click**. jules190. 28 Jul 2003 ...
   www.oscommerce.com/community/contributions,1395 - 17k - Cached - More from this site - Save - Block

3. CodeLifter.com - JavaScript No-**Right-Click** Script
   Get the code! With CodeLifter 5.0 -- the ultimate tool for viewing page code, even on no-**right-click** protected pages, referer pages, and more. ... Basic No-**Right-Click** Script. With Alert Message ... **Click** here to select the code in the window below ... Basic No-**Right-Click** Script Functions: Blocks **right-click** on mouse and ...
   www.codelifter.com/main/javascript/no**right**click1.html - 0 - Cached - More from this site - Save - Block

FIGURE 14.23 *Search results for 'disable right click'*

Using graphics software

We will now look at adding graphics to the website.

Converting file types

The first consideration is to ensure that your graphics will work with web browsers. Therefore, we will start by discussing how to convert graphics into .jpg, .png or .gif format. You will remember that this is because many web browsers will only work with these three graphic formats.

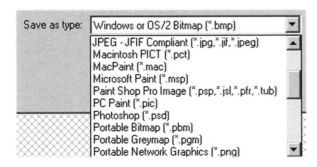

FIGURE 14.24 *The Save as type drop-down list from Paint Shop Pro*

How to...

Convert graphics files to .jpg, .gif or .png format

1 Open a graphics software package. This should be one of the more powerful packages so that you can work with a range of different graphics types.

2 Open the graphics file you wish to convert.

3 Choose Save As from the File menu.

4 Use the Save As Type drop-down list to select either .jpg, .gif or .png.

Optimising graphics

We have talked about compression in other sections of this unit and you should know that it is possible to reduce the file size of a graphic with little effect on quality. This process is called optimising a graphic, and is a further change that you should consider making to any graphics that you wish to include on your website.

Set jpg compression rates

This is a straightforward process in most of the more advanced packages. However, this facility is not offered in all packages.

The following explanation is for Paint Shop Pro, but the process is similar for other packages.

1 In your software package, click Save As from the drop-down menu, and choose the jpeg format.

2 If you now click the Option button, you will be presented with a slider and two radio buttons. The slider is used to set the compression ratio. The accepted quality for use on the web is 75%. This will dramatically reduce the file size, but will not affect the quality of the graphic.

3 The two radio buttons govern how the image builds when seen on the Internet.

When saved in standard encoding, the image builds top to bottom. With progressive encoding, the image starts as a rough image but becomes sharper as the image builds.

Adding graphics

There are a few ways that you can add graphics to your web page. However, as you are eventually going to publish your website, you will need to make sure that you always use graphics that are stored in the images folder you have created. This is because, when you come to publish your website, the folder structure for your website (which will include the images folder) will be transferred to the web server.

Add graphics to your website

Before you add any graphics to your web page, it is a good idea to add a few blank lines. This will make it easier to add text above the graphics later on.

Using a WYSIWYG package

If you are using a WYSIWYG web authoring package, such as Microsoft FrontPage, you will usually use the Insert, Picture tool to insert a picture into your web page.

You may also wish to add graphics using HTML once you have created your website. This would be a useful example of how you are able to work directly with HTML to change the layout of a web page.

Using HTML

1 Find the section of code that refers to the area where you wish to add the graphic.

2 Add the following code:

```
<img src="images/Madrid.jpg">
```

This will insert a graphic file called Madrid.jpg, which is stored in the images folder, into your web page.

In both cases, your graphic will appear left-aligned. This alignment may be changed easily when in Normal View.

Working with image size

It is worth remembering what was said above about graphics size. When we are considering layout, we are really talking about how many pixels wide and tall a graphic is, rather than the file size. It is possible to change how big a graphic appears on your web page, but this only changes the amount of pixels wide or tall the graphic is and does not affect the file size. If the graphic with which you are working takes up too many pixels, the best plan is to resize it in a graphics package and then insert it into your web page. Not only will this reduce the number of pixels the graphic covers, but it will also reduce the file size of the graphic and, subsequently, the time taken to download the web page.

Alternative text

Add alternative text to images

Alternative text can either be added as part of the property of an object when using a web page authoring package or may be added directly into the HTML code for a website.

Figure 14.25 shows the properties for a graphic. Alternative text can be added by typing into the box labelled Text.

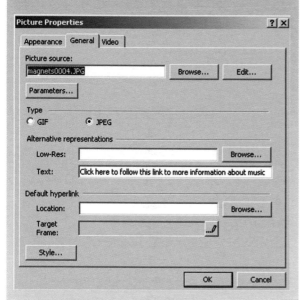

FIGURE 14.25 *Adding alternative text to an image*

Alternatively, you could amend the tag that places the graphic on the web page. The tag below has had alternative text added to the Madrid.jpg graphic.

```
<img src="images/Madrid.jpg"
alt="A picture of Madrid">
```

Adding alternative text to other objects

Each of these methods may also be used to add alternative text to other elements that may be included in web pages, such as embedded videos.

The website about Madrid needs some graphics. The brief has asked us to have a range of colour photographs of the city.

1 Before you add graphics to each page, add a few blank lines at the top of the page so that you can more easily add text later.

2 Choose suitable graphics and add them to your images folder whilst in Folders View. This is best done using cut and paste.

3 Add graphics to your website from the images folder. These will, by default, appear on the left of the page and, depending on their size, either below or alongside each other. If necessary, resize your graphics using graphics manipulation software.

4 Add a short descriptive piece of alternative text for each graphic.

FIGURE 14.26 *Index.htm of the Madrid website*

Animated GIFs

An animated GIF is a set of graphics that are collected together and played in order to create a moving picture. They are fun to create and can improve a website by adding some movement to an otherwise static website.

It is possible to download a range of animated GIFs from the Internet, but anyone with graphic software and animation software can create an animated GIF. Packages such as Paint Shop Pro and Animation Pro can be combined to create quite powerful animations.

How to...

Create an animated GIF

The process of creating an animated GIF begins by creating the graphics you are going to combine together to make your animation. To create the illusion of movement, there should be a small change between each graphic. For an animated GIF of a ball rolling across the screen, for example, the ball may move gradually from left to right in the frame.

When you have created the individual graphics or frames, they should be combined together.

An animated GIF may be added to a web page in the same way as any other graphic file.

An Internet search on 'creating animated GIFs' will bring up many sites that explain this process further.

Theory into practice

Create the following animated GIFs:

* a ball rolling across the page
* the text 'hello' appearing letter by letter in a frame.

Add the 'hello' animated gif to index.htm of your website. Resize it as necessary.

Adding text and numbers

We will now add further detail to our website and will start by giving each page a title.

Naming web pages

Web pages have filenames, which is the name used to save them, such as index.htm. Web pages also have titles, which is the name that is displayed at the top of the web browser page when the page is accessed.

The title of any web page is contained within the following tags:

```
<title>...</title>.
```

These tags will appear between the <head>...</head> tags.

How to...

Name your web pages

1 Open each of your web pages.

2 Choose the HTML View.

3 Add the code <title>*page name*</title> between the <head>...</head> tags. (Use the name shown in your plan for the website.)

4 Name the remaining web pages using the names shown in your plan.

Adding text

Text may be written directly into the Normal View of a WYSIWYG program just as it would be when using a word processor or desk top publishing (DTP) package. This text can also be formatted using similar toools. Alternatively, text may be copied and pasted directly onto your web page from a word-processing package. This method allows you use tools such those explained in the planning section of this unit.

When you create your web page, you will need to add headings and subheadings, as well as standard-sized text. Text may be formatted to achieve these goals by accessing the options from the Style drop-down list. Apart from headings and subheadings, most text on your page will be of the Normal style.

Your website needs some titles. It is a good design tip to start by adding these to your web page and then add the text content later.

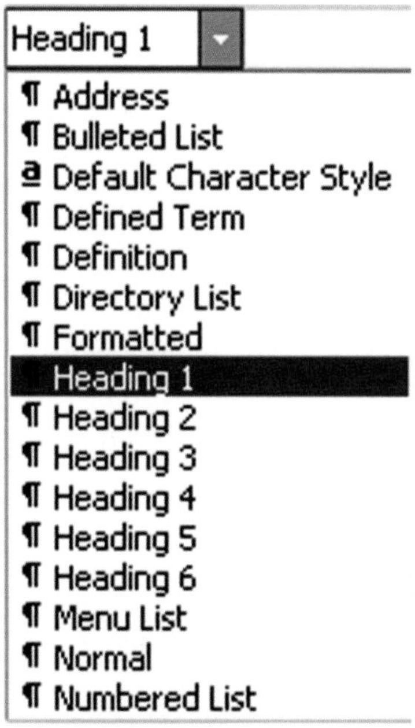

FIGURE 14.27 *The Style drop-down list*

How to...

Add headings and subheadings to your web pages

1 Open index.htm.

2 The first item on your page will be the blank lines you added above your image. You will probably want your title to go into this area.

3 Add some welcoming text. This may be an informal 'Welcome to my website' or may be more formal. This will depend both on your brief and the target audience.

4 Highlight this text and, from the Style drop-down list, select Heading 1.

5 Add two more blank lines to the web page and add a subtitle. Something like 'Introduction' or 'All about this website' would do.

6 Highlight this text and, from the Style drop-down list, select Heading 2.

Theory into practice

Use the techniques described above to add the headings shown in Table 14.5 to your website about Madrid.

WEB PAGE	HEADING 1	HEADING 2
Index	Welcome to my website	All about Madrid!
History	The history of Madrid	Early Madrid Madrid in the Civil War
Geography	The geography of Madrid	Where is Madrid? Physical geography
People	The people of Madrid	(None at this stage.)

TABLE 14.5

Adding lists

When working in the Normal View, the process of adding a numbered list to your web page works in exactly the same way as inserting numbers in a word-processing or DTP document. Your only concern is finding the shortcut button. As with most Microsoft packages, FrontPage has an icon on the main toolbar at the top of the page. Other packages, such as Macromedia Dreamweaver, have theirs at the bottom of the page.

It is worth checking the HTML code for adding a numbered list to your website, as it is a relatively easy piece of code. The numbered list is created by adding the <ol> tag. This tells the browser that a numbered (*ordered*) list is starting. Every separate element on that list then begins with the tag <li> (*list item*). As with other HTML features, the tag </ol> signifies the end of the numbered list. It is equally simple to create an unnumbered list. To do so, replace the <ol> tags with <ul>.

Theory into practice

You should now add suitable text and any lists you require to the Madrid website.

Follow the structure of the website to decide on the content of each page. You might decide to add extra subtitles of your choice as you create the website.

FrontPage defaults to Times New Roman, size 12. Change this in the usual way if your plans require it.

Background and foreground features

Until now, we have only dealt with one layer of your web page. However, you can add elements both to the foreground and the background of your web page. Elements in the foreground will appear on top of elements in the background.

Adding a background

Backgrounds can be graphics or single colours. A background may be added to a page as a whole or to a table or cell within a table. If you are using web page development software, this is a matter of working with the properties of the table or cell. However, if you are working with HTML code, it is simply a matter of inserting the code within the page or cell tags. We will come back to this when we discuss tables and cells later.

How to...

Add a graphic as a background to a page

Software packages differ greatly in how they add backgrounds to web pages. Some packages, such as Dreamweaver, let you change the background by working in the Page Properties interface, whilst others, such as FrontPage, insert a background graphic by using the Format menu.

Adding a background is a task that may be easily accomplished using HTML and is another change to a web page that you could make to show your use of HTML whilst developing your website.

The HTML code to insert a background is included *within* the <body> tag discussed above. Therefore, if we were using an image called XYZ.jpg, in the images folder, the <body> tag would become

```
<body background="images/XYZ.jpg">
```

Instead of using a background image, you may decide to use a background colour. The tag for this is slightly different:

```
<body bgcolor="red">
```

Note the American spelling of 'color' here.

Layering

Layering is not unlike adding a background, but is actually the technique of adding one element on top of another. The ability to lay foreground elements in front of each other is a relatively new concept in web pages and, until fairly recently, layered elements had to be created using graphics software and inserted into a web page as graphic elements. Not all web authoring packages handle layering well. For example, Dreamweaver includes an easy-to-use layer to tool, whilst FrontPage seems to ignore the facility.

Layering is a reasonably complex task and is probably best done using WYSIWYG software if at all possible.

How to...

Add layers to your web page

The following applies to Dreamweaver. You should check if your web authoring package supports this tool. If it does not, you should consider creating your element using graphics software.

There are two stages to creating a layer. The first is to define the layer and the second is to include the required element in that layer.

Add the layer
You will need to be in Design View when working in Dreamweaver to add the layer.

1 Choose Layout Objects from the Insert drop-down menu. Choose Layer from the Layout Objects menu.

2 A box will appear on your web page. Drag the box to where you want the layer to appear.

Add the content
Stay in Design View for this task.

1 Select the layer you have just created.

2 Add your element as you would normally add an element to a web page.

Cascading style sheets

Cascading style sheets have been developed to overcome two problems. Firstly, they allow a web page author to have far more control over what the web page looks like, whatever browsing software is being used. This is achieved by allowing the author to define certain elements that, if not defined by the author, may be interpreted by browser software. A good example is the use of headings. In the section above, we looked at creating headings on our web pages. One example was to add Heading 1 to the web page. When we add this heading, the following HTML code is added to the web page:

```
<h1>...</h1>
```

Any text that appears between these tags then becomes the heading. The problem with this is that different browsers will present this heading in different ways. By defining what Heading 1 is in the style sheet, the author is able to overcome this problem and any text included within the <h1> tags will be presented in exactly the same manner when shown on browsers that work with style sheets.

The second advantage of working with style sheets is that it cuts down on the amount of code included within a web page and therefore speeds up the loading time. This is because fonts and styles may be declared once only, rather than having to be redefined throughout the web page.

Key terms

Cascading style sheet: A set of formatting rules that allow the web author to have greater control over how the website will look on any number of different web browsing software packages.

One further advantage of using cascading style sheet (CSS) styles is that any change to a CSS style is automatically applied to all web pages that are governed by the style sheet. With this in mind, if you want to make some changes to a style sheet but do not want these to apply to all the web pages that use the style sheet, you should create a new style sheet based on the original, but save the updated style under a different name.

* Remember

Whilst the vast majority of web browsers will support cascading style sheets, this is not true of all web browsers and some will ignore your settings and will portray your website using their own settings.

Types of style sheet

There are three types of style sheet:

* external
* embedded
* inline.

An external style sheet keeps the style rules in a separate file. This allows you to apply the rules to all pages in your website if you wish. An embedded style sheet is held within one page only and applies only to the page on which it is held. This allows you to use an external style sheet for your website as a whole, but to change one page to achieve a different effect. This would allow you to have a different structure on a home page, for example.

The inline style sheet allows you to set a style for one element on the page, rather than the page as a whole. This is achieved by setting style rules within the HTML code directly governing that element.

Whilst it is important to understand what embedded and inline style sheets can do, it is just as easy to set your preferences for individual pages or elements included within a web page as you would for a page or an element created using a DTP or word-processing document, so we will leave these two types of style sheets to one side and concentrate on external style sheets.

Creating a cascading style sheet

Most web page development packages will include a range of CSS styles. However, you may decide that the style sheets offered by your web page development software do not suit your needs. If this is the case, you may decide to create your own style sheet. You could do this by using your web page creation software, but the procedure very much depends on the package you are using. However, it is a straightforward task when working with HTML, so we will concentrate on this method. If you want to use your web page creation software, you will need to check the help files included with the package.

Create a style sheet

A style sheet defines standard variables, such as the default font and how items such as headings will appear. We will now create a style sheet that defines the following elements:

* background colour

* normal text

* Heading 1.

1 Create a new text document.

2 To set the background colour and the values for the font, add the following:

```
body {background-color: red;
font-family: Arial, Helvetica,
sans-serif;
color: blue; font-size: 36}
```

Note that the instructions within the document are enclosed within curly brackets ({}). Also note the gaps between instructions and the use of semi-colons to define where instructions end.

These style rules work as follows:

* The background colour for the page is set to red.

* Text will appear in Arial, Helvetica or, if these do not exist on the viewer's computer, any sans serif font will be used.

* Text will be in blue and size 36.

3 To set the value for Heading 1, add the following in the next line:

```
h1 {color:yellow; font-family:
Times New Roman; font-size:48}
```

4 Save your style sheet as style1.css and ensure it is in the same folder as the rest of your website.

Applying a CSS style

As with creating CSS style sheets, the means of applying style sheets differs widely between different packages. If you want to apply a style sheet using the WYSIWYG approach, you will need to check the help files included with your web creation software.

However, applying a style sheet to a document is a relatively easy task when working in HTML.

Style sheets are applied by creating a reference within the document head using a <link> tag.

We will now apply the style sheet you have created to your Madrid website.

Apply an external style sheet

1 Open the index page of your web page in HTML View.

2 Add the following code to the document head, immediately below the title tag.

```
<link rel="stylesheet"
href="style1.css">
```

The style sheet is now linked to the web page and any changes you make to the style sheet will automatically be applied to that web page.

3 Repeat for the other web pages that make up your site.

Many aspects of your web page can be dictated by style sheets, ranging from the size, colour and font used for any text, though to the width and weight of borders used in boxes. An Internet search for cascading style sheets will bring up many sites that will be of great help to you.

✳ Remember

Cascading style sheets can be used to dictate the style of certain tags used in a document. However, these tags may be overwritten by HTML code included in a document. For example, the html code

```
<font size="2">
```

applied to text within the main body of the document would override the style rule set by the style sheet.

Adding tables, forms, interactive features and other components

You will have planned to add a range of interactive features to your website. This is a relatively straightforward process when using web page creation software, as you simply create the element and the software creates what is essentially quite complicated code for you.

In this activity, you will create a CSS style sheet to use on the Madrid website. This will be based on how you view yourself. You may describe this as the beginning of a voyage of self discovery!

1 Open the Madrid website project.

2 You are going to create a new CSS style that will be unique to you. This style sheet will be applied to the website as a whole.

3 You should now have an idea about what rules you can apply in a CSS style. Before you set any, spend some time thinking about what *you* like. What is your favourite colour? Do you have a favourite font?

4 Now create your own style sheet. Just to prove that it is yours, use your name as the name for the style. As you work through making changes to the settings, apply all of your favourites. Save your style sheet in the same folder as your website.

5 Apply your new style sheet to your website.

6 Save the pages in your website.

How to...

Create a table using HTML

The first stage of creating a table is to add the table tags. These are <table> to start the table and </table> to end it. Without both of these tags, your table will not work as intended. Anything between these tags is in the table.

Once you have created your table, you need to create the rows. Each row is created by adding the <tr> tag and closed by adding the </tr> tag. Every time you use these two tags, you create a new row in your table.

Lastly, you need to create the cells within a row. These are created with a <td> tag and closed with a </td> tag.

So, to create a two-by-two table, you would need the following HTML code:

```
<table>
<tr>
<td></td><td></td>
```

Tables

Tables may be used to give you greater control over the layout of your web page, as they divide the web page into a series of cells. If you create a table with a border size of 0, your page will still have a cell structure, but, once published, the table will not be visible. However, elements inserted into cells will be arranged across the page in an organised fashion.

How to...

Add tables

Tables are added to web pages in exactly the same way as you would add tables to a word-processing document. The similarity does not end there, as once you have chosen to add a table to your web page, you will be asked to decide on how many columns and rows you require, as well as the thickness of the borders around each cell. Once you have made your decisions, the table will be created for you.

One of the elements you could add using HTML code is a table. A table is quite easy to add, as long as you have an understanding of HTML tags and adopt a logical approach to creating the element.

```
</tr>
<tr>
<td></td><td></td>
</tr>
</table>
```

To add the title shops to the top left cell of this table, the code would become:

```
<table>
<tr>
<td>shops</td><td></td>
</tr>
<tr>
<td></td><td></td>
</tr>
</table>
```

Note that 'shops' has been enboldened in this example so that it stands out from the rest of the code. The web browser would not show this text as bold unless you added the <b> HTML tag.

This activity will look at adding a table to a web page. You will *not* work on the website you have been creating for this exercise and you should *not* use web page creation software.

1. Open a text editing package. At the top of the page, add the tag <html>.
2. Set up a head section. The title for this page will be **table practice**.
3. Set up a body section.
4. Create the table below within the body of your web page.

Pets	Cost
Dog	£20
Cat	£15

Once you have created your web page, save it as 1.htm and open it in a web browser.

In this activity you will add structure and layout to your website.

1. Open your Madrid website project in the Normal View.
2. Suppose you have decided to use a table to improve the layout of the graphics included on your website. On the index page, create a table with border width set to 0. You will need two columns and as many rows as you have pictures on your page.
3. Move each graphic on your index page to a separate cell in the left-hand column of the table you have created. This can usually be done by dragging the graphic into the correct cell.
4. For each graphic, add a piece of descriptive text in the cell to the immediate right of the graphic.
5. Repeat for the other pages in your Madrid site.
6. Save your website.

Forms

As we have discussed earlier, forms allow you to gather information from visitors to your site.

You should know that there are different types of forms for a range of purposes. Each of these was discussed in the section on planning a website.

When you are creating a form, it is usually best to create the form on the page and then add the elements to that form. This will then allow you to work on alignment around other elements and any text or graphic you choose to include in the form.

Do not forget to add the interactive Submit or Cancel buttons once you have completed your form. You should plan to test that all buttons included on your website work as intended.

Add a form to your web page

Forms are added in essentially the same way as tables. You choose to insert a form and then add the components. These components will range from areas that may be used to enter text (either a text box or a text area) through to components to register decisions (check box or option box).

FrontPage and Dreamweaver both use the Insert, Form menu to create a form and to add further elements. The advantage of using web page creation software to create a form is that the CGI scripts will be automatically created for you.

In this activity you will make your website interactive.

1. Open your Madrid website project.
2. You need to gather some information about how viewers feel about your site. Create a new web page called 'feedback'.

Your feedback form will include a large text area for visitors to add comments.

Create a form and add the text 'Do you like my website?' at the top of the form. Add a text area for visitors to add comments.

3. Add a Submit button to your form.
4. Save your website.

Table of contents and full text search form

Both of these elements were discussed in the interactive elements section. Whilst it is not necessary to include either of these two elements, if they are used properly, they do give a professional feel to your website. This is especially true of the full text search facility.

Theory into practice

1 Open your Madrid website project.

2 In Normal View, go to the index page.

3 Add a table of contents immediately below the 'Welcome to my website' text on this page. Base the table of contents on the navigation structure and start the list from the Geography page.

Other components

The specifications for this unit require you to include other components such as ActiveX controls, Java applets and CGI scripts. Each of these components would be sufficient for a book of its own! CGI scripts and, more recently, scripts written in other languages, such as JavaScript and VBscript, are used to cope with feedback from online forms and are automatically created when you are working with web page authoring software.

Similarly, you would not be expected to create Java applets. It is far more likely that you would be able to find small applications on the Internet that you could include within your website, as you would do with JavaScript.

Hyperlinks

Creating hyperlinks

As we have seen, hyperlinks may be added to many elements on a website. We will start by looking at text links.

Just about all web page authoring packages will have the Add a (text) hyperlink option within the Insert menu. Once clicked, this will

---

How to...

Add a table of contents and a search form to your website

These components are both dealt with as one, because FrontPage lists both components under the Insert, Web Components menu.

1 Select where on your website you wish these components to appear.

2 Use the Insert, Web Components menu to select the component you wish to add.

Inserting a table of contents

3 Choose the Table of Contents from the menu.

4 Choose how you want the table to be organised.

5 When prompted, choose the starting point for the table. This will default to the index page. If you are inserting this table onto the front page, you probably do not want to start with this page, so you should browse to another page on your website and choose this as your starting point.

6 Click OK.

Inserting a search form

7 Choose Web Search from the menu.

8 Choose the text you wish to appear on your form. This dialogue box is shown in Figure 14.28.

9 Click OK.

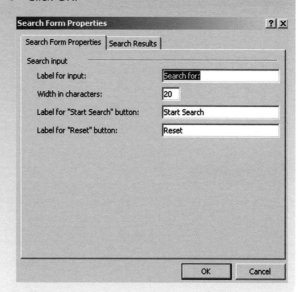

FIGURE 14.28

bring up a user interface form, which will ask you for details about the link, such as what text the link should display and where the link should take the user.

Your only task is to type in the link. This may be a link to a page within your website, in which case you should navigate to the file by using the Select File icon.

Alternatively, you may link to a web page on the World Wide Web. To do this, type the URL for the web page into the link section. This can be a bit tricky, especially for longer URLs, so you may want to copy the URL from the website itself (using CTRL+C) and paste it into the link section (using CTRL+V).

Theory into practice

Before you do this activity, find

* a website about Spain

* a website about Madrid.

Then follow the instructions on creating buttons (see page 265) to create a relevant button for each link. You could base these buttons on the flag of Spain and the flag of Madrid, for example.

1 Open your Madrid website project.

2 Open the index page and add a new table below the graphics that are already on the page. This table should have two cells. Set the border to 0.

3 Insert the button you will use for the link to the Spain website in the left-hand cell and the link to the website about Madrid to the right-hand cell.

4 Add hyperlinks to each button.

✱ Remember

URLs can be long and so you may make errors when entering a URL as a link. To avoid the risk of making a mistake, navigate to the web page to which you want to link and then highlight the URL of the page. You can then copy the URL using CTRL+C and then paste it into the link box using CTRL+V.

How to...

Create graphics links

This is done in much the same way as setting up a text link. The process is the same for any type of graphic, including a button created as a graphic.

To set up a graphic as a hyperlink, you first need to insert it into your document. Once you have inserted the graphic, what you do next will depend on the web page creation software you are using. Some packages will treat any link as part of the properties of a graphic, in which case the link will be added to the graphics properties in the Properties Interface box, whilst other packages will allow you to add a hyperlink by either right clicking on the image or selecting Hyperlink from the Insert menu.

Theory into practice

Now is the time to make your Madrid website navigable. We will concentrate on text-based hyperlinks at the moment. We will start by giving the website a hierarchical structure.

1 Open your Madrid website project. You are going to add a hyperlink from your index page to each of the other pages on your website.

2 In Folders View, open the index page and then switch to Normal View. Move to the area below the table you added in the task above and add a further table, this time with three cells. Set the border to 1. Add the text 'History' to the first cell, the text 'Geography' to the middle cell and the text 'People' to the right-hand cell. Each of these words will become your hyperlinks to the other pages.

3 Select the text History and insert a hyperlink to the History page. Add a link from the Geography text to the Geography page and a link from the People text to the People page.

4 Now return to the Folders View and select the History page. Return to Normal View and add the text 'home' at the bottom of the page. Make this a link back to the index page (the home page).

5 Insert a link back to the index page on all other pages on your site.

6 Save your website.

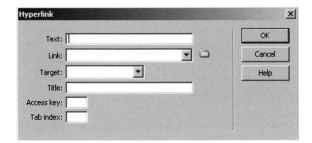

FIGURE 14.29 *Adding a text hyperlink to a Dreamweaver document*

Other links
Email links
It is a good idea to include an email link in your website. An email link is included in a website in much the same way as any other link.

Including video and audio

Before we continue with this section, you will need to be clear about whether you want to include the video or audio on your web page, so that the video or audio is handled by the web page browser, or you want to include a link to the video or audio, so that the web user can download it. The two different tasks are treated very differently.

Embedding a video or audio file
This is the option where the video or audio file is shown by the browser. Sound and video are basically added in the same way, so we shall look at both together.

You have decided to add a sound or video to your web page. Now for the second question. Do you want the sound or video to run when the web page is accessed, or do you want the visitor to control when the sound or video is played?

Let's deal with running a sound or video when a page is accessed. This is a variation on the insert technique used for graphics and other elements. Obviously, different web page creation packages will deal with this in different ways, but, usually, videos are added to a web page as part of the Images menu.

Sound is treated slightly differently, in that it is generally treated as a specific media plug-in. However, once you find the tool to add the sound plug-in, the process is as straightforward as adding any other element.

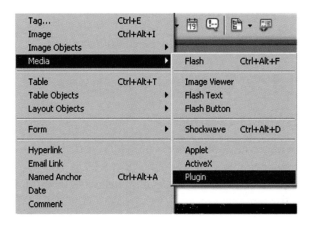

FIGURE 14.30 *The drop-down menu to add a sound file in Dreamweaver*

Because both of these elements have been added in this manner, they will sit on the web page and play independently of the viewer. However, it is possible to have sound and video playback controlled by Stop, Play and Pause buttons. When creating a web page using Microsoft FrontPage, for example, this is achieved by inserting a plug-in as part of the Insert Web Component menu.

Linking to a video or audio file

If you just want the user to be able to download the video or audio file, you can simply create a hyperlink to it.

Working with HTML

Throughout this unit, you have been given instructions on how to add elements to your website using web page creation software. Alongside some of these instructions, you have been given the HTML code required to create these elements.

It is a requirement of this unit that you show that you can work with HTML code. At the most basic level, you need to highlight code used on your website and explain what it does. However, to achieve the higher mark band, you will need to change the layout of a page and to add elements to your website using HTML code. You should refer to the assessment section at the end of this unit for further information on this requirement.

Allowing for non-standard users

We have already discussed the arrangements you should make for the visually impaired visitor to your website. This topic has been dealt with in the section on working with speech synthesisers.

14.5 Testing a website

What is testing?

Before you publish your completed website, you must test it to check whether it works as you intended. There are three main tasks you should perform:

* testing all links and pathways
* proof-reading text

* checking the layout and alignment of all elements.

Testing is an extremely important part of the creation of a website, but is often one that is either ignored, or left until the very end and then rushed. However, it seems silly to put many hours into creating a website, only to have it fail because a link does not work or because an image does not appear.

The best way to ensure that you test all of these elements is to create a **test plan** before you start testing your website. This test plan will list what elements will be tested and how.

> ### Key terms
>
> *Test plan:* A plan showing which parts of your website will be tested. It will also show how each part will be tested and what the expected outcome of each test will be.

Testing for different hardware and software

As you create your test plan, remember to build in testing using different hardware and software. As you will remember, when you are creating a website, you are writing the HTML code that web browsers then interpret. Different web browsers will interpret this HTML code in different ways. You must be sure that your website is not unduly affected by these differences of interpretation.

It would seem unreasonable for you to test every aspect of your website on every possible piece of web browsing software available. However, you should be aware that there are two market leaders in the field and you should at least show some evidence of testing your website on both of these. It would also seem reasonable that you do the majority of your testing using one browser, but repeat some tests, especially those checking the layout of the page and how elements may be viewed, on the other.

We have also discussed the effect that using different hardware to view your website may have on how the viewer experiences your website. You may choose to include a comment about the best screen resolution to use when viewing your website, but you must accept that not all viewers will be able to change their screen resolution settings, so you will need to test how your website appears with a range of different screen resolutions. Screen resolutions are accessed from the Display options within the Control Panel. Generally speaking, most viewers will have their screen resolutions set to 1280 by 1024 pixels, 1024 by 768 or 800 by 600, so you will need to test your website using at least these three resolutions.

You should also be aware that your website may have large elements that will take some time to download. Most web page creation software will give you some indication of how long your page will take to download. You should look for a piece of text saying something like '101 seconds over 56.6' or '46 seconds over ISDN'. This piece of text is telling you how long your web page will take to load using different web connections. For example, '101 seconds over 56.6' means that your web page will take 101 seconds to load over a 56.6k modem.

If you find that your website will take too long to download, refer back to the section on graphics, where we discussed ways of reducing the time it takes to download a website.

Is the meaning clear?

You should check your website and consider whether the meaning is clear. You should ask yourself whether the website as a whole and its different web pages help the reader to understand the information being presented.

You should also consider the elements in your website. Look again at the images you chose to include. Do these improve the understanding of your website? Is text well presented and clearly written? Have you written too much? Remember the design tip about less being more. If, by reducing the amount of text, you could make your website easier to understand, reduce the number of words!

Does the website work as intended?

Your website will include many different elements. To ensure that you test all of these elements, you will have to create a test plan before you start testing your website.

You will need to create a test plan that will test all parts of your website. These tests are explained below.

Testing all links and pathways

✳ Plan to click on each link in your product. The expected result of these tests is that you should go to the planned area of your product.

✳ A subsection of this test is to test other events that will be run by clicking on buttons or other areas within your product. For these tests, the expected result is that the planned event will happen. For example, this may be a video or sound file playing.

Checking the layout and alignment of all elements

This test is largely self-explanatory. You should simply go through and test that images, boxes and other set shapes line up as you intended at the start. You will want your product to appear as professional as possible and alignment, as well as spelling, are both areas that can make a product look unprofessional if not completed with care.

Proof-reading

Before you finally publish your website, you should give it a final read through. This may actually be considered part of the testing process and is one of the most simple of all tests, but possibly the most effective. Most web page creation packages include a spell checker, but a simple read through will still highlight some problems. Remember that a spell checker may not test grammar, so look out for the standard errors, such as 'there' and 'their'.

14.6 Uploading a website

This is the final stage of creating a website and was, traditionally, the most complicated, as you needed to know about the File Transfer Protocol and manage files yourself.

However, with web page authoring software came easy web publishing and all web page authoring packages will allow you to publish your website without the requirement for any real understanding of File Transfer Protocol or to spend hours managing files.

How to publish your site – a step-by-step guide

The step-by-step guide below explains the process of publishing a site authored in Microsoft FrontPage. However, the process is similar for all web page authoring software.

Step 1: Decide whether you are publishing to a web server, an FTP server or to your local computer. It is likely that you will be publishing to a web server.

Step 2: Choose Publish web from the File menu.

Step 3: You will be asked for the location to which you are going to publish your website. This is not the web address for your website, but the address of the web server you will be using. Type the details in and click OK.

Step 4: You will then be asked which pages you wish to publish. As you are setting up a new website, you will probably want to publish all of the pages you have created. To do this, click Options and then click on the Publish tab. You can now choose to publish all the pages. Later, when you have updated the website, you may wish to publish only those pages that you have changed.

Step 5: Now click Publish, and you will have a live website that you can visit and experience as if you were a visitor to the website.

14.7 Evaluation

You will need to provide a written evaluation of your website. You will find it useful to include comments made by visitors to your website to help you in this process.

Your evaluation should cover a list of different topics, as follows:

* A full explanation of why elements were included in the website.
* An analysis of the strengths and weaknesses of your website.
* A discussion of any improvements that could have been made to your original designs and how you used your designs to create the website.
* A discussion of the quality your website as a whole.
* A discussion of how easily you worked with the web page creation software.

Whilst some of the above list are self-explanatory, some need some further clarification.

Identifying the good and bad points

You will need to re-use all the skills and techniques you used to criticise commercially produced websites in order to criticise your own. You will need to comment on how well the completed product meets the original brief. This analysis will be based on your interpretation of your completed product, for which you may want to refer back to your original designs, as well as the original brief. However, as well as your opinion, you should ask others their opinion of your completed product and any supporting materials, such as user guides, and use these comments to inform your general overall opinion of the completed product.

Did you plan and implement well?

Whilst a well-produced plan makes it more likely that your completed website will include all that it should, there is no guarantee that this is the case. It could be that you are excellent at creating plans, but poor at carrying them out. Alternatively, you may actually have real problems with planning, but find that because of other skills you possess, things have a habit of working out. Of course, it could also be that you are excellent or poor at both!

Wherever your skills lie, you will need to comment on the production of your storyboard and the way this influenced how the final website was made. This is not so much a discussion of where you put individual pictures, but rather an explanation of how useful the storyboard was in allowing you to create a working website.

How good is your website?

There are four main areas to consider:

* Does it meet the original needs?
* Does it attract the target audience?
* Does it put the right information across?
* Is it easy to use?

Does it meet the original needs?

For this section of your evaluation, you will need to go back to the original brief. This will allow you to compare your website with the website that the brief asked for.

There are many ways in which you could write this section of your report, but possibly the best way would be to break the brief down into each specific target. For each of these targets, you should then explain how your website met the target. This might be a specific element within your website, such as a piece of text or a graphic, or may be the website as a whole.

Does it attract the target audience?

This is a very important question and is one that you may wish to use other people to help you answer. If your website fails to include elements that attract the target audience, then, to a large degree, you may consider that your website has failed to achieve what it set out to do. This may have been caused by a problem with your interpretation of the brief or by the brief itself.

As you are the author the website, you will have included a range of elements and made design decisions. Hopefully, you will have made these decisions because you thought that they satisfied an element of the brief. This may explain why you chose to include a certain graphic, or chose to have a certain background image. However, the elements you chose to include may not actually be as effective as you assumed they would be. This may be because you have not chosen wisely, or that the original brief, which may have included design considerations set by a customer, was equally flawed. Because you created the website, you may not be aware of these problems. It is therefore good practice for you to invite comments from representatives of the target audience and use these comments as part of your evaluation.

Does it put the right information across?

As you review your product, ask yourself whether what is being said is what needs to be said. Does your product get its message across accurately? You may have chosen to include certain statistics in your website. You should check that these are accurate and also that they are the best figures to use. You may have been asked to include a photograph of a certain location. Have you chosen the best photograph? There may be better choices or there may not, but at least, by considering the issue, you will be sure that you have made the best decision about what to include in your website.

Is it easy to use?

This is a simple question really, but one which may prove difficult to answer without some thought. It is very likely that you will consider your website extremely easy to use; but then, you would, wouldn't you? You have, in your mind, created one of the best websites possible, and, whilst that bit on the third page is a bit weak, overall it is fantastic!

Unfortunately, not everyone may agree that your website is as good as you think, and some may even claim that the weak bit on the third page completely ruins it. You should therefore get others to test it. To do this effectively, you should ask people from different groups to test your website. The first person to review how easy your website is to use should be a friend or colleague. This person will take a quick look over the website and be able to give you immediate feedback that you can apply straight away. The second person should be someone you know who will take a bit more time and may make suggestions that show more depth of thought than those made by your colleague.

The last person, or maybe even people, to test your website should be from the target audience. By the stage your product reaches them, most of the silly mistakes and obvious issues will have been removed. This means that any criticisms made by these testers really will be based on what they think as members of the target audience, rather than just average users of the website.

Issues with using the software

Finally, you will need to comment on how easily you used the web page authoring software. Whether you are new to website creation or have created websites before, there is still a commentary to be given here, especially as just about every user will find new tricks and techniques when they really get to grips with a piece of software.

14.8 Laws and guidelines

The main laws and guidelines that affect website creation are those of Copyright, Data Protection and the Misuse of Computers. You should refer to the section in *Unit 1: Using ICT to Communicate* for specific instructions on how any laws may affect your production of websites.

Knowledge check

1 Explain the following terms:

  a) URL

  b) domain name

  c) home page.

2 What is the difference between web authoring software and web browsing software?

3 What is the difference between using web authoring software and text editing software to create a website?

4 (a) What is meant by the term 'web server'?

  (b) Explain the difference between websites which use the HTTP protocol and those which use the FTP protocol.

5 The time taken to download a website may influence the effectiveness of a website.

  (a) Explain three factors which may affect how quickly a website downloads.

  (b) Explain how the author of a website may affect how quickly their website is downloaded.

6 Why is it important that a web site author tests their website using a range of different software and hardware?

7 (a) What is meant by the term 'alternative text'?

  (b) Explain why a person creating a web page may include alternative text in their website.

8 Write a step-by-step guide to naming and publishing a website.

9 What is the difference between a mesh and a hierarchical structure? State one application for each of these structures.

10 Explain why it is important to test your product once it has been completed.

UNIT ASSESSMENT

You have been asked to produce a multiple-page website for Fastway Travel. The completed website will give information on a range of popular holiday destinations. The website should also include elements intended for clients to use to make enquiries and request further information, such as a copy of Fastway's brochure.

Fastway has been experiencing increased bookings from families, but would like to increase the bookings received from young couples and single people. As well as general information about resorts, Fastway would like you to include specialist information that would appeal to these two target groups.

Task A

Choose *at least* two existing websites with elements you may wish to include in your own website. Write a report discussing the good and bad points of each website. Your report should identify which elements have provided you with ideas for inclusion in, or exclusion from, your website.

Mark Band 1

As a minimum, you should comment on the features found in the websites you choose to review.

Mark Band 2

You must fully explain your reasons for including some features you have found and excluding others.

Mark Band 3

Your report should fully describe and evaluate the design and structure of *at least* two websites and must explain your reasons for choosing to include some elements you have found and to reject others.

Task B

This task concentrates on the design decisions and choice of domain name and the location (URL) of your home page.

The decision about which Mark Band is appropriate is based on how well you deal with the following tasks:

The planning process

You should include the following documents:

* a structure diagram
* a storyboard
* an index of pages
* an index of files used in the website
* a task list or action plan.

Design considerations

You should explain the reasoning behind your choice of:

* font style
* graphics
* colour
* hyperlinks.

Domain name and URL

You should identify the domain name you have chosen and the URL for your home page. You should fully explain the choice of domain name and URL and suggest alternatives that you could have used for both.

Mark Band 1

The planning process: You must include all the documents listed, except the index of files used in the website.

Design considerations: Little or no justification of your choice of font, graphics, colour or hyperlinks is required.

Domain name and URL: You should identify the domain name and URL of the home page.

Mark Band 2

The planning process: Your plan must be for a hierarchical or mesh website, and you must include all the documents listed.

Design considerations: You must produce some justification of your choice of font, graphics, colour or hyperlinks.

Domain name and URL: You should identify the domain name and URL of the home page and clearly explain why you chose these.

Mark Band 3

The planning process: Your plan must be for a hierarchical or mesh website, and you must include all the documents listed.

Design considerations: You must produce a clear justification of your choice of font, graphics, colour or hyperlinks.

Domain name and URL: You should identify the domain name and URL of the home page and clearly explain why you chose these. You should also give alternative options that you could have used.

Task C

You will now create a multiple-page website. Once you have completed your website, you will write a report that addresses the following:

* design techniques used
* hyperlinks
* multimedia features
* interactive features.

All three mark bands require you to create a multiple-page website. The differentiation in this task is how well you write the report. This is explained below.

Mark Band 1

You must produce a multiple-page website.

Your report will *identify* the design techniques, hyperlinks, multimedia features and interactive features included in your website.

Mark Band 2

You must produce a multiple-page website.

Your report will *describe* some of the design techniques, hyperlinks, multimedia features and interactive features included in your website.

Mark Band 3

You must produce a multiple-page website.

Your report will *fully explain* the design techniques, hyperlinks, multimedia features and interactive features included in your website.

Task D

You need to show that, as well as creating a website using web page authoring software (which you did in task C), you have also gained knowledge of HTML code.

Mark Band 1

As a minimum, you should explain three different HTML script commands included in your website.

Mark Band 2

You must show that you have edited HTML script commands to change the page layout for your website.

Mark Band 3

You should show that you have edited HTML script commands to change the page layout for your website and that you have *added* HTML script commands for *two* from

* graphic
* table
* hyperlink.

Task E

When you have completed your website, you will need to test that it meets the design specifications and that it works as intended. You will now produce a test plan to check your product and then carry out testing, making changes to your product as issues arise.

Mark Band 1

You must at least test your website to ensure that it meets the initial design specifications.

Mark Band 2

You must test that your website meets the design specifications and that it works as intended.

Mark Band 3

You must test that the website meets the design specifications and that it works as intended. Once you have completed your testing, you should make the changes necessary to ensure that the errors which your design plan identified are corrected. You should then test that the changes you have made correct the errors.

Task F

Your final task is to review both the website and the role you played in producing it. The review should fully discuss how effective the website is in meeting the needs of the users and should include some feedback from visitors to the site. There should also be some indication about how the product could be improved in the future.

Your review of your own effectiveness in producing the product will identify strengths and weaknesses and will include a discussion of how you would overcome any sortcomings in the future.

Your review should be written in Standard English and contain few, if any, spelling mistakes.

Mark Band 1

You must comment on how good the website is in meeting the needs of the user. You should also comment on the effectiveness of the software you used to produce the website. Your self-review will include a few comments about how well you did and will highlight areas in which you could have done better. Your report may contain errors in spelling, punctuation and grammar.

Mark Band 2

You will review your completed website and identify its strengths and weaknesses. You will also review the approach you took to the designing, implementing and testing of your product and will comment on the strengths and weaknesses of how you carried out these tasks. Your report into your effectiveness will then give some suggestions for how you could do better in the future. Your report will contain few spelling, punctuation and grammar errors.

Mark Band 3

Your review of the completed product should be full and critical. You must justify your decision to include the elements you chose to build into your website. You must gather feedback from visitors to the website and use this, along with your own analysis, to discuss the strengths and weaknesses of the elements you included and the website as a whole.

Your analysis of your own performance starts by identifying the strengths and weaknesses of your performance and uses these points to fully explain how you would do better if you were to do this project again. Your report will be consistently well-structured and there will be few, if any, spelling, punctuation or grammar errors.

Software development

By studying this unit, you will

* understand the principles of software development

* apply the principles of software development to design a software system to meet the needs of an end-user and to provide a solution

* apply the principles of software development to develop and test a software system to meet the needs of an end-user and to provide a solution.

Introduction

The process of developing software to meet the needs and requirements of end-users has various stages that need to be completed. There are many different methodologies that can be used when developing software, but all of them have pre-defined stages that need to be completed.

How this unit will be assessed

This unit is assessed through an external assessment. A case study and tasks will be released before the external assessment. You will need to examine the case study, complete the tasks and take them into the test with you. In the test, you will be asked questions on what you have produced and on other aspects you have covered. The mark on that assessment will be the mark for the unit.

What you need to learn

You need to learn about

* initial/feasibility study
* analysis and design
* implementation and maintenance.

15.1 Introduction to the systems life cycle

All software development projects go through a number of stages before they are completed – the systems life cycle. As the term 'cycle' suggests, there is no clear start or finish point, but it is often helpful to think of the start as the point at which a new software system is being considered. Think of the life cycle as a continuous loop with each stage leading into the next.

It may be that the existing system is unable to cope with the increased demands of the end-users. For example, a business may have expanded its functional base – increased the range of goods and services it offers or expanded to other regions, or the volume of work may have increased – leading to a reduction in the efficiency of the current system.

There are many different methodologies that can be used when developing a new software system. In *Unit 6: Software Development – Design*, you learned about **SSADM**, also known as the waterfall model, which is the foundation from which all other methodologies have been developed. You will, if you continue your study of this subject area, learn about these. It is important that you learn about the waterfall model so that you can build on this knowledge in your future studies.

If you have studied Unit 6, some of the concepts, terms, tools and techniques will be familiar to you, *but it is very important that you revisit these areas to reinforce your knowledge*. In this unit, you will build upon the knowledge you developed whilst studying Unit 6.

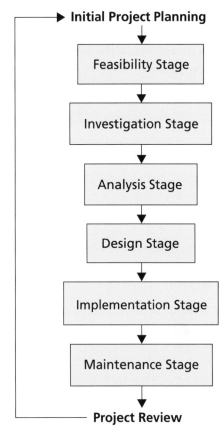

FIGURE 15.1 *The systems life cycle model*

Key terms

SSADM: Structured systems and design methodology.

Each stage within the life cycle has a dependency on the stages that occur immediately before and after it. If you look at Figure 15.1, you can see that the analysis stage will depend upon the investigation stage (the stage before) and the design stage (the stage after).

In this unit, we will be looking at all the stages within the system life cycle:

* Feasibility
* Investigation
* Analysis
* Design
* Implementation
* Maintenance.

The investigation stage is sometimes combined with the analysis stage, but the methods used for investigation are very important, as is the understanding of what is to be achieved by the investigation. The tasks completed within the analysis stage will be based on the findings from the investigation stage.

In Figure 15.1, you will see two stages that are outside of the systems life cycle. These are initial project planning and project review. Usually, the initial project planning stage is considered to be part of the feasibility stage, but the **systems analyst** will have to be prepared for the main investigation as to the feasibility of the proposed changes to the system. This preparation may include investigations into the organisation/business and the current system in place.

Today, most systems analysts are known as systems analysts/designers where they are responsible for both the analysis and the new system design. This change has occurred over time as the boundaries between the stages of feasibility, investigation, analysis and design have become blurred.

> **Key terms**
>
> *Systems analyst:* The person who is responsible for the analysis of a system to assess its suitability for the proposed changes.

Feasibility study

The **feasibility study** is the initial look at the existing system to see how it can be improved, or if it is possible to meet the needs and requirements of the end-users. The end result of this stage is a **feasibility report**.

> **Key terms**
>
> *Feasibility study:* An initial look at an existing system to see how it can be improved.
>
> *Feasibility report:* The final product from the feasibility stage.

The feasibility study answers some very important questions:

* Can the need for a new software system be justified?
* Is it technically feasible and economically desirable to the end-users?

During this stage, a number of important questions may be asked, including the following:

* Can the solution be designed and implemented within the given constraints of timescale and budget?
* Will the solution have a positive impact on the end-users?
* Will the new system bring benefits?
* Will the solution fulfil all the needs and requirements of the end-users?

For the project to continue, the answer to all these questions must be yes. If there is the time, money and resources, the impact of the proposed solution will be positive.

A new system may bring the following benefits:

* greater efficiency
* reduced costs and overheads
* standardised way of working and sharing of information across the organisation
* increased end-user satisfaction.

Feasibility report

During your study of this unit, you will need to investigate a system and produce a feasibility report.

You may be asked to produce a feasibility report as part of the assessment evidence for this unit. You may be asked questions about the feasibility report for Section A of the exam paper.

A feasibility study should include:

* the purpose of the system
* functional and non-functional requirements
* process constraints
* a list of deficiencies of the current system
* the user requirements of the new system
* recommendations for the development of the new system.

The feasibility study begins with an initial investigation that involves the systems analyst obtaining some general information, including:

* the system currently being used, its benefits and limitations
* the additional requirements the end-users need from a new software system.

The purpose of the system

The analyst must identify why a new software system is needed and what the purpose of the software system is.

The analyst must identify why the current system is not meeting the needs of the organisation. There are many reasons why a new system may be required:

* The organisation wants to computerise a part of its operations that is currently done manually.
* The capacity of the existing software system is too small to carry out the work now demanded of it.
* The existing system is now outdated and no longer suits the needs of the organisation.
* The existing system has come to the end of its life and needs to be replaced.

Typically, the end-user will define specific tasks that must be carried out using the new system. Examples of these might be:

* to keep customer records
* to calculate and print invoices
* to record the financial transactions of the organisation.

The analyst must be able to clearly identify the general reasons why a new software system is required and the specific requirements detailed by the end-users.

Once the reasons for a new software system have been identified, the analyst must describe the role of the current system. Based on these findings, the analyst, in consultation with the end-users and management of the organisation, must state what the new system needs to do. This is called a **statement of purpose**.

> **Key terms**
>
> *Statement of purpose:* A statement defining what the new system must do.

Functional and non-functional requirements

Functional requirements specify what the end-users want the system to do. These requirements may include the ability to enter data, and to display data/information on the screen or in printed format.

Non-functional requirements are concerned with two main areas:

* response time
* specified hardware/software/programming languages.

Both these areas are dictated by the end-users and must be considered by the systems analyst during the development of the feasibility report and the new system.

> **Key terms**
>
> *Functional requirements:* What the end-user wants the system to do.
>
> *Non-functional requirements:* The limitations relating to response time/hardware/software/programming language given by the end-user.

Using the case study, Tennis Time, it is possible to define the functional and non-functional requirements.

The functional requirements are to:

* display all the courts that can be played upon
* display the courts that are available at the time requested
* enter the details of the member
* provide a booking reference number.

The non-functional requirements are:

* the system is to run on the existing network
* the operating system to be used is Windows XP
* the software package to be used is Microsoft Access.

Theory into practice

Based on the information given in the case study, write a statement of purpose for Tennis Time.

In many cases the functional requirements and the specific requirements of the end-users (as detailed in the purpose of the new software system) will be very similar. If this is the case, the analyst will be simply redefining and clarifying that the requirements of the new system and the defined functional requirements are correct and cover all the requirements of the new system.

Remember, it is important at this point in the systems life cycle that the requirements of the new software system are clearly defined. The rest of the systems life cycle depends upon the purpose of the new software system and the functional and non-functional requirements being clearly defined and agreed between the analyst and the end-users of the system.

Process constraints

There are four main process constraints that the analyst will have to be aware of and take into account when making recommendations for the proposed solutions:

* budget

* time

* hardware choice

* software choice.

The end-users will normally provide the analyst with a budget – the amount of money that is available to be spent on the project. This budget will be set by the management of the organisation requiring the new software system. During the feasibility stage, the analyst may not be aware of the budget. The feasibility study will need to estimate the cost of completing the project, including the cost of any new hardware that may be required, the cost of developing and implementing the software required and any training costs for the end-users of the new software.

The end-users will also provide the analyst with a deadline for the implementation of the new software system. It may be that the organisation has a target date to meet its needs, such as expansion or a special event. For example, if the new software system needs to be implemented within six months, this deadline may form part of the contractual agreement between the analyst and the organisation, with financial penalties imposed by the organisation if the deadline is not met.

If the new software system is to be integrated into a current system used by the organisation, the hardware and software that can be used may be given. The organisation may specify that a particular hardware platform or software package is to be considered and used by the analyst during the development of the new software system. It may be that the organisation needs the software used throughout the different departments to be standardised or that the new software system is to be run using an existing software package.

It may be possible that the organisation requires extra hardware components, such as laptops, or the peripherals used within the organisation to be upgraded or standardised.

When the analyst is considering the feasibility of the new software system, it is important that the process constraints given by the client are considered. The process constraints given by the client may link with the non-functional requirements already defined by the analyst.

> ### ✳ Remember
>
> The client defines the process constraints to the analyst. The main process constraints are
>
> ✳ time
>
> ✳ budget
>
> ✳ hardware choice
>
> ✳ software choice.

Deficiencies of the current system

The analyst must draw up a list of what is wrong with the current system. This list can be based on initial investigations already completed by the analyst or given by the client.

It is important also that the analyst identifies and notes those parts of the current system that are working well so that these can be included within the new system.

User requirements of the new system

During this initial stage in the life cycle, the user will define their requirements for the new system. These requirements may fall into two categories:

✳ Generic, e.g. keep records of suppliers, customers and stock levels in a database.

✳ Specific, e.g. reports should be printed on a daily basis to show stock levels.

Most organisations will define requirements that fall into both categories. For example, in the Tennis Time case study, it has been defined that one of the requirements of the new system is that the club's courts and their operational status should be displayed.

Another requirement defined by Tennis Time is that a report should be printed to show the peak times that the courts are used.

> ### Theory into practice
>
> Using the case study, Tennis Time, define the other user requirements that have been given.

Following investigation, the analyst may feel that some of the user requirements are not feasible. In consultation with the organisation and end-users, an alternative set of requirements should then be developed.

Once the requirements have been agreed by the organisation and the analyst, it is important that these user requirements are constantly referred to throughout the rest of the life cycle. By doing this, the analyst can be assured that the new system, once implemented, will meet all the user requirements.

If the requirements are not referred back to, the system may not fully, if at all, meet the needs of the end-users. If this situation occurs, the new system will not be useful to the organisation; it may not be used, resulting in a waste of money for the organisation.

Recommendations for the development of the new system

Once all the information has been collected, the analyst will be able to draw conclusions and make recommendations. The recommendations will have to be achievable within the given timescale and budget (if known). If a sensible solution cannot be achieved within the constraints of time and money, the analyst must explain why. If a solution is possible based on the given constraints, the analyst must recommend solutions to the problem.

In the feasibility report, the analyst has to make recommendations for a proposed solution. Usually, analysts will provide more than one solution to the problem, all of which will meet the needs and requirements but may have different budget implications.

Software approaches

There are three main software approaches that the analyst can use to provide the solutions. These are to use:

* bespoke or custom-written software
* off-the-shelf software
* customised off-the-shelf (COTS) software.

Bespoke software

Bespoke or custom-written software is developed to meet the needs of a single organisation. It is specially written to meet the end-user's specific requirements. Although it is very expensive and time-consuming to produce, a bespoke system is designed to meet the exact needs of the end-users and the organisation. For example, the software written to handle customer transactions using Chip and PIN cards is bespoke software. It has been specially written for an organisation – a bank – to meet a specific requirement. It is not only large organisations that will use bespoke software. Smaller organisations may also require bespoke software to be written, as their needs and requirements of the software will be specific to the nature of their business.

Off-the-shelf software

Off-the-shelf software has already been written, developed and tested. It is available from high-street stores, through e-commerce or a mail-order software supplier and can be installed and used immediately. These software solutions are normally sold as whole packages. They are supplied on a CD-ROM or DVD-ROM with any

updates to the software being supplied on storage media or through downloads from the Internet. Off-the-shelf software can be used in many different types of organisations. These solutions are generally cheaper to buy than bespoke or COTS and have the advantage of having been fully tested. As this software can be installed and used almost immediately, this approach has a time advantage over the other two approaches. The main disadvantage with this approach is that the software may not fully meet the needs and requirements of the organisation and end-users.

Customised off-the-shelf (COTS) software

Customised off-the-shelf (COTS) software has the advantages of both bespoke and off-the-shelf software and is often sold to specific organisations that perform the same activities. For example, all DVD and video rental shops will need software that handles customer records and keeps records of loans and returns, stock lists and borrower requests, but each shop will also have specific needs that will not be shared with other shops; for example, some may stock games or sweets and drinks as well. An off-the-shelf solution is not appropriate as it will not be flexible enough to meet all the needs of every shop, whilst a bespoke system will probably be too expensive for a single shop. A customised solution can be bought from a software house that will be able to modify the software, selecting from a range of pre-written functions, to fully meet the needs of an individual shop. The user interface will then be tailored to suit the end-users of the software and to give the impression of a bespoke software package.

Key terms

Bespoke or custom-written software: Software that is specially developed to meet the needs of a particular organisation.

Off-the-shelf software: Software that has already been developed and is ready to buy, install and use on a computer system.

Customised off-the-shelf (COTS) software: Software that is purchased off the shelf as a package and then modified to meet the needs of a particular organisation.

As the feasibility report is written by an analyst for the management of the organisation needing the new software system, it is very important that it is written, as far as possible, in non-technical language so that the contents of the report can be clearly understood. The feasibility report should describe the system from an end-user's perspective.

The analyst is essentially the 'middle man', providing a bridge between the management of the organisation and the technical people who will develop and implement the system.

Investigation of the system

During the development of the feasibility report, the systems analyst must carry out some investigations.

During the investigations, the analyst must discover how the current system is used, the processes that are carried out using the current system and the needs and requirements for the new software system.

The analyst may find out that the end-users are already carrying out the processes using software but that the effectiveness of the current system is no longer adequate. The proposed software solution will simply replace the current system. However, it may be that the current system is a manual one, or that the proposed software solution will add additional functions to an existing software system.

The analyst needs to investigate how data is put into the current system (input), how the data flows around the system, how it is processed and what types of output are produced.

The main topics that need to be considered during investigation are:

✱ the people involved

✱ the data capture methods

✱ data types, sources and flows

✱ decisions taken and types of processing

✱ storage methods

✱ documents used

✱ types of output

✱ manual and automatic processes currently carried out.

There are different methods of investigation that can be used to gather the information on these topics. They include:

✱ interviews

✱ observations

✱ shadowing

✱ questionnaires

✱ document/record analysis and inspection.

The analyst will select the most appropriate method of investigation. Which method of investigation the analyst will use will depend on the following factors:

✱ the people involved

✱ the type of information being gathered

✱ the place in which the investigation is to be carried out.

Each method of investigation has benefits and limitations. Based on these and the factors given above, the analyst may use more than one method during the investigation stage.

Interviews

Through interviewing users, the analyst can clarify that the information already gathered is correct. Interviews, if the questions are planned in advance, can reveal new information and give the analyst the opportunity to understand the system from the end-user's perspective. The analyst should always plan an interview in advance.

However, one of the main benefits of interviewing is that questions can be modified as the interview progresses; an answer might be given that raises some relevant additional information that the analyst has not considered.

It is very important when interviewing that the analyst ensures they can talk to all different types of end-users, from management to staff, and that the interviewee feels comfortable and at ease with the questioning. A good interview will enable a rapport to be developed between the interviewer and interviewee. This rapport may prove to be important if further interviews are needed or further information has to be gathered.

There are four factors which should be considered when arranging interviews:

* who to interview
* where and when to conduct the interview
* what questions are to be asked
* how the answers to the questions are to be recorded.

If all these points are carefully considered, the interview should go well and all the information required by the analyst will be gathered.

Observations and shadowing

If several activities are taking place in the system being investigated, observation and shadowing may be the best methods for collecting the information.

Shadowing is the technique of working with a 'host' – the person you are shadowing. Shadowing enables the analyst to work with someone and to complete parts of that person's job role.

Observing someone doing their job is better than asking someone to describe it, and by observing someone over a period of time the possibility of anything being forgotten is reduced. For example, on a factory production line there will not be much documentation that can be analysed and, because of the nature of the activity, interviewing or questionnaires will not be appropriate.

When the analyst observes or shadows an end-user of the current system, they will be able to identify all the processes that occur in the current system, how long it takes to perform a specific task and what hardware, software (if any) and people are involved.

Although the analyst is simply interested in the current system, one thing they must be aware of is that people will be involved. The analyst must always ask the permission of the people involved before beginning their observation or shadowing. To ensure that the observation or shadowing gathers the information required, the following factors should be carefully considered:

* how the findings are to be recorded
* where and when the observation or shadowing is to take place
* what part of the current system is to be observed.

Questionnaires

Questionnaires are an excellent way of gathering information. However, the questionnaire must be structured correctly, it must be sent to the correct end-users and its return should be strictly controlled.

The questionnaire should be structured clearly and provide opportunities for short answers based on facts and figures as well as for descriptive answers. The balance of type of questions will ensure that all the information required by the analyst will be gathered.

The return of a questionnaire may cause a problem to the analyst. One idea might be to put a time constraint on it, such as 'please return within four working days'. Another idea could be to distribute the questionnaires at a meeting and collect them in at the end of the meeting – this is not always feasible and this approach should be carefully considered. When designing a questionnaire, it is important to consider who the questionnaire is aimed at. End-users of a system can interpret questions differently depending on their job role within the organisation.

METHOD	BENEFITS	LIMITATIONS
Interviews	A rapport can be developed with the people who will use the system Questions can be adjusted as the interviews proceed Additional questions can be added to gather more information	Can be time-consuming and costly Poor interviewing can lead to misleading or insufficient information being gathered In a large organisation, it is not possible to interview everyone
Observation/ shadowing	The effects of office layouts and conditions on the system can be assessed Workloads, methods of working, delays and 'bottlenecks' can be identified Potential to experience all aspects of job role	Can be time-consuming and costly Problems may not occur during observation Users may put on a performance when being observed
Questionnaires	Large numbers of people can be asked the same questions, therefore comparisons are easy to formulate (e.g. 72% of people said they were unhappy with the current system) Cheaper than interviews for large numbers of people Anonymity may provide more honest answers	Must be designed very carefully. Questions need to be simple and easy to use Questions cannot be ambiguous Cannot guarantee 100% return rate; may be lower with some groups
Document/record analysis and inspection	Good for obtaining factual information, e.g. volume of sales over a period of time, inputs and outputs of the system	Cannot be used when input, output and information is not document-based

TABLE 15.1 *Methods of investigation – benefits and limitations*

Document/record analysis and inspection

The analysis of documentation used in the current system is a good way of identifying the format of the input, processing and outputs that occur in a system. The drawback is that this method of investigation can only be used when the information flow is document-based. This method can be used to clarify the information given by the end-users and can also trace the source and recipients of a particular piece of information used by the current system. The analyst should collect copies of all documents used by the current system. The documents commonly analysed include invoices, purchase orders, goods received notes, receipts, stock records and customer records.

> **Think it over...**
>
> For each of the systems below, identify five documents that could be examined and describe how the analyst could use the information:
>
> * school/college
> * sports club
> * supermarket
> * dental surgery.

15.2 Analysis and design

Once all investigations have been completed, the information has been collected and the feasibility study has been developed and approved by the organisation, it is possible to move on to the next stage in the life cycle.

In the design stage, data models will need to be completed. If the information collected during the investigation and feasibility stages was full and complete, all the information needed to complete the design stage will be available.

There are various techniques that can be used during the design stage, all of which will enable a system to be developed that fully meets the needs of the organisation and the end-users.

Amongst the tools and techniques used at this stage are:

* data flow diagrams (DFDs)
* storyboards
* rich picture diagrams
* system flowcharts
* entity-relationship diagrams (ERD)
* data dictionaries
* decision trees/tables
* structured English.

The choice of tools and techniques to be used during this stage will depend on the type of system that is being developed. For example, if a website were being developed, an appropriate tool to use would be a storyboard. If this website were to be used for online shopping, it might be appropriate also to use a data flow diagram to show the flow of data that occurs during the process that is not seen or used by the end-user.

You may have studied *Unit 6: Software Development – Design* as part of your AS course, and you are advised to go back and look again at what you learned then about DFDs, ERDs and flowcharts.

> *** Remember**
>
> The tools and techniques used during this stage must be appropriate to the system being developed.

Data flow diagrams

Data flow diagrams (DFDs) focus on the processes that transform incoming data flows (inputs) into outgoing data flows (outputs). The processes that perform this transformation create and use data that is held in data stores.

The DFD will also show who the system interacts with in the form of external entities. Examples of external entities include people and other systems.

There are many different sets of symbols that can be used when constructing DFDs. It does not matter which set of symbols you decide to use to construct your DFD, but what is important is that once the set of symbols has been selected, it is used consistently and is not changed part way through the analysis stage.

Symbols used in the construction of data flow diagrams

In this unit, the symbols we are going to use to construct DFDs are shown in Figure 15.2.

A DFD does not show the hardware or software required to operate the system. The analyst will use the DFD to show:

* the external entities that the system interacts with
* the processes that happen
* the data stores that are used
* the flow of the data and information.

External entities are used to represent people, organisations or other systems that have a role in the system under development but are not necessarily part of it. The external entities either put data into the system or receive data from it.

A **process** represents activities that take place within and are linked to the system. All activities within a system have a process attached to them.

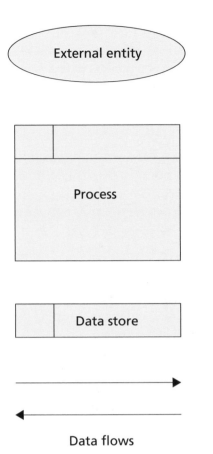

FIGURE 15.2 *Data flow diagram (DFD) symbols*

DATA FLOW LINKS	DATA STORE	EXTERNAL ENTITY	PROCESS
Data store	✗	✗	✓
External entity	✗	✗	✓
Process	✓	✓	✓

TABLE 15.2 *Rules for linking symbols*

Key terms

Data flow diagram (DFD): A diagrammatical way of representing the flow of data and information in a system.

External entities: A source for data that is input into the system or a destination for data that leaves the system.

Process: Activities that take place with or are linked to the system.

Data stores: Where data is stored in the system.

A process models what happens to the data. It transforms incoming data flows into outgoing data flows. Usually, a process will have one or more data inputs and produce one or more data outputs.

Data stores show where data is stored. Examples of data stores include a database file, a paper form or a folder in a filing cabinet. A data store should be given a meaningful descriptive name, for example a 'customer file'.

The data flows indicate the direction or flow of information within the system. Data flows provide a link to other symbols within the DFD. Each flow should be given a simple meaningful descriptive name.

There are certain rules about which symbols can be linked. These are shown in Table 15.2.

So, looking at the table, you can see that in a DFD it is not possible to link an external entity with another external entity or a data store with an external entity.

Identification of symbols used in DFDs

Three of the symbols used in a DFD must also be identified in some way; we will look at these in turn.

Process boxes

Each process box is labelled with a number. Each number given to a process should represent the point in the system when the process takes place. For example, process 4 would come before process 9. The process box should also state what the process is. The example shown in Figure 15.3 shows the process of creating a purchase order.

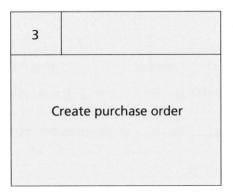

FIGURE 15.3 *Process symbol*

Data stores

Data stores are labelled depending upon the type of data store they are. The two main types are:

✱ D: a computerised data store, such as files in a database

✱ M: a manual data store, such as a filing cabinet or a paper form.

FIGURE 15.4 *Data store – manual*

FIGURE 15.5 *Data store – computerised*

It is possible to have a data store used more than once in a system. These are called repeating data stores. If a data store is repeated, the same numbering and description is used but a second line is inserted, as shown in Figure 15.6.

FIGURE 15.6 *A repeating manual data store*

External entities

These are labelled with the name of the person, organisation or system they represent. The external entity shown in Figure 15.7 shows the customer as an external entity.

FIGURE 15.7 *The customer as an external entity*

It is possible to have repeating external entities. As with the data stores, the original name is kept and a line is used to show that it is repeated.

FIGURE 15.8 *A repeating external entity*

Levels of data flow diagram

In this unit, we are looking at two levels of DFD – the **Level 0 (L0)** or **context diagram** and the Level 1 (L1) DFD. If you go on to study this subject area at a higher level, you will be introduced to many more levels of DFD. Each subsequent level of DFD decomposes a process held in the level before it; for example, a L3 DFD will decompose a process contained within a L2 DFD, and so on.

We will be using the case study, Lovely Lunches, to develop our DFDs.

Level 0 DFD/context diagram

The Level 0 (L0) or context diagram gives a summary of the system. It shows the main external entities and the information that flows into and out of the system.

A Level 0 DFD does not show the processes that occur or the data stores that are used within the system – it simply provides an overview of the system under investigation.

Although there is only one system used at Lovely Lunches, there are two distinct parts. These are the system used in the offices and that used at the kitchen.

During the development of a system, the analyst may be asked to concentrate on the system currently used throughout the organisation or to concentrate on one particular part of the system.

We are going to look at the system as a whole during the development of the DFDs. The skills you learn whilst doing this will enable you to develop DFDs for any small part of a system.

> **Key terms**
>
> *Context diagram (L0 DFD):* A diagram that shows how the system interacts with the outside world.

The first thing that should be done is to identify the external entities. In Lovely Lunches there is only one external entity used in the system under investigation – the customer.

Lovely Lunches

Lovely Lunches is a small business in Manchester. The main function of the business is to deliver filled sandwiches to customers at their workplaces. The sandwiches are made with a variety of fillings. The business also has a range of drinks, salads and snacks that can be delivered to meet the customers' needs. All sandwiches can be ordered either with or without butter and on a range of different types of bread.

The office of Lovely Lunches is in the centre of the business district. Customers can arrange any change to a regular order or businesses can give details of their one-off order by calling into, faxing or phoning this office. Weekly invoices are delivered with the orders every Friday.

The customers call into Lovely Lunches' office to pay their invoices. The owner is based at the office. The sandwiches are made in a kitchen about five miles away from the main office. This is where the delivery scooters are kept and where the orders are put on the correct scooter each morning.

When a customer wants to set up a regular order, they advise the administration staff, based in the office, of the start date, frequency of delivery and products required. These details are then entered into the delivery system and will be used to make up the weekly invoice. A confirmation of the order details is sent to the customer, either by hand, fax or post. The order details are then passed to the kitchen where they are recorded by hand in the appropriate delivery book.

When a customer wants to cancel a regular order, they will advise the administration staff of the final delivery date. A confirmation of the cancellation is sent to the customer, either by hand, fax or post. The administration staff will enter the final delivery date into the order book. The cost of the products received is calculated and totalled. The cost of the products not yet paid for, up to and including the final order, is also calculated and totalled. An invoice showing the total amount due is then produced.

This invoice and the information about the final delivery date are sent to the kitchen. A record of the final delivery date is made – this is done by hand. On the final delivery date, the invoice is left with the delivery. The customer calls into the office to pay the outstanding invoice.

When a customer wants to change a delivery, they will advise the administration staff of the changes they wish to make to their order. This may be, for example, a change of bread or filling, change of other products on their order or a change of frequency of delivery. The administration staff enter the changed order into the order system. The details of the changed order are sent to the customer as confirmation of their request, either by hand, fax or post. The information about the changed delivery is sent to the kitchen. This is recorded by hand in the kitchen.

Following all the changes requested by the customer, the appropriate member of the delivery staff is notified and the delivery changes are actioned.

Some systems will have more than one external entity; the process of constructing the Level 0 DFD will be the same despite the number of external entities and flows involved.

The next thing to be done is to identify the flows of data that occur between the system and the external entity – the customer.

Theory into practice

Using the information given in the case study, identify the flows of information data which occur between Lovely Lunches and the customer.

The main flows you should have identified are:

* regular order details
* confirmation of regular order
* weekly invoices
* weekly payment
* order details changes
* confirmation of changes to regular order
* cancellation of order details
* confirmation of order cancellation
* final invoice
* payment of final invoice.

When the flows of data have been identified, it is important to identify which way the information goes – from the customer to Lovely Lunches or from Lovely Lunches to the customer. This is known as defining the **source** and the **recipient**.

This information may be put into a table. By doing this, the analyst will have a clearer understanding of the flows of information and it may be easier for the client to check that all the flows are present. This table can also be used to construct the L0 DFD.

Theory into practice

Using the headings Data Flow, External Entity and Source/Recipient, construct a table to show the flows of data between the customer and Lovely Lunches.

Once the flows have been identified and checked by the client, it is time to construct the L0 DFD. The L0 DFD for the Lovely Lunches case study is shown in Figure 15.9.

It is convention that the initial flows in the system are shown as the top flows in the

L0 DFD, whilst the flows that happen last are at the bottom.

It is clear from the L0 DFD of the complete system used at Lovely Lunches that the system begins with a customer placing an order for the first time and ends when the customer pays the final invoice following the cancellation of their order.

In the Lovely Lunches case study it would also be possible to construct L0 DFDs for the two component parts of the system currently being used. These parts are the system in use at the office, where the kitchen and the customer would be the external entities, and the system in use at the kitchen, where the external entities would be the office and the customer.

Theory into practice

Construct the L0 DFDs for the systems in place in the office and the kitchen at Lovely Lunches.

Level 1 DFD

The L1 DFD provides an overview of what is happening within the system. The system is represented in the L0 DFD by a process box. The overview includes types of data being passed within the system, documents and stores of data used (data stores), the activities (processes) and the people or organisations that the system interacts with (external entities).

The method you are going to use is only one of a wide range of methods that can be used to construct a L1 DFD. Below is a ten-step plan for constructing a L1 DFD.

1 Read through the information collected during the feasibility and investigation stages.

2 Sort the information into clear sections, identifying the people or organisations external to the system under investigation but who interact with it, the documents used in the system under investigation, and the activities that take place within the system under investigation.

3 Produce a data flow table.

4 Convert external users to external entities.

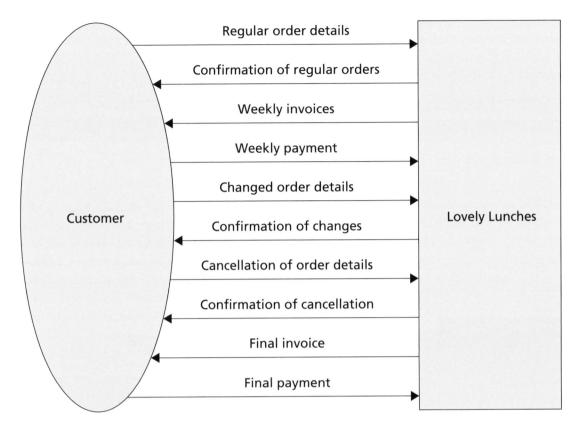

FIGURE 15.9 *L0 DFD for Lovely Lunches*

5 Convert documentation to data stores.

6 Convert activities to processes, identifying when in the system the activity takes place, who is involved and any data stores used.

7 Look at the inputs and outputs for each process with the data stores that are used, and use data flows to 'link' these.

8 Link each data store and external entity with the associated process.

9 Link the processes (remember the rules about the labelling of processes!).

10 Check for consistency – check the initial findings to ensure all documentation has been included, check that the flows between external entities given on the context diagram are included, check with the end-users of the current system to ensure nothing has been forgotten.

Using the 10-step plan, you are now going to construct a L1 DFD for the complete system used at Lovely Lunches.

Step 1: The system under development is the system used in Lovely Lunches.

Think it over...

Re-read the case study, Lovely Lunches. Then look again at the L0 DFD that has been constructed for Lovely Lunches (Figure 15.9).

Steps 2 and 3: The information is sorted and a data flow table is developed. It is useful to include the activities in the order in which they occur in the system. This will help you when you begin to develop your L1 DFD.

Theory into practice

Complete the data flow table for Lovely Lunches. The first two activities have been completed for you (see Table 15.3).

Steps 4, 5 and 6: Using the information from the data flow table and the L0 DFD, the activities are

ACTIVITY NO.	ACTIVITY OVERVIEW	DETAIL	DOCUMENTS USED
1	New Order	Details of new order taken – start date, frequency of delivery and products required	Order book
2	Confirmation	Confirmation of new order produced for customer	Confirmation document

TABLE 15.3 *Incomplete data flow table for Lovely Lunches*

converted to processes, the documents used are converted to data stores and the external entities are confirmed. It is also useful at this stage to give the identifiers to the processes and data stores that will be used in the L1 DFD.

Theory into practice

Using the information given in the case study, Lovely Lunches, and the information you have gathered from steps 1–3, construct a table to show the external entities, data stores and processes.

Identify if each data store is manual or computerised.

Identify any repeating data stores or processes.

Step 7 and 8: Each process now needs to be drawn as a single-process DFD. This is done using the DFD symbols linking the external entities, data stores and the processes together using data flows.

Theory into practice

For each process you have identified in the data flow table, construct a single-process DFD.

If you need to, remind yourself of the rules for linking the components of a DFD – see Table 15.2 on page 311.

Step 9: Link the processes together. You can have more than one process using a data store, but the data flow lines must not cross. You can use repeating data stores to stop the data flow lines

from crossing. Each person will develop a DFD in a different way. This is because we all look at things slightly differently. What is important to remember is that all the processes, external entities and data stores used within the system under investigation must be included, with each process linked to the associated data stores.

✳ Remember

Everyone will construct a slightly different L1 DFD. The important point is that all external entities, processes and data stores are linked correctly.

Theory into practice

Using the single-process DFDs you constructed in steps 7 and 8, link them together to construct a L1 DFD for the system in use at Lovely Lunches.

Remember the rules about flow lines crossing – use repeating data stores and external entities to avoid this happening!

Step 10: Before the DFD is shown to the organisation, the analyst should perform some final checks. These are detailed in the list below.

✳ Does each process receive all the data it needs?

✳ Does any data store have only data flows out and not in?

✳ Does any data store appear to have data in it that is never used?

* Are all data flows consistent across the L0 and the L1 DFD?

* Are all external entities that are shown on the L1 DFD also shown in the L0 diagram? Are all flows labelled? Are they documented in the data dictionary (see page 323)?

* Are there any data flows between two external entities, between external entities and data stores, or between two data stores?

* Do any data flows cross other data flows on the diagram? If they do, use repeating external entities or data stores.

If all the checks completed as part of step 10 are correct, the analyst will be confident that all flows, processes, data stores and external entities are connected correctly and that the DFD shows a true representation of the data flows within the system.

The DFDs must be shown to the organisation for them to check it. It may be that some amendments are necessary, but if the analyst has fully completed the investigations then these amendments are likely to be minor.

Storyboards

A storyboard is defined as 'a small sketch(es) that represents every page in a website'.

If a website were being developed for the organisation that is to be used for, in the case of Lovely Lunches, placing orders, then a storyboard would be used to design and construct the user interface, whilst a DFD would be constructed to show the flow of data that occurs, during the placing of the customer order, that is not seen by the customer.

Like a flowchart, a storyboard shows the relationship of each page to the other pages in the site. Storyboards can be helpful when planning a website, as they allow you to visualise how each page in the site is linked to other pages.

Routes through the website can also be planned using a storyboard to ensure that the user is able to navigate through the website with ease.

Further information about storyboards can be found in *Unit 11: Interactive Multimedia Products* and *Unit 14: Developing and Creating Websites*.

Rich picture diagrams

Rich picture diagrams (RPDs) are an informal method of modelling data flows. An RPD shows what the system is about and is developed using simple 'pictorial' representations of the system under investigation.

It is sometimes easier for end-users to visualise a system in RPD format rather than as a formal DFD. The RPD is sometimes developed prior to the formal DFD being developed. An RPD can be used by the analyst to check that all the activities within the system under investigation are included and are being considered during the analysis stage.

Rich picture diagrams are self-explanatory, as they are designed and developed to help during the analysis stage as well as to help the analyst visualise the system. The RPD has three elements:

* the structure of the system under investigation

* what takes place in the system, the activities and processes

* the relationships between different parts of the system being investigated.

Part of an RPD for the Lovely Lunches system is shown in Figure 15.10.

Theory into practice

Construct a rich picture diagram (RPD) for the system currently in use at Lovely Lunches.

FIGURE 15.10 *Part of an RPD for the Lovely Lunches system*

System flowcharts

A system flowchart shows what processes take place, and where and when they take place.

The system flowchart is divided into columns showing the name of the department, function or people written at the top. Inputs from outside the system under investigation are shown at the left, whilst outputs from the system are shown at the right. The processes and documents used in the system are then put into the appropriate column. The system flowchart can also show any decisions that are taken, who takes them and where.

As with other diagrammatical representations developed during the life cycle, there are many different sets of symbols that can be used. What is important is not which set of symbols is used but that, once the choice has been made, they are used consistently. The symbols used for a system flowchart in this unit are shown in Figure 15.11.

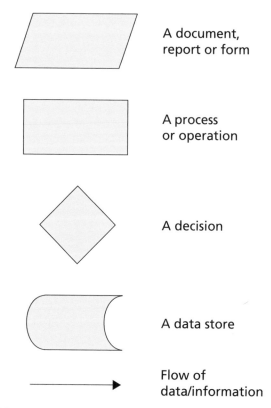

A document, report or form

A process or operation

A decision

A data store

Flow of data/information

FIGURE 15.11 *System flowchart symbols*

A system flowchart is constructed in the following order:

1 Identify the main departments, functions or people involved.

2 Label the column headings.

3 Using the relevant symbols, draw the flow of the data from top to bottom and left to right.

4 Connect the symbols using arrow-headed lines to indicate the flow.

5 Check the system flowchart!

Below are some general guidelines that should be considered when developing a system flowchart:

* Sort out the column headings before beginning to draw the flowchart.

* Keep the flows going from left to right and top to bottom – the system should start at the top left-hand corner and end at the bottom right-hand corner.

* Keep the flow continuous and self-explanatory.

* If multi-part documents are used, such as a two-part order form, both parts of the document should end up at a clearly defined point. Do not have parts of documents 'floating around' the system!

The start of the system flowchart for Lovely Lunches is shown in Figure 15.12.

Theory into practice

Complete the system flowchart for Lovely Lunches (Figure 15.12).

Entity-relationship diagrams

An **entity-relationship diagram (ERD)** is one of the tools and techniques that can be used to produce the logical data model. This tool provides a detailed graphical representation of the information that is used within a system and identifies the relationships that exist between the items of data. As with data flow modelling, a set of tools and documentation is used. In this unit, we are concerned with three elements of ERDs: entities, relationships and the degree of the relationships. The set of symbols we are going to use is shown in Figure 15.13.

Key terms

Entity-relationship diagram (ERD): A technique for representing the structure of data in a software system using entities and the relationships between those entities.

When the analyst is completing the analysis stage, they will have sufficient knowledge and understanding of software development to be able

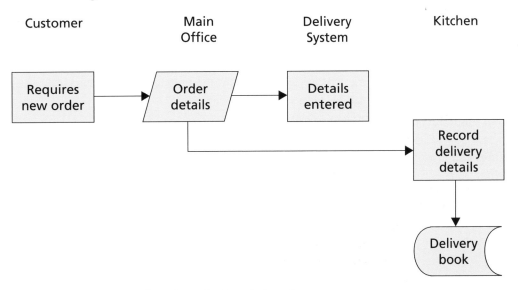

Customer   Main Office   Delivery System   Kitchen

FIGURE 15.12 *Part of the system flowchart for Lovely Lunches*

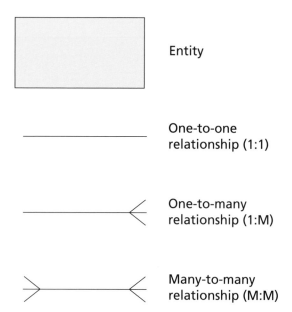

Entity

One-to-one relationship (1:1)

One-to-many relationship (1:M)

Many-to-many relationship (M:M)

FIGURE 15.13 *Entity-relationship diagram symbols*

ENTITY	PRODUCT
Attributes	Product Number
	Category
	Description
	Cost
	Supplier

TABLE 15.4 *The PRODUCT entity*

to identify the entities, attributes and primary and foreign keys that will need to be used in the proposed system. The entities and attributes will be given to you in the pre-release case study for the assessment of this unit. You will develop the ERD based on the information given to you.

Entities are usually real-world things, such as students or products, that need to be represented in the software system.

For example, in the Lovely Lunches system, one **entity** might be products. This is because information is held about the products delivered by Lovely Lunches in the current system. This would be represented by the symbol shown in Figure 15.14.

Each entity has **attributes**. Attributes make up the information that is held in a system about the entity. Table 15.4 shows the information about the products that might be held in the Lovely Lunches system.

The entities and attributes are given in a specific format. There are many different formats

that can be used. As with DFDs, it is important that, once a format has been selected, it is used consistently throughout the ERD development. In this unit, we are going to use the following format:

PRODUCT (ProductNumber, Category, Description, Cost, Supplier)

The entity name is shown in capitals with the attributes contained within brackets ( ).

Each set of attributes for an entity should have a unique field that identifies each **occurrence** of an entity. This unique field is called the **primary key**.

In our example of PRODUCT, the primary key would be ProductNumber as no two products will have the same product number. It is the primary key that provides the links between the entities.

In the Lovely Lunch system, the entities are defined as:

DELIVERY, CUSTOMER, PRODUCT, STAFF, DELIVERY ROUND.

Products

FIGURE 15.14 *Products entity*

The entities will be linked through relationships. Each **relationship** is given a degree. The degrees of relationships that may be used are as follows:

✳ one-to-one (1:1) – shows that only one occurrence of each entity is used by the linked entity. For example, one vet would use one treatment room. This is represented as shown in Figure 15.15.

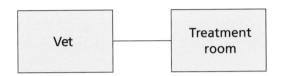

FIGURE 15.15 *One-to-one relationship*

✳ many-to-one (M:1) or one-to-many (1:M) – shows that a single occurrence of one entity is linked to more than one occurrence of the linked entity. For example, one vet would have many appointments. This would be represented as shown in Figure 15.16.

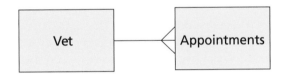

FIGURE 15.16 *One-to-many relationship*

✳ many-to-many (M:M) – shows that many occurrences of one entity are linked to more than one occurrence of the linked entity. Although many-to-many occurrences are common in the real world, a linked entity must be used to break down or decompose the many-to-many relationship. For example, many vets will see many animals. This is represented as shown in Figure 15.17.

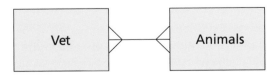

FIGURE 15.17 *Many-to-many relationship*

By using a link entity, a many-to-many relationship can be decomposed to form two 1:M relationships. This is represented as shown in Figure 15.18.

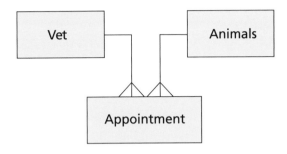

FIGURE 15.18 *Two 1:M relationships*

To define the relationships, the entities and their associated attributes must be clearly defined. In the Lovely Lunch system the entities and attributes are given as:

DELIVERY (<u>DelNumber</u>, *CustID, RoundNumber*, start_date, end_date, frequency, *ProductNumber*)

CUSTOMER (<u>CustID</u>, Forename, Surname, Address1, Address2, Postcode, ContactNumber)

PRODUCT (<u>ProductNumber</u>, Category, Description, Cost)

DELIVERY ROUND (<u>RoundNumber</u>, *DelNumber*, *StaffNumber*)

STAFF (<u>StaffNumber</u>, Forename, Surname, Address1, Address2, Postcode, ContactNo)

This process is known as normalisation. This unit covers the start of this process. For more information on normalisation, see *Unit 18: Database Design*.

The following assumptions have been made when developing these entities:

✳ One member of the delivery staff may do one or more delivery rounds.

✳ One customer may have one or more products delivered.

✳ One product category may have one or more products contained within it.

When the analyst is developing the entities and attributes that will be used in the new system, it is important for him or her to keep referring back to the user requirements that were given during the feasibility stage.

In the entities and attributes defined for Lovely Lunches there is no mention of the supplier of the products used. The user requirements of the new system did not yet include keeping computerised records of the suppliers used.

In some cases the analyst must be aware that, at a later date, the system may be extended to incorporate different needs and requirements of the organisation.

If a database were being built for Lovely Lunches, the analyst would use the entities and their attributes as tables (entities) with each attribute being a field within that table.

There are many different ways of representing the entities and attributes. As before, what is important is that a technique is selected and then used consistently throughout the development of the system.

The format that will be used in this unit is that the primary keys are underlined and are shown as the first attribute in the list. The primary keys for the Lovely Lunches software system are:

DELIVERY (DelNumber

CUSTOMER (CustID

PRODUCT (ProductNumber

DELIVERY ROUND (RoundNumber

STAFF (StaffNumber

In the Lovely Lunches software system, each of the primary keys is a number.

✱ Remember

A primary key uniquely defines each occurrence of the entity.

Think it over...

Why is staff name not used as the primary key of the STAFF entity?

Some of the attributes given for Lovely Lunches are in italics. These are **foreign keys**.

A foreign key is used to link the tables together. It is a primary key in one table that is linked to a field in another table. The data types must be the same.

Key terms

Foreign key: The primary key from one entity used as an attribute in another entity.

For example, the foreign key ProductNumber is an attribute in the entity DELIVERY but is the primary key in the entity PRODUCT.

Once the entities, attributes and primary and foreign keys have been identified, the ERD can start to be developed. The method you are going to use to develop the ERD is only one of a wide range of methods that can be used to construct an ERD.

The entities and attributes need to be shown in boxes. In this diagram the primary keys are shown in **bold** with the foreign keys shown in italics.

For example, the entity DELIVERY ROUND would be shown as in Figure 15.19.

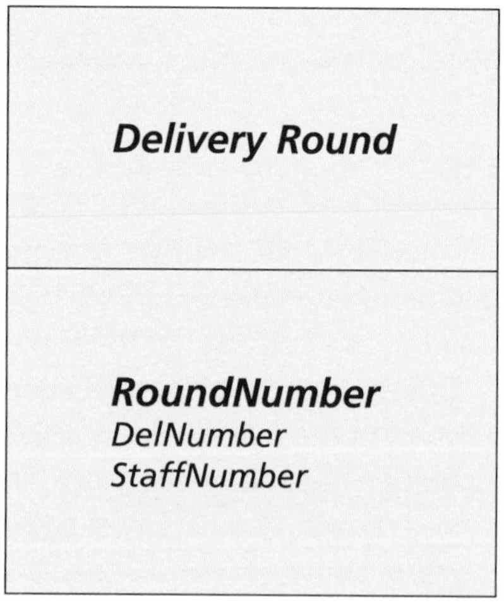

FIGURE 15.19 *The DELIVERY ROUND entity*

Theory into practice

Develop the diagrammatical representation for the other four entities that will be used in the Lovely Lunches system.

We can now begin to think about the relationships that will link the entities together to form an ERD. There are many ways of thinking about the relationships, but it is best to concentrate on one relationship at a time.

There is a link between the DELIVERY and DELIVERY ROUND entities – we know this because the primary key of DELIVERY is a foreign key in DELIVERY ROUND (DelNumber).

The relationship would be:

1   DELIVERY ROUND has many DELIVERYs.

Now the relationships have been defined, it is possible to complete the ERD. Look back at the notation used to represent each type of relationship.

Data dictionaries

As with the DFDs, documentation needs to be developed to clarify and support the ERD. The documentation includes entity descriptions, attribute lists and a **data dictionary**.

Each entity in the ERD should have an associated entity description that details the entity name and description, the entity attributes and any relationships or links associated with it.

The method we used to develop our ERD has already detailed the information that is needed in the documentation. It is simply a matter of putting the information into a format that can be easily understood.

It is necessary to hold data dictionaries about the entities being used in a system. It is also possible to hold data about data elements, data structures, data flows, data stores and processes.

In this unit, we are concerned with developing data dictionaries for the entities used within a system.

A data dictionary may hold the following elements:

* name
* description
* aliases
* type
* format
* values
* comments
* security
* editing.

Not all of these elements will be held – only the ones that are appropriate to the entity should be included in the data dictionary. It is also possible that any validation to be applied is also held in the data dictionary.

As there are five entities being used in the Lovely Lunches system, five data dictionaries should be developed – one for each entity.

The data dictionary for the entity PRODUCT is given in Table 15.5.

NAME	PRODUCT		
Description	The table that contains all general information about a product that is delivered and/or sold by Lovely Lunches		
Aliases	None		
Relationships			
Related to:	Type	Which end?	
Delivery	1:Many (1:M)	Many	
Attributes			
Name	Type/Format	Length	Key
Product Number	Text/String	15	Primary Key
Category	Text/String	15	
Description	Text/String	50	
Cost	Currency	10	

TABLE 15.5 *Data dictionary for the entity PRODUCT*

Defining a process

For any processes required in the new system, a process specification should be produced. There are various methods for defining a process. The most common are:

* flowcharts
* decision tables or trees
* structured English.

The Cars4U case study (see box) will be used throughout this section to illustrate these methods.

Flowcharts

Flowcharts are a method of representing the processes of a system in a pictorial form. They are good for providing a general outline of the processing that is involved in the system under investigation but, generally, do not relate very well to the actual software system that is eventually developed. Different-shaped symbols are used to represent different actions.

There are many different sets of symbols that can be used. As with DFDs and ERDs, it is important that, once a set of symbols has been selected, it is used consistently throughout the flowchart development. In this unit, we are going to use the symbols shown in Figure 15.20.

Flowcharts can be used to model all kinds of systems, not just computer systems. They can be used to break a process into small steps or to give an overview of a complete system. People who are not involved in the ICT industry can easily understand them. However, flowcharts do not translate into code easily and they can sometimes become so complex that they can be hard to follow.

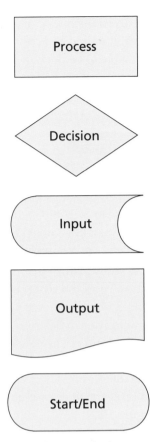

FIGURE 15.20 *Flowchart symbols*

For these reasons, flowcharts are used by the analyst to give a generalised overview of a system or the functions that make up a specific process. Decision tables or structured English can then be used to provide more detailed information.

Below are some rules that must be followed when developing a flowchart:

* Every flowchart must begin with start and finish with end.

* A decision must have two flows coming from it – yes and no.

Before a flowchart is developed, it is important that the analyst clearly defines any input, output, decisions and processes that occur. By doing this they can gain a clear understanding of the system.

In the case study – Cars4U – the process of taking decisions as to whether any action is required has been identified. Based on the outcome of decisions, specified actions must be taken.

These are the decisions that have to be taken:

1 Is it 6 months since the car was last serviced?

2 Has the car done 8,000 miles since the last service?

3 Has the car been hired five or more times since the last valet?

4 Are there any scratches or dents on the car?

Based on these decisions, a range of actions should be taken. It is possible that one or more of the decisions is 'yes' and, therefore, a number of actions may need to be completed on one car.

The actions that may be taken are as follows:

* service the car

* valet the car

* repair any dents or scratches.

* no action needed at this time.

The information needed to make the decisions and take the appropriate actions is found in the car history log.

Once this information has been clearly defined, the flowchart can be developed.

Theory into practice

Draw the flowchart to represent the process that occurs when deciding on what actions need to be taken with a car.

Decision tables and decision trees

Decision tables are useful where there are options/decisions (the conditions) that need to be considered and the analyst needs to identify what happens in each circumstance (the actions). Decision tables are used when the processing that occurs includes a range of true or false conditions.

Depending on the combination of conditions, different actions need to be taken. The advantage of a decision table is that all the combinations of the rules have to be considered, so it is very easy to check that all the rules have been included.

Rules	1	2	3	4
Conditions				
	Y	Y	N	N
	Y	N	Y	N
Actions				

TABLE 15.6 *A decision table*

Decision tables are best used for processes involving complex combinations of up to six decisions. More than six decisions can make the decisions table very large and difficult to read.

There is a standard layout for decision tables, which means that all the information included in the table can be understood by the end-users of the system under investigation.

A decision table is made up of two parts:

✱ The conditions are listed at the top of the table – all combinations of conditions must be listed.

✱ The actions (what to do in each condition) are listed in the bottom part of the table.

An example of a decision table is shown in Table 15.6.

In the case study, Cars4U, there are four conditions that have to be identified in the decision table.

In the decision table, all combinations of the conditions should be provided, but, if all the combinations of these four conditions applicable to Cars4U were provided, the decision table would be very large and difficult to use.

As multiple decisions can be made about an individual car, it would be acceptable for a simple decision table to be developed with the analyst providing a written explaination for the organisation.

Decision trees are another tool that may be used by the analyst to show actions that occur given the conditions and rules. The diagram looks like a fallen tree with a root on the left-hand side and branches representing each decision.

The tree is read from left to right and the actions to be taken are recorded down the right-hand side of the diagram.

The decision tree for the case study, Cars4U, is shown in Figure 15.21.

Once the decision table and/or tree has been developed, the the analyst can use this to develop the structured English.

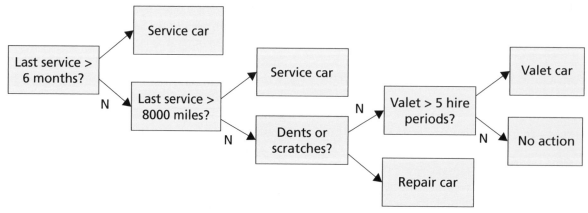

FIGURE 15.21 *Decision tree for Cars4U*

Structured English

Structured English is very detailed; it is a 'half-way house' between actual programming code and normal spoken English. It is used to describe the steps in a process without being concerned about the programming syntax. Structured English is also known as pseudo-code.

Structured English is best used whenever a process combines sequences of actions with decisions and loops. There are no exact rules on how to use structured English, but it is important that it should avoid ambiguity.

There are many constructs which can be used in structured English and the ones you use will depend upon your programming knowledge.

The most common constructs are:

* **If...Then...Else** – used when a choice needs to be made based on a condition. This construct takes the following form:

  If (condition) Then (action)
  Else (alternative action)

* **While Do** or **Do While** – used when a loop must continue until a condition disagrees with the condition given. The construct takes the following form:

  While (condition) Do (action) or
  Do (action) While (condition)

* **CASE** – this is very closely linked with a decision table. The decision table identifies the actions to take in all the different combinations of actions. The CASE construct follows each rule identified in the decision table.

* **Repeat...Until** – this loop is used when a set of commands must be carried out an unknown number of times until a condition becomes true. The construct takes the format:

  Repeat
  any number of instructions put here
  Until a condition is true

Theory into practice

Write structured English for the decision process used in Cars4U.

Physical design specification

The analyst needs to make some recommendations to the organisation about the hardware, software, inputs and outputs of the new system. The recommendations made by the analyst should take into account the needs and requirements of the organisation that were defined at the start of the life cycle process.

These components make up the physical design specification:

* hardware specification
* software specification
* input specification
* output specification.

Note: You will need to know what elements are included within each component of the physical design specification. You will also need to be able to make recommendations appropriate to the organisation and to be able to justify your choices.

Hardware specification

The hardware specification needs to define the following in detail:

* memory capacity
* storage devices
* peripheral specifications
* data capture equipment
* communication equipment.

When the analyst makes recommendations for the hardware to be used by the organisation, it is important that they consider future-proofing the hardware as much as possible and the budget that was set by the organisation at the beginning of the life cycle.

For example, the analyst should recommend storage devices that have the capacity to hold more data than is currently required by the organisation. As the organisation stores more data, it would be inconvenient if the storage devices became full and records had to be deleted or extra storage devices had to be purchased. The analyst must also consider the backing up of the data used by the organisation and how this is going to be done.

Alternative proposals should also be suggested in terms of hardware. The analyst may have suggested a tape streamer as a backup device, as they are able to hold large amounts of data and can be removed for safe keeping. An alternative backup device may be given as a removable external hard drive, as these can be set up to provide real-time replication.

By providing alternatives, the analyst is using his or her professional skills and ability, yet enabling the organisation to make the final decision.

Theory into practice

For the case study, Lovely Lunches, recommend, based on the components of the hardware specification, hardware for the new system. Justify all your choices.

Software specification

The software specification needs to define the following in detail:

* outline program specifications

* system flowchart

* file organisation

* access methods

* error messages

* screen and report layouts.

As the analyst has been analysing and designing the system, most of the components for the software specification should have been covered. The software specification brings together these areas.

The error message that will be produced by the new system should be detailed in the software specification. Any error messages given should be helpful to the end-user. Some indication of why the error message has been displayed, and the action that should be taken by the end-user to rectify the problem, should also be shown.

Access methods and security should also be covered in this part of the physical design specification. Many organisations are concerned about the security of their data when a new system is being developed. Different levels of access to

the data should be detailed, with the rights of each end-user or group of end-users being specified.

For example, only the personnel department of an organisation should be able to access confidential personnel records – this would also include the individual staff member having access to their own records. These access rights should be set by the use of user names and passwords, with each end-user having pre-defined rights to read, write, amend, create or delete.

Whilst setting the access levels, the analyst should also be aware of the legislation that applies to the holding of data, for example the Data Protection Act.

Input specification

The input specification needs to define the following in detail:

* data sources

* methods of data capture

* data input form or screen layouts

* validation methods

* verification methods.

The analyst needs to identify where the information/data to be used in the system will come from. This should have already been identified during the development of the DFDs for the current system. The method of data capture describes how this information/data will enter the system. Understanding where the information/data comes from is important in deciding how it can be captured.

There are many data capture methods available. When making recommendations, the analyst must consider the following:

* accuracy of input

* reliability

* cost

* ease of use, who will use it and where it will be used.

For example, in an office, a keyboard could be recommended as a suitable data capture device. Very little training is needed to use a keyboard and it allows direct input of data/information into the system.

The input screens and forms that will be used in the new system should be clearly detailed in this section of the physical design specification. The analyst should provide designs – hand-drawn in the first instance – that clearly show the layout of the input screens or forms. In addition the analyst should provide:

* a clear description of the purpose of the screen or form
* a list of data items that will be collected using the screen or form
* any data items that are printed or displayed on the screen or report before or during use, with details of where these data items are obtained from
* instructions to assist the user
* related error messages.

It is important that the data entered into the system is accurate. The analyst must define methods for checking that the data has been entered correctly and is reasonable. This is done through **verification** and **validation**.

Verification is the method of checking that the data entered into the system is the same as the source of the data. One method of verification is for the system to request that the end-user enters the data twice – the entries are checked to ensure that they are identical. Another method is to display the data that has been entered and request that the end-user checks it. An action is then taken, such as pressing an on-screen button, to confirm that the data is correct.

Validation checks that the data entered into the system is reasonable and in the correct format. There are many methods of validation including the use of:

* type checks
* input masks
* length checks
* range checks
* presence checks.

These validation checks are usually defined in the data dictionary.

Key terms

Verification: Checks that are made against the original source of the data.

Validation: Computerised checking to detect any data, based on a set of rules, that is unreasonable or incomplete.

Theory into practice

Using the case study, Lovely Lunches:

* Identify the data sources.
* Provide justified recommendations for the data capture methods.
* Design and describe the data input screens.
* Detail any validation or verification methods that could be used in the new system.

Output specification

The output specification needs to define the following in detail:

* data required for output
* printed or screen report layouts
* methods of data output.

The analyst needs to identify where the data to be output from the system will come from. As with the input specification, some of these outputs may have already been identified during earlier stages of the life cycle.

The analyst will follow the same procedures for the output screens and printed report layout as for the input specification. In addition, however, the analyst must consider who the output is for. If the printed report is for a customer, the layout must be clear and unambiguous. If the printed or screen report is to be used within the organisation, the data may be presented in a different way. For example, a report for a manager about sales in different regions will make use of grouping, totals and, in some cases, graphs and charts.

As with other parts of the physical design specification, the needs and requirements of the end-users that were defined in the early stage of the life cycle should be referred to. By constantly referring to the defined needs and requirements, the new system should meet all of them.

There are many data output methods available. The analyst must make recommendations based on:

* accuracy of output
* reliability
* cost
* ease of use, who will use it and where it will be used.

For example, the analyst may suggest a colour laser printer as the output device to produce the printed reports. An alternative would be a black-and-white printer or an inkjet printer.

When the analyst has produced a proposed solution, they must justify it to the end-users. The benefits of the proposed software system must be explained to the end-users along with any potential problems or disadvantages.

Although a proposed solution has been identified and designed, it is good practice to identify alternative solutions that would solve the problems with the current system.

15.3 Implementation and maintenance

Once the new system has been developed and tested, it needs to be implemented. This is the penultimate stage in the systems life cycle.

During this stage the system will be installed, new equipment will be put into operation, software will be installed and set up, data files will be created and end-users will be trained.

Implementation

There are four main strategies that can be used to implement a new system:

* parallel
* phased
* pilot
* direct/big bang.

Parallel

With a **parallel** strategy, the old and new systems are run concurrently. The results from each are compared for accuracy and consistency. The old system is not discarded until there is complete confidence in the reliability and accuracy of the new system.

This strategy has some disadvantages. Staff are effectively doing their work twice. This is very expensive in terms of staff costs and time.

However, if a problem is found with the new system, it is possible for the organisation to function, as the old system is still in place and can be used. This means that there is no detrimental effect on the organisation.

Phased

The **phased** strategy requires selected areas of the organisation to use the new system. The rest of the organisation continues to use the old system. Once confidence in the new system is high, another part of the organisation begins to use it. This continues until the whole organisation is using the new system.

The disadvantages of using this strategy include the potential for double workload if data or information moves between areas of the organisation using the different systems. This may lead to increased workload for staff. The strategy can take a long time to implement and is, therefore, very expensive in terms of staff costs and time.

However, as the old system is still being used in parts of the organisation, if a problem or bug is found with the new system, the organisation will still be able to function. This strategy limits the detrimental effect on the organisation.

Pilot

This strategy requires selected tasks to be completed using the new system. All other tasks are completed using the old system. Once confidence in the new system is high, another task is completed using the new system. This continues until all tasks within the organisation are completed using the new system.

The disadvantages of the **pilot** strategy are that tasks that do not go through the new system at the start of the strategy may be those causing the major problems in the old system. The strategy can take a long time to implement and is, therefore, very expensive in terms of staff costs and time.

However, the old system can still be used in parts of the organisation if a problem is identified with new system. These problems, or bugs, can then be rectified before implementation is continued. Using this strategy limits the dertrimental effect on the organisation.

Direct/big bang

This is seen as the riskiest implementation strategy. The new system completely replaces the old system, on a given day, with no interim parallel, phased or pilot implementation.

The disadvantages of using a **direct** strategy are great and may have potential consequences for the organisation. Any problems or bugs in the new system may lead to total loss of data/information and the failure of the organisation. If this strategy is chosen, the risks may be minimised through careful planning by the analyst. The new system must be thoroughly and completely tested prior to implementation. Staff also need to be fully trained to use the new system. It may also help if the implementation, using this method, is carried out during a slack period to ease the stress and pressure that will be placed upon the staff using the new system.

This strategy is the cheapest in terms of staff costs and time, but the analyst must very carefully consider the advantages and disadvantages of using this strategy.

Key terms

Parallel: The old and new systems operate alongside each other.

Phased: Selected parts of the organisation use the new system. The rest of the organisation uses the old system.

Pilot: Selected tasks are completed using the new system. All other tasks are completed using the old system.

Direct: The new system completely replaces the old system, on a given day.

Maintenance

The final stage of the systems life cycle is that of **maintenance**. During the life of a system (post-implementation) it may be necessary to perform maintenance on it. There are many different reasons for maintenance and the different strategies that are used.

Key terms

Maintenance: The process of ensuring that a software system/product continues to meet the needs of the end-users.

The main reasons for post-implementation maintenance include the following:

* Errors/bugs that may not have been identified during the testing process become apparent when the system is being used.

* After the system has been used for a time, the users may find that parts of the system are not working as they would like.

* Changes in the business environment, such as changes in legislation, may mean that the system is required to perform tasks that were not included at the design stage.

* Security issues may emerge that mean the system requires an extra level of protection.

* The software developer/seller may find a way to make the system run more efficiently – this issue will usually result in the release of a patch/fix.

* New hardware or other software may be purchased that needs to be integrated into the existing system, resulting in essential changes.

There are four main types of maintenance:

* adaptive
* perfective
* corrective
* preventive.

Adaptive

This type of maintenance usually occurs when the organisation using the system has a new need that the system must fulfil. The system may need to be adapted due to changes within the organisation using it, external changes such as legislation (for example tax) or to enable the system to operate with new hardware.

Perfective

Perfective maintenance usually occurs when it may be advantageous to make changes to enhance the performance of the system. It should turn a good system into a better one and is generally undertaken at the request of the end-users.

These requests could include:

* the addition of short-cut keys to help the end-users carry out processes

* an improved screen design – the colours/layout may not be appropriate

* increased levels of online help available to the end-user.

It is important, however, to remember that perfective maintenance does not change the overall functionality of the system.

Corrective

Corrective maintenance is also known as remedial maintenance because it is usually completed if there are errors in the software. These errors can be of two types and are generally known as 'bugs':

* A programming error occurs when the programmer has made a mistake, but this type of error is usually discovered and corrected before the system is released.

* A logic error is more likely to remain undetected during the testing stage of the systems life cycle. With this type of error, the system will appear to work as it was intended to but does not process the data or produce the output it was designed to.

Corrective maintenance is usually resolved through the use of patches. The Y2K problem in 1999–2000 was solved through the use of corrective maintenance and the release of software patches.

Preventive

This type of maintenance attempts to solve any problems before they occur. It is generally completed through a series of routines, procedures and steps that are taken in order to try to identify and resolve potential problems before they happen.

Preventive maintenance is accomplished by a range of tasks, including monitoring the software and hardware and examining computer log files for potential problems. By undertaking preventive maintenance, the 'shelf-life' of the system may be extended and its integrity may also be maintained.

An example of tasks that may be performed as preventive maintenance is running a virus checker and the constant updating of virus checking software.

Training

A very important task that must be completed during this last stage of the system's life cycle is that of training the end-users to effectively, and correctly, use the system.

The type of training recommended and carried out will depend on who is undergoing the training, their job role, current ICT skills and the access they will have to the system.

There are many different types of training that can be considered, including:

* on-site/on-the-job training

* an off-site training provider – part-time classes or day release

* e-learning – self-paced, online learning program

* books.

On-site/on-the-job training

On-the-job training is often used to pass on knowledge and skills from other colleagues and is a very popular training method.

The main advantages of using this method relate to cost and convenience, but there are also disadvantages.

The knowledge and skills passed on may include incorrect knowledge or poor working practices. It may also be that the pressures of the job may not provide a satisfactory time to learn new skills.

There may also be an issue with whether training is to take place in a group or on a one-to-one basis.

Day release

This is a common method for those who are in employment. It combines practical experience of the job with the knowledge or skills taught by a training provider. The training provider might be:

* a further or higher education college or university

* a private training company.

This type of training is best suited to general IT training, such as word processing, presentation and spreadsheets. It would be unlikely that an external training provider will have the knowledge and experience to enable the end-users to use bespoke software.

e-learning

The ICT sector, by its very nature, normally has access to ICT technology. This type of training is frequently used as an addition or supplement to other methods. There are different methods of e-learning, which are discussed below.

Offline e-learning

This is frequently CD- or DVD-based lessons, possibly supported by books. This type of learning requires good time-management skills and motivation. This will appeal to staff who wish to work at a time and pace to suit their learning style or lifestyle. Often there will be an assessment test that can be completed to monitor the effectivness of the learning process. This type of learning may not be appropriate for learning skills related to a bespoke system but would be useful to learn generic IT skills.

Online e-learning

This is generally provided through connection to a central training provider. Usually a learning management system will keep track of the progress of the learner and include the results of assessment tests. There may be accompanying documentation and often the programme will have realistic simulations.

Online e-learning with tutor support

This can overcome the isolation of self-study and has been shown to produce higher completion rates. Access to the tutor may be via email, telephone, video/data conferencing or through seminars.

Advantages of e-learning

* Cost – savings on travel and accommodation.

* Inclusion – this type of learning may be suitable for those who find it difficult to attend a formal training course.

* Availability – normally online at any time.

* Individual – the course can be followed at a pace suitable to the individual.

* Central control of the learning material.

However, this type of learning would not be appropriate if the system were bespoke. As with the other types of training discussed above, this type of training would only be appropriate for generic IT skills training.

Think it over...

Investigate and explain how books could be used as a training method.

Theory into practice

Identify and explain the training methods that could be used for the office staff who work at the Lovely Lunches head office.

End-user documentation

Once the system has been implemented and the staff trained, it is essential that documentation is passed to the end-users. Not all of this documentation will be used on a day-to-day basis, but it should be kept in a safe place in case it needs to be referred to at a later date.

The documentation that may be passed to the end-user includes:

* detailed program specifications

* recovery procedures

* operating procedures
* user manuals
* test plans, data and logs
* security details
* version details.

Detailed program specifications would be passed to the end-user so that, if maintenance were needed at a later date, the programmer completing this maintenance would be able to see clearly how the system was constructed. It would be unlikely, but not impossible, that the same team who developed the system would perform any maintenance.

Security details should be passed to the organisation to ensure that the access rights initially set are maintained. During the life of a system, staff changes will inevitably occur; by passing on security details, the organisation can ensure that the security of the system is not compromised.

Version details should be passed to the organisation to ensure that the organisation is holding and using the most up-to-date set of documents. As with any iterative activity – remember the systems life cycle is iterative – different versions of documentation are produced as changes are implemented. Through using version details, changes made to the system can be tracked and any maintenance can be performed using the most recent set of documents.

Knowledge check

1 Identify the advantages and disadvantages of the three main software approaches.

2 Identify the main techniques used during investigations.

3 Using examples from your school/college, identify a situation when each method of investigation might be used.

4 Explain the benefits and limitations of using questionnaires as a method of investigation.

5 Name the three types of relationship that are used in ERDs.

6 How is a M:M relationship decomposed?

7 Identify the advantages and disadvantages of each of the four system implementation methods.

8 For each maintenance method below, identify a situation when it would be used:

(a) adaptive
(b) perfective
(c) corrective
(d) preventive.

Think it over…

Investigate and identify why the pieces of user documentation listed below should be passed to the end-user. Explain how each piece of documentation may be used during the life of the system:

* recovery procedures
* operating procedures
* user manuals.

Networking solutions

By studying this unit, you will

* understand the advantages and disadvantages of computer networks

* understand the difference between peer-to-peer and client-server networks

* know the differences between LAN and WAN

* be able to design a network using the correct components and topologies.

This unit will help you to understand the need for computer networks, the factors that are considered in their design and the hardware and software needed to build a safe and secure network.

How this unit will be assessed

This unit is externally assessed. To complete the assessment for this unit, you will be required to carry out some pre-release tasks based on a case study and then sit an examination.

Part of the examination will be based on the first pre-release task. The rest of the examination will test your knowledge of the unit.

What you need to learn

You need to learn about

* computer networks
* network design
* network software
* safety and security.

16.1 Computer networks

A computer network is a collection of computers that are connected to each other and can pass data between them.

We use computers for a wide variety of tasks and they are an essential part of the modern workplace. We very rarely work in isolation, so work done on the computer is likely to be shared in some way. A computer network allows data to be shared between users and allows expensive resources, such as printers, to be shared.

There are many examples of the use of networks. Most schools and colleges have networked computers, meaning that students can sit at any computer workstation and access files they have saved on a central file server. Offices will often have networked computers so that all employees can have access to the same files, software and printers. This makes working practices much more efficient and allows people to work more closely together.

Large organisations may have a number of networks in different offices or departments and they may connect these networks together to make one large network of interconnected networks.

The Internet is a very large, worldwide network made up of a very large number of interconnected networks.

Advantages of computer networks

A **stand-alone computer** is a single computer workstation that has no connection to any other workstation or the Internet. It will often have its own set of resources, such as a large hard disk and a printer. As soon as a computer workstation has a connection to another computer, either directly or through a wireless or telecommunications link, it becomes a **networked computer**.

> ### Key terms
>
> *Stand-alone computer:* A single computer workstation that has no connection to any other workstation or the Internet.
>
> *Networked computer:* A computer workstation that is connected to another computer.

A networked computer has a number of benefits over a stand-alone computer, as outlined in the following sections.

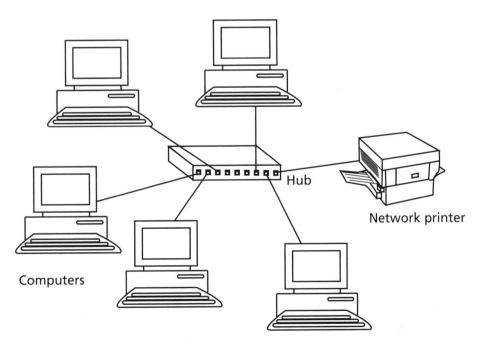

FIGURE 16.1 *Network of computers in an office setting*

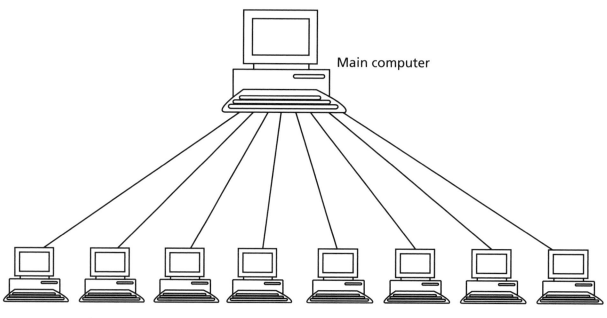

Main computer

Checkouts

FIGURE 16.2 *Network of checkout terminals and main computer*

Sharing hardware resources

A networked computer is able to access hardware resources that are actually connected to other computers. For example, an office might have ten networked computers and one laser printer. As long as all of the computers are connected to the network, they can be set up to access the printer. Each user can print their work from their workstation and only have to move to collect their printout. If all the workstations were stand-alone computers then they would either need a printer each (an expensive option) or each user would need to transfer his or her work to the computer that had the printer attached and then print it from there (an inconvenient way of working).

Other hardware resources that can be shared are:

✱ large hard disks where everyone can store their work together

✱ a router allowing all workstations to access the Internet

✱ other input and output devices – such as scanners, plotters and colour printers – that are only likely to be used every now and then

✱ backing storage devices – such as CD-RW or DVD-RW drives – for backing up data

✱ processors that can share the task of processing intense applications.

Think it over...

SETI@Home (Search for Extra-Terrestrial Intelligence) is an initiative that was set up to operate over the Internet. Satellites in orbit around Earth are collecting signals from outer space constantly and these signals are analysed to see if there is any meaning to them or indication of other life forms in the universe. This requires huge amounts of processing power. So home users of the Internet set up their computers to receive chunks of the data, process it and send the results back to a central computer. This way there are many processors doing a little processing rather than one or two processors doing a large amount of processing.

Theory into practice

Take a look at a network with which you are familiar. This might be at your school or college or in your workplace.

Find out how it is connected together and draw a diagram showing all the workstations and what they are connected to.

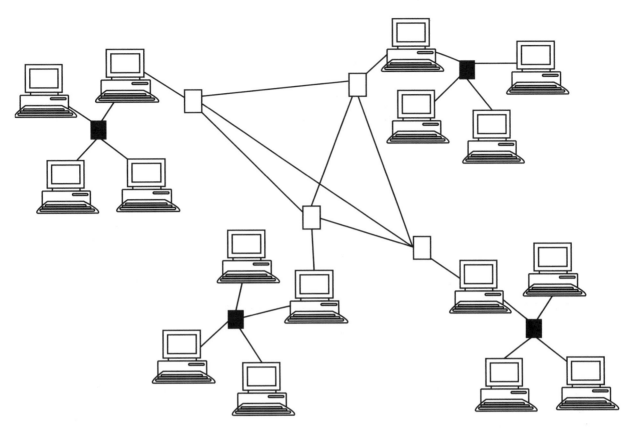

FIGURE 16.3 *Interconnected networks*

Sharing software resources

Most applications software requires a large
amount of hard disk space. For each computer to
have its own software, each must have sufficient
available disk space. It is possible, however, to
have one copy of a piece of software stored on a
central computer (an applications server) which
can be copied and used by each workstation as
it needs it. Network versions of software are
generally cheaper than stand-alone versions and,
when it is time to upgrade the software, only one
copy of it needs to be upgraded.

Sharing common data

This is an important benefit of using networks.
An organisation can allow access to its data for all
employees who need it. This way, all employees
have access to up-to-date data and information.
A company's stock database can be viewed by all
its salespeople so that they know what is currently
in stock. The same database can be updated
regularly by stores people so that the data is
completely accurate and up to date. The World

Wide Web is a very good example of a system
of sharing of data and information over a very
large network (the Internet). A huge amount of
information is available for every user to share.

Some data and information should not be
made widely available, so networks will often
have the facility to restrict access to shared data,
allowing only those who are entitled to use the
data to do so.

There is always the danger that a number of
users will try to change data at the same time and
this could cause it to become corrupt. The ability to
change data can be restricted to a limited number
of users and data can be locked whilst it is being
updated to ensure that it is only changed by one
user at a time.

Potential intranet provision

A network can use Internet technologies even if
it is not connected to the Internet. An **intranet**
can be set up to allow sharing of files, email
facilities and an information service within
an organisation.

When an intranet has been set up, it is possible to make some of it available from outside the network. Certain files can be accessed by users who are given a password and can access them using the Internet. This allows employees to work away from the office or at home. An **extranet** is a network that is private and only available to authorised users, but which can be accessed from any computer with Internet access.

> ### Key terms
>
> *Intranet:* A local private network that uses technology similar to the Internet to provide an information service.
>
> *Extranet:* A private network that can be accessed from outside the network via the Internet.

Email communication between users

Electronic mail (email) can be installed and used whenever a network is set up. Email has many advantages for organisations and their employees:

* It makes it easier to communicate; messages get to their destination quickly.

* It saves the paper that written communications would otherwise use.

* Two users who are communicating by email do not have to be at their computers at the same time, as messages can be stored until they can be dealt with.

* Emails can be sent to groups of people at the same time.

* Emails can save time and postage costs.

* Emails can be organised into folders to make them easier to find.

* Address books or contact lists can be maintained to make contact details easy to find.

Centralised management services

When stand-alone computers are used, it is the responsibility of each user to make sure that they back up their data regularly, delete any old files and protect the work they have on their computer with passwords, which they then have to remember. When new or updated software is needed, it must be installed on each machine individually.

When a network is used, these tasks can be carried out from one central machine:

* If all files are stored on a **file server** then only that computer needs to be backed up. Individual users can assume that their data is safe.

* Regular maintenance can be carried out to remove all old files from the file server. This can often be carried out overnight so that there is no disruption to users.

* The file server will deal with access rights. When a request for a file is made, it will check that the user has access rights before sending it.

* The file server will deal with making sure that a file is not changed by two users at the same time by locking it after one user has opened it.

* When new or updated software is needed, the installation can be controlled from a central machine, saving a lot of time.

> ### Key terms
>
> *File server:* A computer, connected to a network, that has a large amount of hard disk space and on which most data files are stored. The server is asked by individual computers to send files or to save them.

Anti-virus checks and updates to software are much more important on networked computers than on stand-alone computers and these can also be carried out from one central computer. This ensures that all computers have the same level of protection.

Disadvantages of computer networks

There are also a few disadvantages to using networks rather than stand-alone machines.

Potential loss of security

If someone wants to gain unauthorised access to data on a stand-alone computer, they need physical access to that computer.

On a network, they can gain access from any computer connected to the one with the data.

This may be possible even from outside the building that the network is in, especially if the network is connected to the Internet.

Security measures such as anti-virus software, firewalls and anti-spyware are vital on a network.

Loss of speed

When users are sharing resources and data, there will obviously be a reduction in the speed at which they can get their files or print their work, as they may be in a queue. Careful design and management of the network are needed to ensure that it operates at a reasonable speed for everyone. This might include dividing the network into segments so that files shared by a particular set of users are on a special computer that they access first. This way, most data can be retrieved quickly and data that is required less often can be a bit slower to access.

Cost of purchase and set-up

The introduction of a network will bring with it a number of different costs, including the following:

* Computers need to be connected with cables and connectors or wireless connections and these must be bought and installed.

* All computers need extra hardware, such as network interface cards (NICs), to allow them to be connected to a network.

* Many computers will need extra software to allow them to communicate on a network.

* A network will often have one or more server machines, such as a file server – these are extra machines.

* If the network is connected to the Internet then a modem and router are required and there will probably be a fee to be paid to an Internet service provider (ISP).

Maintenance and supervision costs

Even when a network has been installed and is running successfully, it will still incur costs that were not there for stand-alone machines:

* Most networks require extra staff to be employed to manage the running of the network.

* Security software such as anti-virus, anti-spyware and firewall software must be

constantly updated to ensure the best security possible.

* Hardware maintenance costs will be higher simply because there is more hardware to maintain.

CASE STUDY
Your Pets magazine

A company that publishes a monthly magazine, *Your Pets*, has 15 writers, three editors and two administration staff.

Currently, all staff have a stand-alone computer on their desk with all the software they need. There are two printers, connected to the administration staff machines. Writers and editors pass their work to an administrator on a memory stick when they need something printed. A scanner is connected to one machine and, again, writers will request a scan and receive the file on a memory stick.

The company's managing director thinks it is about time they install a network but realises that there are costs involved as well as benefits.

Knowledge check

Prepare a presentation for a meeting at which you will describe advantages and disadvantages of introducing a network and will recommend whether or not it is a good idea.

Types of network

Networks are built to suit the organisations that need them. Some networks are small – an office might have three computers that they want to connect together to share data, for example. Some networks are much larger – a large supermarket might have 25 point-of-sale terminals all connected to one central computer that processes all the sales and stock data. Some networks are huge and cover a wide geographical area, such as a multi-national company requiring a network that is able to operate throughout all its sites around the world. The size of the network will often govern the type of network that is chosen. Peer-to-peer and client-server networks are two types of network that can be chosen to suit the networking needs of an organisation.

Peer-to-peer networks

These are usually very small networks, often connecting together only three or four computers at a time. All computers in a peer-to-peer network are equal and are generally used in the same way as if they were stand-alone computers, except that they can make some files and some resources available to other computers on the network.

A **peer computer** can:

* request data from another computer
* send a file to another computer to be printed
* use a device connected to another machine on the network
* send a file to another peer computer
* print a file sent to it by another peer computer
* allow another peer computer to use a device that is connected to it.

Every computer on a peer-to-peer network can request **network services** from any other computer and can provide network services to any other computer on the network.

Key terms

Peer computer: An individual computer on a peer-to-peer network.

Network services: The services provided by one computer in response to a request from another computer. The services might be to use a device attached to the servicing machine, or to send a file of data to a requesting machine.

There is no central control of a peer-to-peer network. All peer computers must manage their own security by:

* making sure that only those who should have access to data are able to get to it
* carrying out regular back-ups of their own data

* making sure that any necessary anti-virus, anti-spyware and firewall software is installed and up to date.

Because of these requirements being spread throughout the network, it can be less secure. If one peer computer fails to manage its own security then the security of the whole network can be undermined.

Advantages of peer-to-peer networks

There is very little cost involved in setting up a peer-to-peer network with existing stand-alone computers. Each computer will need a network interface card, some cable or communicating media, protocol software to allow it to communicate on the network, and an operating system that can cope with sharing files and resources. Most modern operating systems, such as Windows 98 onwards, have networking capabilities built in; they only need to be activated.

If all machines are equal, the network does not depend on one machine. If one machine stops working, all other parts of the network are still useable.

Disadvantages of peer-to-peer networks

If one machine is not secure, it can allow unauthorised access, or the spread of viruses through the whole network. This will compromise **network security**.

If a resource such as a printer is shared by too many computers, it will slow down the computer that the printer is connected to. If one machine holds a database file that is used by users on all other machines on the network, that computer will be slowed down by the constant access to its hard disk and the need to keep track of who is changing the database and when.

Key terms

Network security: This involves managing access to data and resources, protecting against threats to data from malicious software and users, and keeping regular back-ups in case of loss of data.

Client-server networks

This type of network has one or more **server** machines that provide services to all the other computers on the network. The services they might provide include:

* storing files on request

* sending files on request

* setting access rights for files and folders

* printing files on request

* storing applications and giving copies of them on request

* providing access to the Internet for a number of other computers.

Server computers only provide services to other computers on a network; they are not used for any other function.

All other computers on the network are called **clients** and will request network services from the server.

A client computer requests network services from one or more servers. It does not provide any network services itself. A client may request a copy of a data file and a file server will provide it. A client might want to print a file and a print server will carry out this task.

Key terms

Client: An individual computer on a client-server network that uses network services.

Server: A computer on a client-server network that provides network services to other computers.

Advantages of client-server networks

All security can be carried out on a server machine and is therefore done centrally. There will generally be a member of staff responsible for maintaining the performance and security of the server computer. Central management of security will mean that a client-server network should be more secure than a peer-to-peer network.

Servers can manage access to files and to resources by a large number of clients without too much loss of speed. Servers manage security efficiently. If a file has been copied to a client computer, the server will not allow another client to change that file until the first client has closed it.

Users of client-server networks have much less responsibility for the daily management of their computer systems. They will not need to remember to back up their work, to update their anti-virus software or to carry out other administrative or security tasks. These will all be done by the network administrator from the server machines. This leaves users with more time to do their main work.

Disadvantages of client-server networks

There is a high level of cost involved in setting up a client-server network. The costs might include the following:

* Server machines are not used as clients, so there will always be at least one more machine than was needed before the network was installed.

* Server machines are high-specification machines and will be expensive.

* Both server and client computers will need network interface cards, some cable or communicating media and protocol software to allow them to communicate on the network.

* Client computers will need an operating system that can cope with sharing files and resources.

* Server computers will need a full network operating system, such as Windows NT.

There will need to be at least one member of staff available to run the network and to be responsible for the server machines. Often this is an additional member of staff, and so this will add to the running costs.

Think it over...

Look at the following scenarios and decide whether you would recommend a peer-to-peer network or a client-server network in each case.

1 An office has four computers and will be sharing all files and resources across the network.

2 A company has 30 computers spread between eight offices. Many files and resources will be shared across the network.

3 A group of 16 writers share an office but work independently. They will use a network only for sharing printers.

4 An organisation has one office with five computers. Their network will be used to share a printer and to move files across the network only very occasionally.

Knowledge check

Describe the benefits and limitations of peer-to-peer and client-server networks and recommend a network type for *Your Pets* magazine.

Local and wide area networks

Networks are categorised into local area networks (LANs) and wide area networks (WANs).

LANs are private networks that cover a relatively small geographical area, such as an office, a building or a group of buildings on one site. Computers in a LAN are connected by network cables or by wireless connections. LANs usually have fast data transfer speeds because they have full use of their own cables or wireless frequencies at all times.

WANs are networks that cover a large geographical area. Computers in a WAN may be in different towns, or even in different countries. In general, computers in a WAN will be connected using public telecommunications systems such as:

* the telephone system
* public cable systems
* public wireless systems such as the mobile telephone network.

Some WANs will use leased telephone lines so that they have their own private connections, but these are still part of the public telephone network.

Types of local area network

A single LAN has all computers and resources connected to each other. Data is shared between all computers on the network. Figure 16.4 shows a network connected by cables. Each computer is connected to the network by a cable. The cable might be connected to a network device such as a hub or switch, and this forms the connection between one computer and all the others.

Cabled networks tend to have fast data-transfer rates and are generally reliable. All cables must be installed so that they do not pose a tripping hazard, and will often be attached around the walls of a building. Once cables are installed, they are fixed, and adding new computers requires extra cabling.

Wireless LANs

Sometimes LANs use wireless technology. Each computer has a radio receiver and transmitter and each communicates with a wireless hub or wireless access point.

All components in a wireless network will be capable of receiving and transmitting radio signals.

Wireless local area networks (WLANs) are particularly useful in buildings where it would be

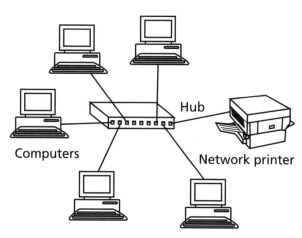

FIGURE 16.4 *A cabled network*

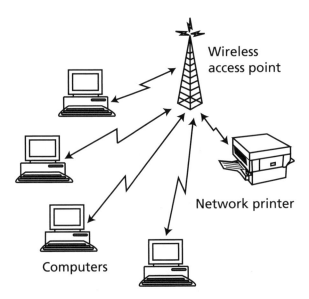

FIGURE 16.5 *A wireless local area network*

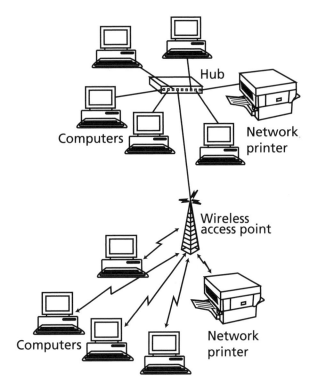

FIGURE 16.6 *A virtual LAN*

difficult to install cables, or for organisations that need their staff to be mobile. Installation is easier because there are no cables to fix. It is also easier to add new computers to the network and computers can be sited anywhere within range of the wireless access point.

In comparison to cable technology, wireless is relatively slow. There can also be difficulties with interference to the radio signals. Interference can cause the network to become slow and unreliable. Wireless signals can pass through walls, which can be an advantage, but they could be picked up by equipment outside the building or office, which is a security risk. Wireless networks are more expensive to buy than many cabled networks, but the advantage is the mobility of the computers in the network.

Many hotels, conference centres and other public areas now provide wireless Internet access through their own servers. This means that people travelling for business can, at least, contact their offices by email and can often access their organisation's extranet or other services.

Virtual LANs

Like the road system in rush hour, too much traffic causes delays to journeys. As LANs become larger, with more computers connected and more data travelling across the network, things can slow down.

To overcome this problem, LANs are often divided into segments. Each segment becomes a separate LAN and can have its own shape and connection type. Segments are connected together and can pass data between them. Each LAN, although separate, is not entirely disconnected from the main LAN and so each is called a virtual LAN (VLAN).

A VLAN is a segment on a network of two or more segments, connected by a backbone cable. As far as the computers on a VLAN are concerned, they are connected to the main LAN and can communicate with all other machines. Most data on a VLAN is passed between computers on that VLAN. Therefore, each VLAN will only receive incoming messages for computers that are part of that VLAN, rather than for every computer on the network, which reduces the traffic. The device that connects each VLAN to the main LAN will pass across any data that needs to travel between VLANs. In general, the network is made faster by splitting it up. If a fault develops on a VLAN, other parts of the wider LAN are not affected.

It is a little more complicated to add a computer to a VLAN than to one single LAN.

Each part of the wider LAN has to be configured to recognise the new machine and which VLAN it belongs to.

VLANs are often used in large organisations where a LAN must serve a large number of computers. Where organisations are divided into separate departments, each can have their own VLAN.

Types of wide area network

Wide area networks cover a wide geographical area and use public communications systems for transmitting data. Wide area networks are generally made up of a number of LANs that are then connected together by telephone, satellite or other communications links.

Public WANs

The biggest WAN in existence is the Internet, a world-wide network connecting millions and millions of computers. The Internet is a public WAN. Telecommunications lines are shared between users. Because of this, there is always the risk that any data sent across the Internet can be intercepted by other users sharing the link.

Private WANs

WANs can be private networks, where one organisation uses private leased telephone lines to ensure that they have sole use of the communications link.

Virtual private networks (VPNs)

An organisation that has two offices in different parts of the country might want to connect the LANs in each office so that they can pass data between them. A private WAN is one option, but the cost of leasing private lines is quite high. It is much cheaper to use the Internet, but this is less secure. It is possible to set up a connection between two LANs on the Internet that uses the shared communications line but has a secure path on that line. A VPN is a way of setting up a private WAN using an existing public network.

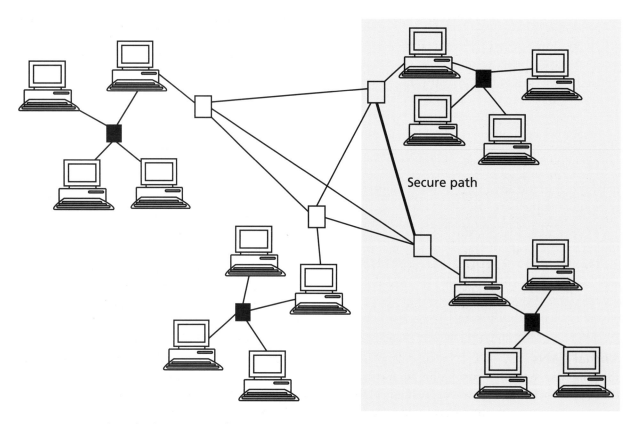

Secure path

FIGURE 16.7 *A virtual private network*

Network services

Every network provides a number of services to its users. A LAN will provide some or all of the following services:

* printer sharing
* other resource sharing (scanners, disks, etc.)
* email
* file sharing
* network-wide communication, often using an intranet
* network-wide file management
* network-wide security.

Email allows users to send messages to each other, to a group of other users, or to everyone on the network. A LAN that provides email will have a machine that is dedicated to managing the flow of messages between users. Each user has a mailbox on the mail server machine. All messages that are sent to that user are placed in the mailbox. When the user logs on with username and password, they are given access to their mailbox where they can retrieve their messages. From here they can reply to messages, forward messages to other users or send new messages, which the mail server places in the correct mailbox.

A user's mailbox will contain all messages they have received and sent, any they have written but not sent and a list of contacts saved by the user. It is generally the user's responsibility to manage their mailbox by deleting old messages and organising messages into folders if necessary.

Networks are ideal media for communicating information around an organisation quickly and efficiently. An **intranet** is a communication system used on a LAN that allows authorised users (with a username and password) to view information in a similar way to the way it is done on the Internet, using a browser. An intranet uses the same technology as the World Wide Web, so users familiar with the Internet do not have to learn a new system. A network might provide email, bulletin boards and information pages on its intranet.

Additional services provided by a WAN

A WAN provides the opportunity for users to access additional services.

Email

Email is available to a wider number of users on a WAN than it is on a LAN. When a LAN is connected to the Internet, it might have its own mail server and will manage its own emails, passing them between LAN and WAN. If a LAN does not have a mail server or an individual computer is connected to the Internet, a webmail application will be used through a browser. A user's mailbox is kept on a server on the Internet, such as the Hotmail server or the Yahoo server; the user has to access the server through their browser and then log in.

Video-conferencing and teleconferencing

Video-conferencing and teleconferencing can be achieved on a WAN if the communications lines are capable of transferring data fast enough. To hold a video-conference, a number of users must be accessing the WAN at the same time. Each has a video camera, a screen and speakers. Using special software, a user is able to talk to the camera and have a stream of video images sent to all other users who are using the same software and connection. Each user receives the video images from every other user and transmits their own images instantly.

Video-conferencing requires a high-speed link between the computers on the WAN, and specialist software to transmit, receive and display the video images and sound.

Teleconferencing works in the same way, but uses only sound, so a microphone and speakers are all that is required, and the communications link does not need to be quite so fast.

Access to the World Wide Web

This is probably the most common use of the Internet. The **World Wide Web** is a worldwide information service that is available using the Internet. Special computers called web servers hold files of information in a special format. These files can be requested by anyone using a browser such as Internet Explorer, Netscape Navigator, Mozilla Firefox or Safari.

Files or pages of information are accessed by typing the address of the web server that holds the file, followed by any folders the file might be in, and the file name.

Web pages contain text and graphical information and may also contain video images and interactive elements. They also contain hyperlinks, which allow users to jump from one page to another by clicking on a part of the page that is a hyperlink.

A variety of search engines can be accessed on the Internet. These keep databases of all the websites they know about, with keywords attached to each page. Users can type in keywords and the search engine will produce a list of all the web pages it knows about that have that keyword.

Access to public domain software

The Internet can also be used to access **public domain software**. Public domain software is software that can be downloaded, copied and distributed freely. It is placed on servers on the Internet and users can ask to download the software. Other, similar, types of software are available in the same way:

* freeware – free to use but can't be copied or distributed

* shareware – free for a given period of time only

* open source – licensed freeware with its source code, which can be modified.

Data file exchange

Data file exchange is the process of copying a file from one computer to another over a WAN. There are different ways that this can be done.

A file can be attached to an email. The receiver can then save the file on their own computer. Most file types can be sent as file attachments to emails, and this is a convenient way to transfer one or two files at a time from one computer to another.

When more files need to be copied at the same time, another method is to use file transfer protocol (FTP) software. FTP software runs on a WAN, such as the Internet, and operates as file management software, allowing the user to copy files to and from their own computer and a remote computer. The user must be given access rights to the remote computer. Once the FTP software is running, the user can transfer files in much the same way as they might on a LAN or even between disks in their own computer. Files can be copied, deleted and organised into folders.

Commercial transactions

Commercial transactions often take place on the Internet. Many people shop online and make payments with credit or debit cards. Online banking is now widely available. It is also possible to fill in tax returns online and to make a wide

Threads in Forum : News Forum			Forum Tools ▾			
Announcement: Things You Need to Know Sayon (Death)				Views: 8,339 ⤵ 08-14-2004		
	Thread / Thread Starter	Rating	Last Post ☑	Replies	Views
✉ ➜	Sticky: Christmas Lectures (uk) YT	🔖	12-20-2005 12:20 PM by YT ⤵	0	18
✉	Top ten buzzwords (and phrases) for 2005 Mart		Yesterday 01:21 PM by He ⤵	7	86
✉	Skin color gene identified (NYT--Science magazine) Mart		12-19-2005 12:23 PM by worm ⤵	10	66
✉	"It's a near certainty that black holes don't exist" (▤ 1 2) bli		12-15-2005 04:22 PM by [Ty?] ⤵	27	1,060

FIGURE 16.8 *A discussion forum*

variety of other transactions. **E-commerce** is the name for commercial transactions that take place on the Internet. For commercial transactions to take place, the provider (the shop making the sale, the bank or the tax office) must have a server that runs the software to make the transactions. Users access the software through their browsers. Organisations that provide e-commerce systems must ensure that the access to the systems is secure.

Bulletin boards and discussion forums

These are ways to share information between groups of interested users. A **bulletin board** is a messaging system set up by an organisation on a server and made publicly available. The bulletin board works as an electronic noticeboard. Users post messages on the board and can look at, and reply to, the messages posted by other users. Some bulletin boards are freely accessible; others are accessed by subscription. The boards can sometimes be used to exchange software and files and to play multi-player games.

A **discussion forum** is a message board that is made available to authorised users (who have a username and password). Users join discussion forums where they can post messages and read and respond to messages posted by other users. Discussion forums are generally moderated to ensure that an acceptable code of conduct is followed by all users.

A string of replies to a particular message is called a thread. Users can follow a thread to read all messages on a particular topic.

Web-based marketing and advertising

Web-based marketing and advertising is a way of getting advertising and marketing materials to a large number of potential customers. Organisations can produce, or get someone else to produce, their marketing and advertising materials in a form that can be accessed on the World Wide Web. The organisation needs to store the materials as web pages on their own web server or one provided by an Internet service provider. Once materials are accessible as web pages on the Internet, they can become available to anyone, anywhere in the world. This means that a larger number of people can get to know the organisation and that materials can be seen without having to be printed and sent out by post.

The organisation can attach keywords to all its web pages and can register these keywords with a search engine. Once the search engine has the keywords and web page addresses in its database, it will place the pages in lists given to people searching for a particular product or service. This means that more customers can be found with little effort and cost.

One further facility that can be available to users of a WAN is an **extranet**. This is a part of an intranet that is made available to users on a public network such as the Internet. Some pages of information are accessible from computers outside an organisation's LAN. These are only available to authorised users who are provided with a username and password and use a secure connection.

Key terms

Video-conferencing: A fast communications link transmits video images to a number of people simultaneously so that they can have a discussion as if they were all in the same room.

World Wide Web: An information service available on the Internet.

Public domain software: Software that is free and can be downloaded or copied without charge.

Data file exchange: The process of transferring a file from one computer to another over a WAN. The file can be sent as an attachment to an email or can be copied using FTP software.

E-commerce: Commercial transactions such as sales, transfer of money or submission of forms over a WAN.

Bulletin boards: Electronic message boards where people can post, read and reply to messages.

Discussion forums: Like bulletin boards but available to a closed set of users.

Web-based marketing and advertising: Making brochures, catalogues and advertising materials available on the World Wide Web and ensuring that they can be found by a search engine.

Extranet: Part of an intranet made available to authorised users over the Internet.

Knowledge check

Explain the Internet services that the company might make use of, the benefits they will gain from each and the hardware and software required for each.

Connecting a LAN to a WAN

Special equipment is required to enable a LAN to be connected to a WAN such as the Internet. Communication takes place using a public communications system such as the telephone network, the TV cable network or the mobile telephone network.

Dial-up modem

A computer or LAN can be connected to the public telecommunications system by dial-up connection or by permanent 'always on' connection. A dial-up connection works in the same way as a telephone call. The computer has a modem that dials the number for the computer it needs to attach itself to. Once the connection is made, the modem does all the transmitting and receiving of data. When the connection is no longer required, the modem hangs up and is disconnected from the line. A charge is made for the duration of the call only. While the computer is connected to the Internet, the telephone line is in use and so normal telephone calls cannot be made or received.

Dial-up connections can be charged as a regular fee for all calls or on a pay-as-you-go basis. The choice of service will depend on the estimated amount of time the Internet will be used. Because of the speed of the connection, it is only really feasible for one computer to be connected to the Internet with a dial-up connection.

Broadband

Permanent 'always on' connections use a dedicated communications line. This is generally an extra telephone line for which a monthly fee is paid. Permanent connections use broadband technology, which allows data to travel much faster than a dial-up line allows. A broadband connection uses the full bandwidth of the communications line to allow the fastest possible data transfer. At the time of writing, the fastest broadband connections are around 8–10 Mbps (8 to 10 million bits per second) compared to a dial-up connection which might achieve 64 Kbps (64 thousand bits per second), so broadband can be over 100 times faster than dial up. High-speed access means that it is feasible for all computers on a LAN to use one Internet connection. If this is to be done, the network will need a router; this will determine which computer requested each web page or other service and will route pages back to the correct computer.

Broadband uses a dedicated communications line and so the normal telephone line is always available. A broadband adapter, sometimes called a broadband modem, connects the computer or the router to the communications line.

Types of broadband connection

There are a number of broadband technologies available.

A digital subscriber telephone line (DSL) can be used. A splitter is installed so that the telephone line can be used for voice and data at the same time. This option is available to any line that is connected to a digital telephone exchange and can achieve speeds of up to 8 Mbps.

An asymmetric digital subscriber line (ADSL) is the type of DSL line most commonly used for connecting to the Internet. This type of line has more space for data going to the connected computer than for data going to the ISP. Most Internet users download large amounts of data but rarely upload data to the ISP server, so it is an advantage if data transfer is fast for downloading and slower for uploading.

Many broadband users are able to connect using the cable television network. This type

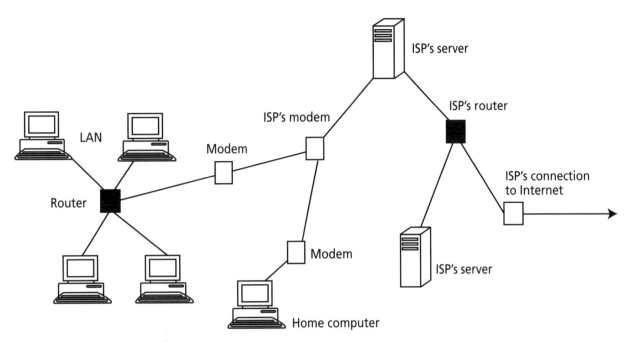

FIGURE 16.9 *An ISP connection*

of connection is only available to people or businesses in areas where cable has been laid. Speeds of up to 10 Mbps are possible. Another option is the Integrated Services Digital Network (ISDN). This is an extra telecommunications line connecting a house or business to the local telephone exchange. This option is available to anyone who has a telephone, regardless of whether their local exchange is digital or not. ISDN can achieve speeds up to 2 Mbps; slower than cable and DSL, but available to everyone.

Making the connection

Whatever type of connection, dial-up or broadband, cable, DSL or ISDN, a modem or adapter suitable for the type of connection is needed.

To make a connection to the Internet, an internet service provider (ISP) is also needed. ISPs provide server machines that users can log on to in order to access the Internet. The ISP will provide:

* Internet access
* the software required to make the connection between the computer and ISP's server
* other services, including email and web page hosting.

When a computer or LAN is connected to the Internet, it becomes part of the ISP's network.

16.2 Network design

When designing a network, you will need to make a number of decisions, including:

* the way the computers will be connected together – the *topology*
* the cables, connectors and transmission methods to be used
* a suitable network interface card
* the connecting equipment required
* the technologies to be used
* network client software
* protocols
* network hardware and servers
* the services to be provided and the hardware, including servers, needed to provide those services.

These decisions will allow you to design a network that fulfils the user's needs and provides the required services.

You may already have decided on a peer-to-peer or a client-server network. This will help to determine the type and number of servers you will need.

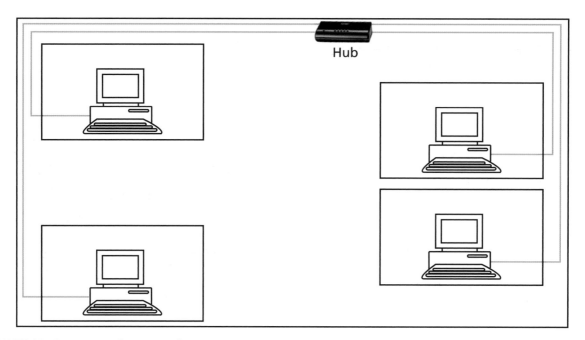

FIGURE 16.10 *Layout of a network*

You may also have decided that connection to the Internet, for the services it offers, is necessary. This will lead to decisions about the type of Internet connection required and will determine some of the connection equipment and protocols needed.

When all decisions are made, you will be able to draw a diagram to show the layout of the network and how all the components are connected together.

Network topologies

The way a network is laid out is called its topology. The topology determines how computers are connected together and what connecting equipment is required by the network. The topology defines the map of the network. There are several topologies in common use; each has its own features, types of connecting equipment and method of moving data.

Every network needs a map. The map shows where all the computers are and how the cables are arranged. A map can also show how data flows around a network. To make the map simple to follow, it may not be to scale nor completely accurate in its placing of computers and cables. In this case, the map is showing the

logical topology, a simplified representation of the network layout.

The most commonly used topologies are:

* bus
* ring
* star
* mesh.

The logical representations of each of these are described in the following sections.

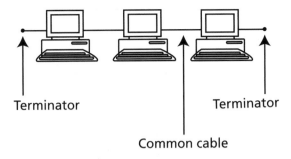

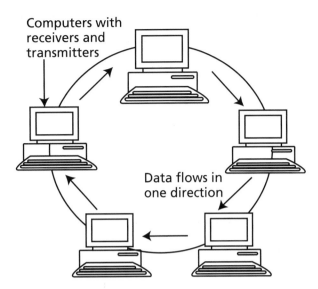

Computers with receivers and transmitters

Data flows in one direction

FIGURE 16.11 *Bus topology*

Bus topology

Computers are connected in a line. Each computer is connected to a common cable that allows data to pass in both directions at once and for data to be sent (or broadcast) from one computer to all computers. The cable is terminated at each end. Each computer must have the facility to send and receive on the common cable.

This is a very easy topology to set up and use. Apart from the terminators, it requires no special connecting equipment and it uses the minimum amount of cable. If a new computer is added, it can just be slotted into the line. If a computer is switched off or unable to work, this does not affect other computers, except that they cannot contact that one computer.

Network operation can sometimes be slow because all computers are using the same cable, and this causes congestion and corruption to data. This topology is not suitable for very large or very busy networks but can form part of a larger network. There is a limit to the length of the common cable, which means that the network cannot cover a very large area. There is also a limit on the number of computers that can be attached to one cable, and, when new computers are added, there can sometimes be problems with finding where to add them.

The network is dependent on the cable. If there is a break in the cable, the whole network will stop working. Finding the break in the cable is often quite difficult.

Ring topology

Computers are connected in a continuous ring and data flows in one direction only. Each computer has a receiver that receives data

FIGURE 16.12 *Ring topology*

from the computer before it in the ring and a transmitter that sends data to the computer after it in the ring. The computer will inspect each set of data to see if it is addressed to it. If not, it will simply pass the data on.

This type of network can be very fast. Data travels in one direction only and so there is little chance of collision with other data. Computers will have a limited waiting time however much traffic there is on the network. If a computer is switched off or unable to work, there will generally be some way for data to be passed through so that the ring does not cease operation. Each computer transmits the data as a new set of signals, so it is boosted each time it goes through a computer on the ring; this allows the ring to cover a much larger area than some other topologies. If a cable stops working, it is very easy to find where in the ring this cable is. It will be just before the computer that does not receive data. The topology is fairly simple to set up and use. No special connecting equipment is required for a ring network.

A ring network uses a cable for each computer and this can cause it to be quite expensive. The shape of a ring network makes it quite inflexible. New computers can be added into the ring, but they have to be placed in a position where they can be connected between two other computers. This can sometimes cause difficulties.

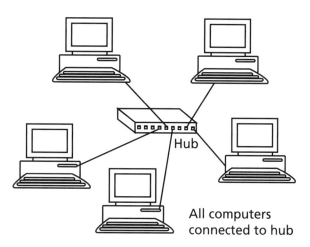

FIGURE 16.13 *Star topology*

All computers connected to hub

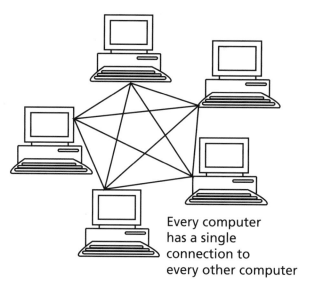

Every computer has a single connection to every other computer

FIGURE 16.14 *Mesh topology*

Each packet of data has to travel all the way round the ring so that the sender knows it reached its destination; it can't travel back the way it came. If there is a break in one cable or one receiving/ transmitting device, it can't do this and the whole network stops.

Star topology

All computers in a star topology are connected to a single hub. All data passes through this hub.

This network is easy to set up and it is very easy to add another computer to the network. It is simply plugged into the hub. If one computer or cable fails, this does not affect the network. It is relatively easy to find a faulty machine or cable, as it will be the one that is unable to use the network.

A star network uses one cable to connect each computer to the hub and so cabling costs are relatively high.

The network is dependent on the hub. If the hub fails, the network fails.

Mesh topology

Every computer in a mesh topology has a single connection to every other computer. The network is very fast as each device can send data as soon as it is ready; the only waiting it will have to do is if the receiving device is already receiving data from another machine. Each computer has its own switch, which allows a number of other computers to be connected to it.

It is possible to only partially connect a mesh. In this case, routers are needed to allow

computers to figure out how to send data to each machine on the network.

The mesh network is very fast and highly fault tolerant. A cable failure breaks a connection between two machines only, but it is possible to route data through other machines to make up for this.

Due to the high number of connections, a mesh network is very expensive. A small mesh network of five computers will require ten cables. Every computer must know which computers it is connected to. When a new computer is added, a number of extra cables are required. To add a sixth computer to the illustrated mesh would require an extra five cables. Every computer would need to be reconfigured so that it knew about the new computer and how to get to it if the cable fails.

Physical topologies

The logical topologies shown so far are unlikely to be implemented in real life. When a real network is installed, the position of the cables is determined by where the computers need to go and where the cables can be attached to walls or chanelled under floors.

A star topology will not have cables trailing across the room, and will, most probably, not have the hub in the centre. This connection equipment must go where it is more convenient and safe.

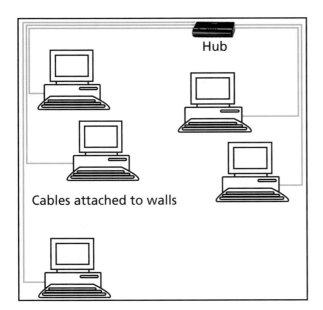

FIGURE 16.15 *A physical star topology*

The principle is the same – all computers are connected to a central hub. In Figure 16.15 it is more difficult to see the individual connections.

Connections in a network

All networks have some way of sending data from one machine to another, regardless of the topology being used. When designing a network, the type of connection will be considered and will be chosen depending on whether a WAN or LAN is being set up, how big the network needs to be, the required speeds of

FIGURE 16.16 *A digital signal*

data transmission and any cost limitations. Data is transmitted as a set of signals along a cable, a telecommunications link or across a wireless connection.

Types of signal

Most signals are transmitted as frequencies. Signals used by computers are digital. They can have two voltages only. One voltage represents 1 and the other represents 0. Digital signals are read easily by computers.

For a computer to send digital signals, it must have an interface card that can translate a 1 in computer terms into the frequency that represents a 1 on the transmission medium, and it must do the same with a 0. This process is called **modulation**. A receiving computer must translate what it receives on the transmission medium into what represents 1 and 0 in computer terms. This process is called **demodulation**.

Some telecommunications systems use different types of signals which are not digital. **Analogue signals** are different in that they can transmit a wide range of frequencies, not just two. Analogue signals use a constantly changing set of frequencies (see Figure 16.17). If digital data is going to be transmitted on a medium that can only carry analogue signals, then it has to be converted into a set of analogue signals that are understood to represent that digital data.

Again, the signals need to be modulated to change what represents a 1 in computer terms to what represents a 1 in analogue signals on the transmission medium.

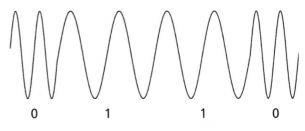

FIGURE 16.17 *An analogue signal*

Many standard telephone lines are still analogue and if a computer is connected to a telephone line, it will need a **modem**. A modem will perform the digital to analogue conversion and will modulate the signal so that the correct signals for 1 and 0 are sent. A computer at the other end will also have a modem. This will demodulate the signal and convert it from analogue to a **digital signal**.

FIGURE 16.18 *Unshielded twisted pair cable and RJ-45 connector*

Cables

All networks require computers to be connected together in some way. For a LAN, this might be by cables or by wireless transmission.

Different types of network use different types of cable. Some types of cable are faster than others and more expensive. Some networks are unable to use cables because they cannot be put anywhere. These networks might use radio broadcasts instead.

Unshielded twisted pair (UTP) cable

Twisted pair cable consists of a number of individually insulated wires that are twisted together in pairs and covered with an outer sheath. Twisting the wires together minimises

the amount of electrical interference (crosstalk). UTP is the most commonly used cable for LANs. UTP cable uses an RJ-45 connector.

UTP is cheap, easy to work with and fast, with data speeds up to 1000 Megabits per second (Mbps).

Shielded twisted pair (STP) cable

Less commonly used, STP cable is very similar to UTP, but the twisted pairs of wires are covered by a metallic shield that gives extra protection from interference and means that data transmission is more reliable. STP also uses RJ-45 connectors.

FIGURE 16.19 *Shielded twisted pair cable*

Both types of twisted pair cable are prone to electrical interference, which causes data to get lost during transmission.

Fibre-optic cable and fibre transmission

Fibre-optic cable uses light pulses rather than electrical signals and is therefore immune to electrical interference. Fibre-optic cables can be used where other cables cannot because of the electrical interference, such as in lift shafts. The cable is made either of glass or of plastic.

Glass can carry signals a greater distance, but plastic is cheaper. A glass or plastic core is covered in a layer of PVC or Plenum, which protects it from light interference.

Fibre-optic cable is not especially fast. It can reach speeds as fast as the fastest twisted pair cable, but its advantage is in the distance it can carry signals: up to 10 kilometres as opposed to a maximum of 100 metres for twisted pair cable. Fibre-optic cable uses either SC (subscriber connector) or ST (straight tip) connectors that look like the connectors on a television aerial cable.

FIGURE 16.20 *Fibre-optic cable with ST connector*

Connectors

Every cable has a particular type of connector. Cable and connector pairs must be matched.

> **✱ Remember**
>
> UTP cable uses RJ-45 connectors.
> STP cable uses RJ-45 connectors.
> Fibre-optic cable uses either SC or ST connectors.
> Telephone cable uses RJ-11 connectors.

Wireless transmission

Wireless transmission uses radio signals, so no wiring is required. A wireless network card is connected to a PCI slot, to a PCMCIA slot or through a USB port. The network card sends and receives radio signals at a particular frequency.

Wireless transmission has the advantage that no wires are needed, but it is often subject to interference from signals that just hang around in the air, and it can be slow and unreliable. It is possible that signals can be received outside the area they are intended for, causing some problems with security.

Typical wireless speeds are 11 Mbps to 54 Mbps.

> **✱ Remember**
>
> All data is sent as a set of individual bits (1 or 0). A megabit is approximately a million bits. Speeds given in Mbps indicate the number of millions of bits that can be transferred each second.

Transmission methods

Data travels along all transmission media in individual bits (1s or 0s represented by a particular voltage or frequency). Computers deal with data in sets of eight bits at a time and so need to receive it in multiples of eight bits.

When data is sent, it needs to be put into sensible sets of bits so that they can be understood. Each set of data needs to be packaged up with an address of where it is going to, where it has come from and some information to allow the receiver to check that the contents of the packet are correct.

If you order items from a mail order company they will be sent to you in a packet with

* your address (so that it reaches the correct person)

* the mail order company's address (so that it can be returned if it does not reach the correct person)

* the items you ordered

* a delivery note so that you can check that the order is correct (the mail order company's address can also be used to report any errors in the order)

* a postmark (so that it can be monitored if the parcel does not get delivered in a certain time).

Data packets are sent in a similar way.

Different types of network will organise data differently, but all data packets have some common elements:

* sender's address

* receiver's address

* data in sets of eight bits

* some checking data

* some control data.

Data packets

The following information describes the format of the packets on different network technologies. The technologies are described later and the examples here are given as examples of the different layouts for data packets.

FIGURE 16.21 *A network interface card*

Ethernet packet

Number of Bytes					
8	6	6	2	(variable)	4
Control data	Destination address	Source address	Length of data	Data	Check data

The control data is a set of 1s and 0s that indicate that this is the start of the packet. This allows the receiver to be ready to catch the data. The 'length of data' field allows the receiver to know how much data it should be expecting to read. The 'check data' field allows the receiver to perform a calculation on the data it has received and to check that the results match the check data. If they do, it assumes that the data was correct. If not, it will ask for the packet to be sent again.

Token ring packet or frame

Number of Bytes						
2	1	2 or 6	2 or 6	up to 5000	4	2
Control data	Frame control	Destination address	Source address	Data	Checking data	End of frame data

Packets in a token ring network are called frames. The control data marks the start of the frame, frame control data contains checking information and the checking data allows the receiver to check that the data was received correctly. The end of frame is a special sequence of 0s and 1s that are recognised as the end of the frame.

FDDI packet

Fibre-distributed data interface (FDDI) is a very similar standard to the token ring standard but is intended for high-speed token ring networks that use two rings of fibre-optic cables. FDDI rings can cover large distances and achieve high speeds. They can use the two rings to send two lots of data at a time (usually one in each direction) or to keep one as a backup in case the first ring breaks.

The packet format on an FDDI ring network is the same as on the token ring network.

Bandwidth and transmission rate

When data is sent along any type of transmission media, it is sent as frequencies. Each type of transmission has a range of frequencies that it can handle. The bandwidth is the range of frequencies that can be used for the transmission of data. The wider (or bigger) the range of frequencies, the more data can be sent.

Broadband connections are able to use a range of frequencies of over 3 kHz and can be divided into a number of channels, meaning that a number of computers can use the broadband cable at the same time, all being able to transmit and receive data at high speed.

Baseband (or narrowband) connections use a range of frequencies of much less than 3 kHz and are only able to allow one connection at a time.

The bandwidth that is available for a single connection will affect the speed of that connection. Wider bandwidths allow higher speeds as more bits can be sent at a time. The speed of data transmission is measured in bits per second (bps) and is generally given as kilobits per second (Kbps), megabits per second (Mbps) or even gigabits per second (Gbps).

Calculating the estimated time for transferring a file

If you know the size of a file and the transmission rate, you can estimate how long it will take to transfer the file from one computer to another.

For example, suppose a file's size was 8 KB and it was being sent over a communications channel with a speed of 64 Kbps. The calculation would be:

$$\text{Transfer time} = \frac{\text{File size (in bits)}}{\text{Channel speed (bps)}}$$

The file size must be calculated in bits.

There are 8 bits in a byte, 1024 bytes in a KB and this file is 8KB. The size of this file is:

$$8 \times 1024 \times 8 \text{ bits} = 65536 \text{ bits}$$

The channel speed is 64 Kbps (1 Kbps = 1024 bps). The speed in bps is:

$$64 \times 1024 \text{ bps} = 65536 \text{ bps}$$

Transfer time is 65536/65536 seconds or 1 second.

Think it over...

How long will it take to transfer a 16MB file over a broadband connection with a speed of 2 Mbps?

(A MB is 1024 KB, which is 1024 × 1024 bytes)

File size in bits = 16 × 1024 × 1024 × 8 bits
= 134217728 bits

(1 Mbps = 1024 Kbps which is 1024 × 1024 bps)

Channel speed = 2 × 1024 × 1024 bps
= 2097152

Transfer time = file size/channel speed
= 134217728/2097152
= 64 seconds

Knowledge check

A 4 MB file takes 4 seconds to be transferred over a broadband connection with a speed of 8 Mbps. How is this calculated?

Servers

All client–server networks will need at least one server to provide services for client computers to use. These services might include managing network files, printer sharing or providing application software or Internet access. As well as a file server, networks may also include a print server, an application server and a proxy server. These servers are described in the section on network hardware later in this chapter.

Network interface cards (NIC)

Every networked computer will have a network interface card (NIC) or adapter that will form the connection between the computer and the network.

In some personal computers, the NIC plugs into a PCI slot, in others it is incorporated in the motherboard. Some wireless adapters plug into PCMCIA ports on laptops or might plug into a USB port.

A NIC will have:

* at least one connector for a cable to plug into or a receiver/transmitter for a wireless network
* circuits that translate the data into the correct format for transmission
* circuits that manage the process of getting the data onto the network and checking that it has arrived safely
* circuits that manage the process of receiving data from the network and acknowledging that it has been read correctly or asking for it to be retransmitted.

Every NIC has a unique address so that each can be uniquely identified. This is known as its media access control (MAC) address. A MAC address looks similar to this:

06:37:AA:2F:C3:46

MAC addresses cannot, generally, be changed. This means that no two NICs will have the same address and all can be uniquely identified.

Connecting equipment

A network will consist of a number of computers, each with a network interface card, and a number of items of connecting equipment, depending on the type and size of the network.

Star and mesh networks need hubs or switches and patch panels. Large networks use bridges to allow them to be split into smaller sections. Ring networks and large networks of all topologies use repeaters. Mesh networks, wide area networks and LANs that are connected to WANs, use gateways and routers.

Hubs

Each computer in the network is connected to the hub by a cable which plugs into a socket (or port) in the hub. The hub receives data from a computer in the network and broadcasts it to all its connected computers. The computer whose address is in the data packet will read it; the rest will ignore it.

FIGURE 16.22 *Three hubs*

Passive hubs just broadcast the data directly; active hubs will receive the data and re-transmit it. This way the data signal is boosted and is less likely to become lost.

The number of computers that can be connected to a hub is dictated by the number of ports the hub has.

Switches

Whereas a hub is a relatively simple device that just receives data and broadcasts it, a switch is an intelligent device that can make a 'virtual' connection between two computers.

Switches are used in star and mesh networks to make connections between a number of connected computers. A switch has a number of sockets (or ports). Cables from each connected computer are plugged into the ports.

A switch is an intelligent device. It looks at data sent by one computer, works out which computer needs the data, and sends it only

FIGURE 16.23 *A switch*

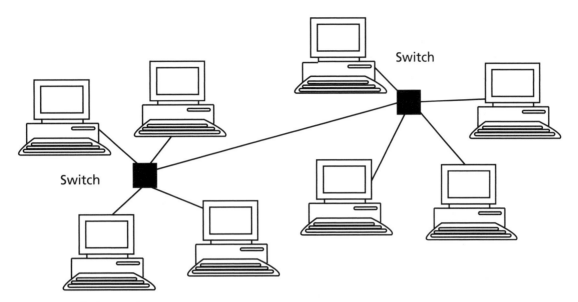

FIGURE 16.24 *Switches and segments*

through the port that the receiving computer is plugged into. The switch needs to have the ability to store information about the MAC address of the NIC in each computer and which port its cable is plugged into.

As networks become larger, a switch will slow down. It has to constantly inspect all its ports to look for incoming data and this process takes longer the more ports it has. Larger networks can be divided into segments. Often, a network consists of a number of groups of computers that do a lot of communicating within the group, but only a small amount of communicating with computers in other groups. Each group can become a segment with its own switch.

Each segment in a large network will have its own switch to which all computers will be connected. The switch will be connected to the switches in the other segments.

Each switch stores information about which computers are attached to it and which are attached to each of the other switches. When a packet of data is sent to a switch, it will inspect the data for the destination address and will forward the packet either to the destination computer or to the switch that the destination computer is attached to.

Packets of data can also be filtered so that damaged data can be removed and data can be blocked from or to particular computers.

Patch cables and patch panels

Wiring of networks causes many problems, especially when long lengths of cable are needed between computers and the hub or switch (UTP cables can be up to 100 metres long).

Once the cable is installed, especially if it is boxed in, it would be very difficult to move it. Computers become static and adding a new computer is problematic. A solution to this problem is to install a maximum number of cables in the wall and to use wall jacks to allow computers to be plugged into the main cabling system.

Patch cables are used to connect the NIC in the computer to the wall jack. Drop cables connect the wall jacks to the hub.

For further flexibility, a patch panel can connect the individual drop cables to one or

FIGURE 16.25 *A wall jack*

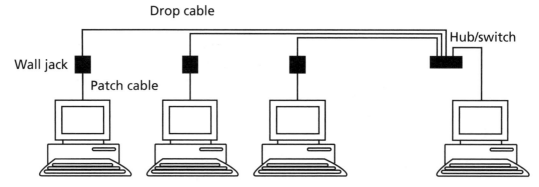

FIGURE 16.26 *Patch cables connect NICs to wall jacks; drop cables connect wall jacks to the hub*

more hubs using more patch cables. The patch panel allows a large number of drop cables to be plugged into it and so is a central wiring point.

Repeaters

Cabling can restrict the size of the network. UTP has a maximum transmission distance of 100 metres. Over this length, data signals get lost. To increase the distance that data can be sent, a repeater can be used. Repeaters simply receive packets of data and re-transmit them. The re-transmission process means that the signal is regenerated and can travel the maximum distance again.

Bridges

An organisation might have a number of small networks in different departments or different parts of a building. It may be useful to connect the networks together so that some data can pass between them.

A bridge can connect two separate networks together as long as they are of the same type. An Ethernet bridge can connect two ethernet networks.

Many wireless networks use wireless Ethernet as their main technology. This makes it possible to use a wireless bridge to connect a cabled and a wireless network together.

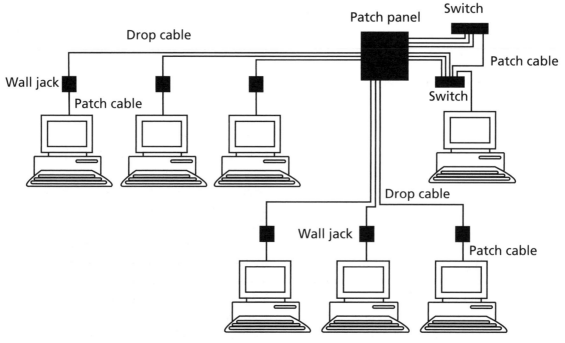

FIGURE 16.27 *A patch panel in a network with segments*

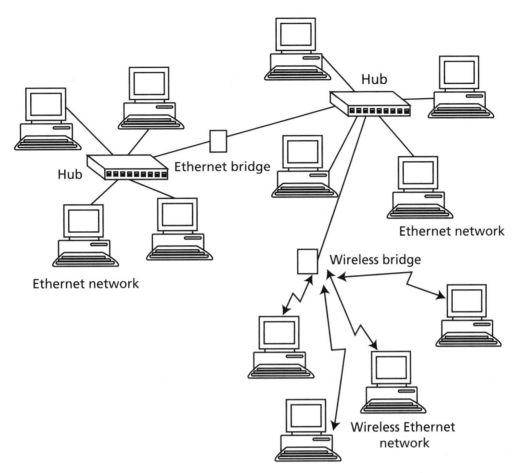

FIGURE 16.28 *An Ethernet bridge and a wireless bridge*

Gateways

Where two different networks are joined together, a gateway is used. The gateway converts the signals and data packet format from one technology to another and so can allow data to pass from one network to another.

Gateways are generally computers connected to both networks. The gateway computer runs software that does the translation from one network format to another. The translation takes place at many levels. At the lowest level, one network may use a different type of signalling and a different packet format to the other. The gateway must be able to receive data in one format and send it in another. At a higher level, the gateway might perform translations between different types of operating system or between different types of software.

Gateways are often used to translate emails from the format used on a local network to the SMTP format used on the Internet.

Routers

Many organisations connect their LANs to the Internet so that every user can access the Internet through one single connection. The trouble with this is that when one user has requested a web page, it needs to appear only on their computer.

A router is a device that stores and uses information about which computers are connected to it. As web pages are downloaded, it routes them to the correct computer using a special address format called an Internet Protocol (IP) address. This type of addressing is used by all computers on the Internet.

A large WAN might have a number of routers. Each router knows which computers are connected to all other routers in the network. When a router receives data for a computer connected to another router, it will know where to send it, even if this is through one or more other routers.

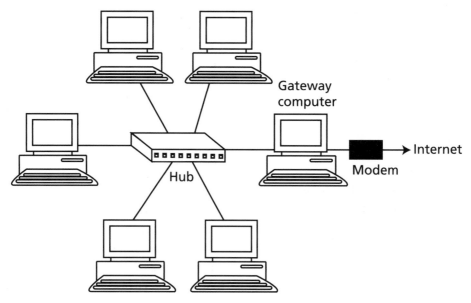

FIGURE 16.29 *A gateway*

LAN technologies

There are various technologies available, including Ethernet, token ring, fibre-distributed data interface (FDDI) and wireless. Each technology has its own methods of transmitting data on the transmission media it uses.

A LAN will generally use one particular technology and all its components will use the same technology. If a star network is cabled and using Ethernet technology, it will have Ethernet network interface cards installed in each machine, an Ethernet hub or switch and Ethernet cabling.

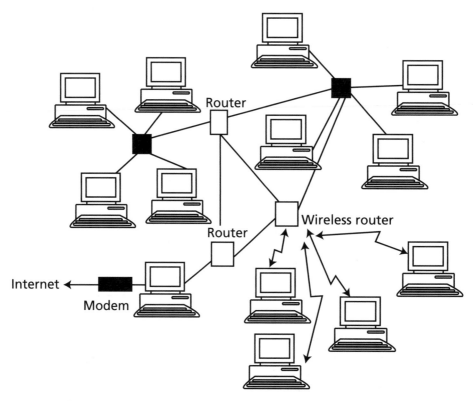

FIGURE 16.30 *A network using routers*

STANDARD	LAN TECHNOLOGY
802.3	Ethernet
802.5	Token ring
802.8	FDDI
802.11	Wireless

TABLE 16.1 *Standards for local networks*

A token ring network will use token ring network interface cards and cabling for a token ring network. An FDDI network will only use FDDI components.

The Institute for Electrical and Electronic Engineers (IEEE) has produced a set of standards for local networks and these standards cover the available LAN technologies. A standard will describe a set of rules that all devices working to that standard must conform to. The rules cover the format of a data packet, how computers access network media and how data is acknowledged.

802.3 Ethernet

Ethernet networks can be bus or star networks and can use coaxial, UTP or even fibre-optic cable. They can have transmission speeds of 10, 100 or 1000 Mbps. An Ethernet network uses a method called Carrier Sense Multiple Access with Collision Detection (CSMA/CD) for computers to access network media.

Using the CSMA/CD method, any computer that wants to send data on the network will first listen to its network connection to see if any other computer is already sending. If it detects that there is data already on the network, it will wait and try again a little later. If it detects that there is no data on the network, it will send its data. The sending computer will then listen to the network to see if the data it sent is still the same or if it has been muddled up with another set of data because both were sent at the same time. If it detects that its data has clashed with other data, it will wait for a short while and try again.

When data is sent on an Ethernet network, it is sent using the Ethernet packet format. All devices on the network communicate in the same way, using CSMA/CD and use the same packet format and transmission speed.

802.5 token ring

Token ring networks can use a variety of cable types but mostly use UTP or STP. They can have transmission speeds of 4 or 16 Mbps. A token ring network uses a method called 'token passing' for computers to access the network media.

The token passing method uses a 'token', which is a signal that is passed round and round the network. Computers can only send data if they 'catch' the token. When a computer wants to send data, it waits for the token to reach it. When it gets the token, it attaches its packet of data behind the token and sends it on around the ring. Whilst the data is attached, no other computer can use the token. The token and the data reach the destination computer, which reads the data, adds an acknowledgement and sends it on. When the sending computer gets the acknowledgement, it empties the token and sends it on so that another computer can use it.

802.8 fibre-optic LANs and FDDI

This standard covers any network that uses fibre-optic cabling, whether it is an Ethernet network, a token ring network or any other type of network. FDDI is not covered by one 802 standard. It is a fibre-optic network that uses token passing on a logical ring network and has transmission speeds of 100 Mbps.

802.11b and 802.11g wireless networks

Wireless networks use radio frequencies rather than cables for transmitting data. Transmission speeds are 11 Mbps in standard 802.11b and 54 Mbps in standard 802.11g.

Publicly available wireless networks, such as those in hotels and conference centres, often use the 802.11b standard and are commonly known as WiFi networks. These networks allow a constantly changing number of users to have access. A new computer will send a signal to the network with its address and a connection will

---

Theory into practice

The publishers of *Your Pets* magazine have decided to install a network to connect their computers in one large office. You have been asked to design a network for them.

Produce a network design which includes

* a logical topology diagram
* a network technology
* all connecting devices, cables and connectors.

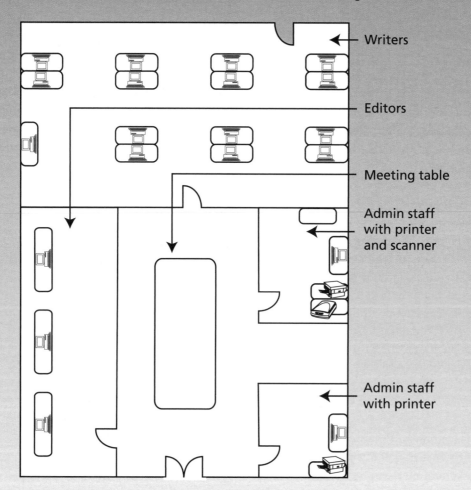

FIGURE 16.31 *Office layout*

be made. At the end of the session, the computer sends another signal to indicate that it is leaving the network.

Wireless networks use a method known as Carrier Sense Multiple Access with Collision Avoidance (CSMA/CA). This method is very similar to CSMA/CD used in Ethernet networks, but, whereas the CSMA/CD involves whole data packets sent and then inspected for collisions, the CSMA/CA method involves sending a 'request to send' message and then waiting for a 'clear to send' message. If it is clear, the data packet will be sent with the assumption that nothing will collide with it.

Network software

All devices in a LAN will generally use the same technology. This will ensure that data is in the correct format and using the right signals. Various software is needed to make a network operational using the selected technology.

Network adapter software

Each device in the network must have a network interface card (NIC) or network adapter. The card or adapter does the sending and receiving of data, but it needs software to drive it. Driver software must be installed on the machine that the card or adapter is intalled on. Driver software manages the conversion of data between the network operating system and the card or adapter.

Network client software

Part of the network design involves choosing the operating systems that all machines on the network will use. The choice of operating system will depend on what each machine is required to do.

Client machines on a client–server network need network client software. Operating systems such as Microsoft Windows have network client software included in the overall system.

Network client software is a set of programs that allow the operating system of one machine to communicate with the operating system of another machine. The other machine might be another client or it might be a server.

Client software must be installed on top of the operating system software and can be configured

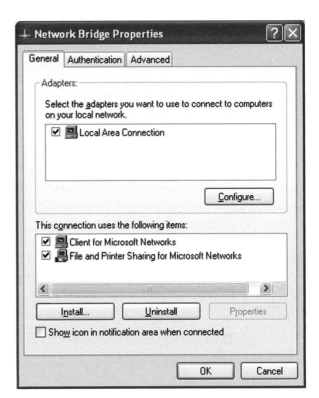

FIGURE 16.32 *Network client software*

to start up when the computer is switched on to allow the computer to join the network straight away.

Network client operating systems

An alternative to installing network client software on top of a standard operating system is to install a network client operating system. This is a specialised operating system that allows the computer only to operate as a networked computer and not as a stand-alone computer.

> **Think it over...**
>
> When you log on to a computer in your school or college's network, you will generally get a home area and will be able to access other drives such as the hard disk in the computer you are working on. If you were using a specialised network client operating system, you might have only a home area and no ability to access a hard disk inside your computer. Your computer might have a very small hard disk, just big enough to hold the operating system software.

Protocol software

In order for computers to be able to fully communicate with each other, they must be able to understand the data itself and must know how to receive and acknowledge that the data is correct. This is called a 'protocol'.

Every protocol that is used by the network will need protocol software. All network client operating systems and many standard operating systems come with protocol software, which must be loaded if it is going to be used.

Each NIC will be configured by its driver to use a specific protocol. This might be NetBIOS, NetBEUI, IPX/SPX or TCP/IP.

All NICs in the network must use the same protocol so that they are able to communicate effectively.

Communication protocols

There are several commonly used protocols, described below. All computers on the network must use the same protocol.

NetBIOS

This is an acronym for Network Basic Input/Output System. NetBIOS is a program that runs in the background, alongside the operating system. It provides the facility for all applications to access the network in the same way. Application software simply needs to request network services and the NetBIOS software will provide those services.

NetBIOS will deal with sending a message from one computer to another (for example, when a file is saved to a file server). It can also, at times, deal with broadcasting messages to all computers in a LAN (for example, when a Win pop-up message is broadcast).

NetBIOS is used on Ethernet and token ring networks and is generally included with all Microsoft operating systems.

NetBEUI

NetBEUI is an extension of NetBIOS, called the NetBIOS Extended User Interface. It provides the facility to split data into frames, which can be sent separately and reassembled at the other end.

NetBEUI is faster, more flexible and more reliable than NetBIOS and is generally included with all Microsoft operating systems.

IPX/SPX

This protocol is similar to NetBIOS and NetBEUI but is generally used on Novell networks rather than Microsoft networks. Internetwork Packet Exchange/Sequence Packet Exchange (IPX/SPX) is a protocol used on LAN and WAN. It can deal with sending a message from one computer to another on a LAN, by making a connection between the two computers, or it can do the same on a WAN, by routing messages from one computer to another through a series of other computers.

This protocol is capable of operating on the Internet but is not commonly used, even though it is supported by a number of operating systems, including some of the Microsoft operating systems as well as Novell network systems. It is not properly supported by the Unix operating system and some others. As support is not universal, it has not become the standard protocol used on the Internet.

TCP/IP

NetBIOS and NetBEUI are both LAN protocols. They are capable of sending data between computers on a LAN but are unable to cope with routing, which is required on a WAN. Transport Control Protocol/Internet Protocol (TCP/IP) is a protocol designed to work on a WAN as well as a LAN and is used throughout the Internet.

Where NetBIOS, NetBEUI and IPX/SPX are protocols specific to particular operating systems, TCP/IP is independent of any hardware or operating system software. TCP/IP works with most network technologies, such as Ethernet, token ring and FDDI and works on all Internet connections. TCP/IP is also supported by all operating systems capable of running networks.

TCP/IP uses routing, a method of deciding a path across a network via a number of different computers. It can decide to send data on a particular route to spread the traffic throughout the network. It can even split a large message up and send it on a number of different routes to its destination. A message is split into a number of datagrams. Each has a TCP header that identifies it as a datagram and gives its sequence number. The datagrams are assembled together in the correct order at the other end to form the original message.

The Transport Control Protocol defines the method for transporting messages between computers on a network. It defines how the messages are divided up into datagrams and how they are sent from one device to another within the network. On networks like the Internet, a datagram will generally travel through a number of different devices to get to its destination. The IP part of the protocol adds a special IP header to each datagram sent from one computer to another. The header contains data that is used by the routers in the network to work out how to get the data to its final destination.

← 32 bits →			
← 8 bits →			
IP version (4 or 6)	Internet header length	Type of service	Total length of datagram
Identification information to allow datagrams to be reassembled		Flags	Offset
Time to live	Protocol	Header checksum	
Source IP address			
Destination IP address			
TCP header and data			

FIGURE 16.33 *IP header*

Key:
Flags – these indicate if a datagram must not be divided up (fragmented) by TCP or if this is the last datagram in the sequence making up a message.

Offset – the position in the sequence of datagrams making up the whole message.

Time To Live – the number of routers that a datagram can pass through before it is considered lost. This number is decreased by each router. If it reaches 0, the message is destroyed and will be considered to be lost.

Protocol – IP works with TCP and with other protocols such as User Datagram Protocol (UDP) used on LANs using Network File System (NFS).

Header checksum – an error-checking value, calculated to allow each device to check that the datagram has not become corrupted on its journey. Each device will recalculate the checksum as fields such as Time To Live change.

IP addressing

Each computer or device on the Internet is called a host and has a unique address. This ensures that messages are sent to the correct host every time. When a host joins the Internet, it is given an IP address. Routers within the Internet learn that this host has this particular IP address and they store information about how to get messages to that address.

The IP address has a particular format that helps the routing decisions. There are two types of IP address: IPv4 and IPv6. IPv4 is the system most commonly used. An IPv4 address consists of four parts, each separated by a decimal point; for example:

195.80.125.203

Each part is a number between 0 and 255 (the numbers that can be represented by sets of eight binary digits).

An IPv6 address consists of eight parts, each separated by a colon; for example:

3FEE:0B00:1000:0004:0000:0000:0000:000D

Each part is a hexadecimal number between 0 and FFFF (the numbers that can be represented by sets of 16 binary digits). There are many, many more IPv6 addresses available than IPv4 addresses, but, at the time of writing, IPv4 is the most commonly used addressing system.

IP addresses identify individual hosts on a network. Unlike MAC addresses, they are stored by software and can be changed. If an organisation wants to connect its internal network to the Internet, it must get IP addresses for all its hosts and these must be totally unique. If any two hosts have the same IP address, there will be a conflict and data may not reach either host, or may reach the wrong host.

Internet IP addresses are assigned by regional Internet registries, such as Réseaux IP Européens (RIPE), American Registry of Internet Numbers (ARIN) and others. Each keeps a database of all IP addresses and to who they are assigned. A worldwide organisation, Internet Assigned Numbers Authority (IANA), ensures that no IP address is duplicated anywhere in the world. Each organisation that applies for IP addresses will need a number of individual addresses. For very large networks, this will be a very large number of addresses.

IP address classes

IP addresses are divided into five classes, which identify the size of the network they are assigned to.

Binary versions of IP addresses

There are occasions when it is useful to be able to see an IP address in a different format.

Each part of an IP address is called an octet. Each octet is a decimal number between 0 and 255. The term octet refers to the fact that each is a binary number of 8 bits. The address 195.80.125.203 is represented in binary as

11000010 01010000 01111101 11001011

The decimal numbers 0 to 255 are represented in binary as the numbers 00000000 to 11111111. Each binary digit has a decimal value depending on where it is in the sequence of 8 digits. The digit on the right has the value 1, the second from the right has the value 2 and the third from the right has the value 4. Each digit then has a value that is double the value of the digit on its right.

128	64	32	16	8	4	2	1

To convert a decimal value between 0 and 255 to its binary equivalent, perform the following steps:

1 Is the number 128 or above? If so, put a 1 in the 128 column and subtract 128 from the number. If not, put a 0 in the 128 column and leave the number as it is.

CLASS	DESCRIPTION
A	Used for very large networks of up to 16 million hosts. The first part of the IP address can only have values from 0 to 127. If a network were allocated 127 as its first number, every host on the large network would have an IP address beginning with 127 (e.g. 127.xxx.xxx.xxx) and every possible address beginning with 127 would be allocated to that network. There can only be up to 128 Class A networks, and all are already allocated.
B	Used for medium-sized networks. These can have the numbers 128 to 191 as the first number, 0 to 255 as the second and are each allocated all available IP addresses following this (e.g. 128.80.xxx.xxx). This allows for around 16,000 different networks, each with up to around 64,000 hosts. All Class B networks are aready allocated.
C	Used for smaller networks. These can have the numbers 192 to 223 as the first number, 0 to 255 as the second, 0 to 255 as the third and are allocated all possible addresses following this (e.g. 195.80.125.xxx). This allows for around 2 million networks each having up to 254 hosts.
D	These are available for individual hosts not on networks and have the number 224 to 254 as the first number (e.g. 234.xxx.xxx.xxx). There are 268 million possible addresses.
E	Experimental addresses 255.xxx.xxx.xxx

TABLE 16.2 *Classes of IP address*

Example – 194

128	64	32	16	8	4	2	1
1							

194 is at least 128, so put a 1 in the 128 column
194 – 128 = 66

2 Is the number now 64 or above? If so, put a 1 in the 64 column and subtract 64 from the number. If not, put a 0 in the 128 column and leave the number as it is.

128	64	32	16	8	4	2	1
1	1						

66 is at least 64, so put a 1 in the 64 column
66 – 64 = 2

3 Is the number now 32 or above? If so, put a 1 in the 32 column and subtract 32 from the number. If not, put a 0 in the 32 column and leave the number as it is.

128	64	32	16	8	4	2	1
1	1	0					

2 is smaller than 32, so put a 0 in the 32 column
Leave the number as 2

4 Is the number now 16 or above? If so, put a 1 in the 16 column and subtract 16 from the number. If not, put a 0 in the 16 column and leave the number as it is.

128	64	32	16	8	4	2	1
1	1	0	0				

2 is smaller than 16, so put a 0 in the 16 column
Leave the number as 2

5 Is the number now 8 or above? If so, put a 1 in the 8 column and subtract 8 from the number. If not, put a 0 in the 8 column and leave the number as it is.

128	64	32	16	8	4	2	1
1	1	0	0	0			

2 is smaller than 8, so put a 0 in the 8 column
Leave the number as 2

6 Is the number now 4 or above? If so, put a 1 in the 4 column and subtract 4 from the number. If not, put a 0 in the 4 column and leave the number as it is.

128	64	32	16	8	4	2	1
1	1	0	0	0	0		

2 is smaller than 4, so put a 0 in the 4 column
Leave the number as 2

7 Is the number now 2 or above? If so, put a 1 in the 2 column and subtract 2 from the number. If not, put a 0 in the 2 column and leave the number as it is.

128	64	32	16	8	4	2	1
1	1	0	0	0	0	1	

2 is at least 2, so put a 1 in the 2 column
2 – 2 = 0

8 If the remaining number is 1, put a 1 in the the right-hand column. If not, put a 0 in the right-hand column.

128	64	32	16	8	4	2	1
1	1	0	0	0	0	1	0

Remaining number is 0, so put a 0 in the right-hand column

Theory into practice

Convert the following decimal octets to their binary equivalents:

✳ 125

✳ 32

✳ 203.

Write down the binary equivalent of the following decimal IP address:

192.224.127.68

Converting a binary IP address to decimal

The process for converting a binary octet to its decimal version is more straightforward. The binary octet will always have eight digits and these have the same place values as shown above. To convert a binary octet, write it in table form and add up all the column values where there is a 1.

Example:
Convert 11010110 to its decimal equivalent:

128	64	32	16	8	4	2	1
1	1	0	1	0	1	1	0

There are 1s in the 128, 64, 16, 4 and 2 columns

$128 + 64 + 16 + 4 + 2 = 214$

Theory into practice

Convert the following binary octets to their decimal equivalents:

✳ 00110101

✳ 10010100

✳ 11111101.

Write down the decimal equivalent of the following binary IP address:

11001100 00010001 10100101 11111110

IP subnets

There are millions of hosts on the Internet. Every time data is transferred between hosts, the IP address must be examined by every router it passes through. The destination host will often be a computer on a network. All computers on this network will have similar IP addresses; only the final part of the address identifies the individual computer, the rest identifies the network.

So, once the message has reached the destination network, the first part of the address is no longer needed. The rest of the IP address identifies one host, but there could be thousands of hosts on this one network and a lot of routing will still be needed to find the right one.

Subnetting is a method of using the IP address to divide the network up into segments. Each segment uses a set of IP addresses that are even more similar than whole network addresses.

Example:
A Class C network uses IP addresses of the form 195.80.125.xxx and has 250 hosts on its network.

It uses subnetting to divide its network into four segments, each with its own set of IP addresses.

195.80.125.0 to 195.80.125.63

195.80.125.64 to 195.80.125.127

195.80.125.128 to 195.80.125.191

195.80.125.192 to 195.80.125.255

Subnet masks

Routers use masks to isolate the binary digits that they need. A router on the main part of the Internet needs the first three octets of a Class C address. A router on an individual Class C network needs only the fourth octet.

To ignore the host part of the address, routers can use masks. These have the same format as an IP address. If looked at in its binary form, the mask has 1s in the places that are of interest. The subnet mask 255.255.255.0 is:

11111111 11111111 11111111 00000000

in binary. The final octet has all 0s and is the part of address where the host is identified. The mask is like an overlay which blocks out the fourth octet. Once the mask is applied, the IP address becomes 195.80.125.0 and the 0 can be ignored.

If a network has two segments, part of the final octet can be used to identify the two separate segments. This is done by adding the first binary digit of the fourth octet to the mask.

11111111 11111111 11111111 10000000

The decimal equivalent of this is 255.255.255.128. Once the mask is applied, it is possible to tell which segment the host is in and so to route the data to the correct segment, where it can be routed to the correct host.

Think it over...

The IP address 195.80.125.203 is on the network 195.80.125.xxx. When the subnet mask 255.255.255.128 is applied, all host addresses from 128 upwards will give the new address 195.80.125.128 and the rest will give the new address 195.80.125.0. A router will know to send one set of addresses to one segment and the other set to the other segment.

For a network with four segments, the first two binary digits of the fourth octet are used (for example 255.255.255.192). This allows four separate subnets to be identified.

Of course, the more subnets a network has, the fewer hosts it can have on each.

Other protocols

Protocols are designed to provide a set method of communication between devices on a network. The protocols above are designed to standardise the way devices communicate with each other.

Other protocols are designed to standardise the way applications talk to each other. When an email is sent, there might be two different applications dealing with it. There may even be two different operating systems. The email itself must have a format that can be understood by all applications that are likely to have to read it. The Simple Mail Transfer Protocol (SMTP) is a standard for moving emails between email servers. The protocol defines how an email is formatted. As long as an email uses the SMTP format, all servers can read it and convert it into the format they use. Servers will convert SMTP messages to Post Office Protocol (POP) or Internet Mail Access Protocol (IMAP), depending on the type of email software used by the networks they serve.

File Transfer Protocol (FTP)

This is a standard for moving files from one host to another on the Internet or other WAN. FTP defines how files and directories are organised and viewed and allows text files and binary files to be moved from one host to another, even if they are running different operating systems. FTP software is used to transfer whole files from one host to another and is widely used to upload web pages to web servers.

Hypertext Transfer Protocol (HTTP)

Web pages are viewed by many users, on many different types of system. Web browsers are used to request pages and to view them. There are different web browsers, such as Internet Explorer, Netscape Navigator, Safari and Mozilla Firefox. Each must be able to request pages and to understand and display the contents of each page. HTTP is the standard for communication between web browsers and web servers. It defines how a web page is requested (such as by hyperlink), how it is found and how it is displayed. Secure HTTP (HTTPS) is an extension to the HTTP protocol that allows encryption and authentication for extra security of transactions over the Internet.

Network hardware used in LAN and WAN communication systems

In a client–server network, servers will perform certain tasks. Computers within a network can be made dedicated servers whose function it is to provide a particular service to clients. If the network is connected to the Internet, special devices might be considered to provide protection from hackers and viruses. When the network is finally up and running, it would be disastrous for problems with the power supply to affect parts of the network where data is being transferred or stored. Again, devices to stop this happening might be considered.

File servers

For file-sharing, a file server may be used. The function of a file server is to give copies of files, on request, to client computers. The file server will have a network server operating system that will have the facility to manage files, control access to files for all users, and ensure that files are not updated by more than one user at the same time.

Networks with file servers are totally dependent on the server for the operation of the whole network. File servers need fast processors, large amounts of disk space and an operating system capable of carrying out all the functions of a file server.

Print servers

Print servers control one or more printers and have the software to manage printing jobs sent from client machines. The printing jobs are generally files already in the right format for printing. The print server must be able to store all the printing jobs until it is able to forward them to the connected printer.

Application servers

These store and run applications on request from clients. Where an application server is used, client

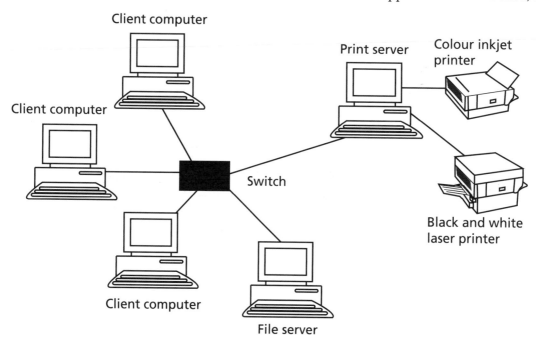

FIGURE 16.34 *A network with a file server and a print server*

computers do not need to have copies of the applications stored on their hard disks. They just send a request to run the software and it runs as if it was on the client computer itself. The application runs on the server but takes its input from the client computer over the network, and sends its output to the client computer. The output needs to be in a format that the client computer can display.

Very fast networks are needed to run applications from servers and to allow them to look like they are running on the client machine.

Applications that run on the Internet, such as applets and servlets, are run from applications servers; the user's requests are sent across the Internet and the results are sent to the user's computer in a form in which they can be shown, such as HTML.

Proxy servers

A proxy server is used to protect a network from problems that can be associated with using the Internet. A proxy server will send packets of data from a host on its own network to a server on the Internet. Before sending, however, the proxy server will take the packet of data apart, check it and reassemble it. It can check for corrupted data, for viruses and for its destination, which can be blocked if necessary.

The proxy server also inspects packets of data being sent to hosts on its network. Again, it breaks the packets up, inspects them and reassembles them. Unwanted data, data from unauthorised sites and corrupted or infected data can be removed.

Sometimes, a proxy server will hide the IP addresses of the individual hosts on the network, exchanging their IP addresses for its own. This adds a level of security from hackers. Sometimes, proxy servers are set up to cache web pages. As a web page is received, it saves a copy of it. If the same page is requested again, even by a different host, it can send the page itself rather than relying on getting it from the Internet. This makes access to pages much faster. Proxy servers can handle FTP transfers and Internet email using SMTP. For both, the proxy server can check all files and emails that pass through it and can remove any that might have viruses or have been received from unauthorised sites.

Firewalls

A proxy server can serve as a firewall, but when a proxy server is not used, a separate firewall is needed.

A firewall will protect a network from unauthorised access over the Internet. It is either a computer on the network or a box with a

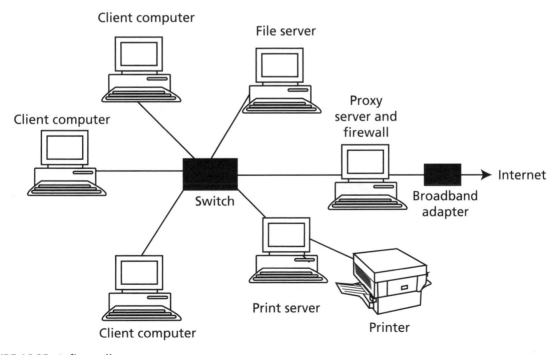

FIGURE 16.35 *A firewall*

dedicated processor installed. The computer or box will have two network cards or adapters. One will connect it to the internal network, the other will connect it to the Internet.

The firewall inspects all data that passes from the network to the Internet and from the Internet to the network. It will remove any packets of data that appear suspicious, either because they are corrupted, they contain a virus or they come from an unauthorised source. The firewall keeps a list of sites that should be blocked and this list can be updated by the network administrator. When a packet is received from a blocked site, it is removed. The firewall can also match packets received against packets requested and can filter out any packets of data that seem to have arrived without being asked for.

Uninterruptable Power Supply (UPS)

When a large amount of data is being dealt with, there will never be a convenient time for a power failure. For individual users a power failure might cause some inconvenience, but if the power supply for the file server fails whilst a large number of files are being updated, this could be disastrous.

An Uninterruptable Power Supply (UPS) works by sitting between the electricity supply (the plug and socket) and the computer. It is a sort of battery that gradually stores power from the power supply and feeds the power from the battery to the computer. The computer only gets its power from the battery, so a power cut or a power surge will not affect the computer. Once the power to the battery is cut, a warning is issued so that there is time to ensure that all work is saved and that the server computer is shut down properly.

Network services

Two major advantages of using networks are the ability to share files and the ability to share resources such as printers. If these services are to be used, the correct software must be available.

File sharing

Network operating systems provide the facility for sharing files. Folders that contain files can be shared with all users on the network, or they can be shared with selected users, identified by their usernames and passwords. Files can also be shared with groups of users. On Microsoft networks these groups are called workgroups. The owner of a file or folder will change the permissions on the file or folder to individual access, group access or access for all.

Files that are shared can be set up in a number of ways. They can be shared for reading only. In this case, the user who created the file can make changes to it. All other users can only read the file.

A file can be shared for reading and writing so that all authorised users can both see the file and change it. The file sharing software will ensure that the file cannot be changed by two users at the same time, as this would cause problems.

Files that are executable (application software files) can be set so that all authorised users can run the software or all may not.

It is also possible to share a file or folder for writing only. Individual users can add files to a folder or add information to a file, but cannot see what is already there. Again, the file sharing software must ensure that two users do not change the same file at the same time.

To enable file sharing, it is necessary to have a network operating system that has file sharing built in, or to have specialist file sharing software installed on top of the operating system.

On WANs, FTP software is often installed to allow the movement and sharing of files between hosts.

FTP software allows users to log in to a host machine with their unique username and password. This will then give them access to all files and folders to which they have permission. Users can then add files, remove files, look at folders and transfer files to their own computer. In order to do this, FTP software must be installed on both machines.

Printer sharing

Sharing resources is one of the primary reasons for using networks. Network operating systems and network client software will have the facility to allow all users on a network to access the same printer. The system software will allow printers to be given names so that users can identify them easily.

Most often, printers are connected to print servers. These run specialist printer sharing software that allows them to control one or more printers. The print server will receive files for printing, add them to a queue if the printer is not currently available, and will print them in turn. The software will often allow some print jobs to have a higher priority than others so that they will be printed first.

Some printers have print server software installed on their NICs so that an extra computer is not required.

Print server software is very specialised, and a print server will often only service printing requests. As the print server computer will not need as many resources, it can often be a low-specification machine or an old machine. As long as it can run the software and has enough hard disk space to store the maximum number of print jobs likely to be sent to it at one time, it does not need much else.

16.3 Network software

Purposes and functions of software

All networks, LANs and WANs use a variety of different types of software. The purpose of each type of software is different. Some are necessary for all networks and some are necessary only for specialised networks.

Table 16.3 lists the different types of software and the purpose of each.

TYPE OF SOFTWARE	PURPOSE
Standard operating system	Every computer needs an operating system. This can often be a standard operating system, like Microsoft Windows, to which network software is added.
Dedicated network operating system	Any computer that is going to act as a server in a network will need a dedicated network operating system. This contains all the software required for communicating over the network and for allowing the computer to perform the required services. Servers and clients can have a dedicated network operating system.
Network adapter software	Each network adapter will need driver software. This software converts data between the format used by the operating system and the format in which the adapter will send or receive it.
Network client software	Sometimes, a standard operating system has the facility for network client software to be installed to work with it. This means that a dedicated network operating system is not needed for computers that will act only as clients.
Protocol software	Software must be installed for each protocol to be used by the network. Protocol software is used to ensure that data is in the correct format for transmission on the network.
Network service software	File and printer sharing are services performed by servers on a network. Each computer performing one of these services will need the software to do so. Other service software that might be needed is the software required to run an applications server and the software for a proxy server.

Connection software for the Internet	When you sign up with an internet service provider (ISP), you will be given some software that will allow you to connect your computer to their network. The software will use the point-to-point protocol (PPP) to establish and maintain a connection. For a dial-up connection, the software will establish the connection by getting the modem to dial the number, detect when the connection is made and open the line. Once a dial-up connection is made, the computer becomes a temporary host on the ISP's network. It is assigned an IP address which it uses until the connection is terminated. The PPP software manages the transfer of data between the connected host and the ISP's server. For a permanent broadband connection, PPP software, again, manages the connection, but the software runs as soon as the computer has booted up and just reinstates the connection each time. A computer with a permanent connection has a permanent IP address and is, again, a host on the ISP's network.
Web browser software	If a network has an Internet connection, users will generally want to view web pages. Web browser software is able to convert the HTML code, which web pages are written in, into text, pictures and other objects to display on the page. The browser software also deals with sending web page addresses (URLs) to request web pages. These addresses are either typed in by the user or are generated by the user clicking on a hyperlink on the current web page. Internet Explorer, Safari and Netscape Navigator are three examples of web browsers.
FTP software	FTP software is used to transfer files from one host to another on a WAN such as the Internet. If websites have been created, then FTP software will be used to transfer all files associated with the site to the web server. Both the web server and the host computer must be able to run the FTP software.
HTML and web page editors	HTML editors and web page editors are used to create the HTML that web pages are coded in. HTML is text-based and can be written using a text editor. Alternatively, there are many web page editing applications available that let the user create web pages graphically and then convert them to HTML code. Macromedia's DreamWeaver and Microsoft's FrontPage are just two examples of this type of software.

TABLE 16.3 *Types of software*

Setting up a connection to the Internet

When you set up an account with an ISP, it will often send you some connection software. This software will run either when you request it (by starting your browser) or when the computer starts up. The ISP's software will make a connection between your modem or broadband adapter and its network. The connection will either be dial-up or broadband. Modern operating systems include software to set up an Internet connection (see Figure 16.36).

This software will allow you to install the connection software and any protocols,

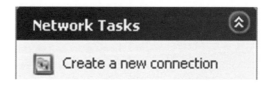

FIGURE 16.36 *Creating an Internet connection*

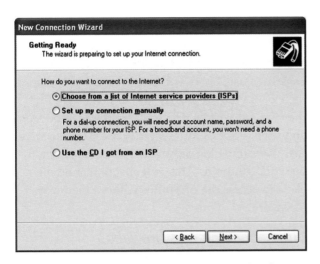

FIGURE 16.37 *Setting up an Internet connection*

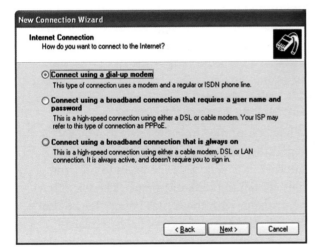

FIGURE 16.38 *Choosing a connection method*

such as point-to-point protocol (PPP), for the communication between computer and ISP, and TCP/IP for all Internet communication.

You will be able to enter the ISP name, any telephone number and any username and password information. These settings will be used every time you connect to your ISP. It is important that you record these settings in case the connection has to be reset at any time.

The ISPs CD may provide FTP and browser software. If not, these can either be downloaded from the Internet or might be already installed on the computer. Again, when the software has been installed, all settings must be written down in case reinstallation is necessary later.

Using web browsing and FTP software

Web browsing software, such as Internet Explorer and Netscape Navigator, has two main functions:

✳ to allow the user to request web pages by typing the uniform resource locator (URL) in the correct area or by clicking on a hyperlink

✳ to find and request pages or services from web servers and display them.

Web browsers understand a variety of types of URL. Each URL has two main parts:

✳ the service required (e.g. http://, ftp://, https://)

✳ the domain name or address of the web server and the required web page that is stored on it.

FTP software is available on the Internet and can be downloaded either as freeware or by licence. FTP software allows you to to log in to an FTP server and to browse through any files that you have permission to browse, in a similar way to the way you browse through the files on your hard disk. It allows you to copy files in either direction while the software is running.

To access an FTP server, you will generally be required to have a user name and password.

FIGURE 16.39 *Internet Explorer is a simple form of FTP software*

16.4 Safety and security

During the design and installation of a network, there are one or two further things to be considered. The network must be installed safely and workstations must meet health and safety standards. The network must also be as secure as possible from viruses, hackers and software or hardware failure.

Health and safety procedures

These considerations will include:

* making sure that each workstation has enough space for users to work in

* using office furniture and equipment that allow the user to reduce the risk of problems like repetitive strain injury, back problems, eye strain and other problems associated with use of computers

* ensuring that equipment is installed safely, cables are routed around walls and are not left trailing across floors where they can trip people up

* ensuring that all electrical equipment is safe and all cables are free from damage.

Security procedures

Backing up data and software

A network will hold a large amount of data for a number of different users. If data is held in one place, it becomes vulnerable if that one place fails. If a file server fails, all data stored on it could be lost. This might be the entire network's data. If an application server fails, no one can use the software it stored. Backing up the data and software regularly will ensure that, at least, the data and software can be put back on the network.

Protecting confidential information

Most networks give passwords to all their users and do not allow use without a valid password. This allows the network manager to configure the network so that access to data is controlled. If access is controlled, confidential data can be protected and the risk of theft of data can be reduced.

Ensuring that passwords are used and kept safe

Most organisations will have policies for password use. Users will be encouraged to change their passwords regularly and to make sure that they are not written down where they can be seen and used. Policies for computer use will also state that users must log off properly before leaving a network computer. This will ensure that no one else can access the computer without their own password.

Virus checking and firewalls

Security software, such as anti-virus software, will generally be installed on a network and will be configured to run at regular intervals and when new files are introduced to the network from the Internet. Firewalls help to keep out unwanted external access and reduce the risk of hackers accessing the network.

Protecting copyright

When computers are connected together, especially when they are connected to the Internet, it is very easy for users to find and copy files containing data or images. There is often no problem with these files being viewed, but organisations must have policies in place to stop users downloading and using files that are copyrighted. Firewalls can be used to block sites where copyrighted data can be accessed and procedures for staff conduct can, at least, make users aware of the need to check copyright.

Avoiding theft

Networks carry important data for the organisations they serve. They can be a target for theft. Table 16.4 describes types of theft and how they can be avoided.

Communications log

When things do go wrong, it is useful to be able to track what was happening at the time and if this particular problem has happened before. A communications log can be used to record information about all data transfers so that the

TYPE OF THEFT	HOW IT CAN HAPPEN	HOW IT CAN BE AVOIDED
Data	Users copying data and transferring it to another network	Strict policies about what can be done with data. Password protection so that only authorised users can access the data
	Hackers accessing the network and its data from outside via the Internet	Install firewalls to help block unwanted access
Software	Illegal copying of software to transfer to home or other computers	Restrict access to software files by password
Equipment	Removal of equipment	Keep rooms containing important network equipment locked with access only to authorised users with keys
		Fix and lock all equipment in place so that it cannot be easily removed

TABLE 16.4 *Types of theft*

exact transfer taking place at the time of the problem can be identified.

A communications log will contain information such as the date, time and length of communication between workstations, the type of connection used (dial-up, broadband, local connection), the protocols used (FTP, SMTP) and information about the files or data that were transferred (source, destination, size, file type).

The log can be referred to so that the exact data transfer that took place at the time of a problem can be traced. The same problem might have happened before, either with the same data, or with data from the same source.

Problem logs

Another type of log is the problem log. This contains records of problems that have occurred and will group the problems into categories so that finding them is easier.

A problem log might be kept in a database or might be in separate files kept in a set of folders. Access to the problem log will be restricted so that it is up to date and useful. A problem log will contain information such as the date and time of the problem, a description of the problem, who was using the computer at the time, who reported the problem, how it was resolved and who resolved it.

The log can be used to spot recurring problems and for reference when similar problems occur again.

CASE STUDY

Your Pets Magazine has 20 staff who will use a new network once it has been installed. The network will connect the 20 existing machines and will allow staff to use the software already installed on their computers. The two printers and the scanner will be shared over the network.

A client server network will be installed for the existing staff. Sales are good and the company may expand in the future. This may require them to take on extra staff.

Knowledge check

Describe the types of server that might be used for the Your Pets network.

Describe the network software, protocols and other software that might be required.

Explain the safety and security implications of using a network, especially when connected to the Internet.

Introducing a new network will often cause disruption and will always require staff to change the way they carry out various tasks. The management of Your Pets Magazine are concerned that the disruption and change in working practices might cause some anxiety. It is important for them to help staff to see the benefits of the new network and the possible improvements it will bring to their daily tasks.

They are also keen to find the best way to connect their network to the Internet and will need to find out how to go about this.

Knowledge check

Describe the services a network can provide for employees, including those services provided by the Internet.

Explain how the network will improve the way day-to-day tasks (such as printing, scanning, research) are carried out.

Think it over...

There are a number of ways that a network can be connected to the Internet. Describe the different ways this can be achieved and describe the equipment and costs required to make the connection.

Glossary

Absolute cell referencing The cell reference will stay the same when the formula is copied to other cells.

Alternate key Candidate key that is not used as the primary key.

Alternative text (alt) Text that appears in place of graphics when a website using graphics is viewed using a text-only browser.

Analogue signals These use constantly changing frequencies. Voice and television signals are analogue. Humans interpret these signals as sounds.

Append To add new records in a database.

Appendices (singular: appendix) Separate numbered or lettered sections at the end of the document that contain additional information that the author refers to but does not want to include in the main text.

Argument The values or cell references that appear in brackets after a function. For example, the arguments for Ceiling are the number to be rounded and the multiple (or significance) it is to be rounded to.

Array function A function that acts on a range of cells and whose results can appear in a range of cells. Pressing CTRL, SHIFT + ENTER signifies an array function and will insert braces {} round the formula in the Formula bar.

ASCII Stands for American Standard Code for Information Interchange. This is a 7-bit code, so provides 128 different possible codes.

Aspect ratio The ratio of an image's height to its width, for example an image with an aspect ratio 2:1 is twice as tall as it is wide.

Asset Anything of value that is owned by a company.

Atomic An attribute that does not need to be broken down any further.

Attribute One of the elements that defines an entity.

Authoritarian A style of management where the manager is fully in control of all decisions and resources.

Awareness of audience The ability to produce work that meets the needs of the target audience.

Banner headline The main headline at the top of a page that goes across the full width of the page, usually in a large font size.

Bespoke or custom-written software Software that is specially developed to meet the needs of a particular organisation.

Bibliography Detailed list of all information sources used in compiling a document. It should enable someone else to locate the same information.

Binomial distribution probability The probability of a number of successes in a number of trials when there are two possible and mutually exclusive outcomes – success and failure.

Bitmap graphics Images created by storing details about each pixel included in the image.

Break even When a company's income becomes equal to the amount it spends (expenditure) so that it can start to make a profit.

Brief The instructions given for a task.

Bulletin boards Electronic message boards where people can post, read and reply to messages.

Camera ready copy (CRC) The final copy of a document exactly as it will appear when it is printed, i.e. it is ready to be photographed to create the printing plates.

Candidate key Attribute that has a unique value in each occurrence and could be a primary key.

Cascading style sheet A set of formatting rules that allow the web author to have greater control over how the website will look on any number of different web browsing software packages.

Cast Anything, other than effects, that will appear in the completed product. Includes sound files as well as images.

Chunking down The process of breaking a large task or project into smaller, more manageable sections or chunks.

Client An individual computer on a client-server network that uses network services.

Colour depth The number of colours that may be represented by a piece of software or a piece of hardware.

Comma separated variable (.csv) file A text file where commas are used to separate data items that would normally be in separate cells in a table. Other separators can also be used, such as a tab. In this case, the file type becomes .tsv – tab separated variable.

Commission A task that is given to an individual or a group. An interactive multimedia product to suit the needs of the brief, or an order for a special, one-off image (or series of images) to be created.

Common Gateway Interface (CGI) scripts Used to analyse the data sent from forms to your web server.

Composite key Occurs when more than one field is required to uniquely identify a record. Or a primary key that is made up of two or more attributes.

Compression ratio The ratio of the file size of the original uncompressed file to the compressed file. The higher the ratio, the greater the amount of compression.

Compression Decreasing the file size.

Confidence interval A range on either side of the mean of a sample. The mean of the population will be within this range with a particular level of confidence.

Contents page Lists the main sections of a document in the order they appear, with page numbers for the start of each section.

Context diagram (L0 DFD) A diagram that shows how the system interacts with the outside world.

Correlation coefficient A measure of the correlation between two variables. It has values between –1 and +1. 0 means the variables are independent of one another.

Correlation The level of dependence between two variables.

Critical friend A person you trust to give you constructive advice in a non-threatening manner.

Critical path analysis The process of identifying how the tasks within a project fit together so that all tasks occur in a logical order.

Crop marks Marks on page proofs that show where the edges of the final printed page will be, i.e. where the paper will be cropped. They consist of a short horizontal and a short vertical line that cross precisely at each corner of the page.

Cross referencing Involves referring the reader to something covered somewhere else in the document.

Customised off-the-shelf (COTS) software Software that is purchased off the shelf as a package and then modified to meet the needs of a particular organisation.

Data capture form A paper form that is used to collect data to be input into a computer. The layout of the form and the data input screen should match.

Data dictionary A file containing descriptions of, and other information about, data. It is a record of data about data.

Data file exchange The process of transferring a file from one computer to another over a WAN. The file can be sent as an attachment to an email or can be copied using FTP software.

Data flow diagram (DFD) A diagrammatical way of representing the flow of data and information in a system.

Data logging The use of sensors to collect physical data electronically, such as the temperature in a room, so that it can be automatically input and analysed by a computer.

Data series One row or column of data in the spreadsheet that is used to create a chart or graph.

Data stores Where data is stored in the system.

Decision points Those points in a product where a decision has to be made. Typically, these decisions would be forced by presenting the user with different possible routes through a product. Any point at which the user has to decide on which path to follow is therefore a decision point.

Decision table A table that specifies the actions to be taken when certain conditions arise.

Decision tree A diagram resembling a fallen tree that represents the conditions and associated action.

Democratic A style of leadership which involves all team members equally.

Demodulation The process of transforming a signal on a cable or telecommunications link into a digital signal that can be understood by a computer.

Depreciation The decrease in value of assets over time.

Digital signals These can have two discrete frequencies only. One frequency represents a 1 and the other represents 0. Computers use digital signals.

Direct The new system completely replaces the old system, on a given day.

Discussion forums Like bulletin boards but available to a closed set of users.

Distortion Changing how an image looks without changing the basic content of an image.

Dithering This is a strange name for a very useful tool. Dithering takes account of the fact that apart from the primary colours, all other colours can be made by combining different amounts of others. For example, the colour green is a combination of the colours blue and yellow.

When you are saving in a format which uses 256 colours or less, you can choose to apply dithering to your image. This will then place colours that are in the 256 colour palette in a pattern which the eye will see as another colour that is not in the colour palette.

Domain name server A database of domain names that direct web users to a computer hosting the requested website.

Domain name The unique name that identifies a website. Sometimes known as a web address.

Drop capitals A feature used in publications where the first letter of a paragraph is enlarged and covers several lines of normal text.

E-commerce Commercial transactions such as sales, transfer of money, submission of forms over a WAN.

Edition One of a number of printings of a newspaper. Several editions are printed each day. For a morning paper, the first edition is printed late on the previous evening with subsequent editions being printed overnight, whilst for an evening paper, the first edition may be printed at midday with subsequent editions being printed during the afternoon and early evening.

Elements The individual parts which are combined together to create a multimedia product.

Ellipsis (...) Used to show that something has been omitted.

Email A messaging system where each user on a network has a mailbox and messages are passed from one user's mailbox to another's using their email address.

En rule (–) Used as a dash. It takes up the same space as a letter n.

Entity An object in the real world that data is stored about.

Entity-relationship diagram (ERD) A technique for representing the structure of data in a software system using entities and the relationships between those entities.

External entities A source for data that is input into the system or a destination for data that leaves the system.

External stakeholders Those groups of stakeholders who are external to the project.

Extranet A private network that can be accessed from outside the network via the Internet.

Fan-fold paper Paper that comes in a continuous strip, rather than separate sheets. There are perforations between each sheet so that they can be separated after printing, and the paper is folded along the perforations, like a concertina. A series of holes along each edge of the paper fit on the printer sprockets to move the paper through the printer. Depending on the application, there may be perforations between the holes and the printing area so that the strip of holes can be removed.

Feasibility report The final product from the feasibility stage.

Feasibility study An initial look at an existing system to see how it can be improved.

Field An individual data item within each record.

File server A computer connected to a network that has a large amount of hard disk space and on which most data files are stored. The server is asked by individual computers to send files and asked to save them.

File transfer protocol (FTP) The protocol created to allow the transfer of ftp resources across the internet.

Firewall Software that restricts the amount of access given to outside users to a computer system.

Fixed cost Costs, such as rent or mortgage payments, wages or the cost of machinery, which stay the same regardless how many items are made or sold.

Foreign key An attribute of one entity that is related to the primary key of another, setting up a relationship between the entities.

Formal and informal interaction Two different forms of communication, bound by different rules. Formal interaction will be more businesslike and less relaxed than informal interaction, which will be more like a conversation between friends.

Forms Included on web pages so that you may gather information from visitors to your website.

Frame rate The number of frames shown per second.

Frame The individual still photograph which, when combined with other frames, makes up a multimedia presentation. Or the smallest part of a completed multimedia product. A completed product will be made up of lots of frames.

Frequency The number of values that fall in particular ranges.

Functional requirements What the end-user wants the system to do.

Future value How much an investment will be worth at a certain time in the future.

Gutter The space between two columns.

Horizontal rules Horizontal lines drawn on a document to separate sections of it, for example to separate the heading and field names from the data in a database report. A vertical rule is a vertical line often used between columns.

House style Corporate image that determines the style that an organization uses for all the documents it produces, so that the documents can be recognised as coming from that organisation.

HTML code The language for describing the structure of a web page. A web browser translates that language into the web page as you see it on the Internet.

HTML tags Instructions to the web browser about how a page should look.

Hyperlink The code that moves the viewer from one section of a website or web page when the user clicks on a button or other interactive element on a page.

Hypertext Transfer Protocol The protocol created to allow the transfer of http pages between web servers and clients.

Index A feature in a database that speeds up queries on the indexed fields as well as sorting and grouping operations. For example, if you search for specific employee names in a LastName field, you can create an index for this field to speed up the search for a specific name. Or an alphabetical list of key words that appear in a document, with the page number(s) on which each word can be found.

Integrity A database that is consistent, accurate and reliable.

Interest rate The monthly or annual rate of increase of an investment, or the monthly or annual cost for a loan.

Interest The money earned by the investment.

Internal stakeholders Those groups of stakeholders who are part of the project.

Intranet A communications system that works in a similar way to the World Wide Web but works on a local area network, not necessarily connected to the Internet.

Investment period The length of time the money is invested.

Investment Money that is put into a bank, business or stocks and shares to make a profit.

Iterative problem solving A method that is sometimes called trial and improvement. This involves entering values and then refining them to obtain the required solution.

Kerning Used to adjust the spacing between letters within a word.

Leader A line, either solid or dotted, that leads up to a tab stop.

Leading Used to adjust the space between lines of text.

Linear When values plotted on a graph form, or are close to, a straight line.

Logical topology A stylised representation of the shape of the network. The logical topology is easy to understand but does not represent the real picture.

Mail merge The process of combining a standard document with a database, usually of names and addresses. Multiple copies of the document are created, each with the details from one record in the database.

Maintenance The process of ensuring that a software system/product continues to meet the needs of the end-users.

Master page A page that includes all the features and the layout that will appear on every page that uses that master page.

Mathematical mean The sum of a set of values divided by the number of values in the set.

Mean The mathematical average of a set of values, i.e. the total value divided by the number of values.

Mind mapping Drawing a diagram of ideas all linked to a central plan or project.

Mirror To reverse an image along its horizontal axis.

Modem A device that connects a computer to an analogue telephone line and converts the signals between digital and analogue and to and from the form that can be transmitted on the line.

Modulation The process of transforming a digital signal in the computer into a form that can be transmitted on a cable or telecommunications link.

Multimedia authoring The process of creating a multimedia presentation.

Multi-part carbonised paper Sometimes called NCR paper. Paper that has two or more sheets attached on top of one another. The paper is treated so that anything written or typed on the top sheet is transferred to those beneath it. This is due to the pressure applied, so does not work with non-impact printers such as lasers or ink-jets. Multi-part paper is often used for invoices and order forms as one copy can be sent to the customer or supplier and the other kept as a record.

Mutually exclusive If one value is true, the other cannot be.

Navigation tool The range of tools that affect the order in which the frames in a multimedia product play.

Net present value The value of a series of investments and/or payments in today's money.

Network security Involves managing access to data and resources, protecting against threats to data from malicious software and users and keeping regular back-ups in case of loss of data.

Network services The services provided by one computer in response to a request from another computer. The services might be to use a device attached to the servicing machine, to send a file of data to a requesting machine.

Networked computer A computer workstation that is connected to another computer.

Non-functional requirements The limitations relating to response time/hardware/software/ programming language given by the end-user.

Normal distribution A distribution of values that produces a symmetrical bell-shaped curve when plotted. Many measurements are approximately normally distributed.

Normalisation The process of ensuring that a database has integrity.

Numerical processing The calculations that will be needed to obtain the required information.

Object libraries Collections of different objects that may be added to a graphic. Object libraries will include stock objects that may be difficult to draw, such as fire, or everyday objects.

Occurrence One example of an entity, e.g. one particular patient.

Off-the-shelf software Software that has already been developed and is ready to buy, install and use on a computer system.

OLE Stands for object linking and embedding; a facility that allows one type of file (A) to be accessed within another (B). Linking means that only a link to file A is included in the file B. Any changes made to the file A will automatically appear in file B, but both files must be available. Embedding means that file A is actually part of file B but can be edited in the original software by double clicking on it.

Orphan Where the last line of a paragraph ends up on its own at the top of a new page.

Page proofs Printed copies of the pages of a publication that can be read and checked for errors.

Parallel The old and new systems operate alongside each other.

Paternalistic A style of management where the leader treats the team as a family and plays out the role of a father, who may allow some discussion but, ultimately, makes most decisions.

Peer computer An individual computer on a peer-to-peer network.

Period The length of time between payments, usually a month or a year. The interest rate and the period must match, i.e. months and monthly interest rate or years and annual interest rate.

Phased Selected parts of the organisation use the new system. The rest of the organisation uses the old system.

Physical topology The actual way a network is connected. A diagram of this topology is difficult to follow.

Pilot Selected tasks are completed using the new system. All other tasks are completed using the old system.

Pixel A small dot of an image; the smallest part of an image that can be displayed. Images are made up of many pixels.

Pixelation The breaking up of an image into the individual pixels so that it appears as an area of coloured blocks. It is caused by trying to enlarge a JPEG image. Sometimes pixelation is used deliberately to hide a person's identity, for example.

Population All possible individuals for a particular statistical measure.

Portfolio Samples of work. Usually used as evidence of the artist's or designer's imagination, ability and skill.

Posterisation Decreasing the levels of colour and light in an image.

Primary data Information obtained through your own research.

Primary key An attribute (or attributes) that uniquely identify an occurrence of an entity.

Process Activities that take place with and/or are linked to the system.

Proxy server A server that appears to serve up the website or any other data requested, but which is actually serving the website on behalf of another machine.

Public domain software Software that is free and can be downloaded or copied without charge (also called freeware).

Radian A unit for measuring angles. If you draw two radii of a circle so that the arc between the two points where they touch the circumference is the same length as the radius, the angle between the radii will be one radian. A right angle is equal to $\Pi/2$ radians.

Range of cells A block of cells that is defined by the addresses of the top-left and bottom-right cells.

Rank The position of a value within a list of values if they were placed in numerical order.

Rate of return The percentage increase or decrease in value of a series of payments and/or incomes over a period of time.

Recipient Where the data goes to.

Record All the data about one person or 'thing'.

Relationship The way in which one entity is related to another.

Relative cell referencing When the cell references used in a formula are relative to the cell that the formula is in. Copying the formula to another cell will cause the cell references to change.

Resolution Describes how clear the image will be and is based on how many pixels are in a fixed area of an image. This may be described as pixels per inch or pixels per centimetre.

Return on an investment Profit made.

Role ambiguity A lack of clear understanding about the specific roles that members of a group may play.

Rotate To turn an image around its centre.

Sample A subset of the population that is measured and assumed to behave like the population as a whole.

Search engine This allows you to search the content of millions of websites simultaneously.

Secondary research Research based on information that already exists.

Server A computer on a client-server network that provides network services to other computers.

Setting priorities The ability to analyse a list of competing tasks and decide which are more important than others.

Source Where the data comes from.

SSADM structured systems and design methodology

Stakeholders Any group of people who are affected by a project or team.

Stand-alone computer A single computer workstation that has no connection to any other workstation or the Internet.

Standard deviation (sd) A measure of the distribution of values or the width of a normal curve; 68 per cent of all values fall within 1sd of the mean.

Statement of purpose A statement defining what the new system must do.

Subeditor On a newspaper, the person responsible for fitting the stories and pictures onto the page.

Systems analyst The person who is responsible for the analysis of a system to assess its suitability for the proposed changes.

Table of contents A list of the main topics or chapters in a publication in the order they appear.

Table Contains all the data about a particular type of person or 'thing'.

Tabulation The process of organising text in a table.

Target audience The audience for which a piece of work has been produced. Each target audience will have different needs, tastes and interests.

Technical documentation In-depth documents intended to allow a more advanced ICT user to understand how the program was created and how it may be updated in the future.

Tempo The speed at which a multimedia presentation runs.

Test plan A plan showing which parts of your multimedia product which will be tested. It will also show how each part will be tested and what the expected outcome of each test will be.

Time management The ability to use the time you have available to complete the most relevant and necessary tasks in an efficient manner.

Top-down design The process of breaking a project down into ever smaller components.

Trend line A line drawn on a graph to fit the measured values.

Unicode 'Uni' stands for universal. It is a 16-bit coding system that includes every character in every language. The first 128 character codes are the same as ASCII.

Uniform resource locator (URL) The address for each item of data on the Internet.

User documentation Documents to help the user use the program more efficiently.

Validation A method of ensuring the data that is input is reasonable, i.e. that it meets the validation rule applied. For example, a rule that requires values between 1 and 20 would reject values outside that range, such as 0 or 21. Validation does not ensure data is correct.

Variable cost Costs, such as raw materials, which will change depending on the number of items made or sold.

Variance The square of the standard deviation.

Vector graphics Images created by storing details of the magnitude and direction of lines that make up shapes within the image.

Verification The process of checking that data has been correctly transferred onto the computer. The data entered may still be incorrect if the original data was incorrect.

Video card The card that converts the data in a computer into a format that may be displayed on an output device such as a monitor or data projector.

Video-conferencing A fast communications link transmits video images to a number of people simultaneously so that they can have a discussion as if they were all in the same room.

Watermark Any picture or text, such as a logo or 'DRAFT', that appears on top of or, more usually, behind existing document text.

Web authoring software WYSIWYG software you use to create a website.

Web browsing software The software you use to view a website.

Web development tools The tools used to create websites.

Web-based marketing and advertising Making brochures, catalogues and advertising materials available on the world wide web and ensuring that they can be found by a search engine.

Widow Where the first line of a paragraph is left on its own at the bottom of a page.

Win–win approach A strategy for avoiding conflict by concentrating on solving the problem rather than arguing about possible solutions.

World Wide Web (www) An information service available on the Internet.

Index

All entries in *italic* refer to Unit 18 which is available from the Heinemann website. Go to www.heinemann.co.uk/vocational, click on **IT & Office Technology** and select **Free Resources**. The password is **A2ICTU18**